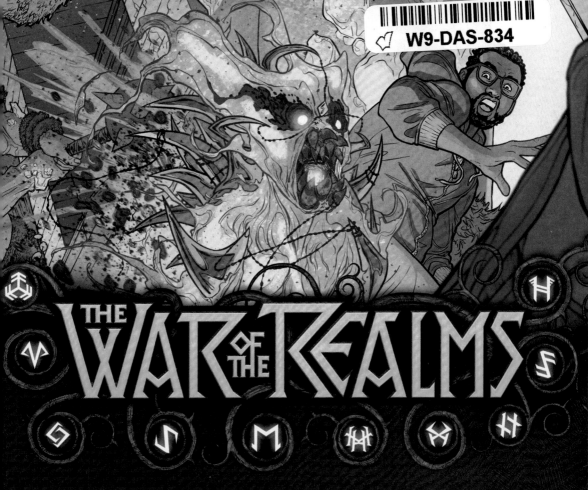

THE WAR OF THE REALMS

Jason Aaron
WRITER

Russell Dauterman
ARTIST

Matthew Wilson
COLOR ARTIST

VC's Joe Sabino
LETTERER

Arthur Adams & Matthew Wilson
COVER ART

Patrick McGrath
LOGO & REALMS SYMBOLS

Sarah Brunstad
ASSOCIATE EDITOR

Wil Moss
EDITOR

Tom Brevoort
EXECUTIVE EDITOR

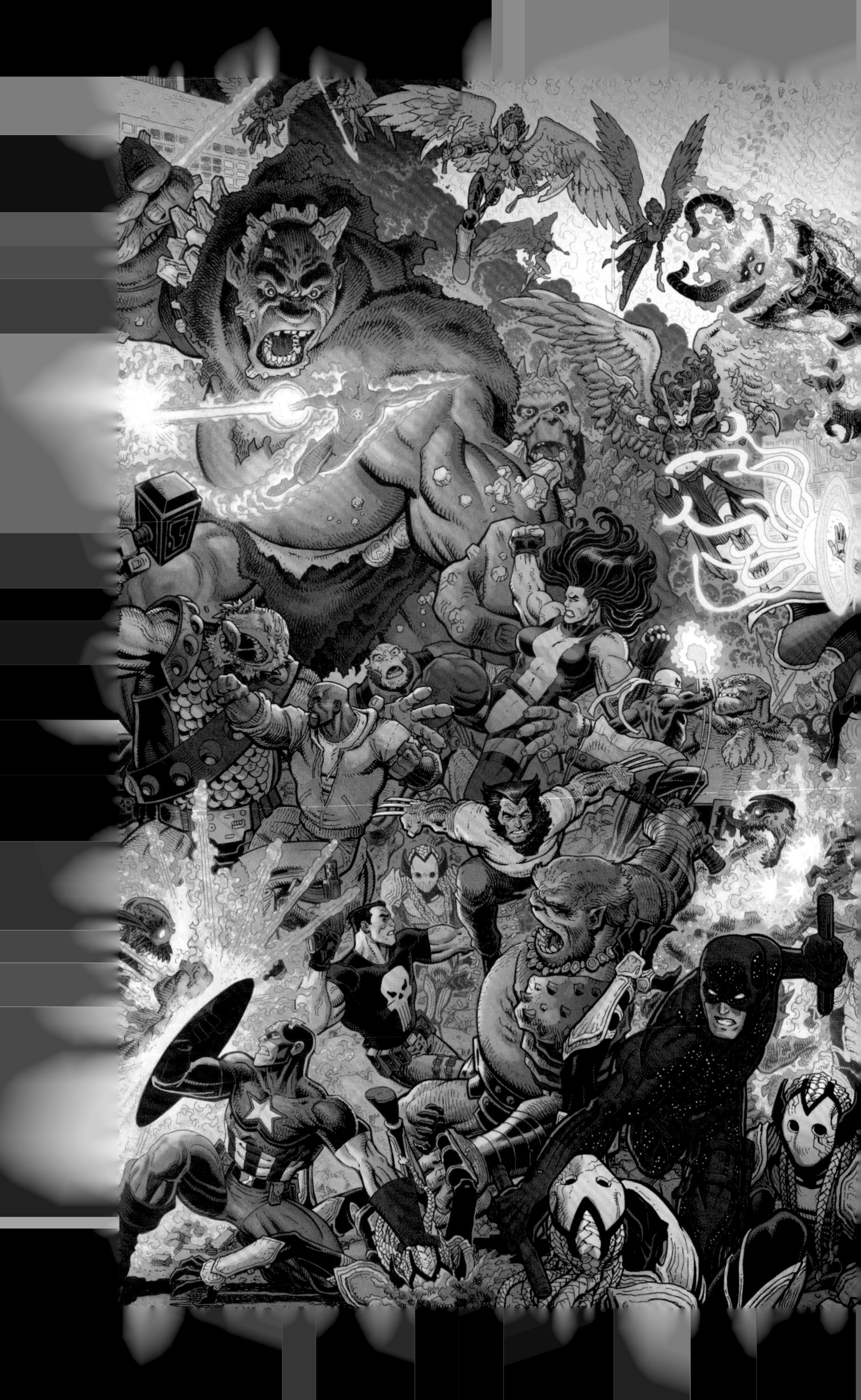

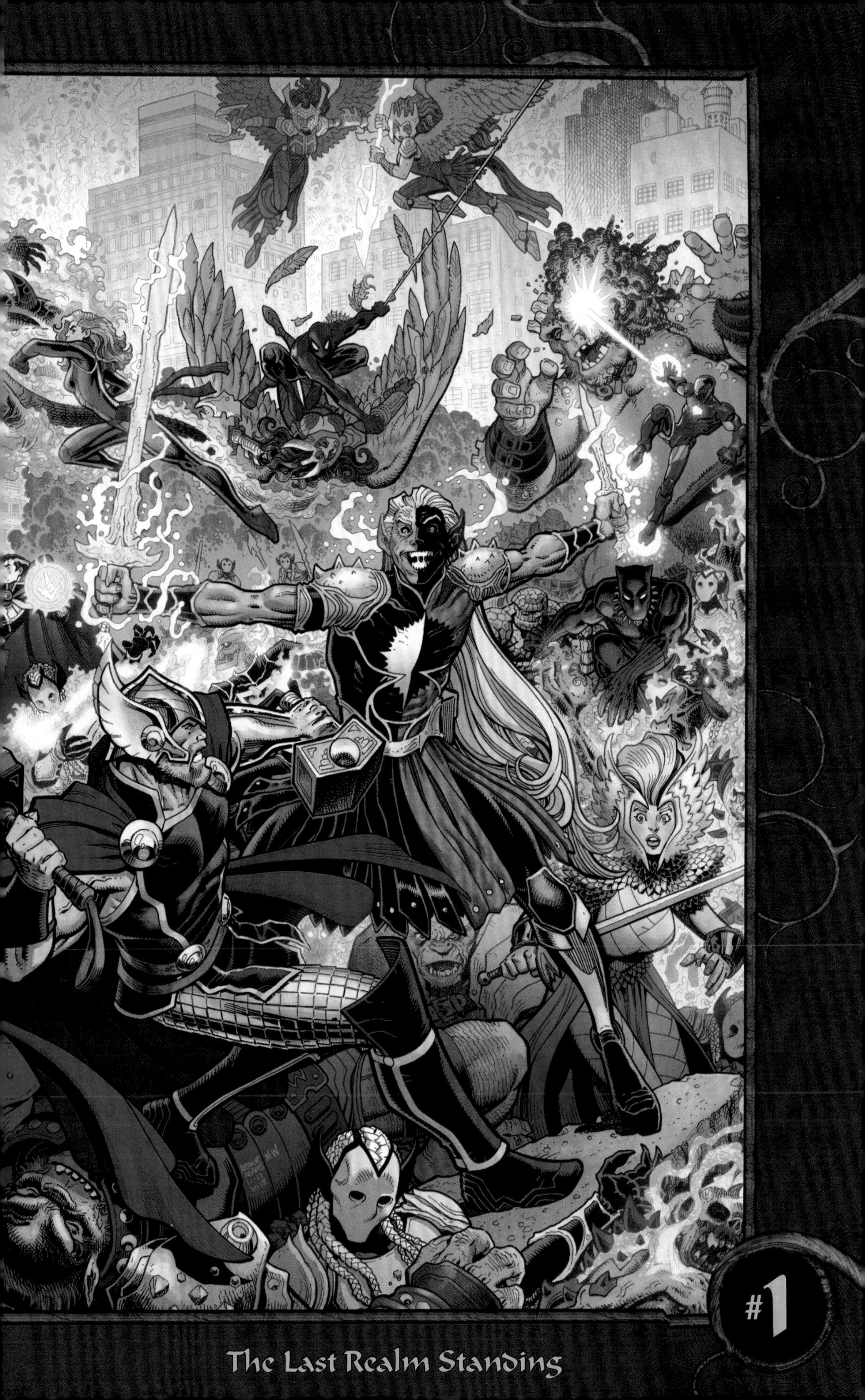

#1

The Last Realm Standing

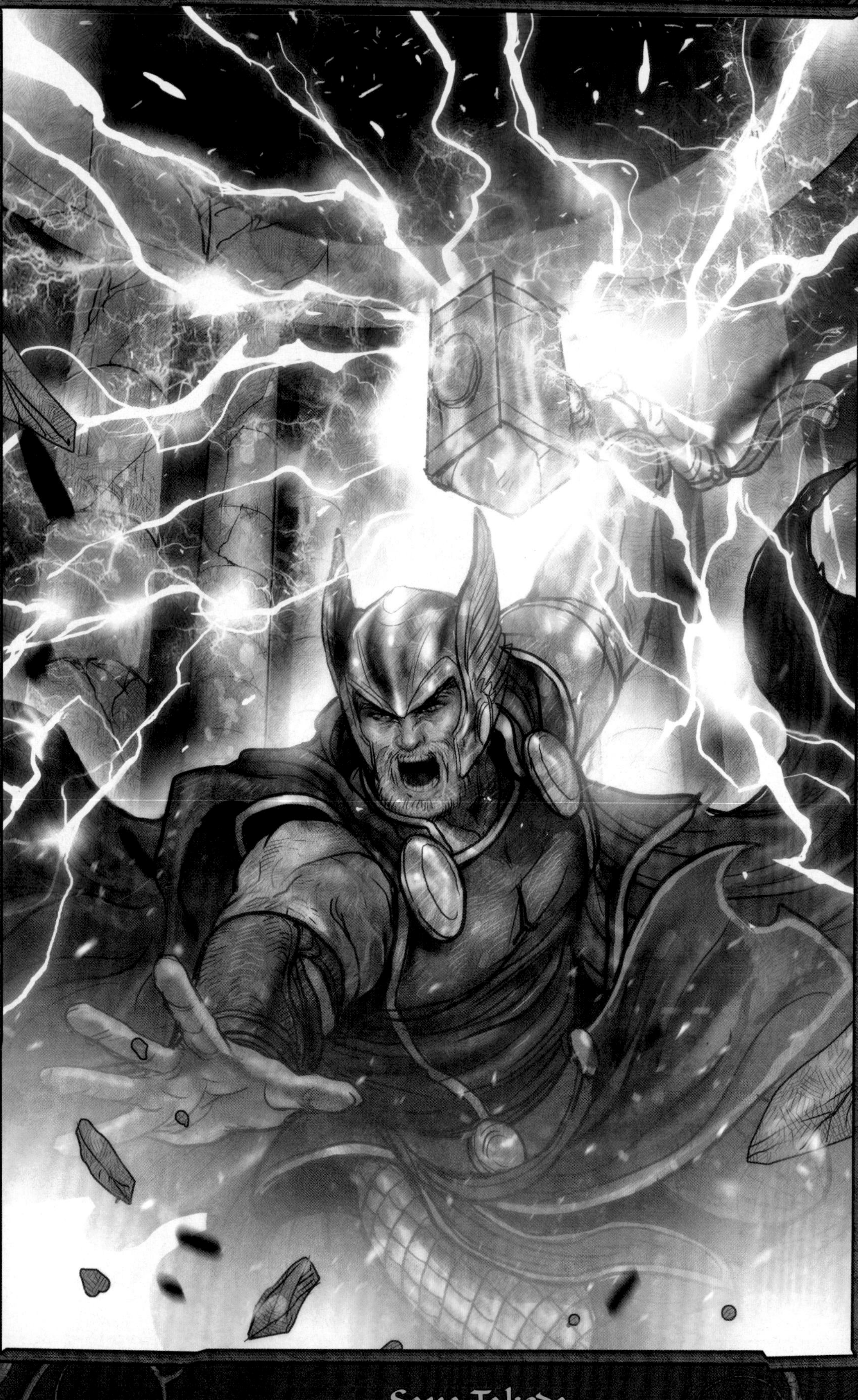

#1 VARIANT BY Sana Takeda

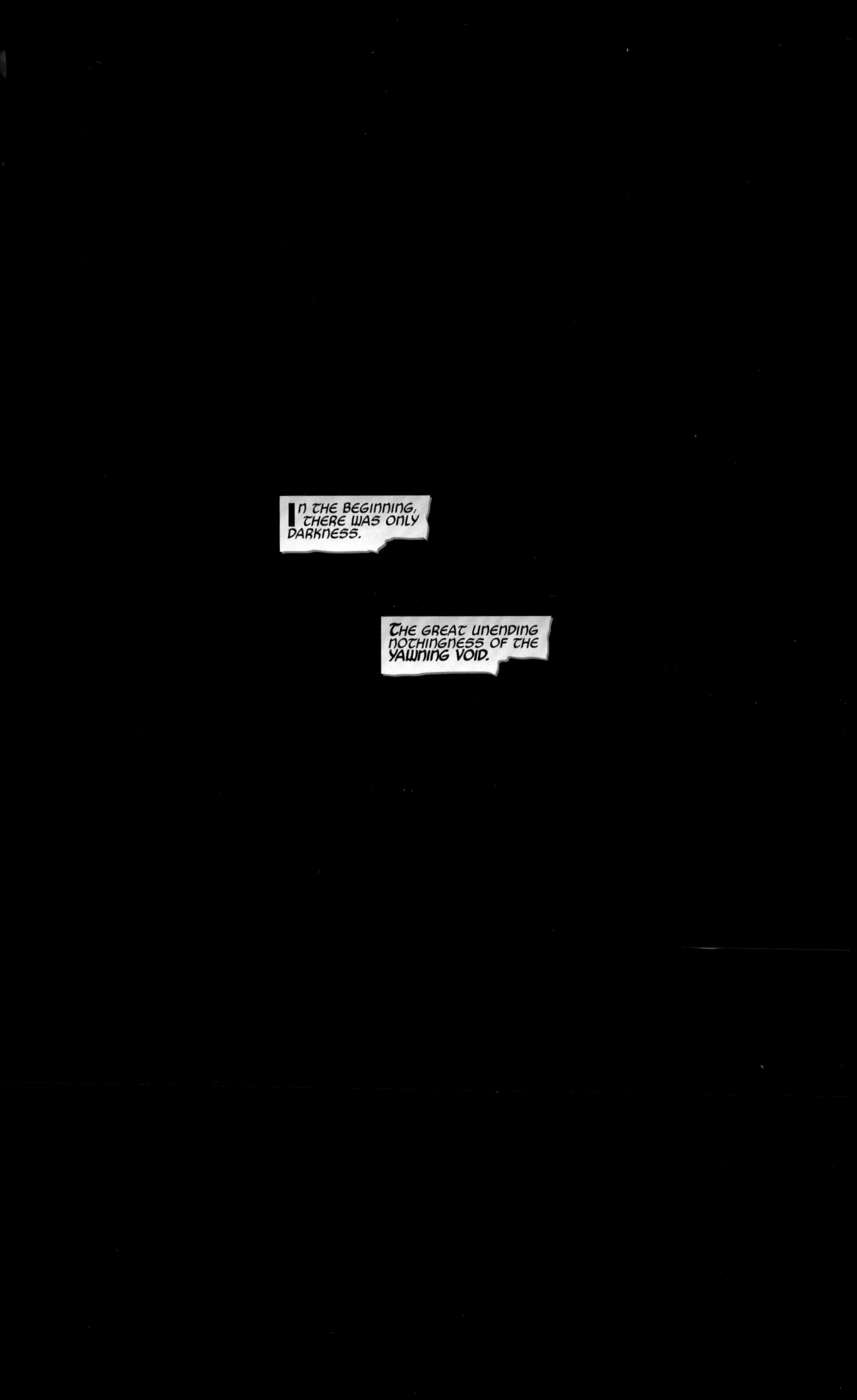
IN THE BEGINNING, THERE WAS ONLY DARKNESS.
THE GREAT UNENDING NOTHINGNESS OF THE YAWNING VOID.

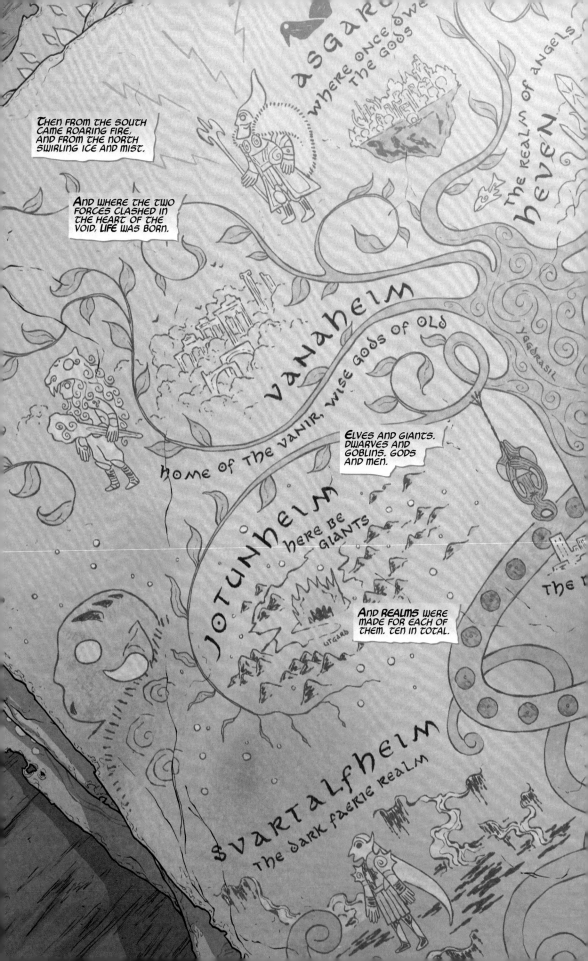

ASGARD
WHERE ONCE DWE
THE GODS

THE REALM OF ANGELS
HEVEN

Then from the south came roaring fire, and from the north swirling ice and mist.

And where the two forces clashed in the heart of the void, LIFE was born.

VANAHEIM

HOME OF THE VANIR, WISE GODS OF OLD

YGGDRASIL

Elves and giants. Dwarves and goblins. Gods and men.

JOTUNHEIM

HERE BE GIANTS

UTGARD

THE N

And REALMS were made for each of them. Ten in total.

SVARTALFHEIM
THE DARK FAERIE REALM

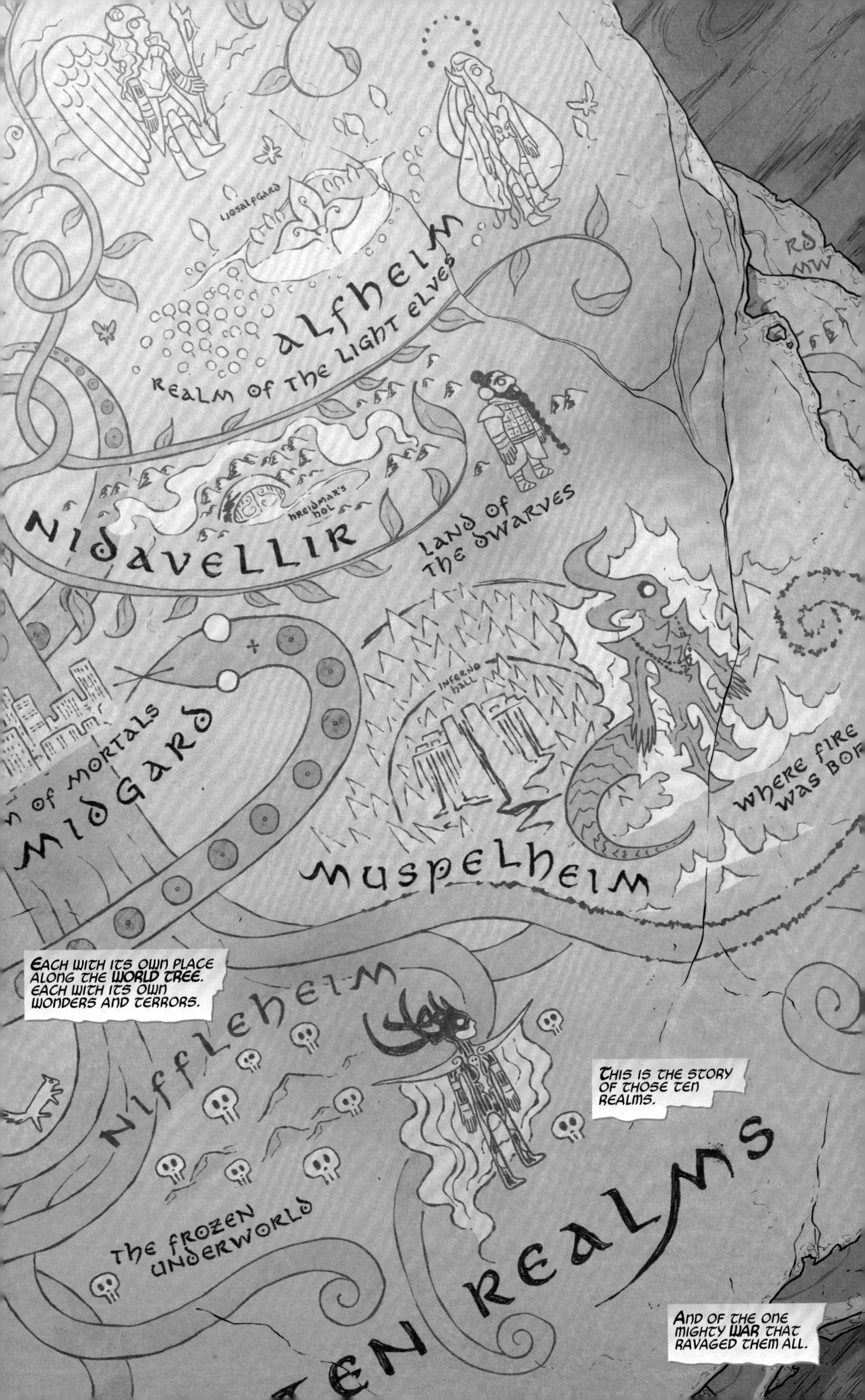

LJOSALFGARD
ALFHEIM
REALM OF THE LIGHT ELVES
HREIDMAR'S HOL
NIDAVELLIR
LAND OF THE DWARVES
OF MORTALS
MIDGARD
INFERNO HALL
WHERE FIRE WAS BO
MUSPELHEIM
EACH WITH ITS OWN PLACE ALONG THE WORLD TREE. EACH WITH ITS OWN WONDERS AND TERRORS.
NIFFLEHEIM
THE FROZEN UNDERWORLD
THIS IS THE STORY OF THOSE TEN REALMS.
EN REALMS
AND OF THE ONE MIGHTY WAR THAT RAVAGED THEM ALL.

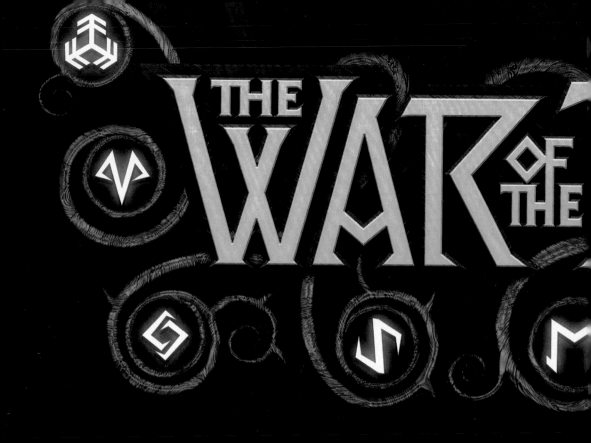

THE WAR OF THE

MALEKITH'S FORCES

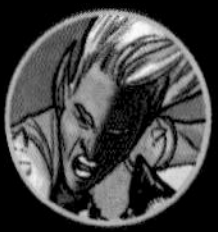

MALEKITH

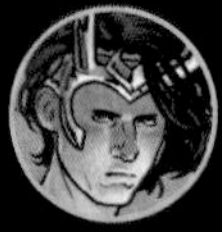

LOKI
Thor's brother

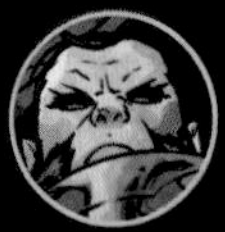

VLIK
Lord of the Trolls

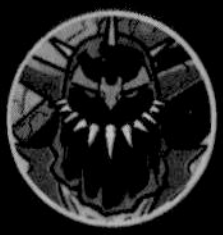

KURSE
Malekith's enforcer

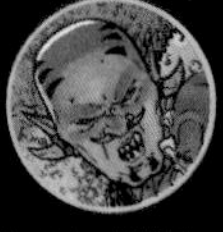

LAUFEY
King of the Frost Giants, Loki's biological father

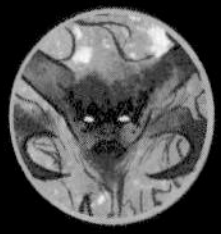

SINDR
Queen of Muspelheim, daughter of Surtur

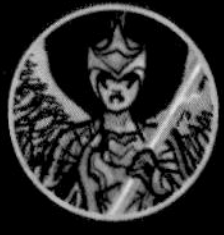

QUEEN OF HEVEN
Ruler of the warrior Angels

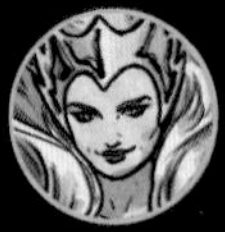

THE ENCHANTRESS
Asgardian sorceress

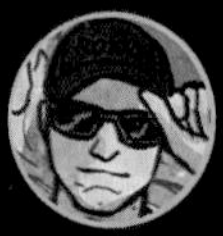

DARIO AGGER
Shapeshifting CEO

REALMS

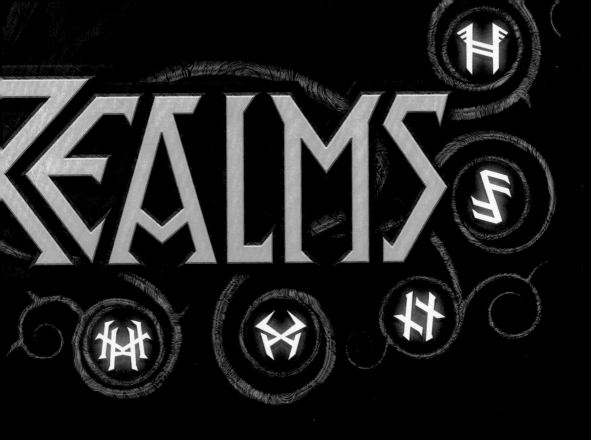

ASGARDIANS

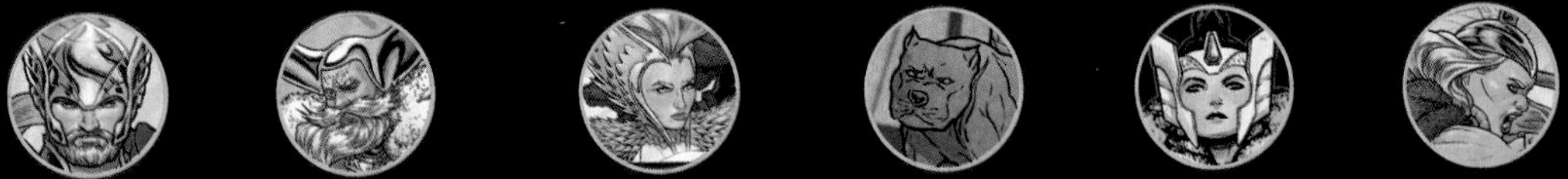

THOR

ODIN
Thor's father, All-Father of Asgard

FREYJA
Thor's mother, All-Mother of Asgard

THORI
Thor's Dog

SIF

HILDEGARDE

HEROES OF MIDGARD

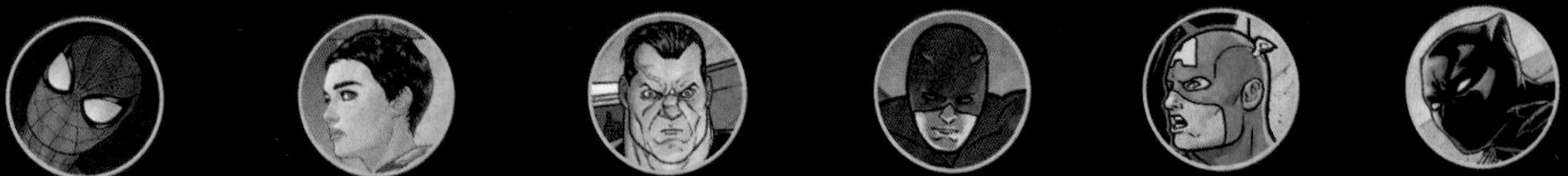

SPIDER-MAN

JANE FOSTER
Former Thor

PUNISHER

DAREDEVIL

CAPTAIN AMERICA

BLACK PANTHER

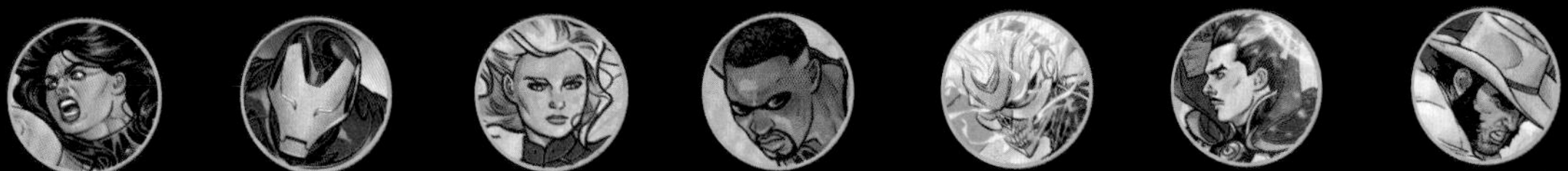

SHE-HULK

IRON MAN

CAPTAIN MARVEL

BLADE

GHOST RIDER

DOCTOR STRANGE

WOLVERINE

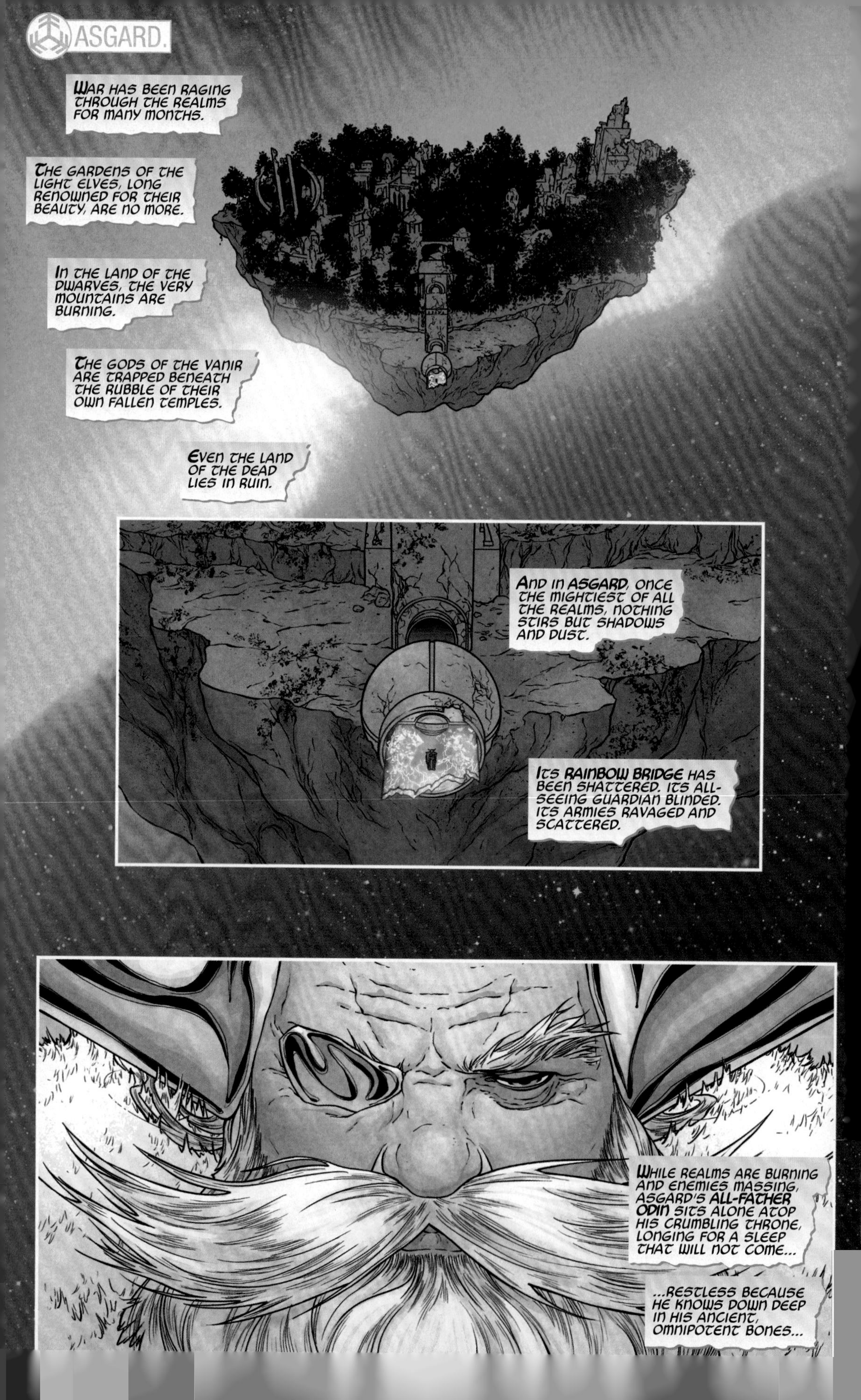
ASGARD.
WAR HAS BEEN RAGING THROUGH THE REALMS FOR MANY MONTHS.
THE GARDENS OF THE LIGHT ELVES, LONG RENOWNED FOR THEIR BEAUTY, ARE NO MORE.
IN THE LAND OF THE DWARVES, THE VERY MOUNTAINS ARE BURNING.
THE GODS OF THE VANIR ARE TRAPPED BENEATH THE RUBBLE OF THEIR OWN FALLEN TEMPLES.
EVEN THE LAND OF THE DEAD LIES IN RUIN.
AND IN ASGARD, ONCE THE MIGHTIEST OF ALL THE REALMS, NOTHING STIRS BUT SHADOWS AND DUST.
ITS RAINBOW BRIDGE HAS BEEN SHATTERED. ITS ALL-SEEING GUARDIAN BLINDED. ITS ARMIES RAVAGED AND SCATTERED.
WHILE REALMS ARE BURNING AND ENEMIES MASSING, ASGARD'S ALL-FATHER ODIN SITS ALONE ATOP HIS CRUMBLING THRONE, LONGING FOR A SLEEP THAT WILL NOT COME...
...RESTLESS BECAUSE HE KNOWS DOWN DEEP IN HIS ANCIENT, OMNIPOTENT BONES...

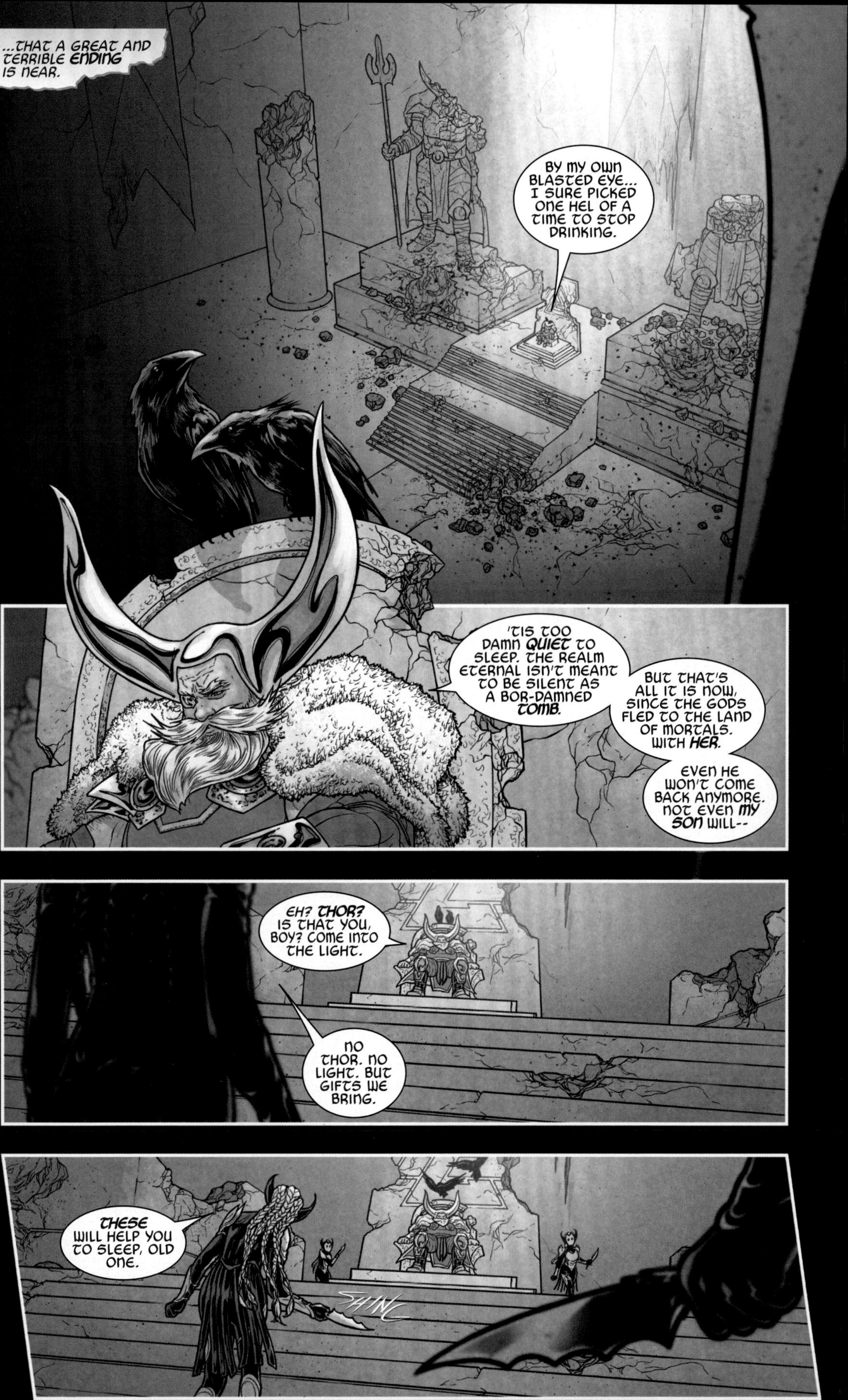
...THAT A GREAT AND TERRIBLE ENDING IS NEAR.
BY MY OWN BLASTED EYE... I SURE PICKED ONE HEL OF A TIME TO STOP DRINKING.
'TIS TOO DAMN QUIET TO SLEEP. THE REALM ETERNAL ISN'T MEANT TO BE SILENT AS A BOR-DAMNED TOMB.
BUT THAT'S ALL IT IS NOW, SINCE THE GODS FLED TO THE LAND OF MORTALS. WITH HER.
EVEN HE WON'T COME BACK ANYMORE. NOT EVEN MY SON WILL--
EH? THOR? IS THAT YOU, BOY? COME INTO THE LIGHT.
NO THOR. NO LIGHT. BUT GIFTS WE BRING.
THESE WILL HELP YOU TO SLEEP, OLD ONE.
SHING

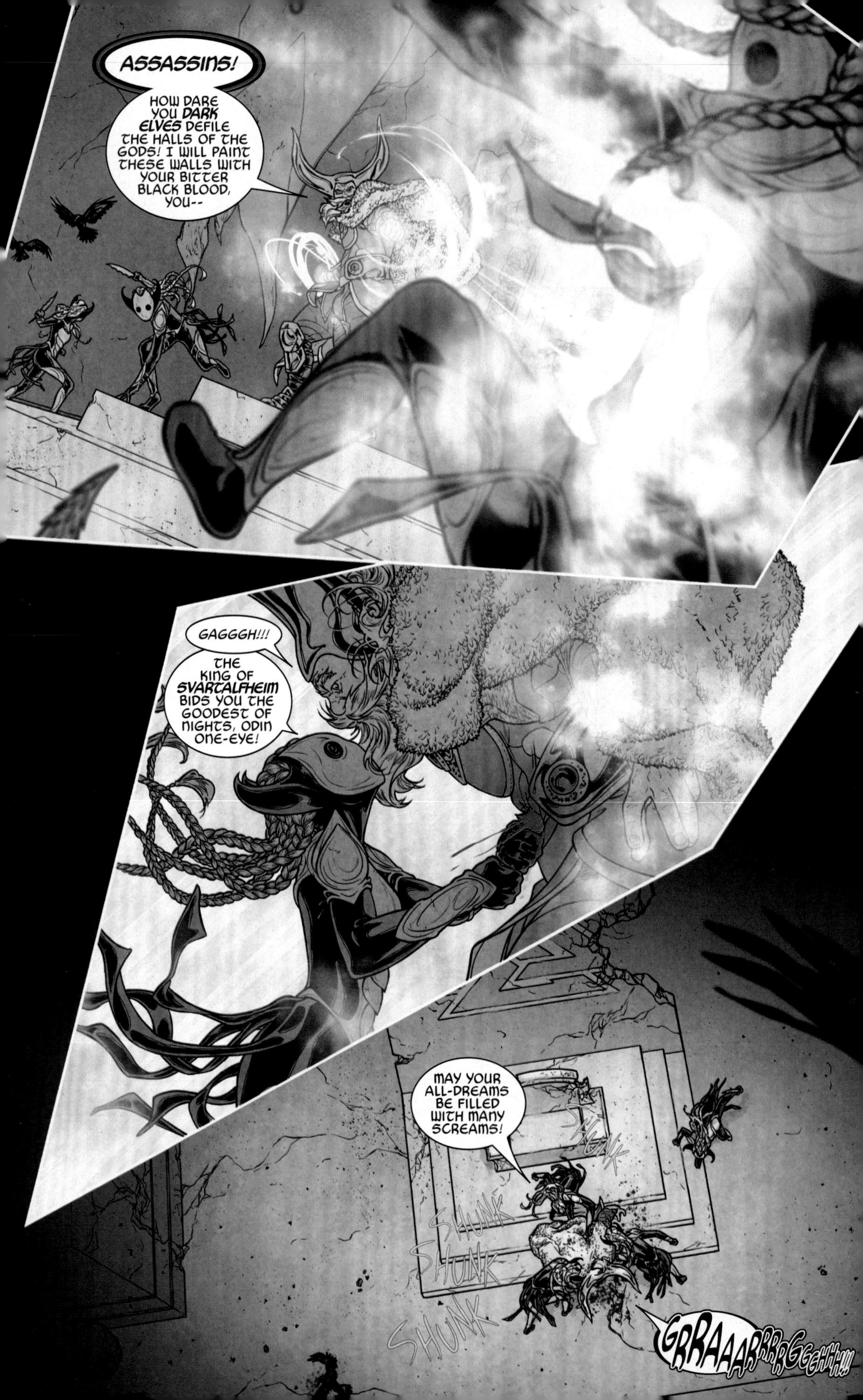
ASSASSINS!
HOW DARE YOU DARK ELVES DEFILE THE HALLS OF THE GODS! I WILL PAINT THESE WALLS WITH YOUR BITTER BLACK BLOOD, YOU--
GAGGGH!!!
THE KING OF SVARTALFHEIM BIDS YOU THE GOODEST OF NIGHTS, ODIN ONE-EYE!
MAY YOUR ALL-DREAMS BE FILLED WITH MANY SCREAMS!
SHUNK
SHUNK
SHUNK
SHUNK
SHUNK
GRRAAARRRRGGEHHH!!!

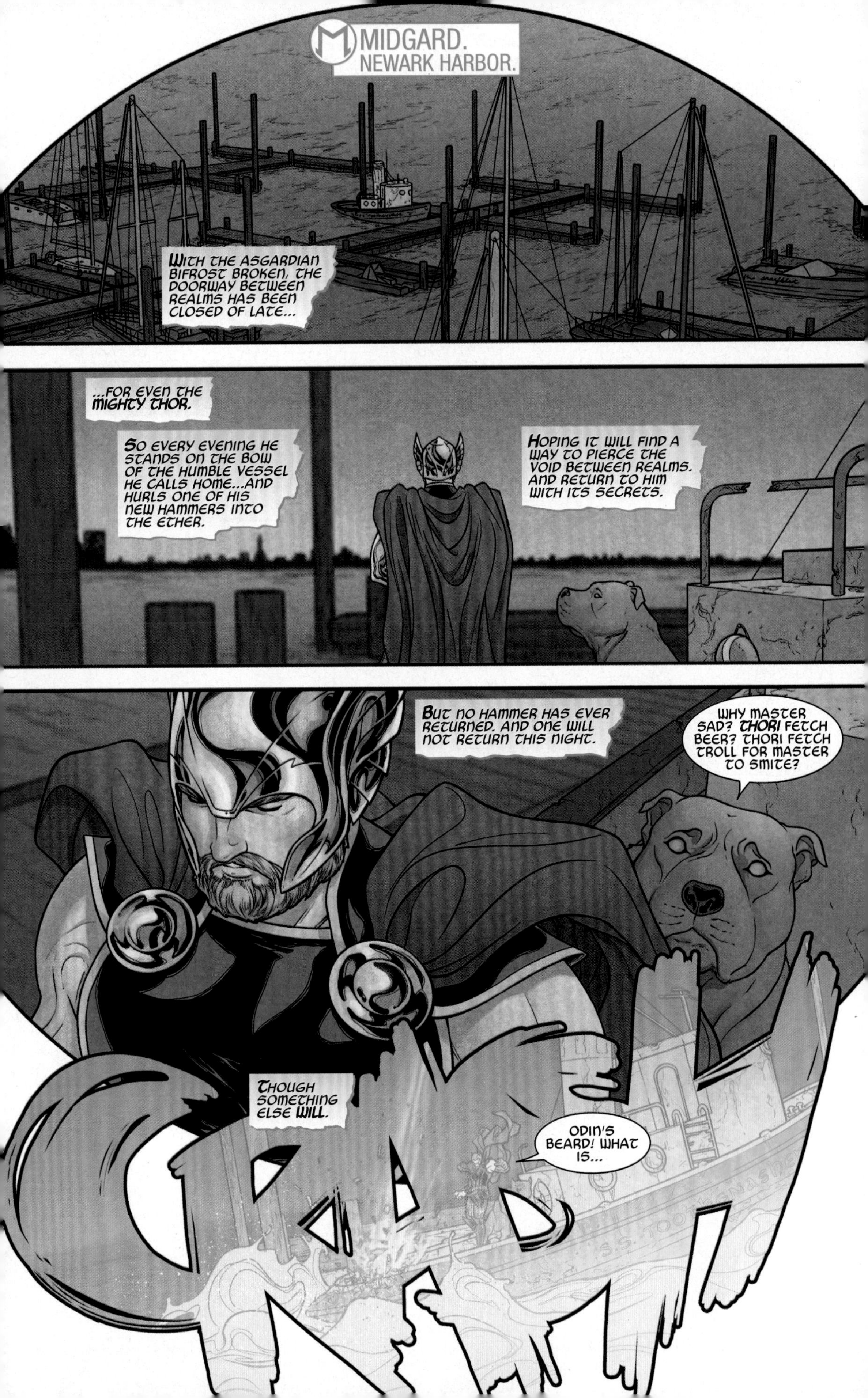
MIDGARD.
NEWARK HARBOR.
WITH THE ASGARDIAN BIFROST BROKEN, THE DOORWAY BETWEEN REALMS HAS BEEN CLOSED OF LATE...
...FOR EVEN THE MIGHTY THOR.
SO EVERY EVENING HE STANDS ON THE BOW OF THE HUMBLE VESSEL HE CALLS HOME...AND HURLS ONE OF HIS NEW HAMMERS INTO THE ETHER.
HOPING IT WILL FIND A WAY TO PIERCE THE VOID BETWEEN REALMS. AND RETURN TO HIM WITH ITS SECRETS.
BUT NO HAMMER HAS EVER RETURNED. AND ONE WILL NOT RETURN THIS NIGHT.
WHY MASTER SAD? THORI FETCH BEER? THORI FETCH TROLL FOR MASTER TO SMITE?
THOUGH SOMETHING ELSE WILL.
ODIN'S BEARD! WHAT IS...
S.S. TOOTH GNASHER

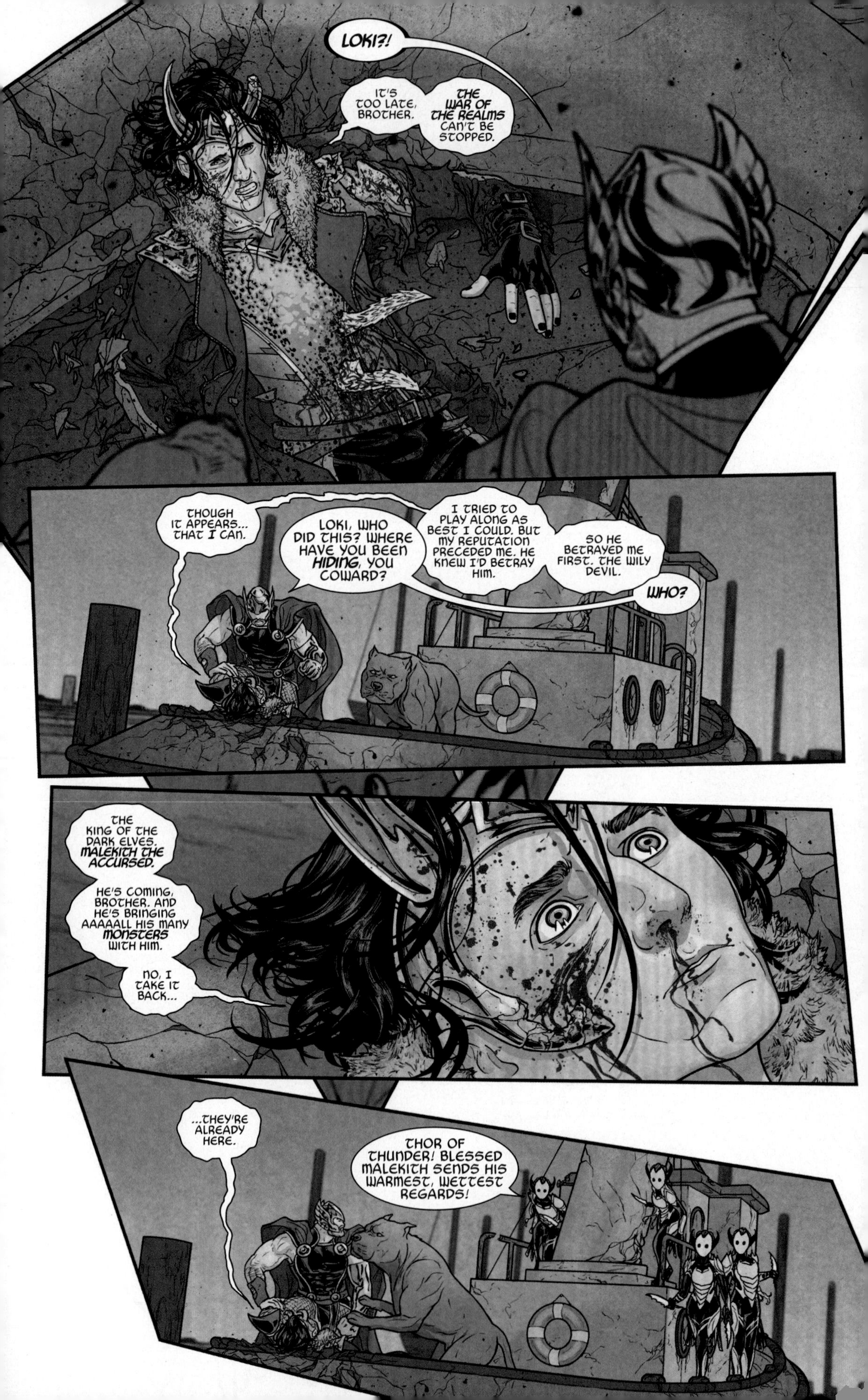
LOKI?!
IT'S TOO LATE, BROTHER. THE WAR OF THE REALMS CAN'T BE STOPPED.
THOUGH IT APPEARS... THAT I CAN.
LOKI, WHO DID THIS? WHERE HAVE YOU BEEN HIDING, YOU COWARD?
I TRIED TO PLAY ALONG AS BEST I COULD. BUT MY REPUTATION PRECEDED ME. HE KNEW I'D BETRAY HIM.
SO HE BETRAYED ME FIRST. THE WILY DEVIL.
WHO?
THE KING OF THE DARK ELVES. MALEKITH THE ACCURSED.
HE'S COMING, BROTHER. AND HE'S BRINGING AAAAALL HIS MANY MONSTERS WITH HIM.
NO, I TAKE IT BACK...
...THEY'RE ALREADY HERE.
THOR OF THUNDER! BLESSED MALEKITH SENDS HIS WARMEST, WETTEST REGARDS!

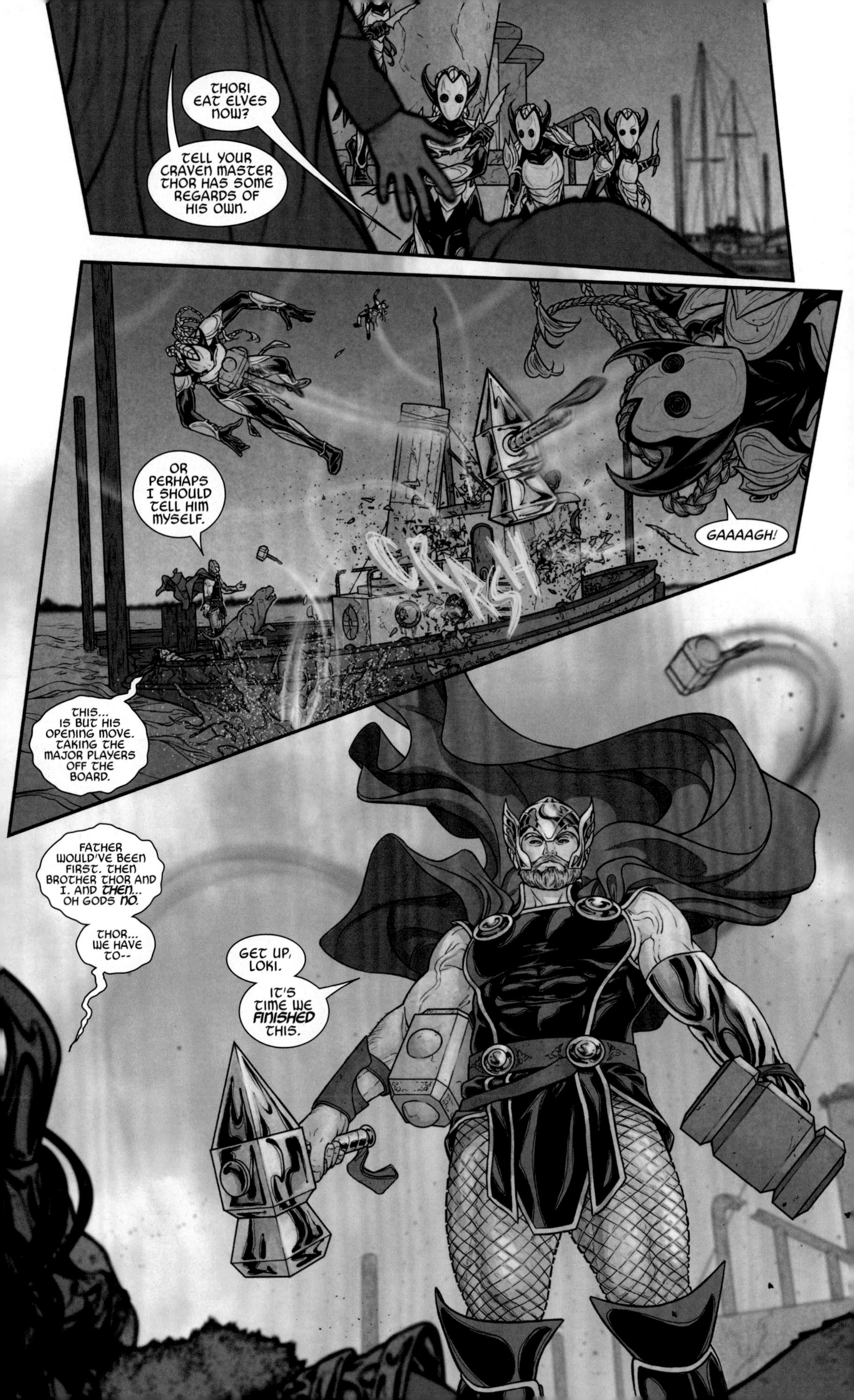
THORI EAT ELVES NOW?
TELL YOUR CRAVEN MASTER THOR HAS SOME REGARDS OF HIS OWN.
OR PERHAPS I SHOULD TELL HIM MYSELF.
CRASH
GAAAAGH!
THIS... IS BUT HIS OPENING MOVE. TAKING THE MAJOR PLAYERS OFF THE BOARD.
FATHER WOULD'VE BEEN FIRST. THEN BROTHER THOR AND I. AND THEN... OH GODS NO.
THOR... WE HAVE TO--
GET UP, LOKI.
IT'S TIME WE FINISHED THIS.

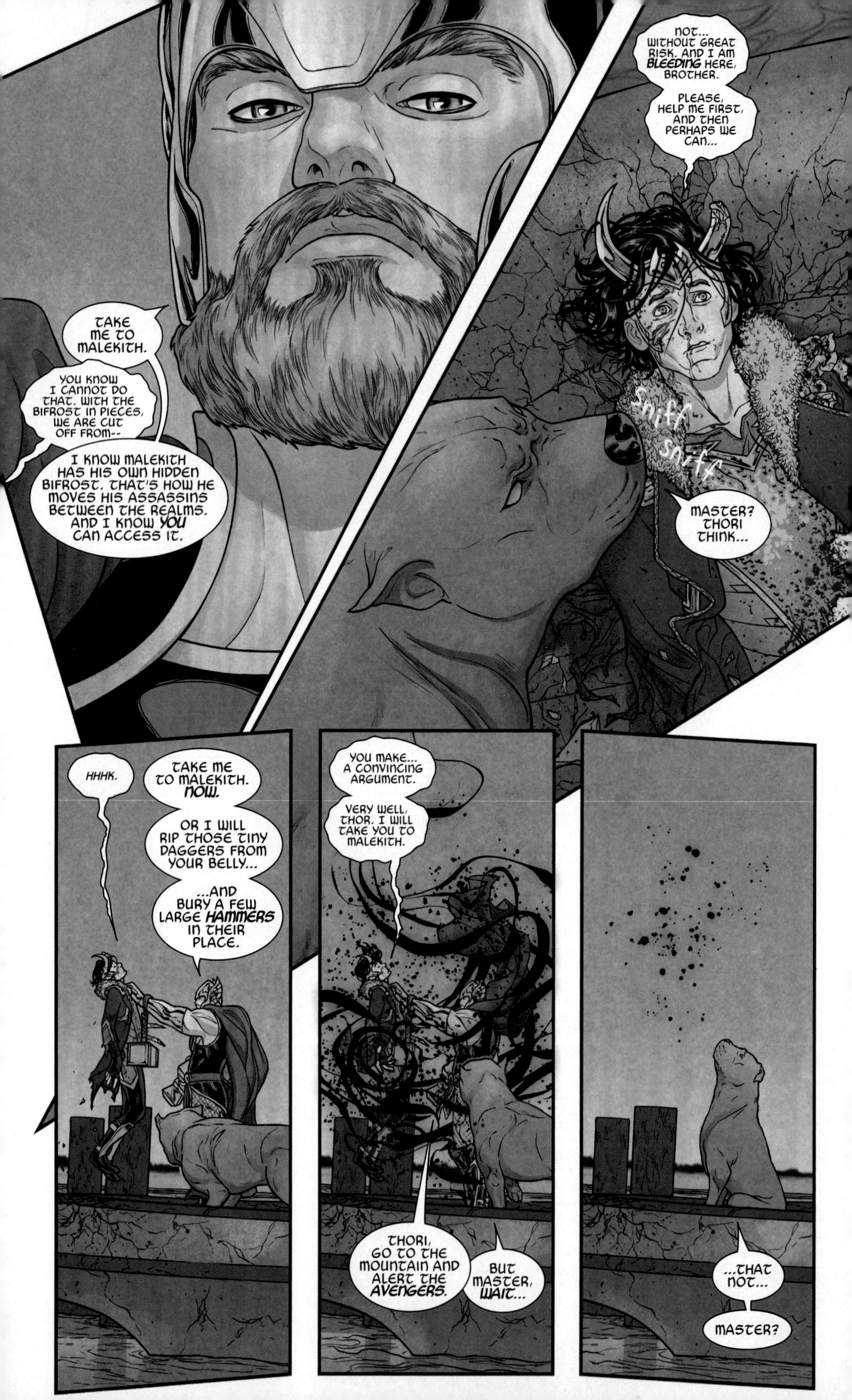

TAKE ME TO MALEKITH.
YOU KNOW I CANNOT DO THAT. WITH THE BIFROST IN PIECES, WE ARE CUT OFF FROM--
I KNOW MALEKITH HAS HIS OWN HIDDEN BIFROST. THAT'S HOW HE MOVES HIS ASSASSINS BETWEEN THE REALMS. AND I KNOW YOU CAN ACCESS IT.
NOT... WITHOUT GREAT RISK. AND I AM BLEEDING HERE, BROTHER.
PLEASE, HELP ME FIRST, AND THEN PERHAPS WE CAN...
SNIFF
SNIFF
MASTER? THORI THINK...
HHHK.
TAKE ME TO MALEKITH. NOW.
OR I WILL RIP THOSE TINY DAGGERS FROM YOUR BELLY...
...AND BURY A FEW LARGE HAMMERS IN THEIR PLACE.
YOU MAKE... A CONVINCING ARGUMENT.
VERY WELL, THOR. I WILL TAKE YOU TO MALEKITH.
THORI, GO TO THE MOUNTAIN AND ALERT THE AVENGERS.
BUT MASTER, WAIT...
...THAT NOT...
MASTER?

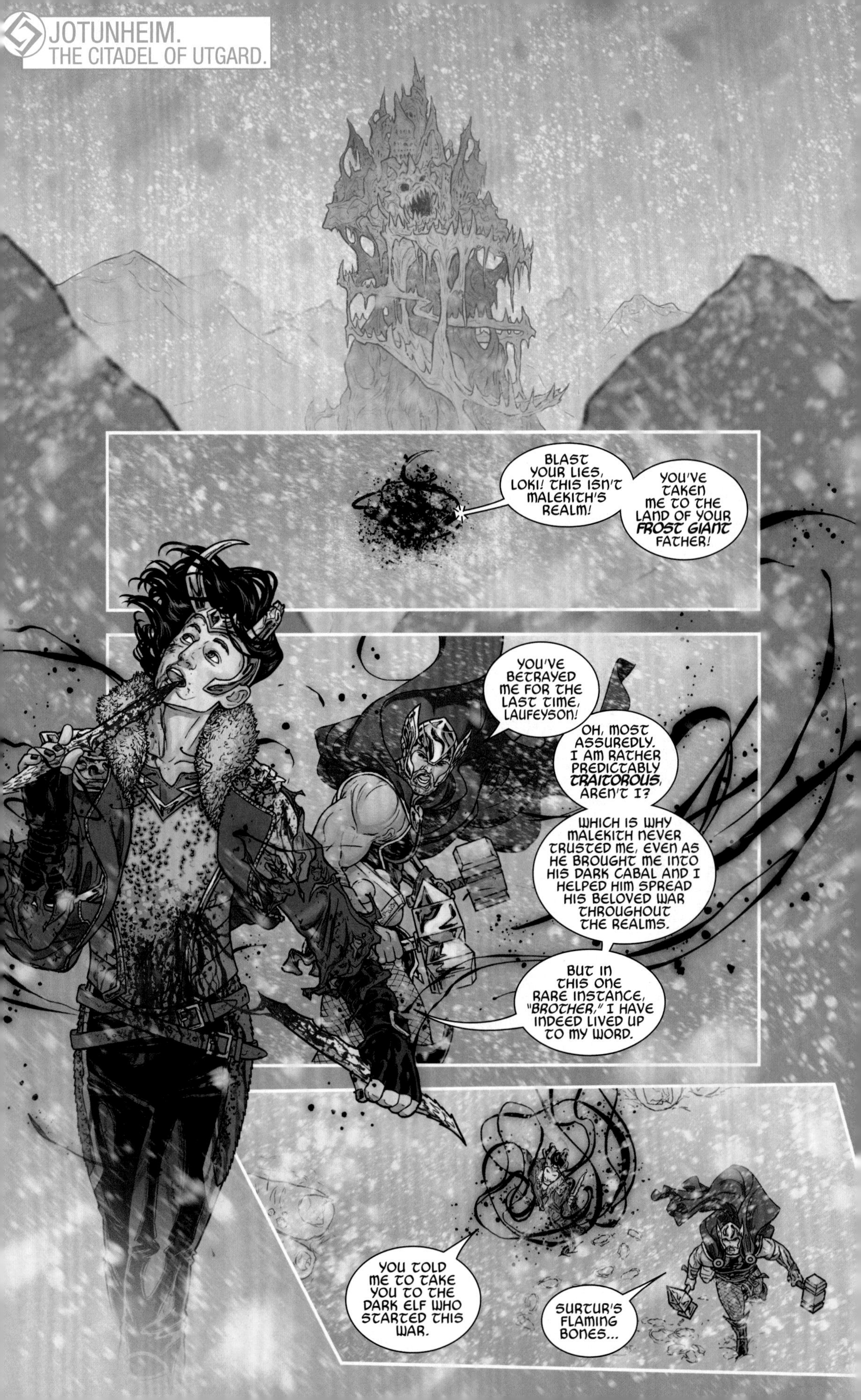
JOTUNHEIM.
THE CITADEL OF UTGARD.
BLAST YOUR LIES, LOKI! THIS ISN'T MALEKITH'S REALM!
YOU'VE TAKEN ME TO THE LAND OF YOUR FROST GIANT FATHER!
YOU'VE BETRAYED ME FOR THE LAST TIME, LAUFEYSON!
OH, MOST ASSUREDLY. I AM RATHER PREDICTABLY TRAITOROUS, AREN'T I?
WHICH IS WHY MALEKITH NEVER TRUSTED ME, EVEN AS HE BROUGHT ME INTO HIS DARK CABAL AND I HELPED HIM SPREAD HIS BELOVED WAR THROUGHOUT THE REALMS.
BUT IN THIS ONE RARE INSTANCE, "BROTHER," I HAVE INDEED LIVED UP TO MY WORD.
YOU TOLD ME TO TAKE YOU TO THE DARK ELF WHO STARTED THIS WAR.
SURTUR'S FLAMING BONES...

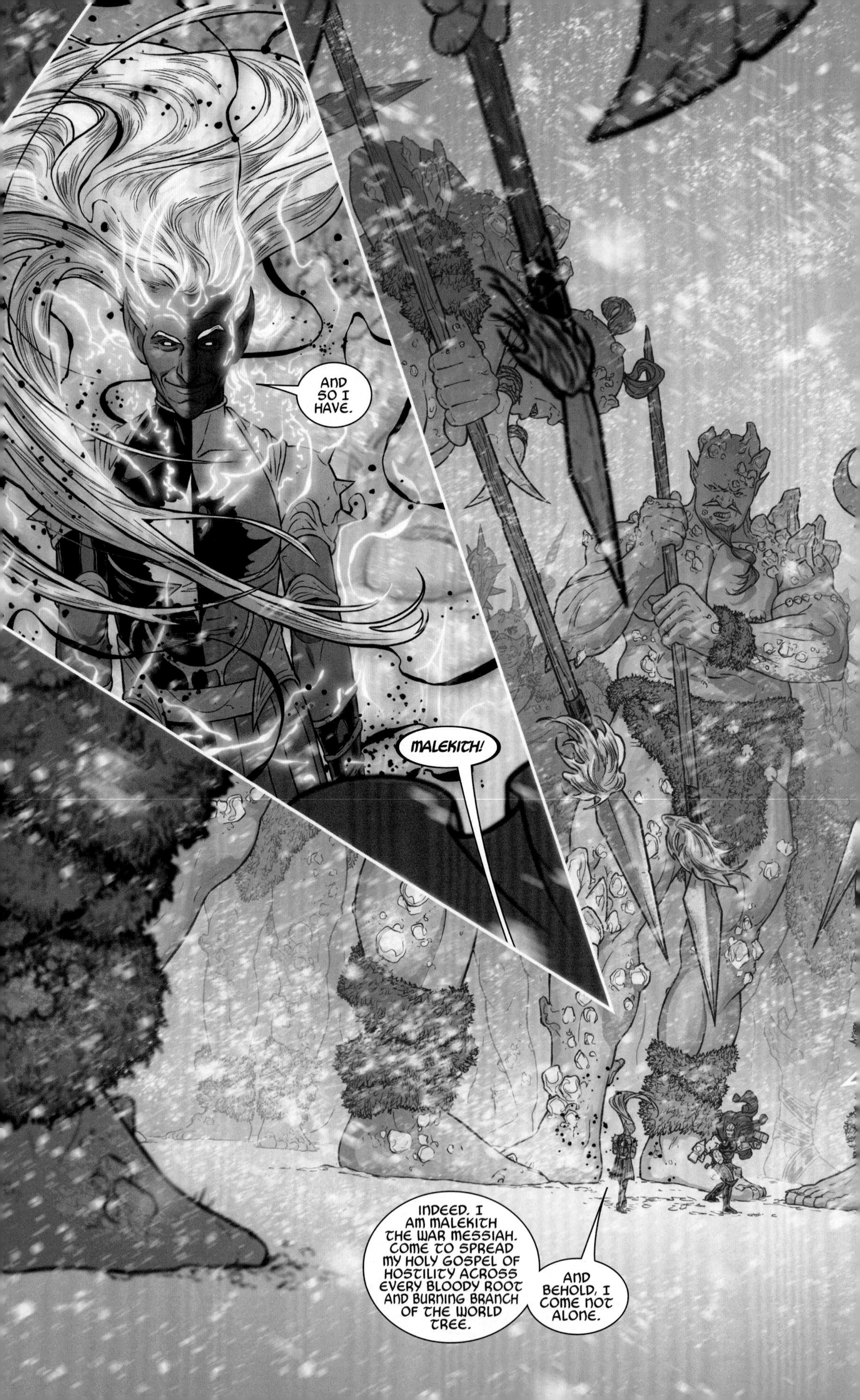
AND SO I HAVE.
MALEKITH!
INDEED. I AM MALEKITH THE WAR MESSIAH. COME TO SPREAD MY HOLY GOSPEL OF HOSTILITY ACROSS EVERY BLOODY ROOT AND BURNING BRANCH OF THE WORLD TREE.
AND BEHOLD, I COME NOT ALONE.

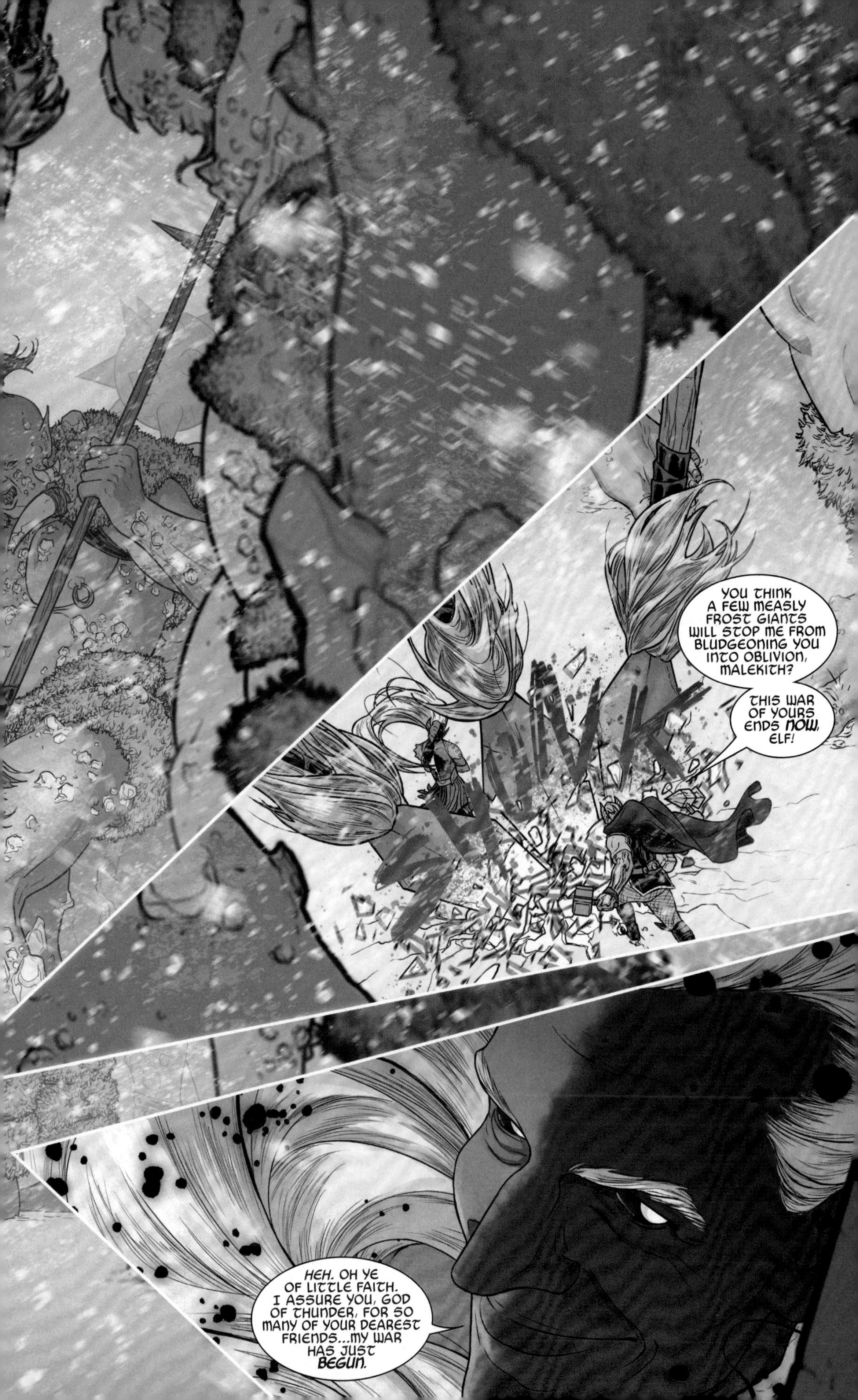
YOU THINK A FEW MEASLY FROST GIANTS WILL STOP ME FROM BLUDGEONING YOU INTO OBLIVION, MALEKITH?
THIS WAR OF YOURS ENDS NOW, ELF!
HEH. OH YE OF LITTLE FAITH. I ASSURE YOU, GOD OF THUNDER, FOR SO MANY OF YOUR DEAREST FRIENDS...MY WAR HAS JUST BEGUN.

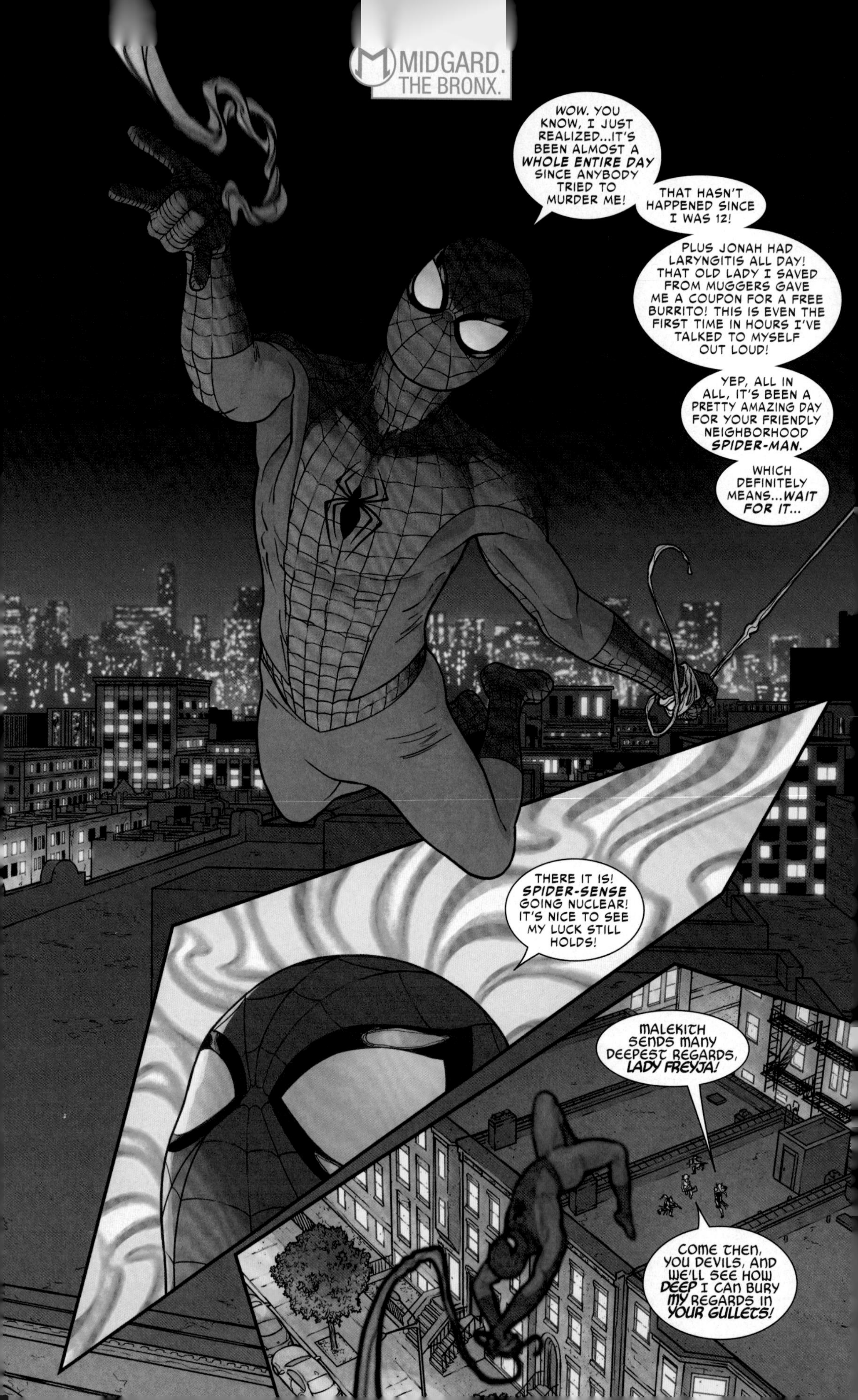
MIDGARD. THE BRONX.
WOW. YOU KNOW, I JUST REALIZED...IT'S BEEN ALMOST A WHOLE ENTIRE DAY SINCE ANYBODY TRIED TO MURDER ME!
THAT HASN'T HAPPENED SINCE I WAS 12!
PLUS JONAH HAD LARYNGITIS ALL DAY! THAT OLD LADY I SAVED FROM MUGGERS GAVE ME A COUPON FOR A FREE BURRITO! THIS IS EVEN THE FIRST TIME IN HOURS I'VE TALKED TO MYSELF OUT LOUD!
YEP, ALL IN ALL, IT'S BEEN A PRETTY AMAZING DAY FOR YOUR FRIENDLY NEIGHBORHOOD SPIDER-MAN.
WHICH DEFINITELY MEANS...WAIT FOR IT...
THERE IT IS! SPIDER-SENSE GOING NUCLEAR! IT'S NICE TO SEE MY LUCK STILL HOLDS!
MALEKITH SENDS MANY DEEPEST REGARDS, LADY FREYJA!
COME THEN, YOU DEVILS, AND WE'LL SEE HOW DEEP I CAN BURY MY REGARDS IN YOUR GULLETS!

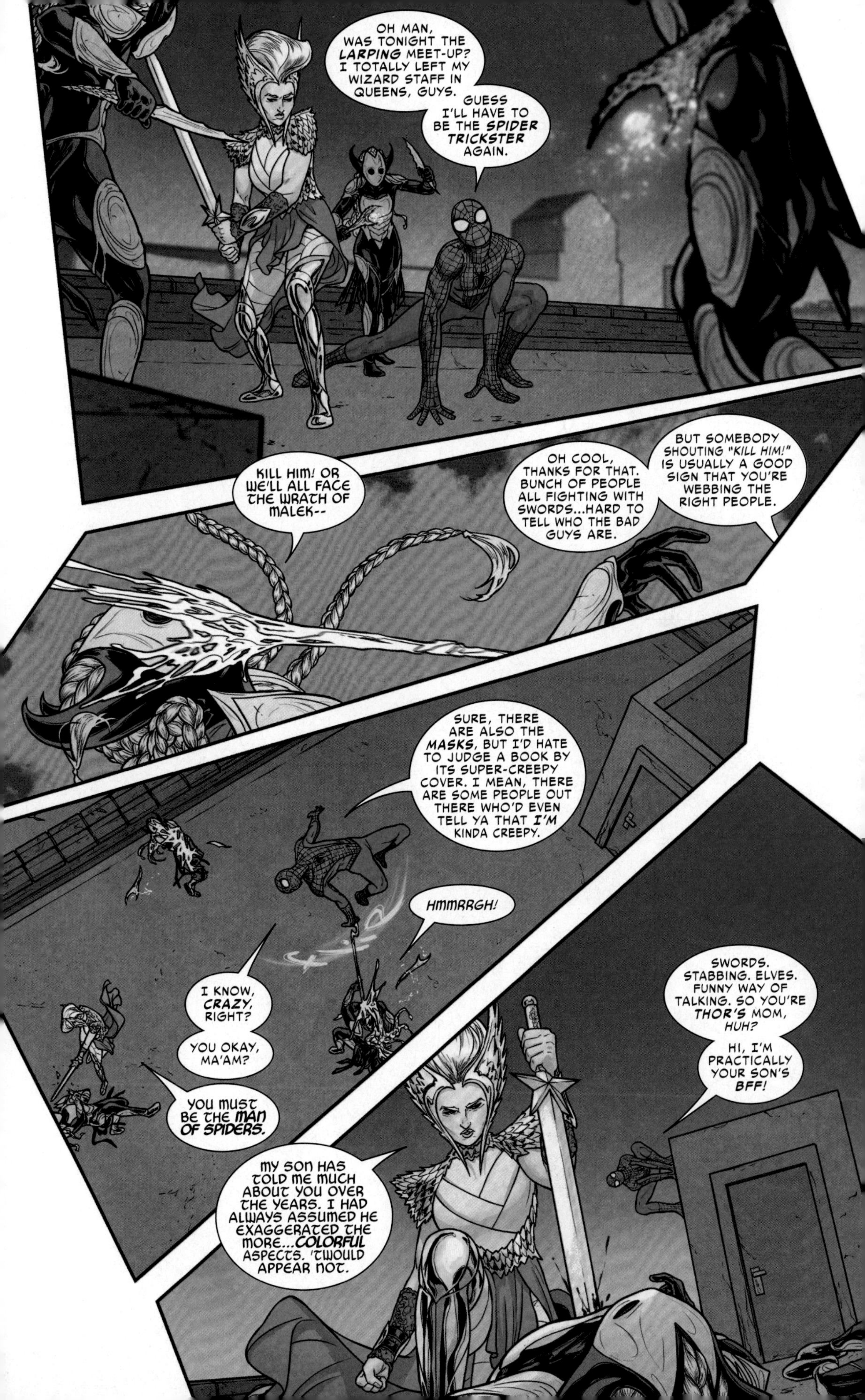

OH MAN, WAS TONIGHT THE LARPING MEET-UP? I TOTALLY LEFT MY WIZARD STAFF IN QUEENS, GUYS.
GUESS I'LL HAVE TO BE THE SPIDER TRICKSTER AGAIN.
KILL HIM! OR WE'LL ALL FACE THE WRATH OF MALEK--
OH COOL, THANKS FOR THAT. BUNCH OF PEOPLE ALL FIGHTING WITH SWORDS...HARD TO TELL WHO THE BAD GUYS ARE.
BUT SOMEBODY SHOUTING "KILL HIM!" IS USUALLY A GOOD SIGN THAT YOU'RE WEBBING THE RIGHT PEOPLE.
SURE, THERE ARE ALSO THE MASKS, BUT I'D HATE TO JUDGE A BOOK BY ITS SUPER-CREEPY COVER. I MEAN, THERE ARE SOME PEOPLE OUT THERE WHO'D EVEN TELL YA THAT I'M KINDA CREEPY.
HMMRRGH!
I KNOW, CRAZY, RIGHT?
YOU OKAY, MA'AM?
YOU MUST BE THE MAN OF SPIDERS.
SWORDS. STABBING. ELVES. FUNNY WAY OF TALKING. SO YOU'RE THOR'S MOM, HUH?
HI, I'M PRACTICALLY YOUR SON'S BFF!
MY SON HAS TOLD ME MUCH ABOUT YOU OVER THE YEARS. I HAD ALWAYS ASSUMED HE EXAGGERATED THE MORE...COLORFUL ASPECTS. 'TWOULD APPEAR NOT.

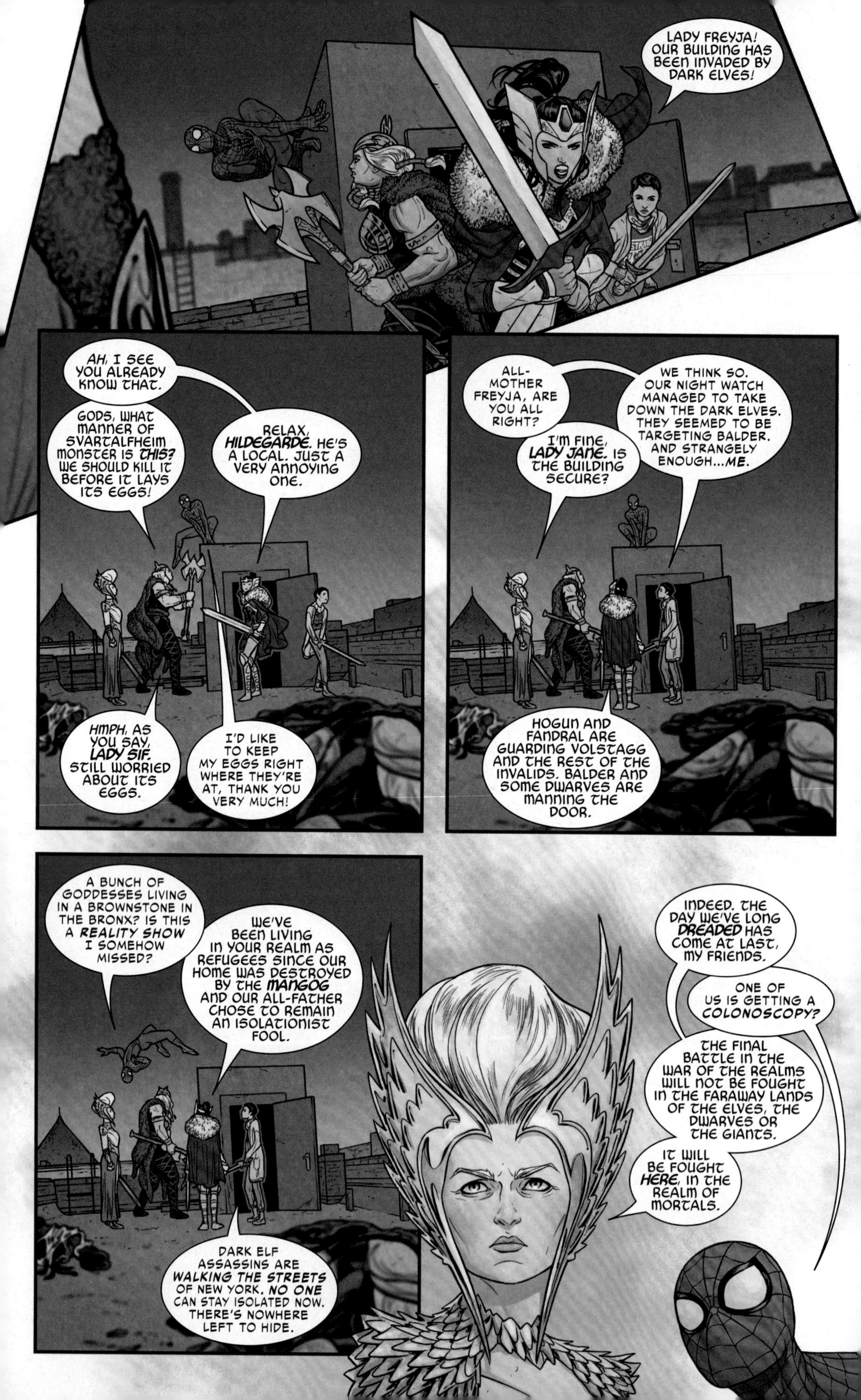
LADY FREYJA! OUR BUILDING HAS BEEN INVADED BY DARK ELVES!
AH, I SEE YOU ALREADY KNOW THAT.
GODS, WHAT MANNER OF SVARTALFHEIM MONSTER IS THIS? WE SHOULD KILL IT BEFORE IT LAYS ITS EGGS!
RELAX, HILDEGARDE. HE'S A LOCAL. JUST A VERY ANNOYING ONE.
HMPH. AS YOU SAY, LADY SIF. STILL WORRIED ABOUT ITS EGGS.
I'D LIKE TO KEEP MY EGGS RIGHT WHERE THEY'RE AT, THANK YOU VERY MUCH!
ALL-MOTHER FREYJA, ARE YOU ALL RIGHT?
WE THINK SO. OUR NIGHT WATCH MANAGED TO TAKE DOWN THE DARK ELVES. THEY SEEMED TO BE TARGETING BALDER. AND STRANGELY ENOUGH...ME.
I'M FINE, LADY JANE. IS THE BUILDING SECURE?
HOGUN AND FANDRAL ARE GUARDING VOLSTAGG AND THE REST OF THE INVALIDS. BALDER AND SOME DWARVES ARE MANNING THE DOOR.
A BUNCH OF GODDESSES LIVING IN A BROWNSTONE IN THE BRONX? IS THIS A REALITY SHOW I SOMEHOW MISSED?
WE'VE BEEN LIVING IN YOUR REALM AS REFUGEES SINCE OUR HOME WAS DESTROYED BY THE MANGOG AND OUR ALL-FATHER CHOSE TO REMAIN AN ISOLATIONIST FOOL.
DARK ELF ASSASSINS ARE WALKING THE STREETS OF NEW YORK. NO ONE CAN STAY ISOLATED NOW. THERE'S NOWHERE LEFT TO HIDE.
INDEED. THE DAY WE'VE LONG DREADED HAS COME AT LAST, MY FRIENDS.
ONE OF US IS GETTING A COLONOSCOPY?
THE FINAL BATTLE IN THE WAR OF THE REALMS WILL NOT BE FOUGHT IN THE FARAWAY LANDS OF THE ELVES, THE DWARVES OR THE GIANTS.
IT WILL BE FOUGHT HERE, IN THE REALM OF MORTALS.

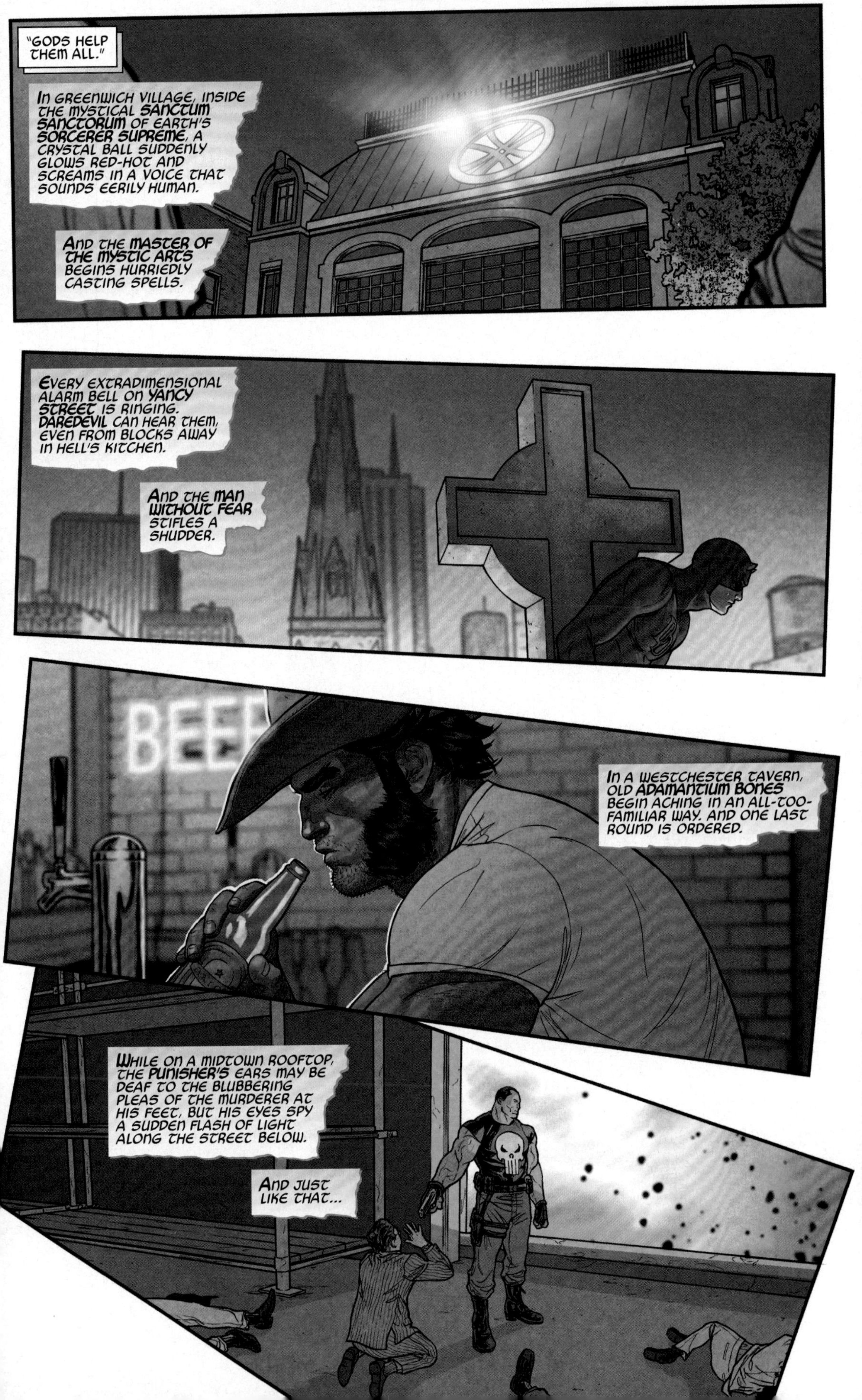

"GODS HELP THEM ALL."
IN GREENWICH VILLAGE, INSIDE THE MYSTICAL SANCTUM SANCTORUM OF EARTH'S SORCERER SUPREME, A CRYSTAL BALL SUDDENLY GLOWS RED-HOT AND SCREAMS IN A VOICE THAT SOUNDS EERILY HUMAN.
AND THE MASTER OF THE MYSTIC ARTS BEGINS HURRIEDLY CASTING SPELLS.
EVERY EXTRADIMENSIONAL ALARM BELL ON YANCY STREET IS RINGING. DAREDEVIL CAN HEAR THEM, EVEN FROM BLOCKS AWAY IN HELL'S KITCHEN.
AND THE MAN WITHOUT FEAR STIFLES A SHUDDER.
BEER
IN A WESTCHESTER TAVERN, OLD ADAMANTIUM BONES BEGIN ACHING IN AN ALL-TOO-FAMILIAR WAY. AND ONE LAST ROUND IS ORDERED.
WHILE ON A MIDTOWN ROOFTOP, THE PUNISHER'S EARS MAY BE DEAF TO THE BLUBBERING PLEAS OF THE MURDERER AT HIS FEET, BUT HIS EYES SPY A SUDDEN FLASH OF LIGHT ALONG THE STREET BELOW.
AND JUST LIKE THAT...

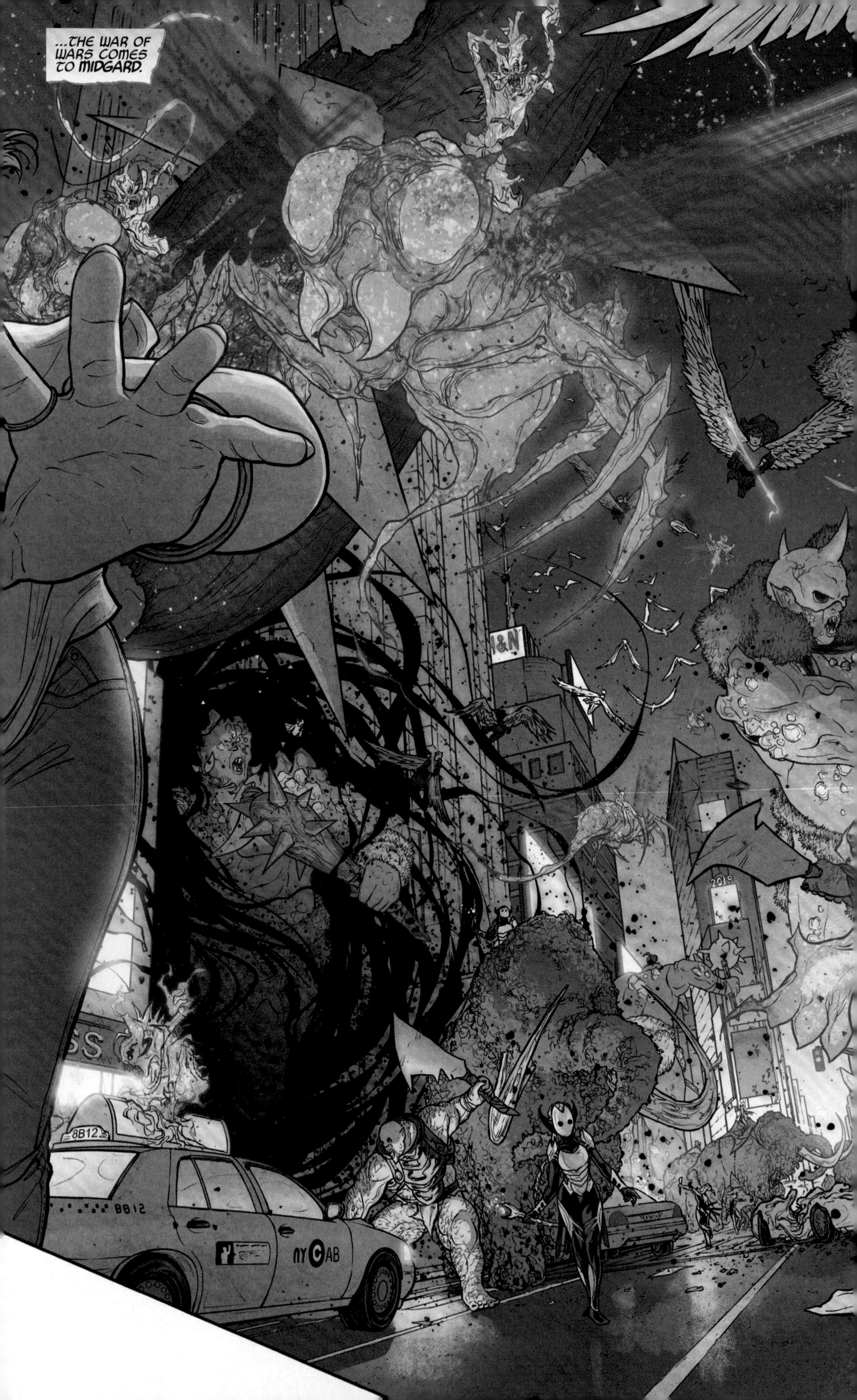
...THE WAR OF WARS COMES TO MIDGARD.
8B12
NYC CAB
2019

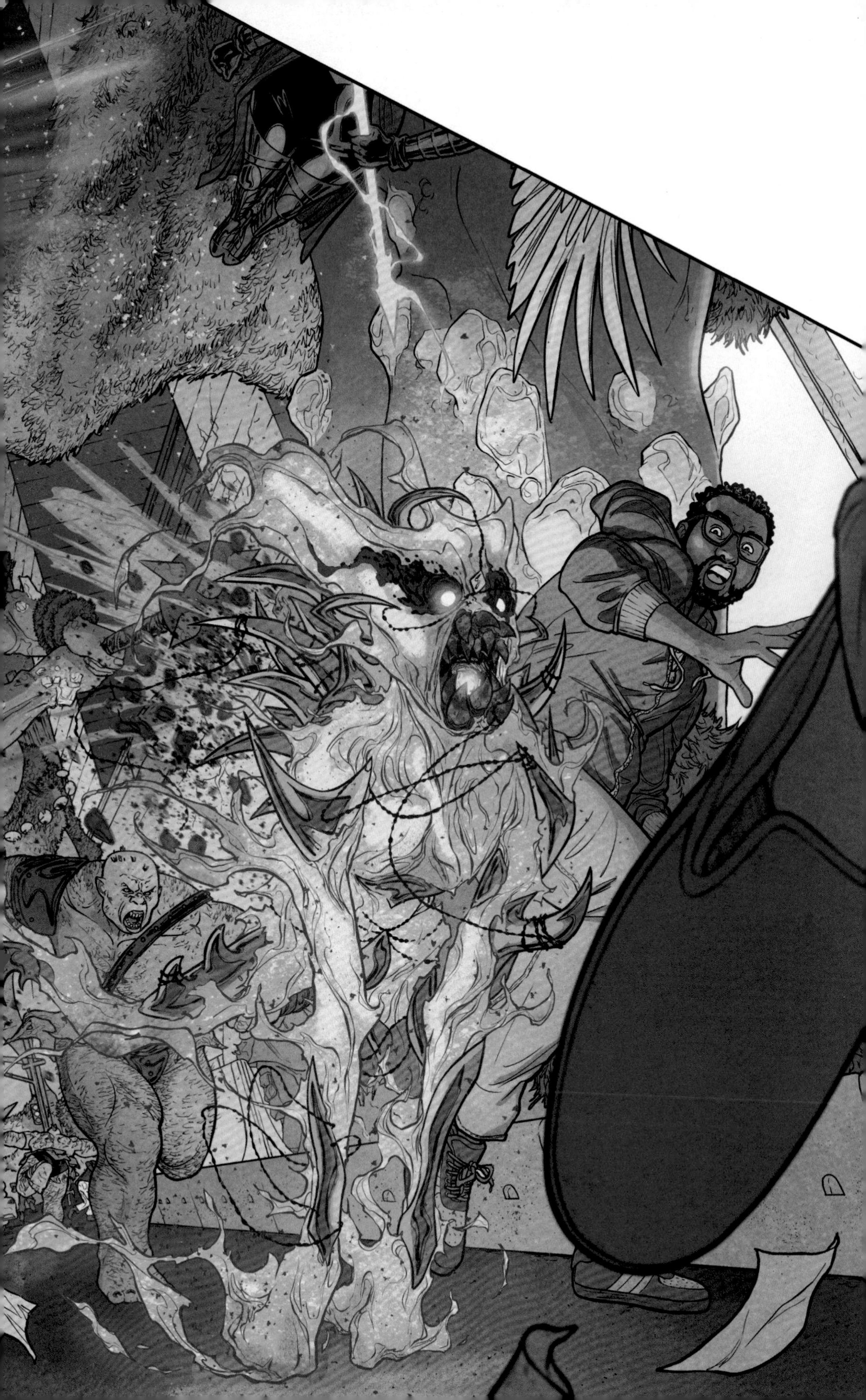

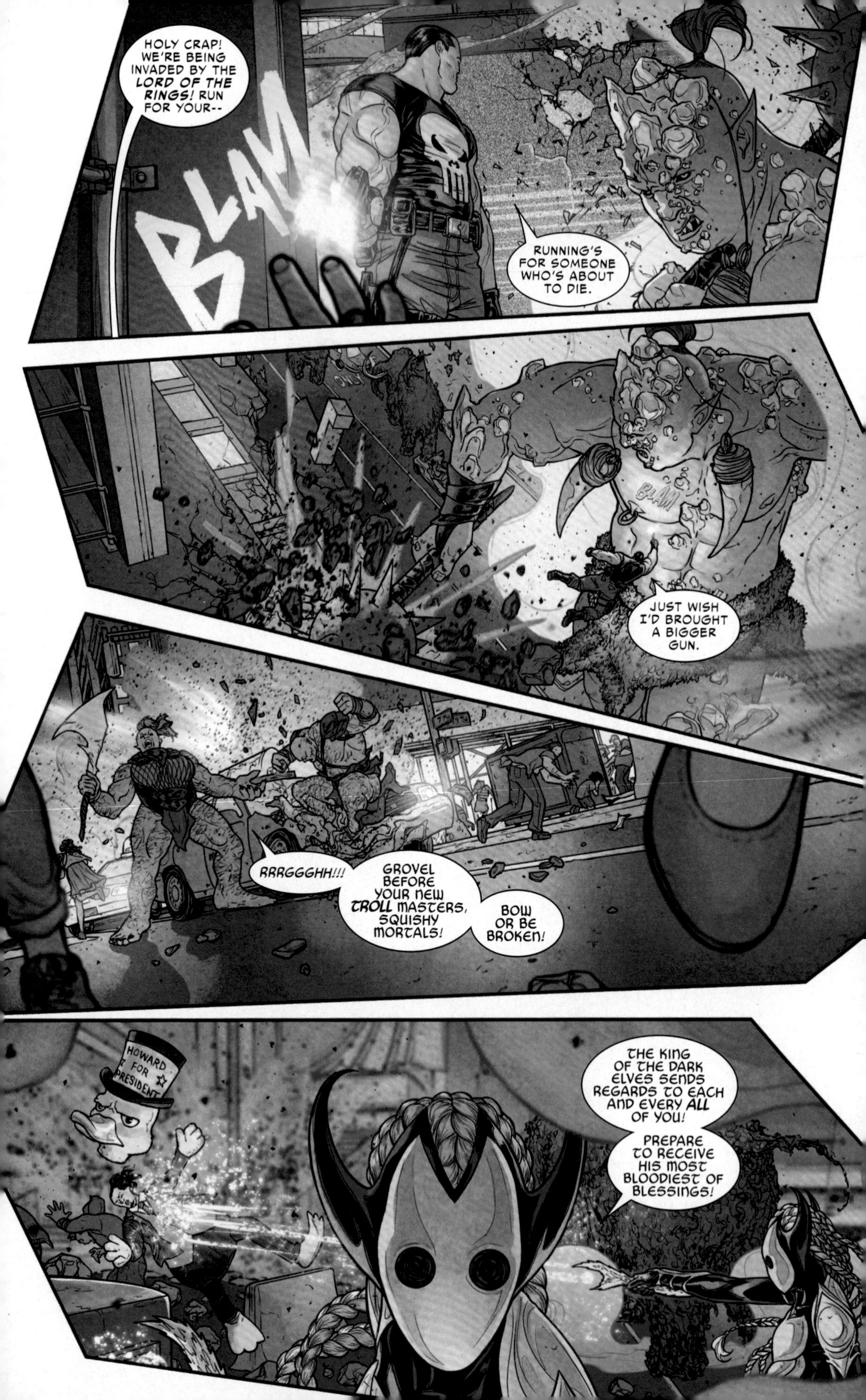
HOLY CRAP! WE'RE BEING INVADED BY THE LORD OF THE RINGS! RUN FOR YOUR--
BLAM
RUNNING'S FOR SOMEONE WHO'S ABOUT TO DIE.
BLAM
JUST WISH I'D BROUGHT A BIGGER GUN.
RRRGGGHH!!!
GROVEL BEFORE YOUR NEW TROLL MASTERS, SQUISHY MORTALS!
BOW OR BE BROKEN!
HOWARD FOR PRESIDENT
THE KING OF THE DARK ELVES SENDS REGARDS TO EACH AND EVERY ALL OF YOU!
PREPARE TO RECEIVE HIS MOST BLOODIEST OF BLESSINGS!

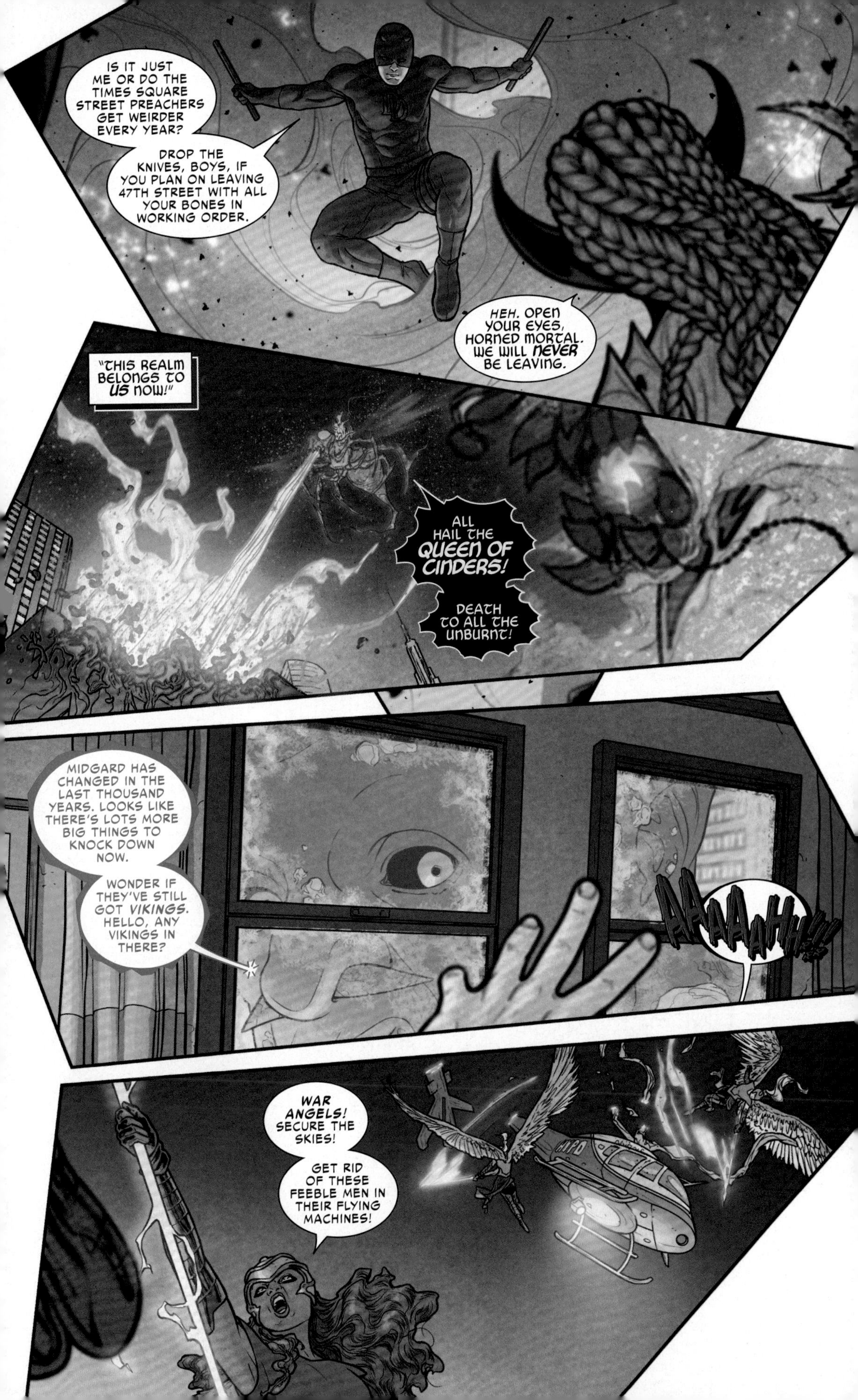
IS IT JUST ME OR DO THE TIMES SQUARE STREET PREACHERS GET WEIRDER EVERY YEAR?
DROP THE KNIVES, BOYS, IF YOU PLAN ON LEAVING 47TH STREET WITH ALL YOUR BONES IN WORKING ORDER.
HEH. OPEN YOUR EYES, HORNED MORTAL. WE WILL NEVER BE LEAVING.
"THIS REALM BELONGS TO US NOW!"
ALL HAIL THE QUEEN OF CINDERS!
DEATH TO ALL THE UNBURNT!
MIDGARD HAS CHANGED IN THE LAST THOUSAND YEARS. LOOKS LIKE THERE'S LOTS MORE BIG THINGS TO KNOCK DOWN NOW.
WONDER IF THEY'VE STILL GOT VIKINGS. HELLO, ANY VIKINGS IN THERE?
AAAAAHH!!
WAR ANGELS! SECURE THE SKIES!
GET RID OF THESE FEEBLE MEN IN THEIR FLYING MACHINES!
NYPD

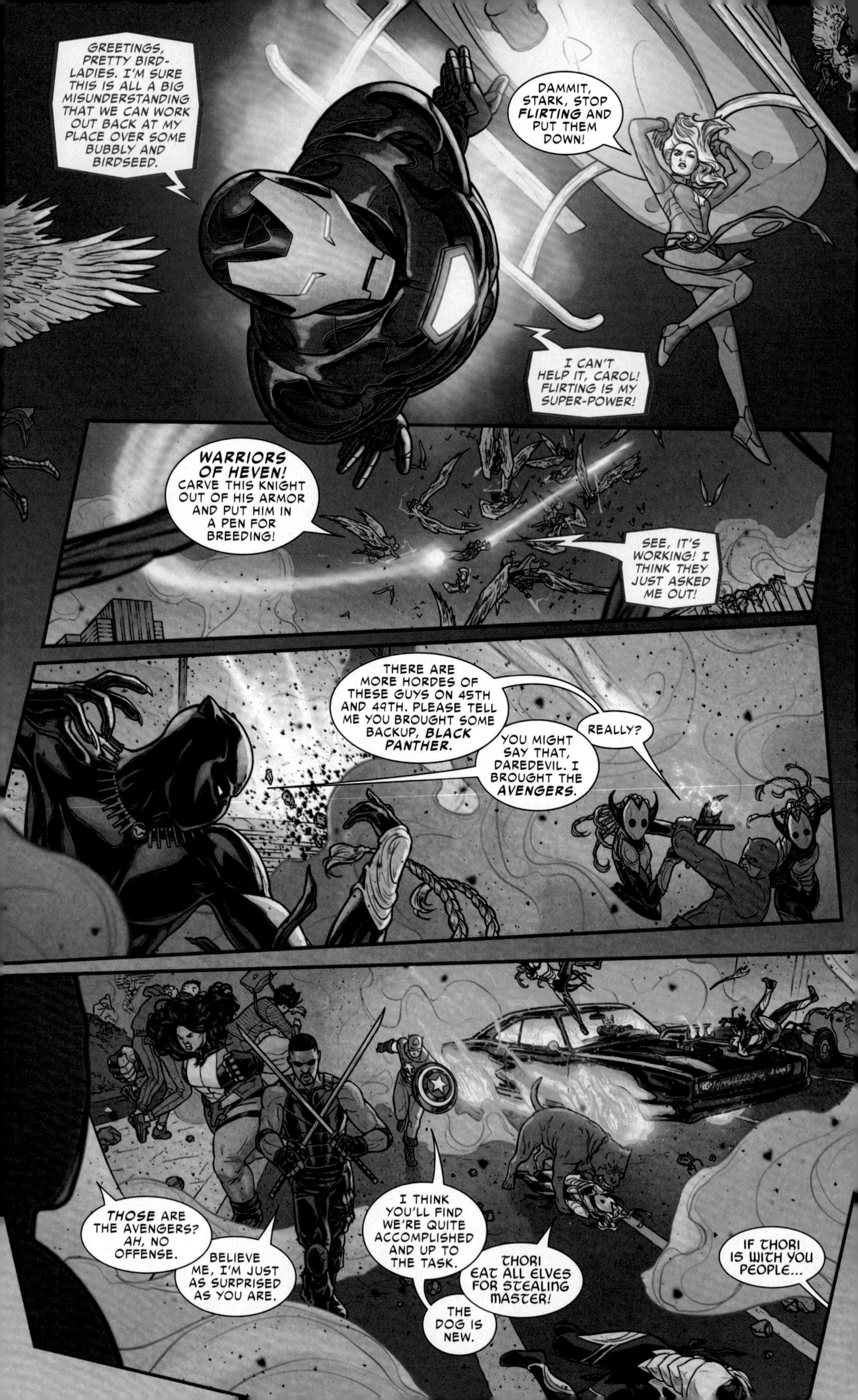
GREETINGS, PRETTY BIRD-LADIES. I'M SURE THIS IS ALL A BIG MISUNDERSTANDING THAT WE CAN WORK OUT BACK AT MY PLACE OVER SOME BUBBLY AND BIRDSEED.
DAMMIT, STARK, STOP FLIRTING AND PUT THEM DOWN!
I CAN'T HELP IT, CAROL! FLIRTING IS MY SUPER-POWER!
WARRIORS OF HEVEN! CARVE THIS KNIGHT OUT OF HIS ARMOR AND PUT HIM IN A PEN FOR BREEDING!
SEE, IT'S WORKING! I THINK THEY JUST ASKED ME OUT!
THERE ARE MORE HORDES OF THESE GUYS ON 45TH AND 49TH. PLEASE TELL ME YOU BROUGHT SOME BACKUP, BLACK PANTHER.
YOU MIGHT SAY THAT, DAREDEVIL. I BROUGHT THE AVENGERS.
REALLY?
THOSE ARE THE AVENGERS? AH, NO OFFENSE.
BELIEVE ME, I'M JUST AS SURPRISED AS YOU ARE.
I THINK YOU'LL FIND WE'RE QUITE ACCOMPLISHED AND UP TO THE TASK.
THE DOG IS NEW.
THORI EAT ALL ELVES FOR STEALING MASTER!
IF THORI IS WITH YOU PEOPLE...

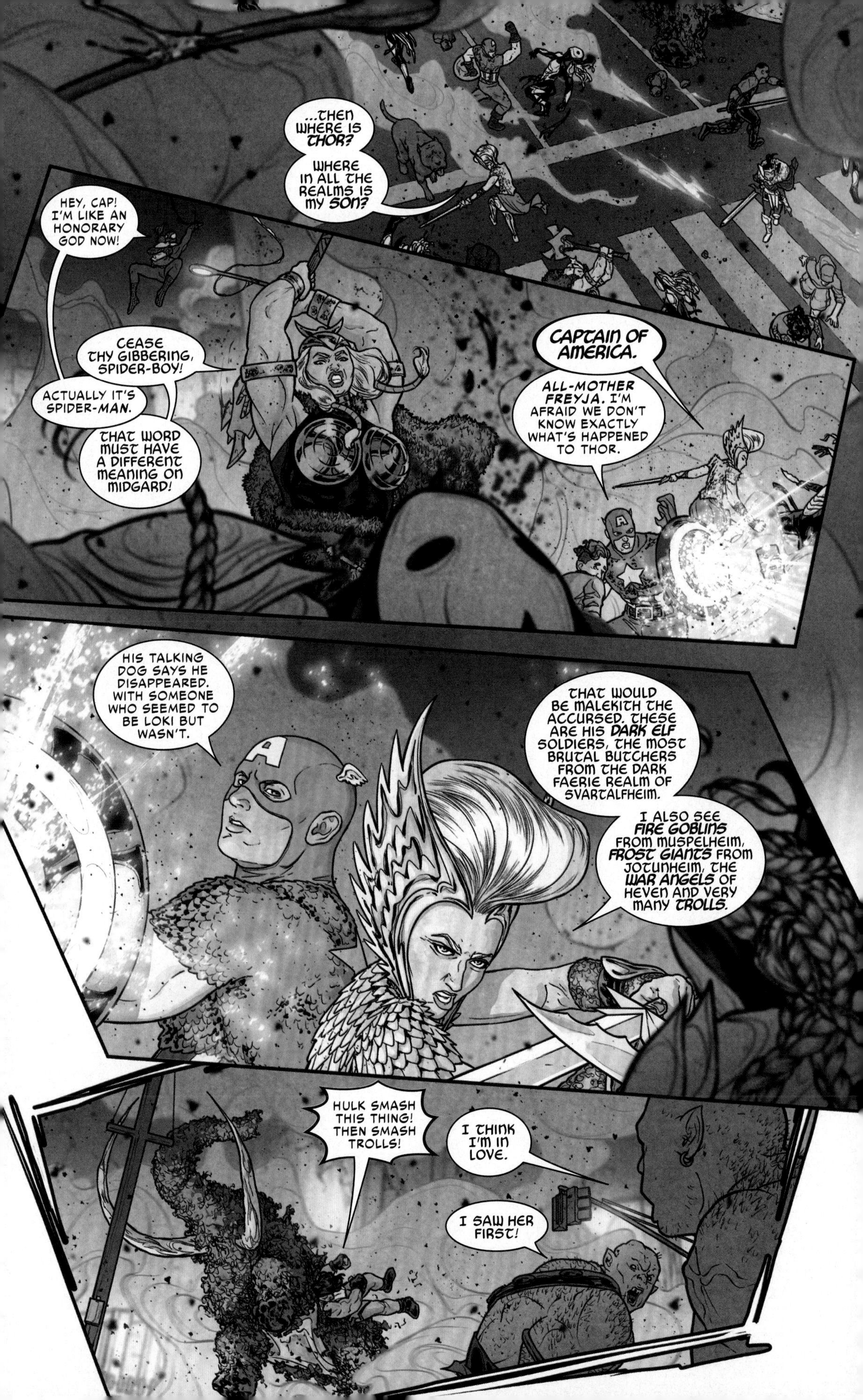
...THEN WHERE IS THOR?
WHERE IN ALL THE REALMS IS MY SON?
HEY, CAP! I'M LIKE AN HONORARY GOD NOW!
CEASE THY GIBBERING, SPIDER-BOY!
ACTUALLY IT'S SPIDER-MAN.
THAT WORD MUST HAVE A DIFFERENT MEANING ON MIDGARD!
CAPTAIN OF AMERICA.
ALL-MOTHER FREYJA. I'M AFRAID WE DON'T KNOW EXACTLY WHAT'S HAPPENED TO THOR.
HIS TALKING DOG SAYS HE DISAPPEARED. WITH SOMEONE WHO SEEMED TO BE LOKI BUT WASN'T.
THAT WOULD BE MALEKITH THE ACCURSED. THESE ARE HIS DARK ELF SOLDIERS, THE MOST BRUTAL BUTCHERS FROM THE DARK FAERIE REALM OF SVARTALFHEIM.
I ALSO SEE FIRE GOBLINS FROM MUSPELHEIM, FROST GIANTS FROM JOTUNHEIM, THE WAR ANGELS OF HEVEN AND VERY MANY TROLLS.
HULK SMASH THIS THING! THEN SMASH TROLLS!
I THINK I'M IN LOVE.
I SAW HER FIRST!

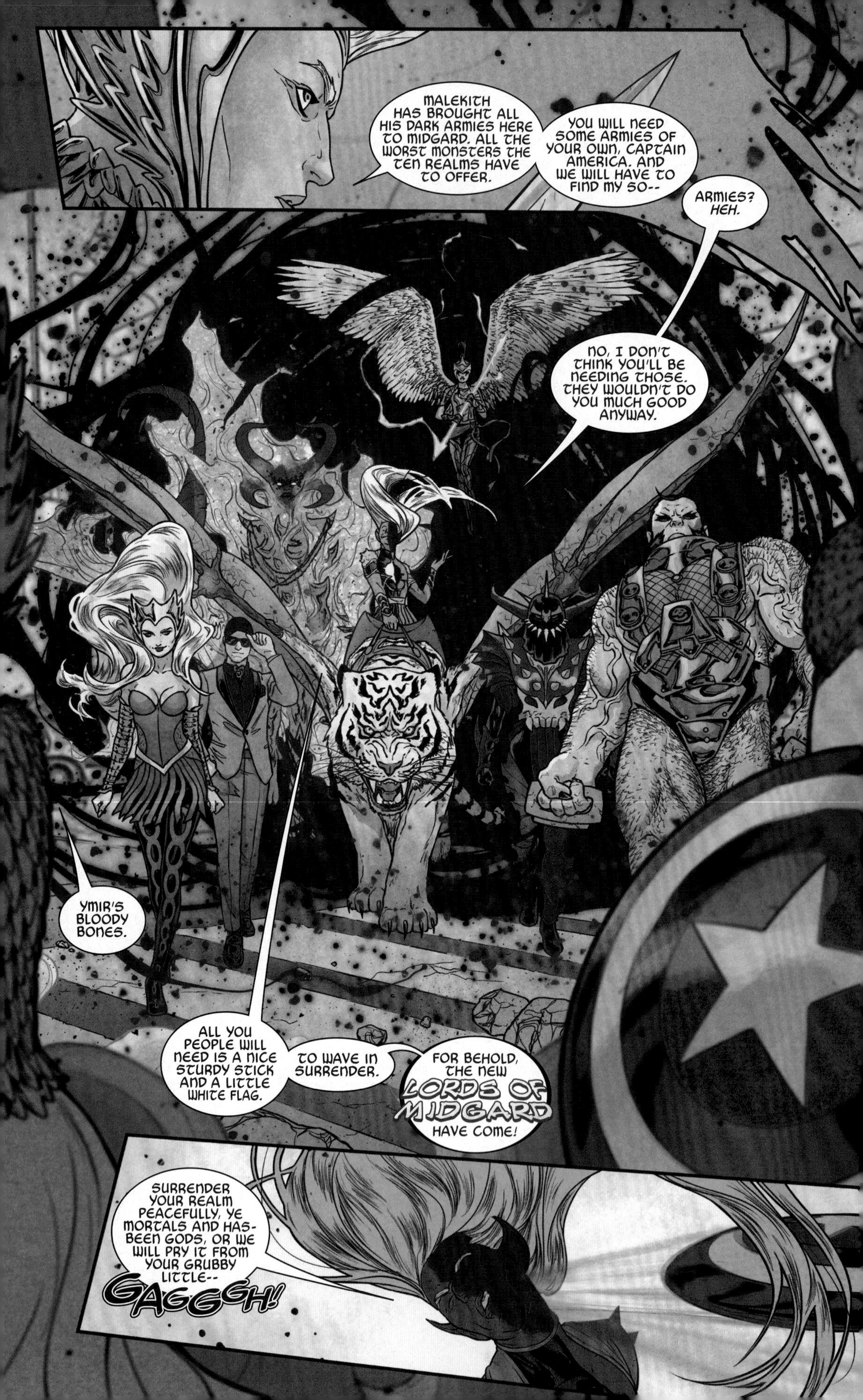
MALEKITH HAS BROUGHT ALL HIS DARK ARMIES HERE TO MIDGARD. ALL THE WORST MONSTERS THE TEN REALMS HAVE TO OFFER.
YOU WILL NEED SOME ARMIES OF YOUR OWN, CAPTAIN AMERICA. AND WE WILL HAVE TO FIND MY SO--
ARMIES? HEH.
NO, I DON'T THINK YOU'LL BE NEEDING THOSE. THEY WOULDN'T DO YOU MUCH GOOD ANYWAY.
YMIR'S BLOODY BONES.
ALL YOU PEOPLE WILL NEED IS A NICE STURDY STICK AND A LITTLE WHITE FLAG.
TO WAVE IN SURRENDER.
FOR BEHOLD, THE NEW LORDS OF MIDGARD HAVE COME!
SURRENDER YOUR REALM PEACEFULLY, YE MORTALS AND HAS-BEEN GODS, OR WE WILL PRY IT FROM YOUR GRUBBY LITTLE--
GAGGGH!

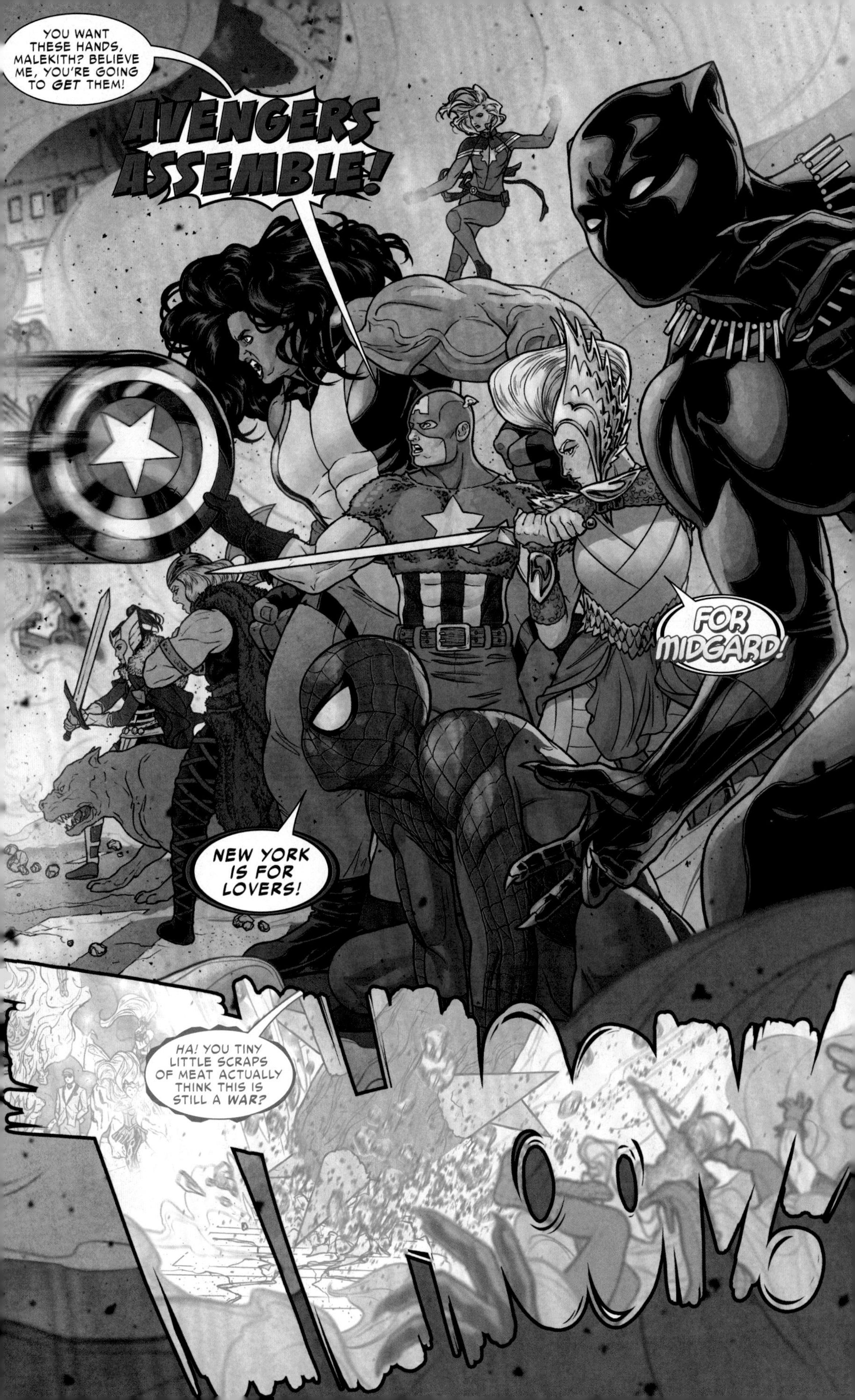
YOU WANT THESE HANDS, MALEKITH? BELIEVE ME, YOU'RE GOING TO GET THEM!
AVENGERS ASSEMBLE!
FOR MIDGARD!
NEW YORK IS FOR LOVERS!
HA! YOU TINY LITTLE SCRAPS OF MEAT ACTUALLY THINK THIS IS STILL A WAR?
THOOM!

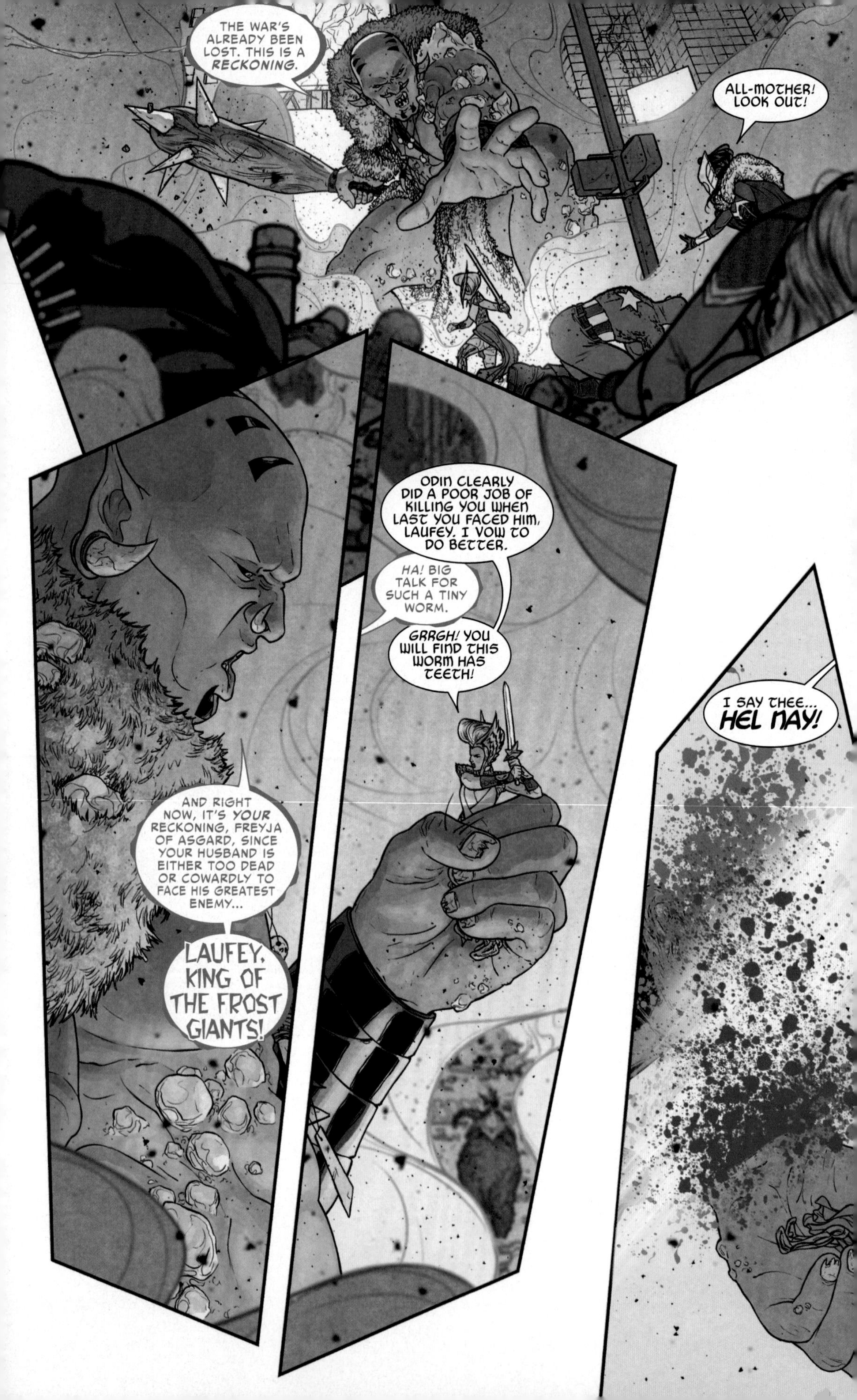

THE WAR'S ALREADY BEEN LOST. THIS IS A *RECKONING.*
ALL-MOTHER! LOOK OUT!
AND RIGHT NOW, IT'S *YOUR* RECKONING, FREYJA OF ASGARD, SINCE YOUR HUSBAND IS EITHER TOO DEAD OR COWARDLY TO FACE HIS GREATEST ENEMY...
LAUFEY. KING OF THE FROST GIANTS!
ODIN CLEARLY DID A POOR JOB OF KILLING YOU WHEN LAST YOU FACED HIM, LAUFEY. I VOW TO DO BETTER.
HA! BIG TALK FOR SUCH A TINY WORM.
GRRGH! YOU WILL FIND THIS WORM HAS TEETH!
I SAY THEE... **HEL NAY!**

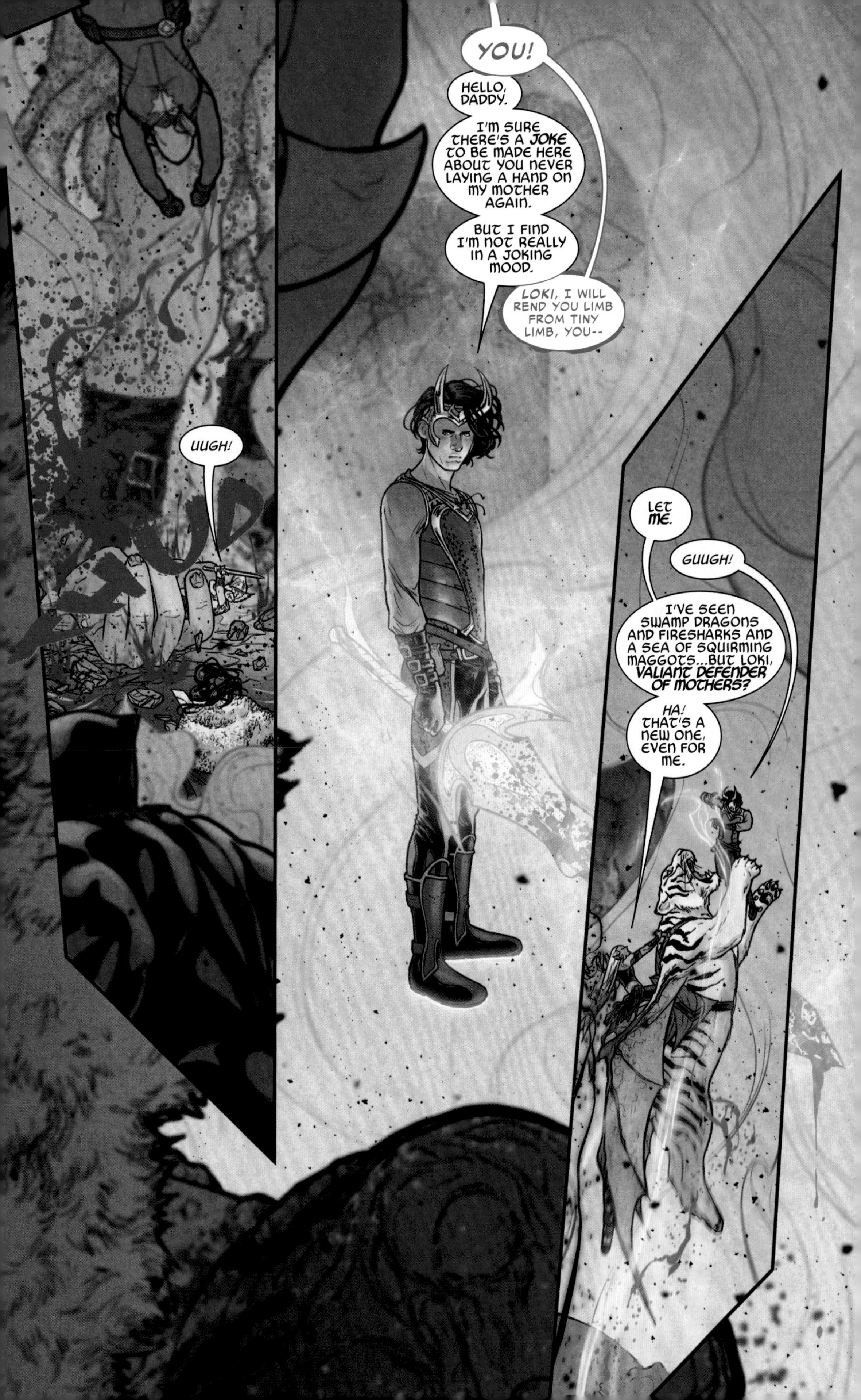
YOU!
HELLO, DADDY.
I'M SURE THERE'S A JOKE TO BE MADE HERE ABOUT YOU NEVER LAYING A HAND ON MY MOTHER AGAIN.
BUT I FIND I'M NOT REALLY IN A JOKING MOOD.
LOKI, I WILL REND YOU LIMB FROM TINY LIMB, YOU--
UUGH!
LET ME.
GUUGH!
I'VE SEEN SWAMP DRAGONS AND FIRESHARKS AND A SEA OF SQUIRMING MAGGOTS...BUT LOKI, VALIANT DEFENDER OF MOTHERS?
HA! THAT'S A NEW ONE, EVEN FOR ME.

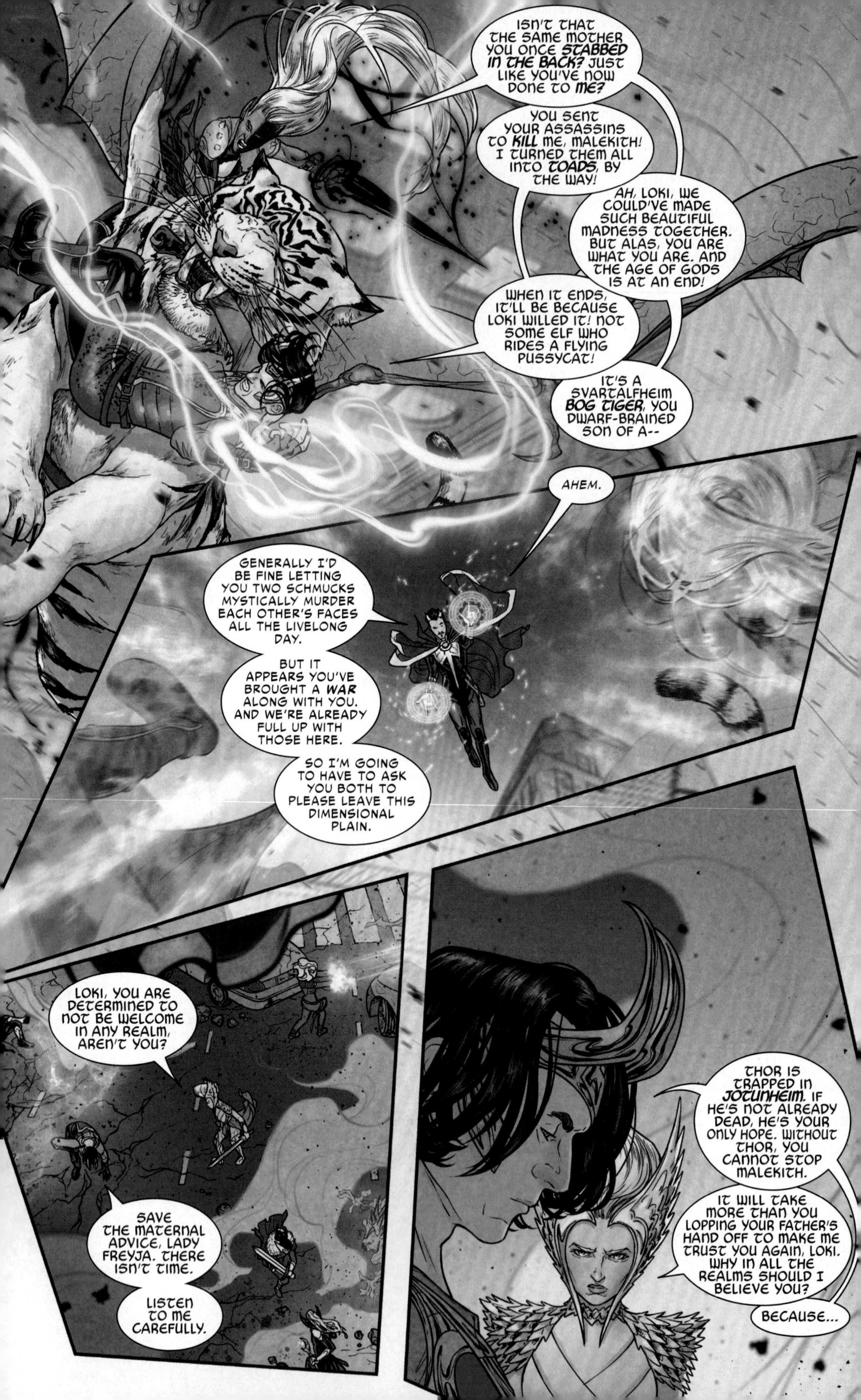
ISN'T THAT THE SAME MOTHER YOU ONCE STABBED IN THE BACK? JUST LIKE YOU'VE NOW DONE TO ME?
YOU SENT YOUR ASSASSINS TO KILL ME, MALEKITH! I TURNED THEM ALL INTO TOADS, BY THE WAY!
AH, LOKI, WE COULD'VE MADE SUCH BEAUTIFUL MADNESS TOGETHER. BUT ALAS, YOU ARE WHAT YOU ARE. AND THE AGE OF GODS IS AT AN END!
WHEN IT ENDS, IT'LL BE BECAUSE LOKI WILLED IT! NOT SOME ELF WHO RIDES A FLYING PUSSYCAT!
IT'S A SVARTALFHEIM BOG TIGER, YOU DWARF-BRAINED SON OF A--
AHEM.
GENERALLY I'D BE FINE LETTING YOU TWO SCHMUCKS MYSTICALLY MURDER EACH OTHER'S FACES ALL THE LIVELONG DAY.
BUT IT APPEARS YOU'VE BROUGHT A WAR ALONG WITH YOU. AND WE'RE ALREADY FULL UP WITH THOSE HERE.
SO I'M GOING TO HAVE TO ASK YOU BOTH TO PLEASE LEAVE THIS DIMENSIONAL PLAIN.
LOKI, YOU ARE DETERMINED TO NOT BE WELCOME IN ANY REALM, AREN'T YOU?
SAVE THE MATERNAL ADVICE, LADY FREYJA. THERE ISN'T TIME.
LISTEN TO ME CAREFULLY.
THOR IS TRAPPED IN JOTUNHEIM. IF HE'S NOT ALREADY DEAD, HE'S YOUR ONLY HOPE. WITHOUT THOR, YOU CANNOT STOP MALEKITH.
IT WILL TAKE MORE THAN YOU LOPPING YOUR FATHER'S HAND OFF TO MAKE ME TRUST YOU AGAIN, LOKI. WHY IN ALL THE REALMS SHOULD I BELIEVE YOU?
BECAUSE...

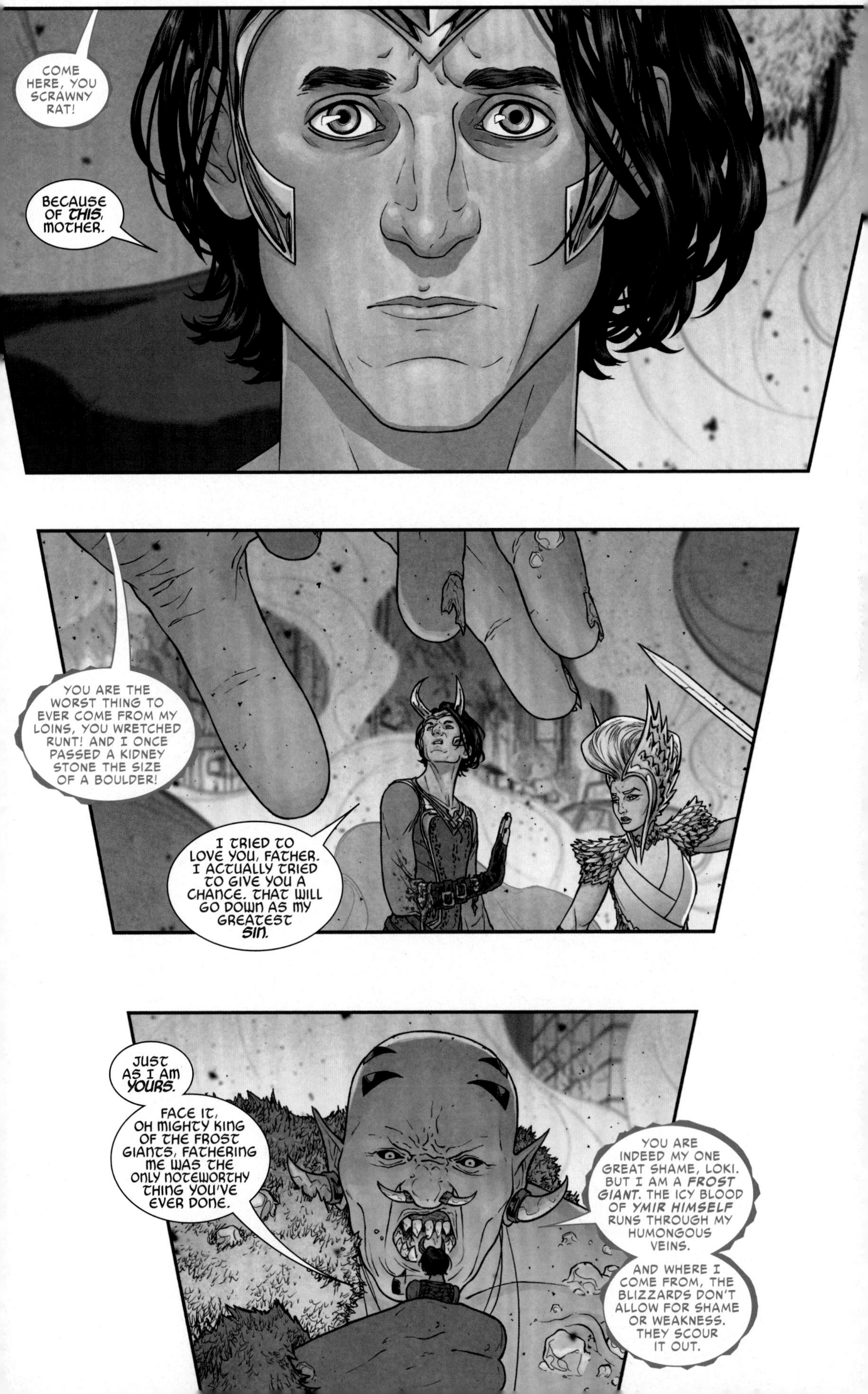
COME HERE, YOU SCRAWNY RAT!
BECAUSE OF THIS, MOTHER.
YOU ARE THE WORST THING TO EVER COME FROM MY LOINS, YOU WRETCHED RUNT! AND I ONCE PASSED A KIDNEY STONE THE SIZE OF A BOULDER!
I TRIED TO LOVE YOU, FATHER. I ACTUALLY TRIED TO GIVE YOU A CHANCE. THAT WILL GO DOWN AS MY GREATEST SIN.
JUST AS I AM YOURS.
FACE IT, OH MIGHTY KING OF THE FROST GIANTS, FATHERING ME WAS THE ONLY NOTEWORTHY THING YOU'VE EVER DONE.
YOU ARE INDEED MY ONE GREAT SHAME, LOKI. BUT I AM A FROST GIANT. THE ICY BLOOD OF YMIR HIMSELF RUNS THROUGH MY HUMONGOUS VEINS.
AND WHERE I COME FROM, THE BLIZZARDS DON'T ALLOW FOR SHAME OR WEAKNESS. THEY SCOUR IT OUT.

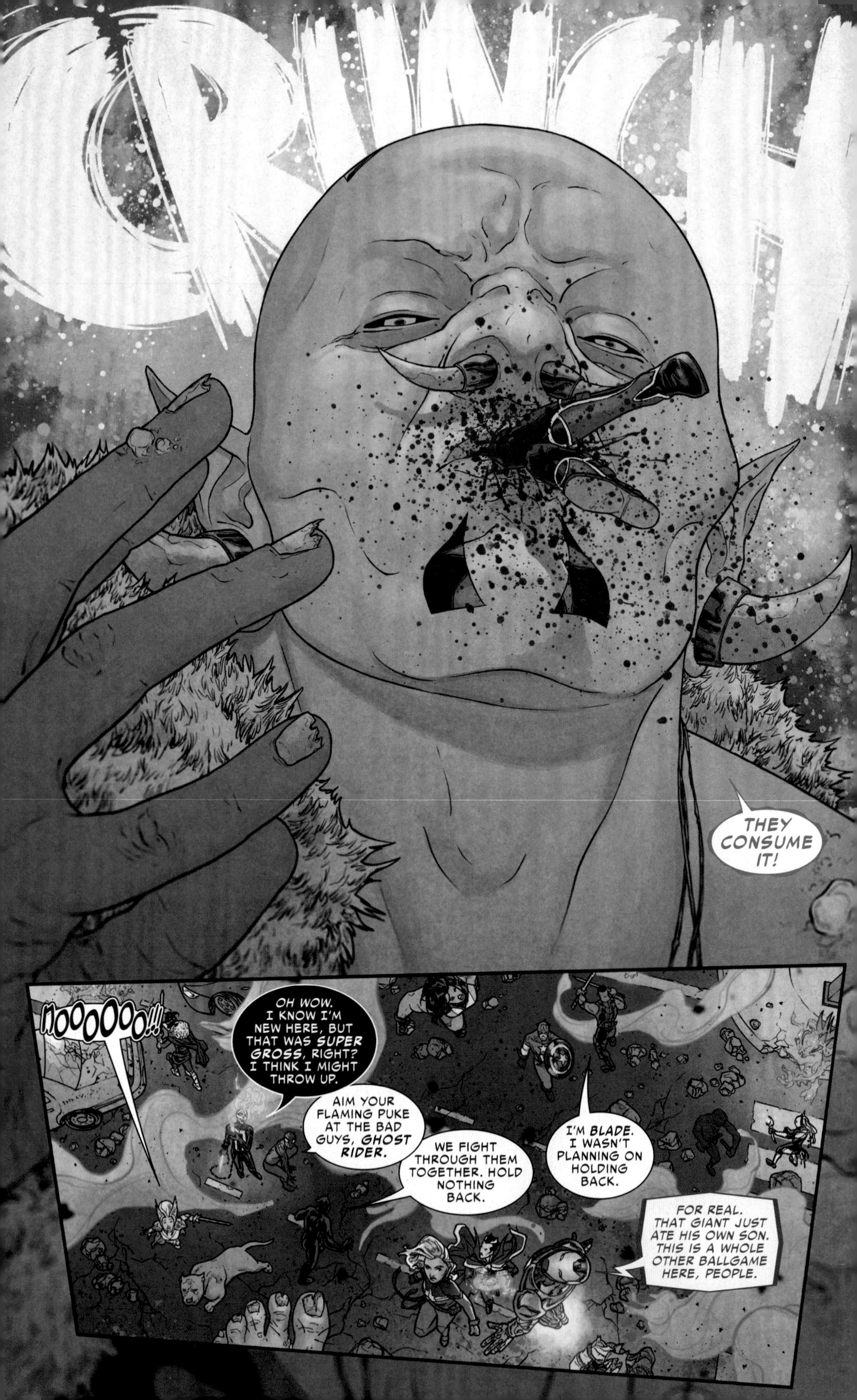
THEY CONSUME IT!
NOOOOOOO!!!
OH WOW. I KNOW I'M NEW HERE, BUT THAT WAS SUPER GROSS, RIGHT? I THINK I MIGHT THROW UP.
AIM YOUR FLAMING PUKE AT THE BAD GUYS, GHOST RIDER.
WE FIGHT THROUGH THEM TOGETHER. HOLD NOTHING BACK.
I'M BLADE. I WASN'T PLANNING ON HOLDING BACK.
FOR REAL. THAT GIANT JUST ATE HIS OWN SON. THIS IS A WHOLE OTHER BALLGAME HERE, PEOPLE.

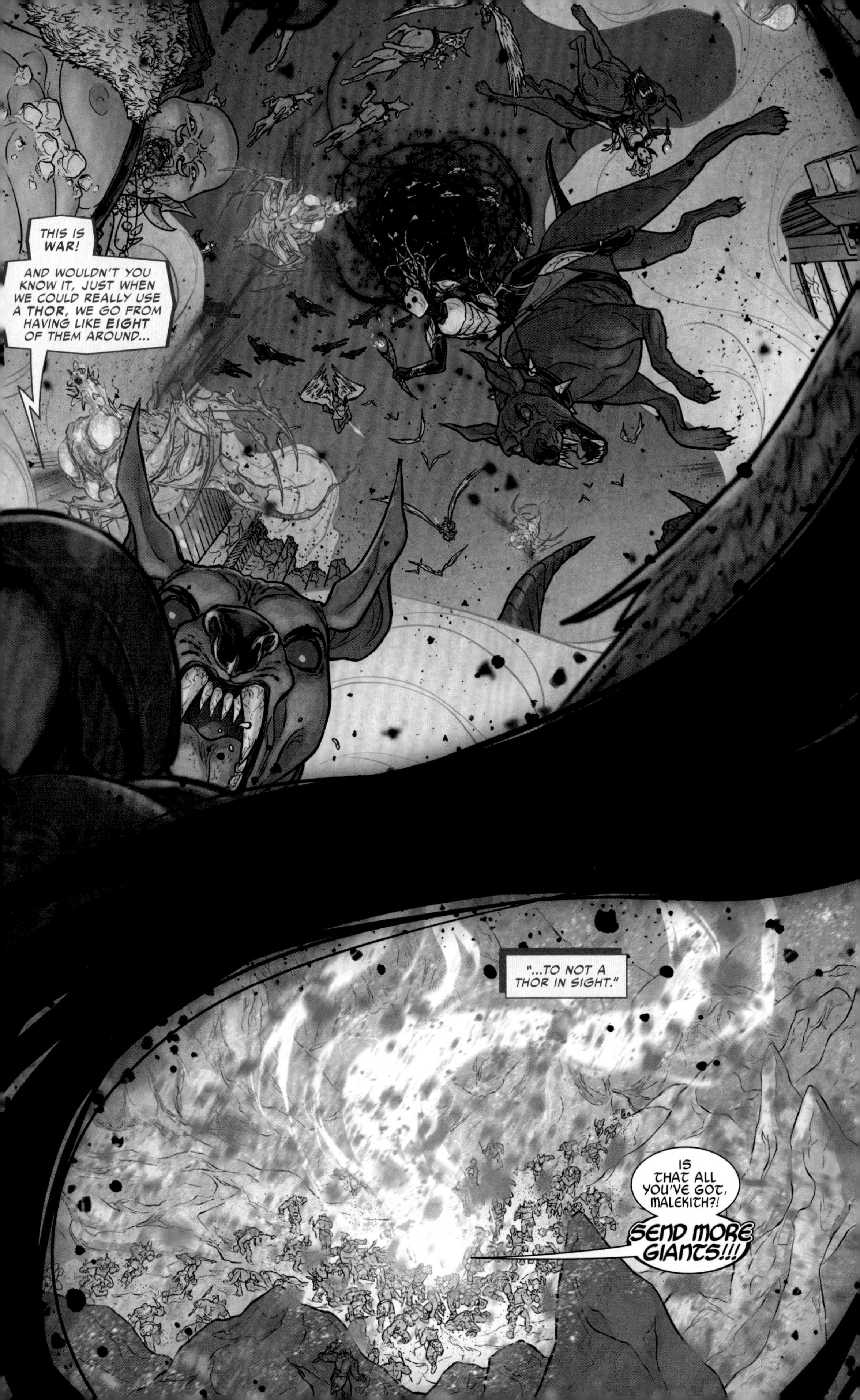
THIS IS WAR!
AND WOULDN'T YOU KNOW IT, JUST WHEN WE COULD REALLY USE A THOR, WE GO FROM HAVING LIKE EIGHT OF THEM AROUND...
"...TO NOT A THOR IN SIGHT."
IS THAT ALL YOU'VE GOT, MALEKITH?!
SEND MORE GIANTS!!!

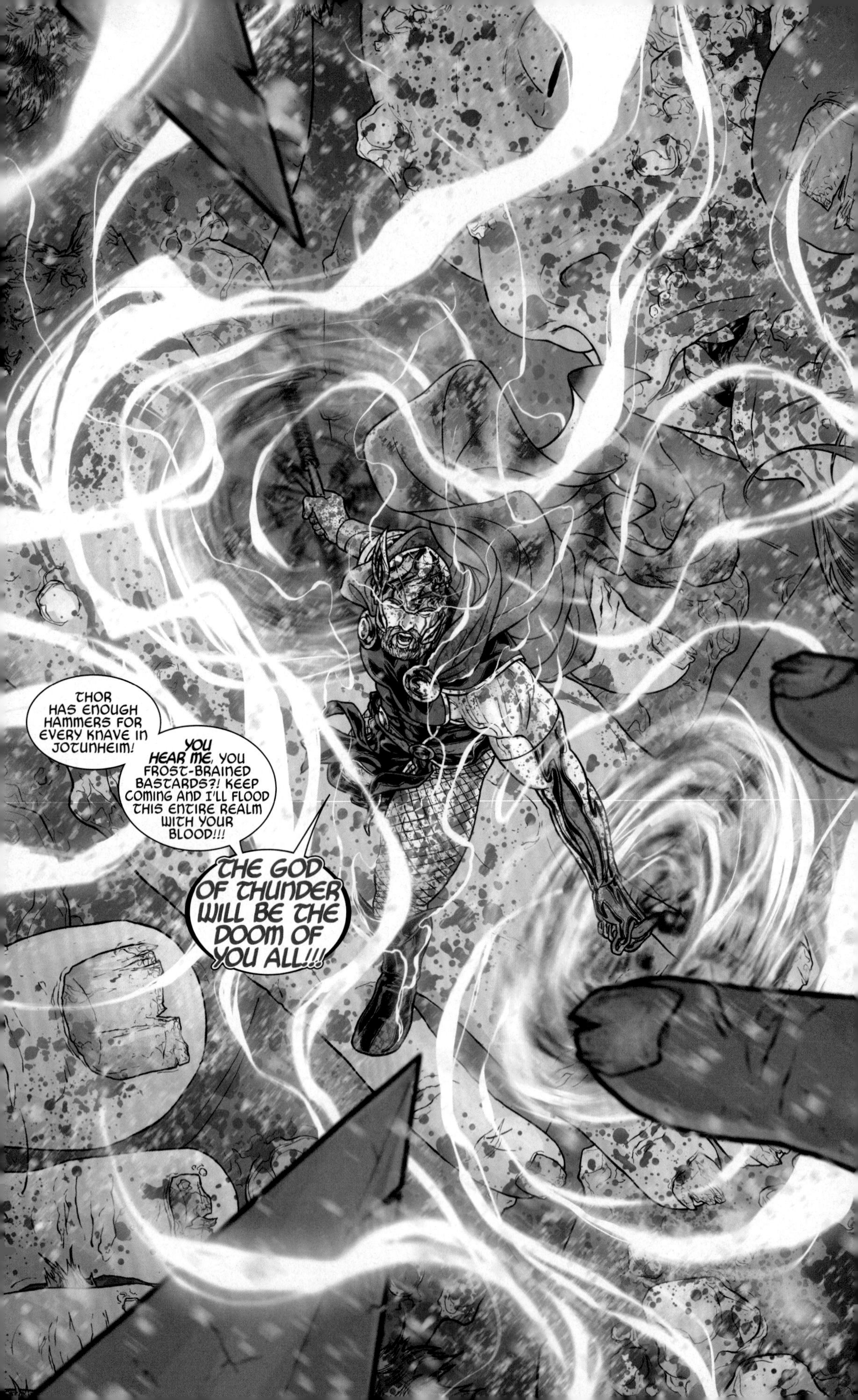
THOR HAS ENOUGH HAMMERS FOR EVERY KNAVE IN JOTUNHEIM!
YOU HEAR ME, YOU FROST-BRAINED BASTARDS?! KEEP COMING AND I'LL FLOOD THIS ENTIRE REALM WITH YOUR BLOOD!!!
THE GOD OF THUNDER WILL BE THE DOOM OF YOU ALL!!!

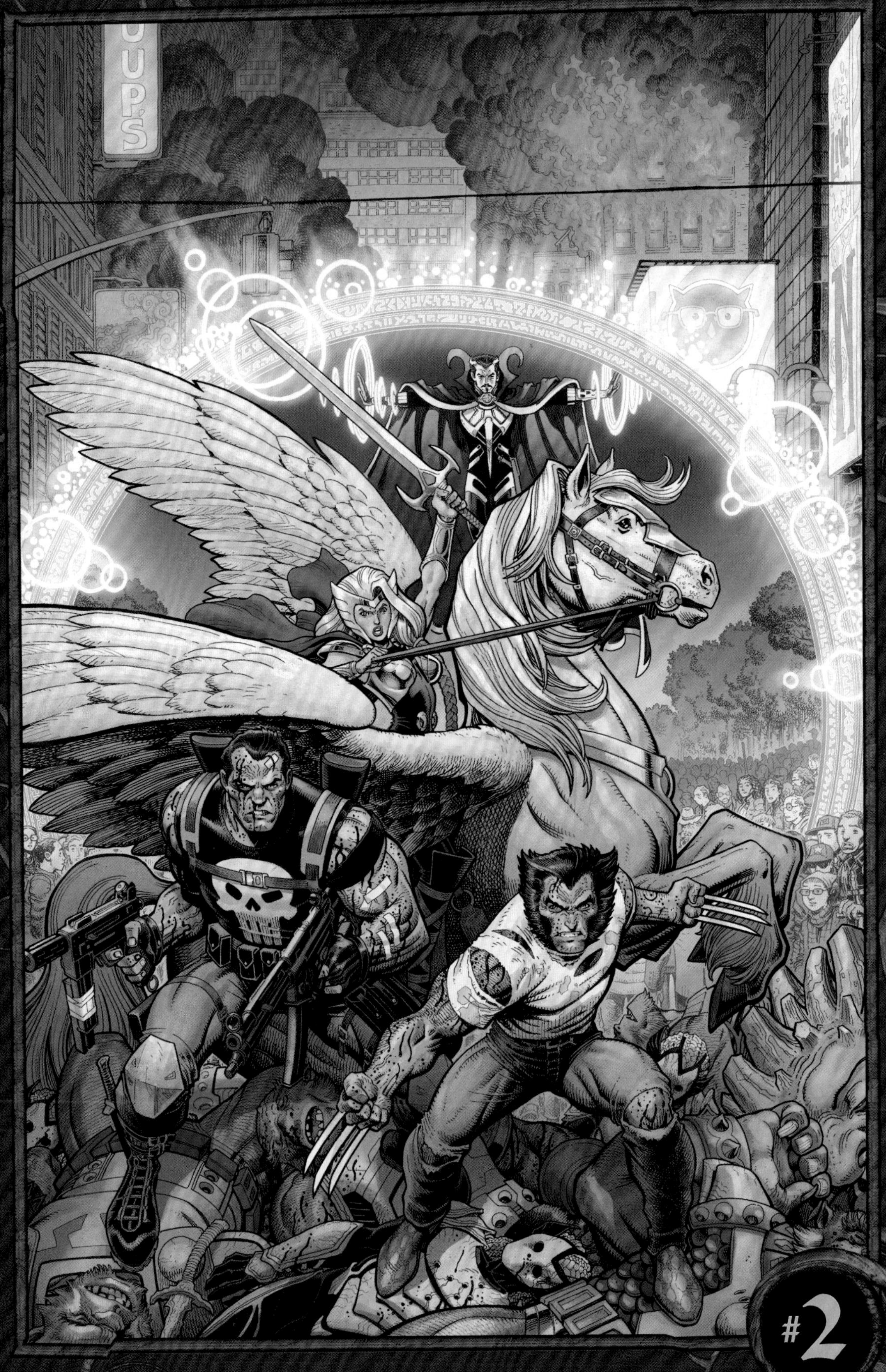
#2

The Midgard Massacre

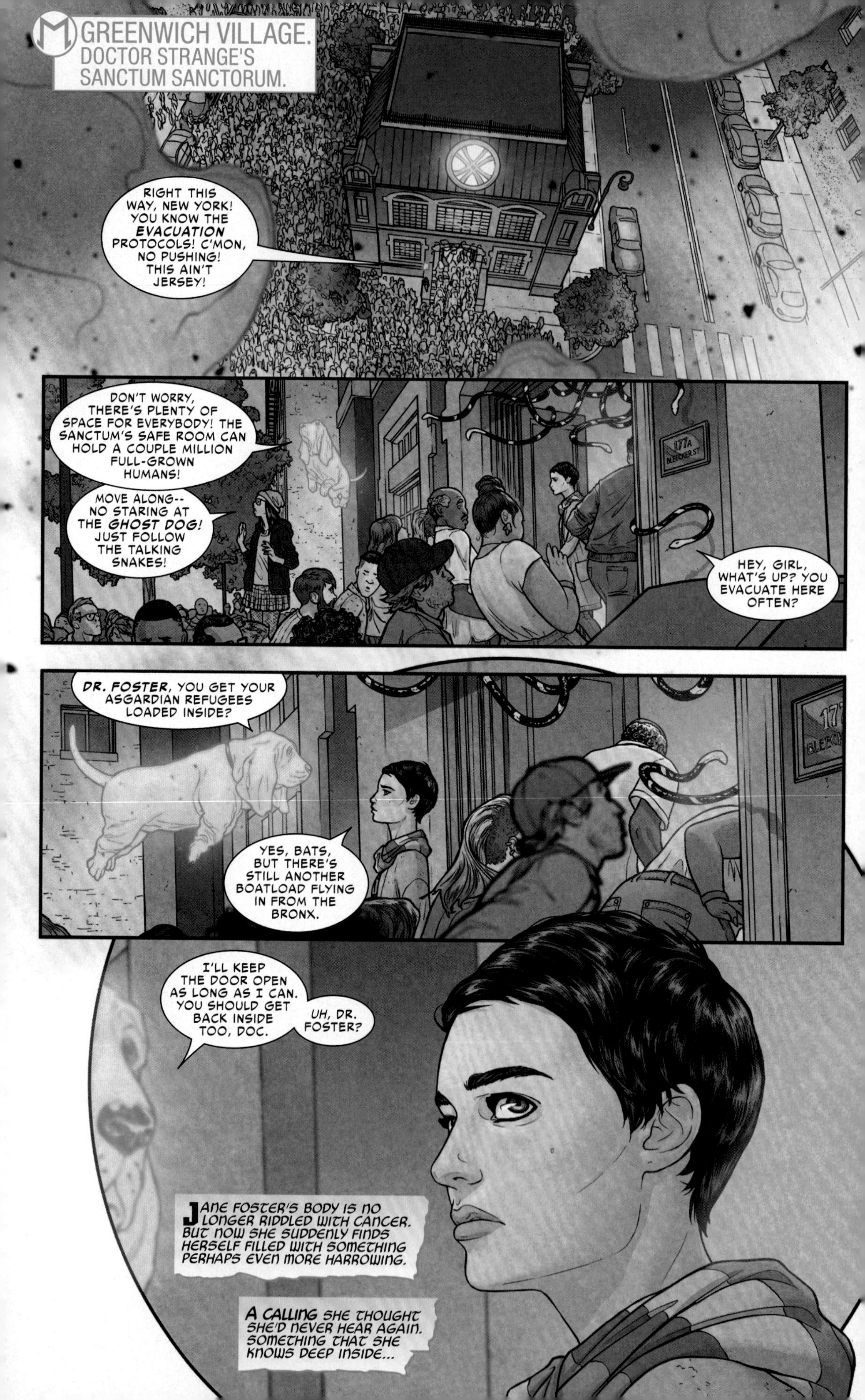
GREENWICH VILLAGE. DOCTOR STRANGE'S SANCTUM SANCTORUM.
RIGHT THIS WAY, NEW YORK! YOU KNOW THE EVACUATION PROTOCOLS! C'MON, NO PUSHING! THIS AIN'T JERSEY!
DON'T WORRY, THERE'S PLENTY OF SPACE FOR EVERYBODY! THE SANCTUM'S SAFE ROOM CAN HOLD A COUPLE MILLION FULL-GROWN HUMANS!
MOVE ALONG-- NO STARING AT THE GHOST DOG! JUST FOLLOW THE TALKING SNAKES!
177A BLEECKER ST
HEY, GIRL, WHAT'S UP? YOU EVACUATE HERE OFTEN?
DR. FOSTER, YOU GET YOUR ASGARDIAN REFUGEES LOADED INSIDE?
YES, BATS, BUT THERE'S STILL ANOTHER BOATLOAD FLYING IN FROM THE BRONX.
I'LL KEEP THE DOOR OPEN AS LONG AS I CAN. YOU SHOULD GET BACK INSIDE TOO, DOC.
UH, DR. FOSTER?
JANE FOSTER'S BODY IS NO LONGER RIDDLED WITH CANCER. BUT NOW SHE SUDDENLY FINDS HERSELF FILLED WITH SOMETHING PERHAPS EVEN MORE HARROWING.
A CALLING SHE THOUGHT SHE'D NEVER HEAR AGAIN. SOMETHING THAT SHE KNOWS DEEP INSIDE...

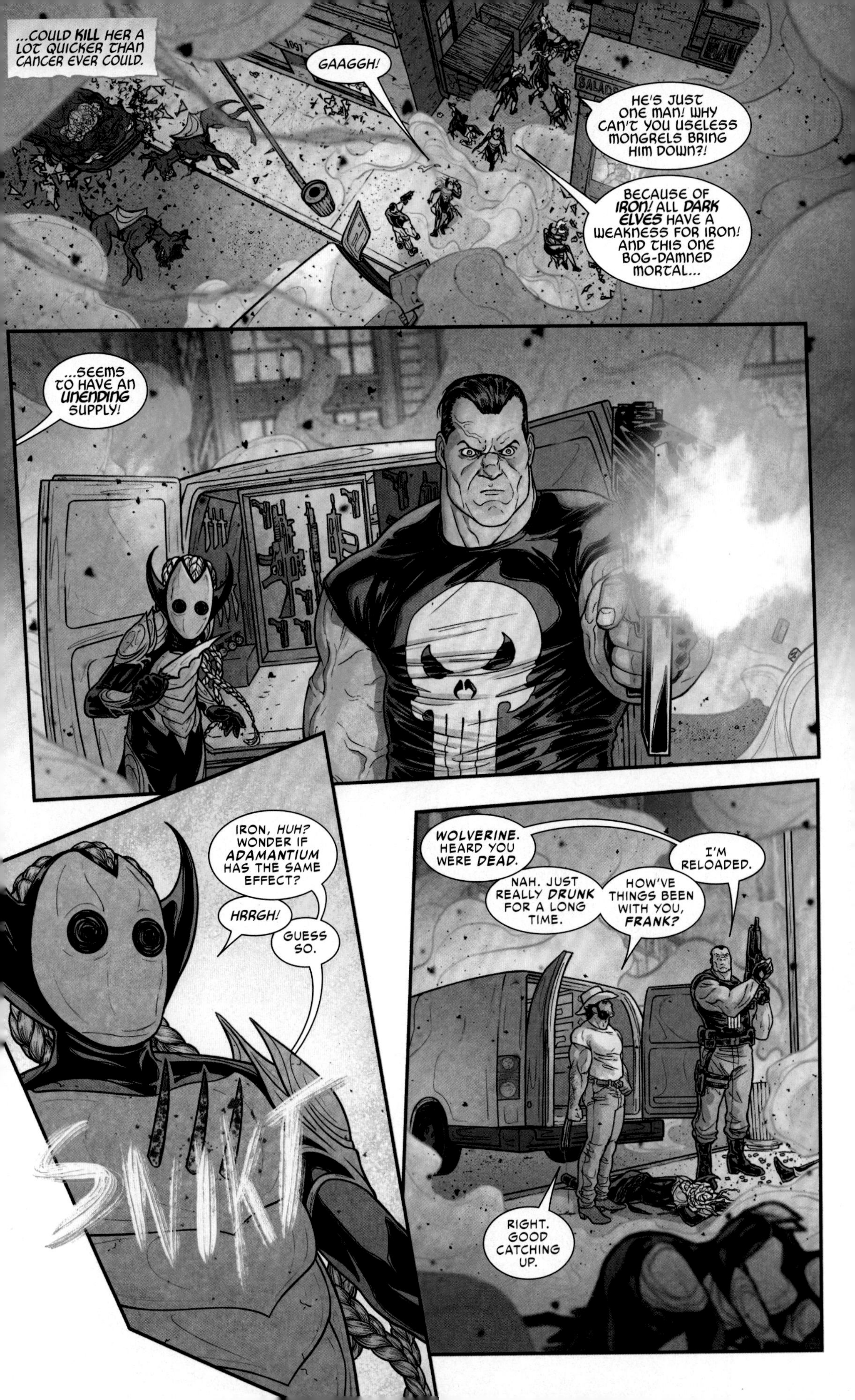
...COULD KILL HER A LOT QUICKER THAN CANCER EVER COULD.
GAAGGH!
HE'S JUST ONE MAN! WHY CAN'T YOU USELESS MONGRELS BRING HIM DOWN?!
BECAUSE OF IRON! ALL DARK ELVES HAVE A WEAKNESS FOR IRON! AND THIS ONE BOG-DAMNED MORTAL...
...SEEMS TO HAVE AN UNENDING SUPPLY!
IRON, HUH? WONDER IF ADAMANTIUM HAS THE SAME EFFECT?
HRRGH!
GUESS SO.
SNIKT
WOLVERINE. HEARD YOU WERE DEAD.
I'M RELOADED.
NAH. JUST REALLY DRUNK FOR A LONG TIME.
HOW'VE THINGS BEEN WITH YOU, FRANK?
RIGHT. GOOD CATCHING UP.

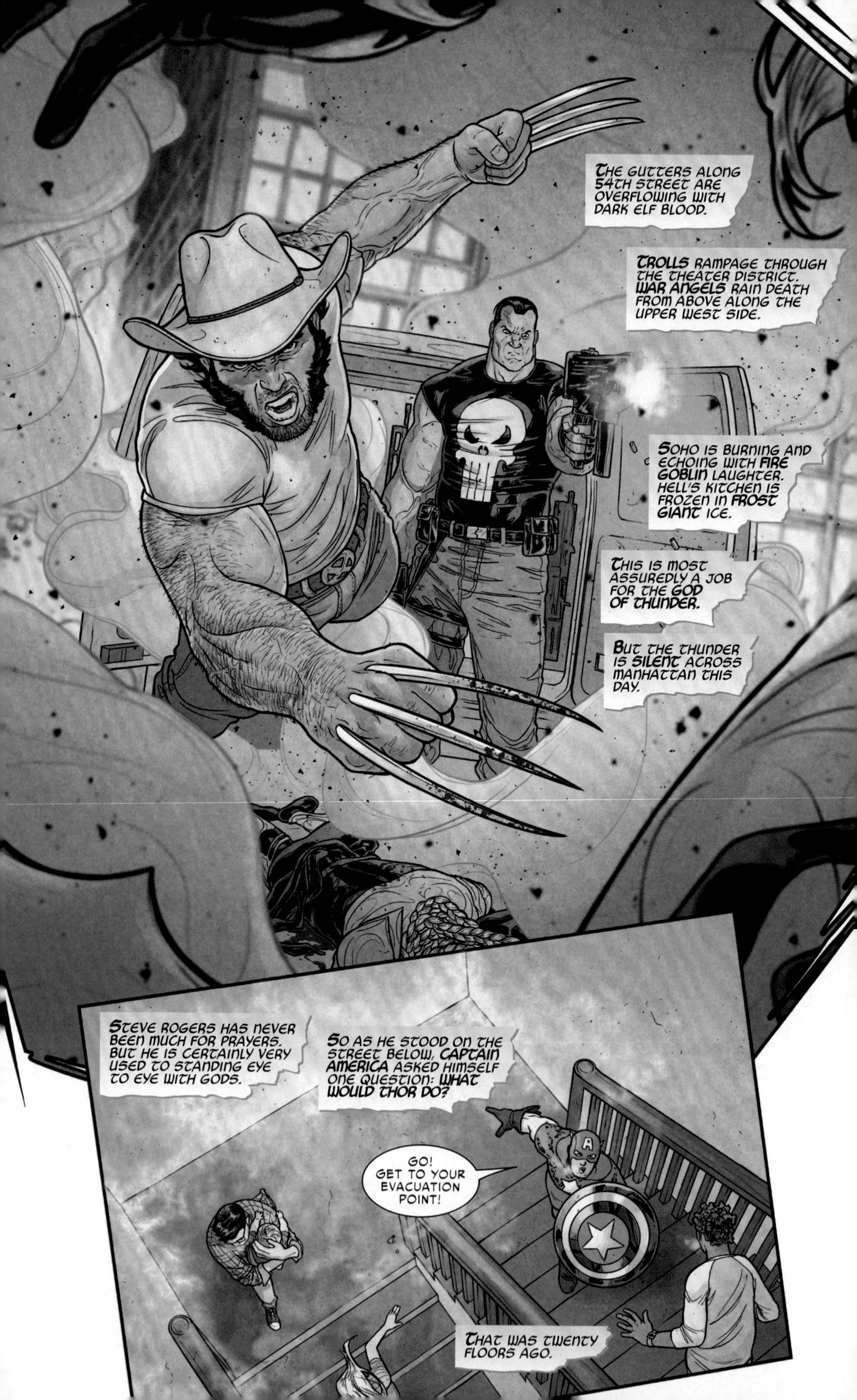
THE GUTTERS ALONG 54TH STREET ARE OVERFLOWING WITH DARK ELF BLOOD.
TROLLS RAMPAGE THROUGH THE THEATER DISTRICT. WAR ANGELS RAIN DEATH FROM ABOVE ALONG THE UPPER WEST SIDE.
SOHO IS BURNING AND ECHOING WITH FIRE GOBLIN LAUGHTER. HELL'S KITCHEN IS FROZEN IN FROST GIANT ICE.
THIS IS MOST ASSUREDLY A JOB FOR THE GOD OF THUNDER.
BUT THE THUNDER IS SILENT ACROSS MANHATTAN THIS DAY.
STEVE ROGERS HAS NEVER BEEN MUCH FOR PRAYERS. BUT HE IS CERTAINLY VERY USED TO STANDING EYE TO EYE WITH GODS.
SO AS HE STOOD ON THE STREET BELOW, CAPTAIN AMERICA ASKED HIMSELF ONE QUESTION: WHAT WOULD THOR DO?
GO! GET TO YOUR EVACUATION POINT!
THAT WAS TWENTY FLOORS AGO.

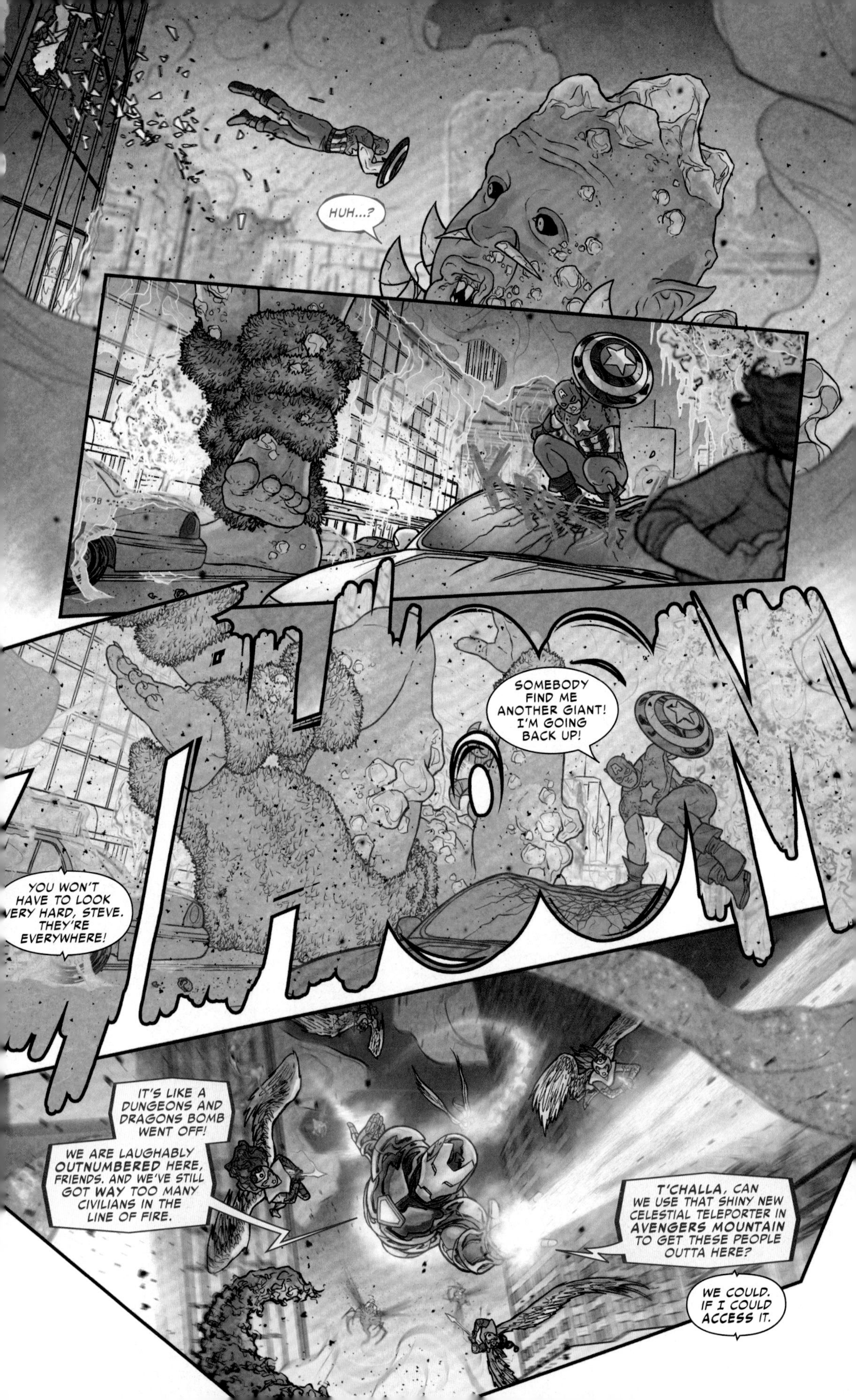
HUH...?
SOMEBODY FIND ME ANOTHER GIANT! I'M GOING BACK UP!
YOU WON'T HAVE TO LOOK VERY HARD, STEVE. THEY'RE EVERYWHERE!
IT'S LIKE A DUNGEONS AND DRAGONS BOMB WENT OFF!
WE ARE LAUGHABLY OUTNUMBERED HERE, FRIENDS. AND WE'VE STILL GOT WAY TOO MANY CIVILIANS IN THE LINE OF FIRE.
T'CHALLA, CAN WE USE THAT SHINY NEW CELESTIAL TELEPORTER IN AVENGERS MOUNTAIN TO GET THESE PEOPLE OUTTA HERE?
WE COULD. IF I COULD ACCESS IT.

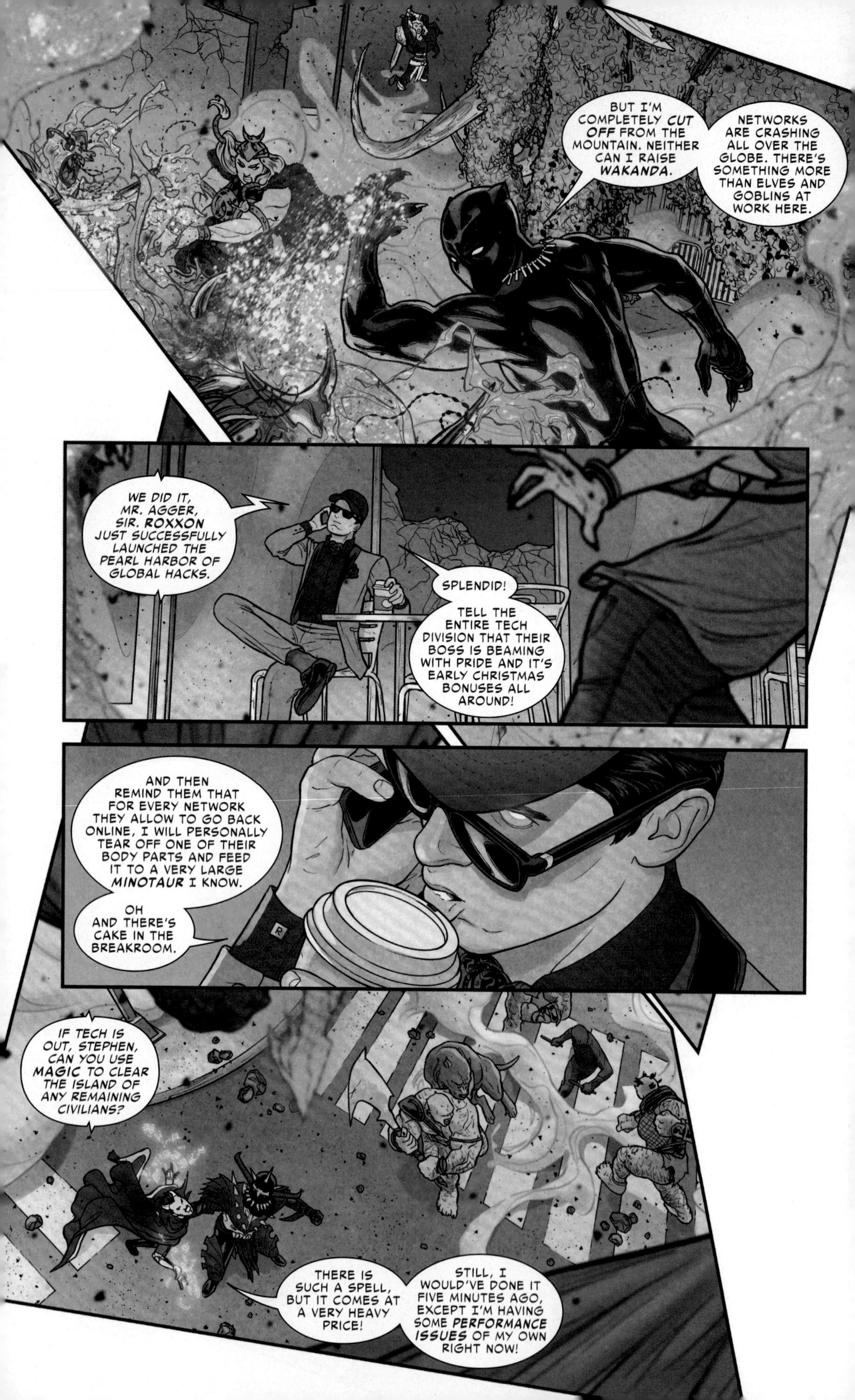
BUT I'M COMPLETELY *CUT OFF* FROM THE MOUNTAIN. NEITHER CAN I RAISE *WAKANDA*.
NETWORKS ARE CRASHING ALL OVER THE GLOBE. THERE'S SOMETHING MORE THAN ELVES AND GOBLINS AT WORK HERE.
WE DID IT, MR. AGGER, SIR. *ROXXON* JUST SUCCESSFULLY LAUNCHED THE PEARL HARBOR OF GLOBAL HACKS.
SPLENDID!
TELL THE ENTIRE TECH DIVISION THAT THEIR BOSS IS BEAMING WITH PRIDE AND IT'S EARLY CHRISTMAS BONUSES ALL AROUND!
AND THEN REMIND THEM THAT FOR EVERY NETWORK THEY ALLOW TO GO BACK ONLINE, I WILL PERSONALLY TEAR OFF ONE OF THEIR BODY PARTS AND FEED IT TO A VERY LARGE *MINOTAUR* I KNOW.
OH AND THERE'S CAKE IN THE BREAKROOM.
IF TECH IS OUT, STEPHEN, CAN YOU USE *MAGIC* TO CLEAR THE ISLAND OF ANY REMAINING CIVILIANS?
THERE IS SUCH A SPELL, BUT IT COMES AT A VERY HEAVY PRICE!
STILL, I WOULD'VE DONE IT FIVE MINUTES AGO, EXCEPT I'M HAVING SOME *PERFORMANCE ISSUES* OF MY OWN RIGHT NOW!

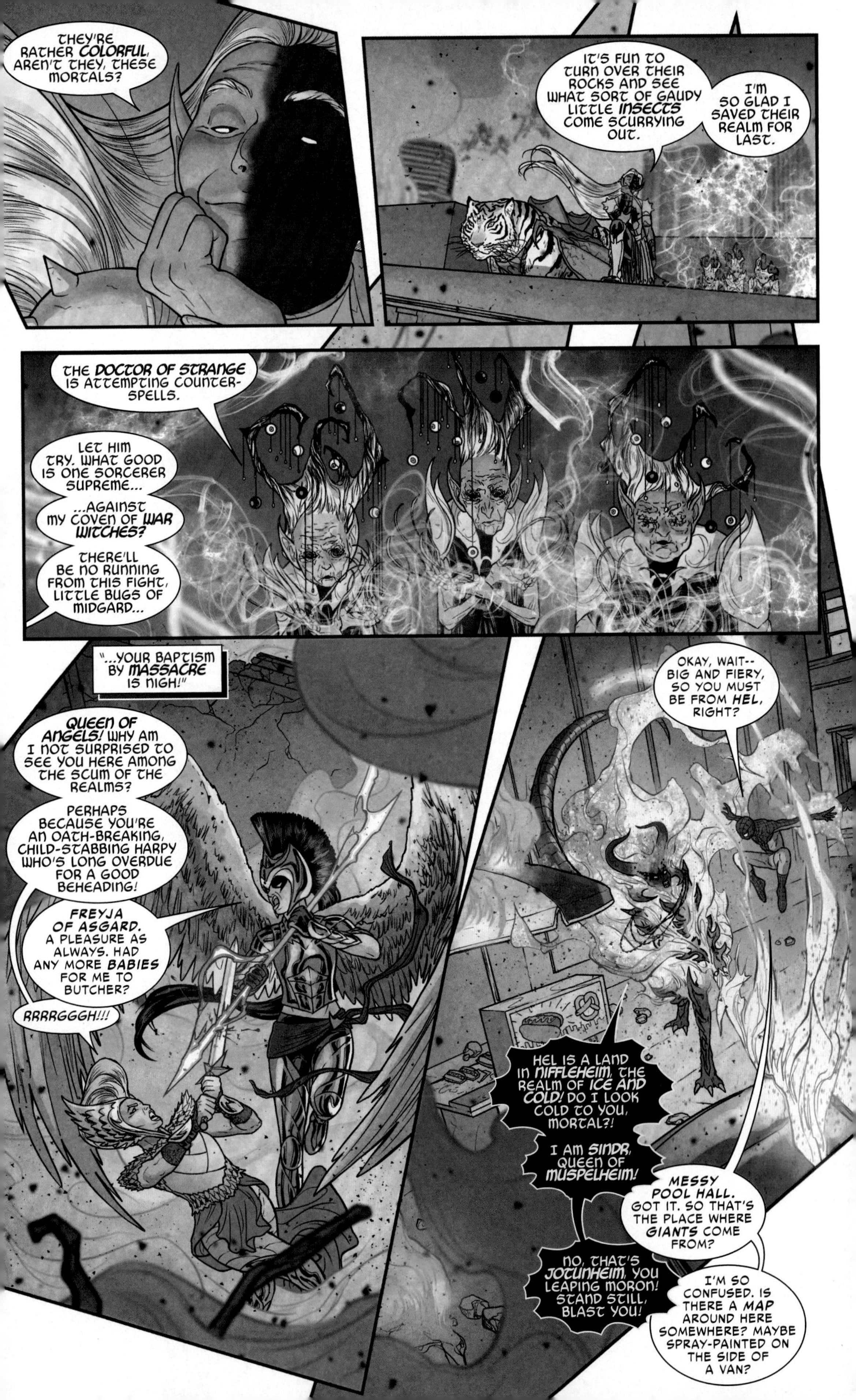
THEY'RE RATHER COLORFUL, AREN'T THEY, THESE MORTALS?
IT'S FUN TO TURN OVER THEIR ROCKS AND SEE WHAT SORT OF GAUDY LITTLE INSECTS COME SCURRYING OUT.
I'M SO GLAD I SAVED THEIR REALM FOR LAST.
THE DOCTOR OF STRANGE IS ATTEMPTING COUNTER-SPELLS.
LET HIM TRY. WHAT GOOD IS ONE SORCERER SUPREME...
...AGAINST MY COVEN OF WAR WITCHES?
THERE'LL BE NO RUNNING FROM THIS FIGHT, LITTLE BUGS OF MIDGARD...
"...YOUR BAPTISM BY MASSACRE IS NIGH!"
QUEEN OF ANGELS! WHY AM I NOT SURPRISED TO SEE YOU HERE AMONG THE SCUM OF THE REALMS?
PERHAPS BECAUSE YOU'RE AN OATH-BREAKING, CHILD-STABBING HARPY WHO'S LONG OVERDUE FOR A GOOD BEHEADING!
FREYJA OF ASGARD. A PLEASURE AS ALWAYS. HAD ANY MORE BABIES FOR ME TO BUTCHER?
RRRRGGGH!!!
OKAY, WAIT-- BIG AND FIERY, SO YOU MUST BE FROM HEL, RIGHT?
HEL IS A LAND IN NIFFLEHEIM, THE REALM OF ICE AND COLD! DO I LOOK COLD TO YOU, MORTAL?!
I AM SINDR, QUEEN OF MUSPELHEIM!
MESSY POOL HALL. GOT IT. SO THAT'S THE PLACE WHERE GIANTS COME FROM?
NO, THAT'S JOTUNHEIM, YOU LEAPING MORON! STAND STILL, BLAST YOU!
I'M SO CONFUSED. IS THERE A MAP AROUND HERE SOMEWHERE? MAYBE SPRAY-PAINTED ON THE SIDE OF A VAN?

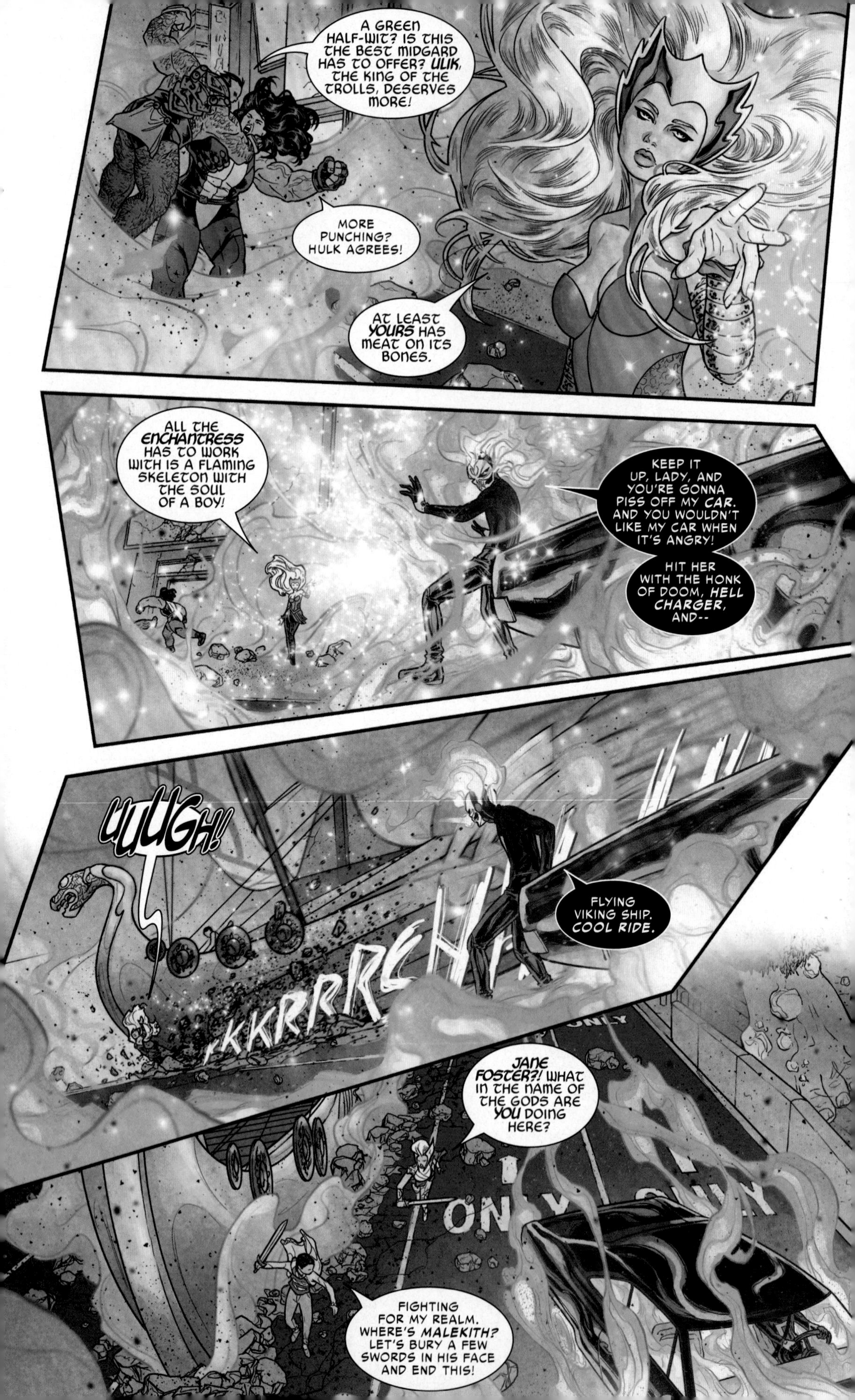

A GREEN HALF-WIT? IS THIS THE BEST MIDGARD HAS TO OFFER? ULIK, THE KING OF THE TROLLS, DESERVES MORE!
MORE PUNCHING? HULK AGREES!
AT LEAST YOURS HAS MEAT ON ITS BONES.
ALL THE ENCHANTRESS HAS TO WORK WITH IS A FLAMING SKELETON WITH THE SOUL OF A BOY!
KEEP IT UP, LADY, AND YOU'RE GONNA PISS OFF MY CAR. AND YOU WOULDN'T LIKE MY CAR WHEN IT'S ANGRY!
HIT HER WITH THE HONK OF DOOM, HELL CHARGER, AND--
UUUGH!
KKRRRCH
FLYING VIKING SHIP. COOL RIDE.
JANE FOSTER?! WHAT IN THE NAME OF THE GODS ARE YOU DOING HERE?
FIGHTING FOR MY REALM. WHERE'S MALEKITH? LET'S BURY A FEW SWORDS IN HIS FACE AND END THIS!

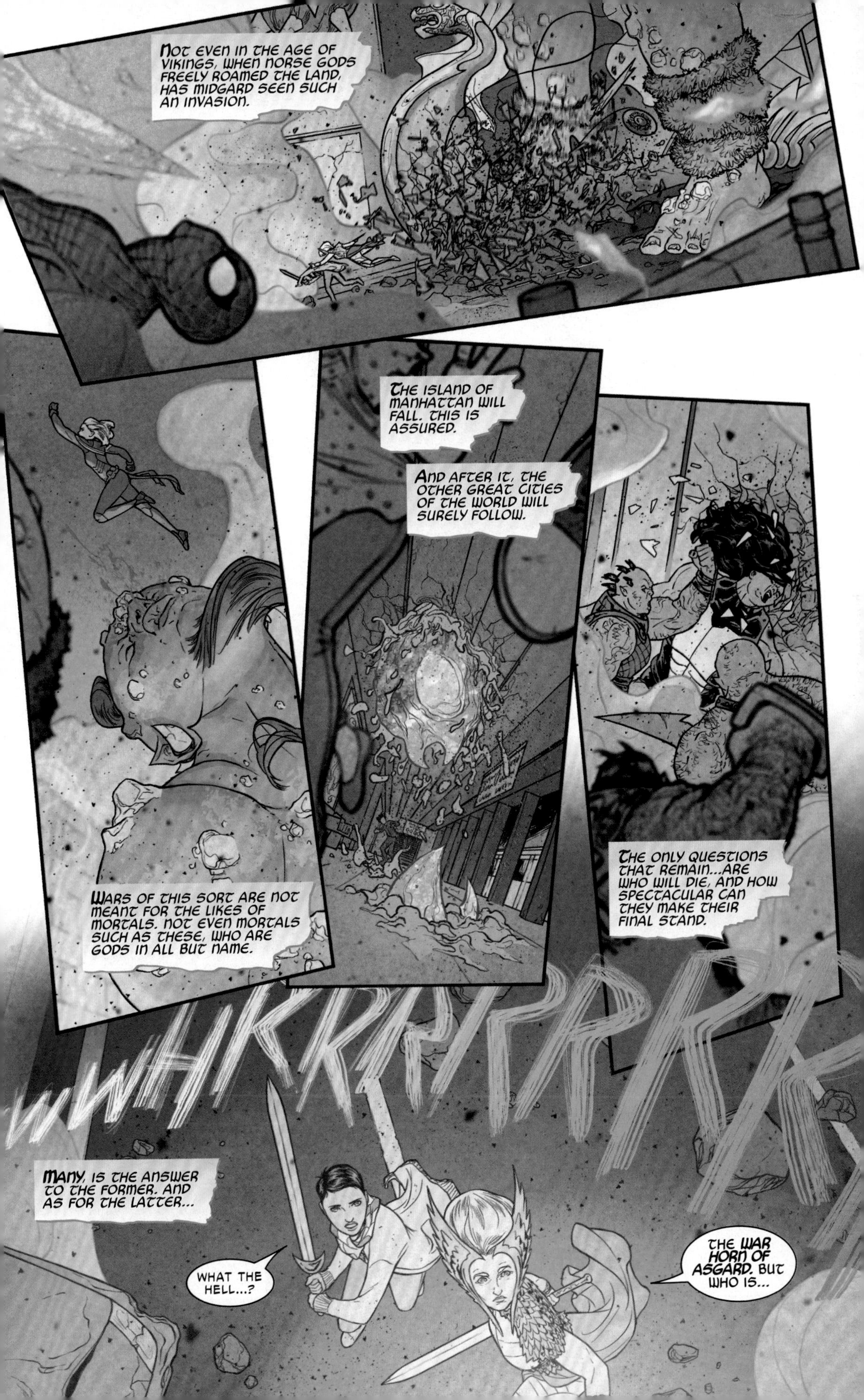
NOT EVEN IN THE AGE OF VIKINGS, WHEN NORSE GODS FREELY ROAMED THE LAND, HAS MIDGARD SEEN SUCH AN INVASION.
WARS OF THIS SORT ARE NOT MEANT FOR THE LIKES OF MORTALS. NOT EVEN MORTALS SUCH AS THESE, WHO ARE GODS IN ALL BUT NAME.
THE ISLAND OF MANHATTAN WILL FALL. THIS IS ASSURED.
AND AFTER IT, THE OTHER GREAT CITIES OF THE WORLD WILL SURELY FOLLOW.
THE ONLY QUESTIONS THAT REMAIN...ARE WHO WILL DIE, AND HOW SPECTACULAR CAN THEY MAKE THEIR FINAL STAND.
WWHRRRRRRRR
MANY, IS THE ANSWER TO THE FORMER. AND AS FOR THE LATTER...
WHAT THE HELL...?
THE WAR HORN OF ASGARD. BUT WHO IS...

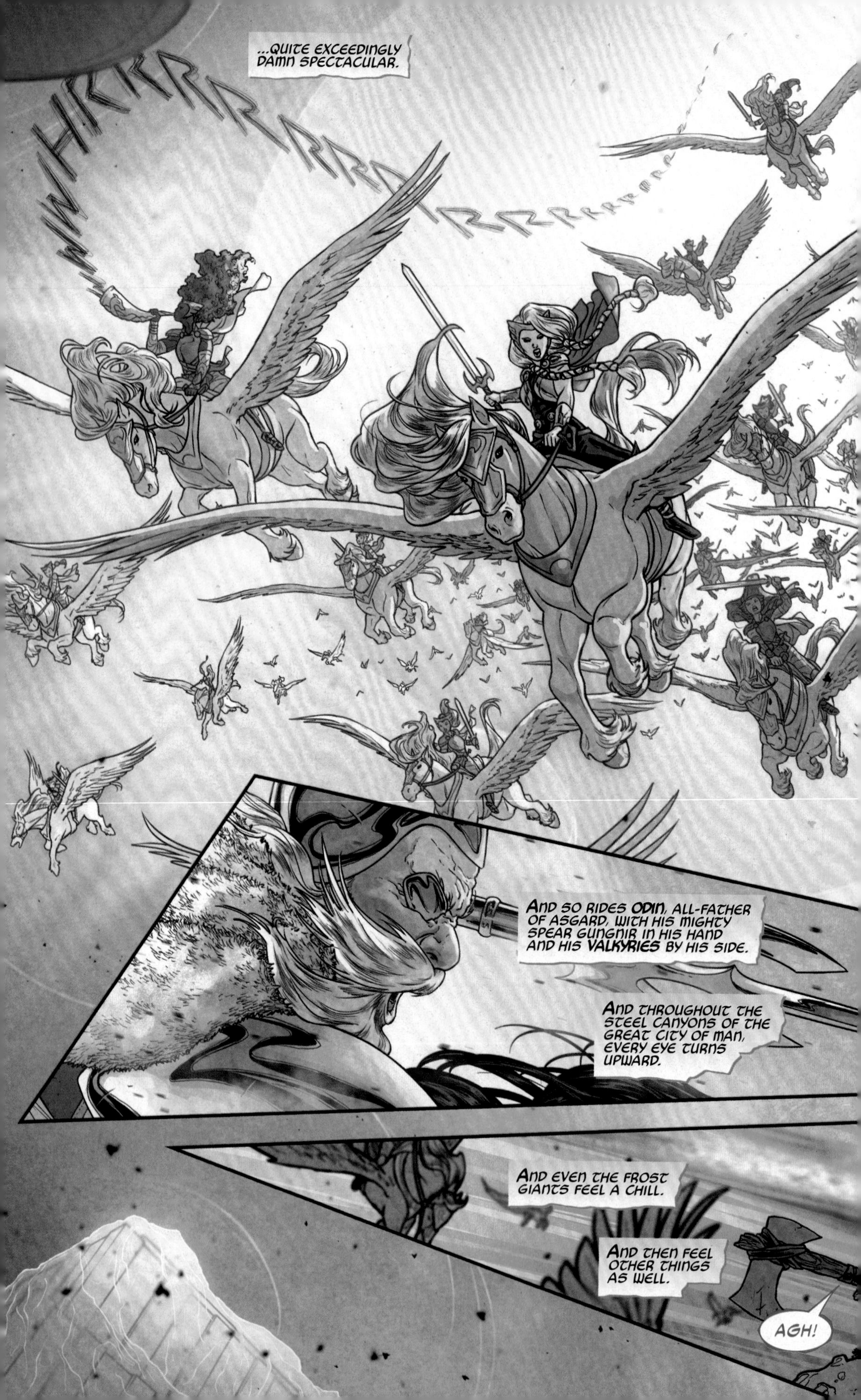
...QUITE EXCEEDINGLY DAMN SPECTACULAR.
WHHKRRRRRRRRrrrrrr
AND SO RIDES ODIN, ALL-FATHER OF ASGARD, WITH HIS MIGHTY SPEAR GUNGNIR IN HIS HAND AND HIS VALKYRIES BY HIS SIDE.
AND THROUGHOUT THE STEEL CANYONS OF THE GREAT CITY OF MAN, EVERY EYE TURNS UPWARD.
AND EVEN THE FROST GIANTS FEEL A CHILL.
AND THEN FEEL OTHER THINGS AS WELL.
AGH!

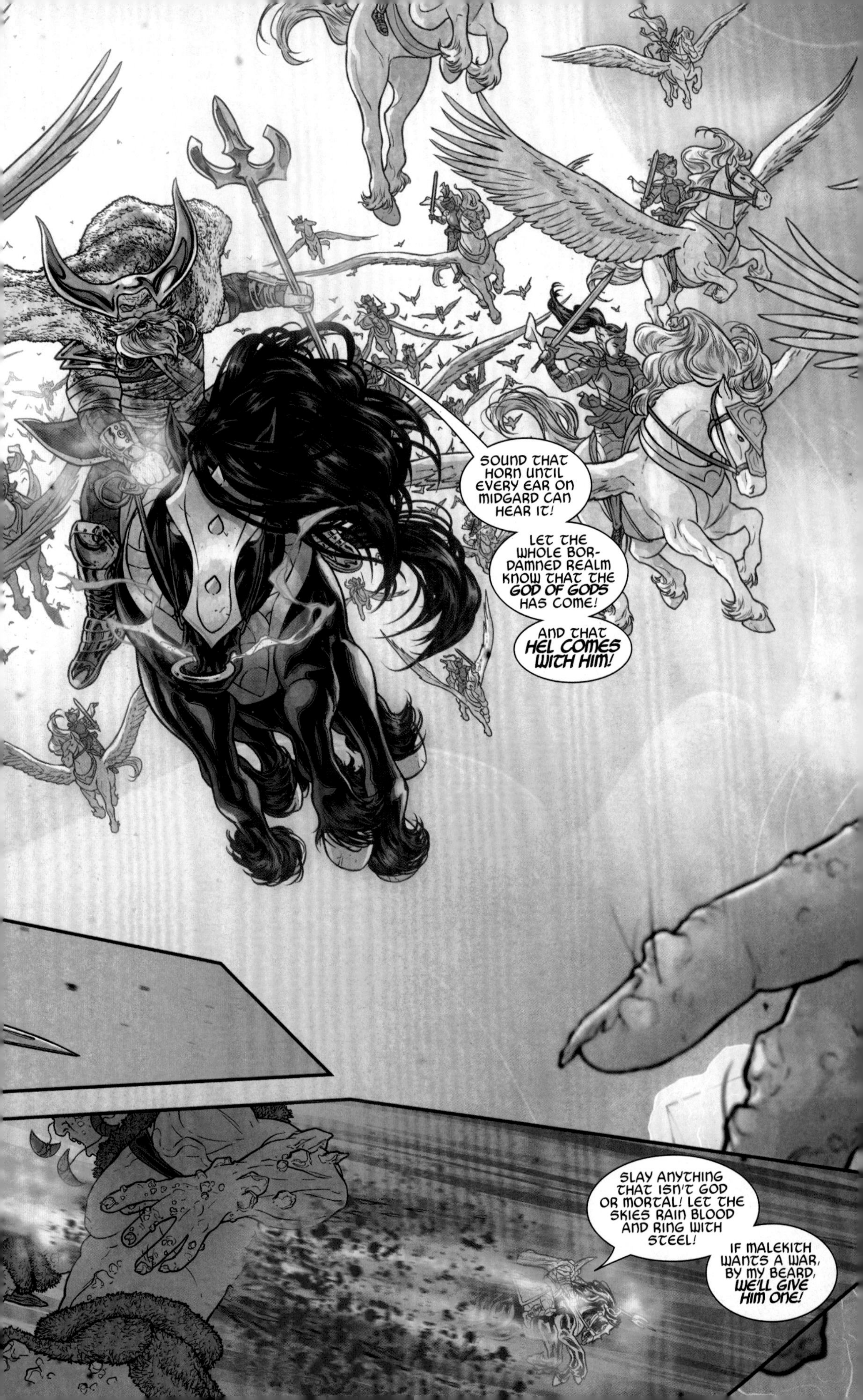
SOUND THAT HORN UNTIL EVERY EAR ON MIDGARD CAN HEAR IT!
LET THE WHOLE BOR-DAMNED REALM KNOW THAT THE GOD OF GODS HAS COME!
AND THAT HEL COMES WITH HIM!
SLAY ANYTHING THAT ISN'T GOD OR MORTAL! LET THE SKIES RAIN BLOOD AND RING WITH STEEL!
IF MALEKITH WANTS A WAR, BY MY BEARD, WE'LL GIVE HIM ONE!

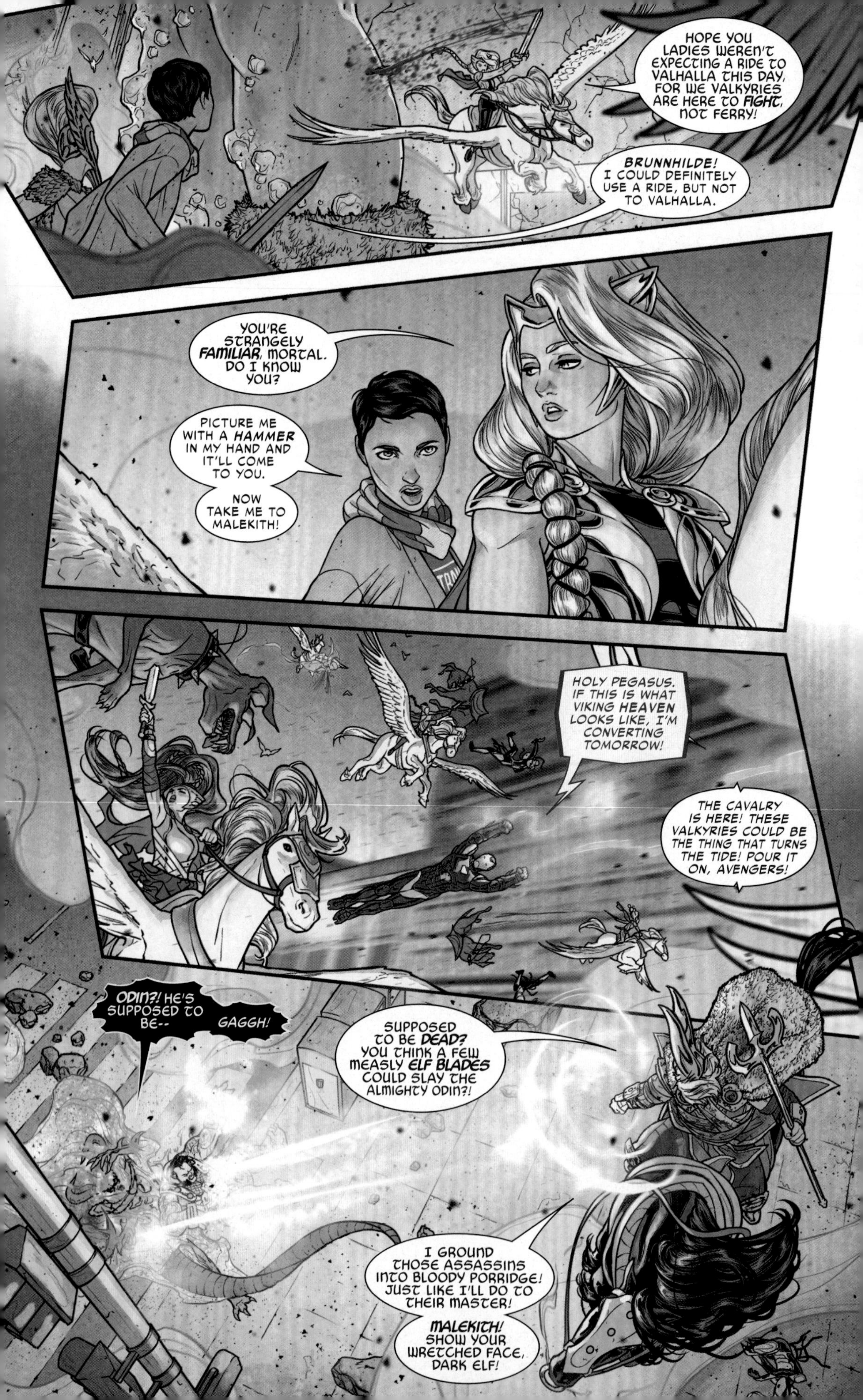
HOPE YOU LADIES WEREN'T EXPECTING A RIDE TO VALHALLA THIS DAY, FOR WE VALKYRIES ARE HERE TO FIGHT, NOT FERRY!
BRUNNHILDE! I COULD DEFINITELY USE A RIDE, BUT NOT TO VALHALLA.
YOU'RE STRANGELY FAMILIAR, MORTAL. DO I KNOW YOU?
PICTURE ME WITH A HAMMER IN MY HAND AND IT'LL COME TO YOU.
NOW TAKE ME TO MALEKITH!
HOLY PEGASUS. IF THIS IS WHAT VIKING HEAVEN LOOKS LIKE, I'M CONVERTING TOMORROW!
THE CAVALRY IS HERE! THESE VALKYRIES COULD BE THE THING THAT TURNS THE TIDE! POUR IT ON, AVENGERS!
ODIN?! HE'S SUPPOSED TO BE--
GAGGH!
SUPPOSED TO BE DEAD? YOU THINK A FEW MEASLY ELF BLADES COULD SLAY THE ALMIGHTY ODIN?!
I GROUND THOSE ASSASSINS INTO BLOODY PORRIDGE! JUST LIKE I'LL DO TO THEIR MASTER!
MALEKITH! SHOW YOUR WRETCHED FACE, DARK ELF!

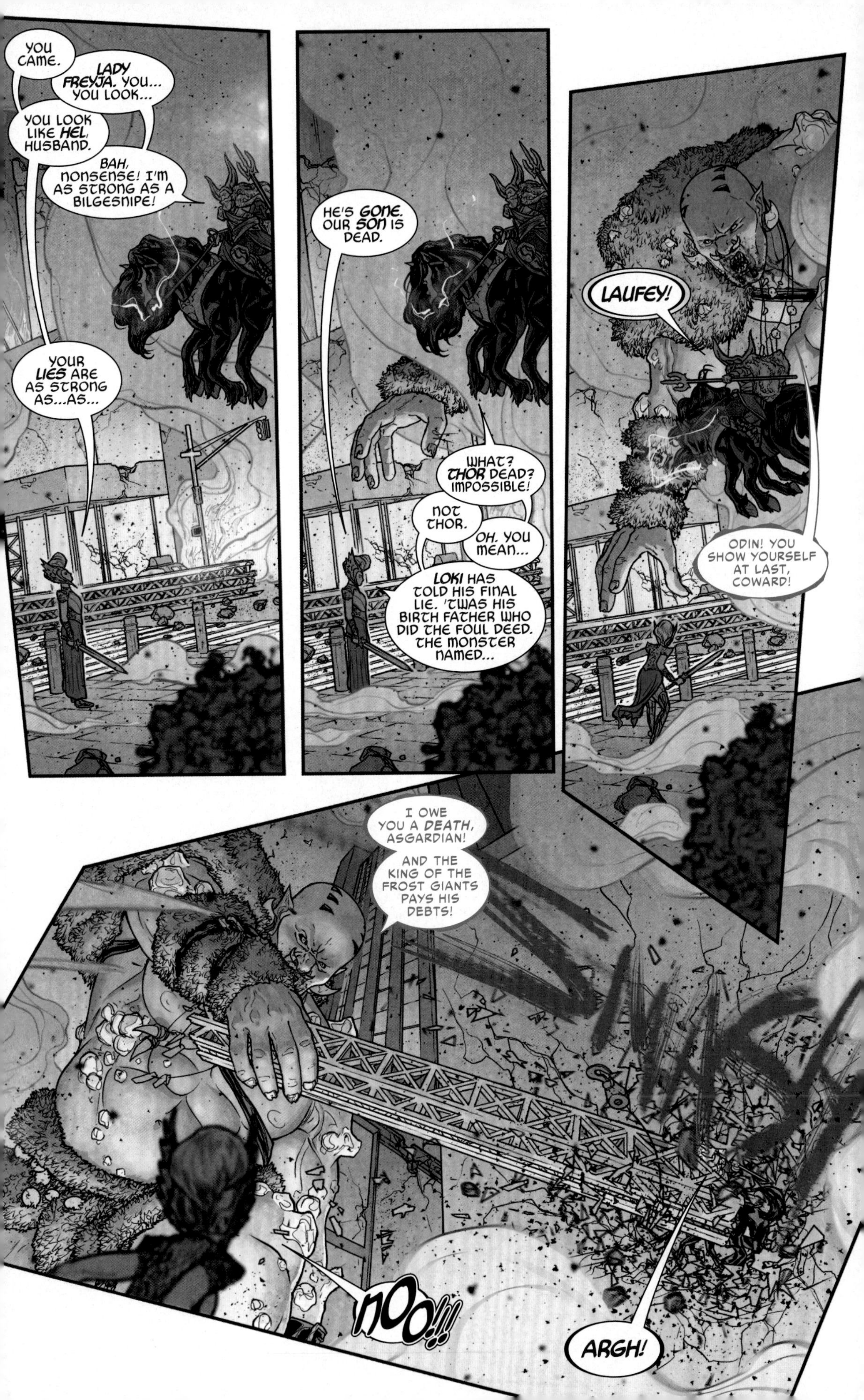
YOU CAME.
LADY FREYJA. YOU... YOU LOOK...
YOU LOOK LIKE HEL, HUSBAND.
BAH, NONSENSE! I'M AS STRONG AS A BILGESNIPE!
YOUR LIES ARE AS STRONG AS...AS...
HE'S GONE. OUR SON IS DEAD.
WHAT? THOR DEAD? IMPOSSIBLE!
NOT THOR.
OH. YOU MEAN...
LOKI HAS TOLD HIS FINAL LIE. 'TWAS HIS BIRTH FATHER WHO DID THE FOUL DEED. THE MONSTER NAMED...
LAUFEY!
ODIN! YOU SHOW YOURSELF AT LAST, COWARD!
I OWE YOU A DEATH, ASGARDIAN!
AND THE KING OF THE FROST GIANTS PAYS HIS DEBTS!
NOO!!!
ARGH!

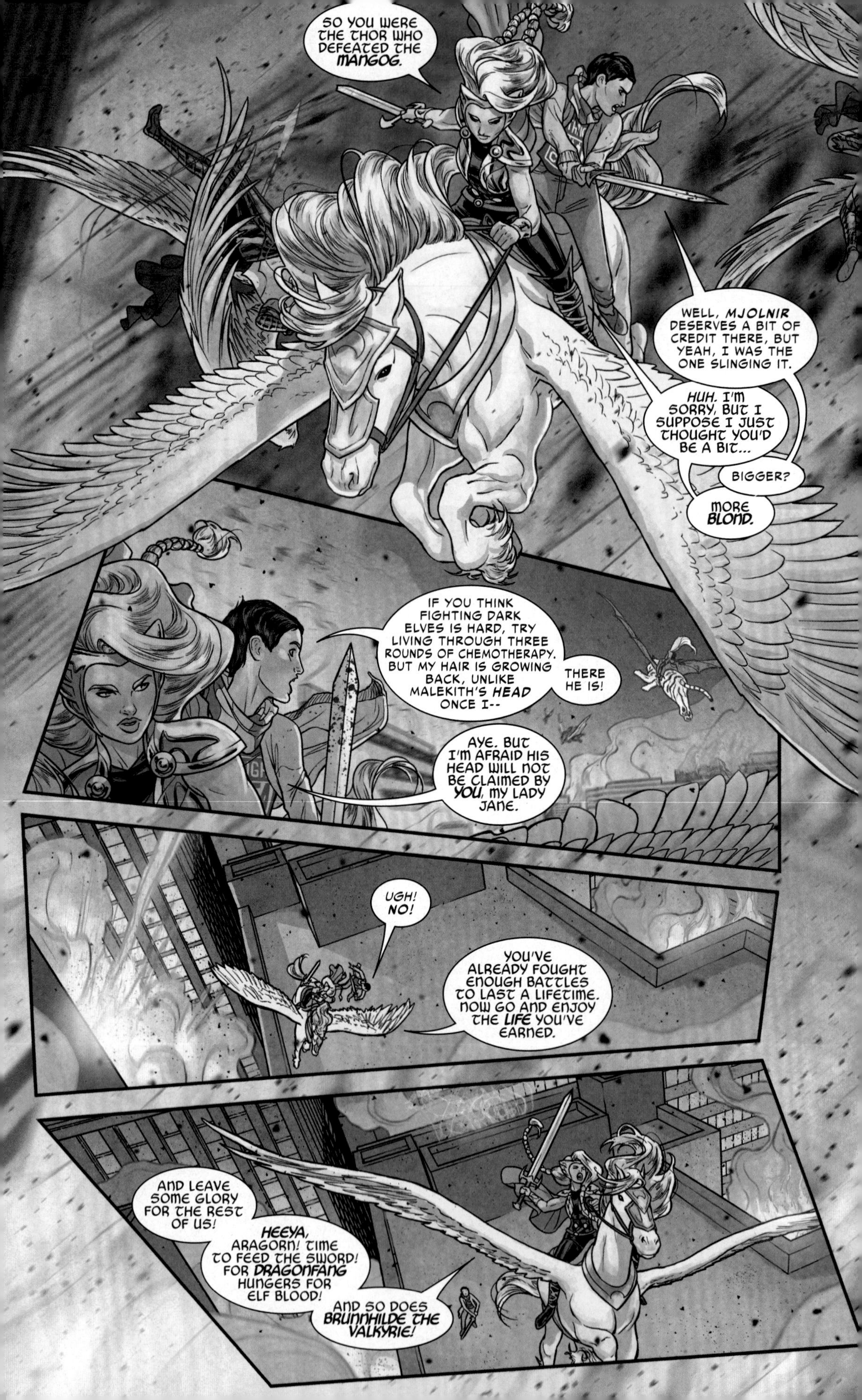

SO YOU WERE THE THOR WHO DEFEATED THE MANGOG.
WELL, MJOLNIR DESERVES A BIT OF CREDIT THERE, BUT YEAH, I WAS THE ONE SLINGING IT.
HUH. I'M SORRY, BUT I SUPPOSE I JUST THOUGHT YOU'D BE A BIT...
BIGGER?
MORE BLOND.
IF YOU THINK FIGHTING DARK ELVES IS HARD, TRY LIVING THROUGH THREE ROUNDS OF CHEMOTHERAPY. BUT MY HAIR IS GROWING BACK, UNLIKE MALEKITH'S HEAD ONCE I--
THERE HE IS!
AYE. BUT I'M AFRAID HIS HEAD WILL NOT BE CLAIMED BY YOU, MY LADY JANE.
UGH! NO!
YOU'VE ALREADY FOUGHT ENOUGH BATTLES TO LAST A LIFETIME. NOW GO AND ENJOY THE LIFE YOU'VE EARNED.
AND LEAVE SOME GLORY FOR THE REST OF US!
HEEYA, ARAGORN! TIME TO FEED THE SWORD! FOR DRAGONFANG HUNGERS FOR ELF BLOOD!
AND SO DOES BRUNNHILDE THE VALKYRIE!

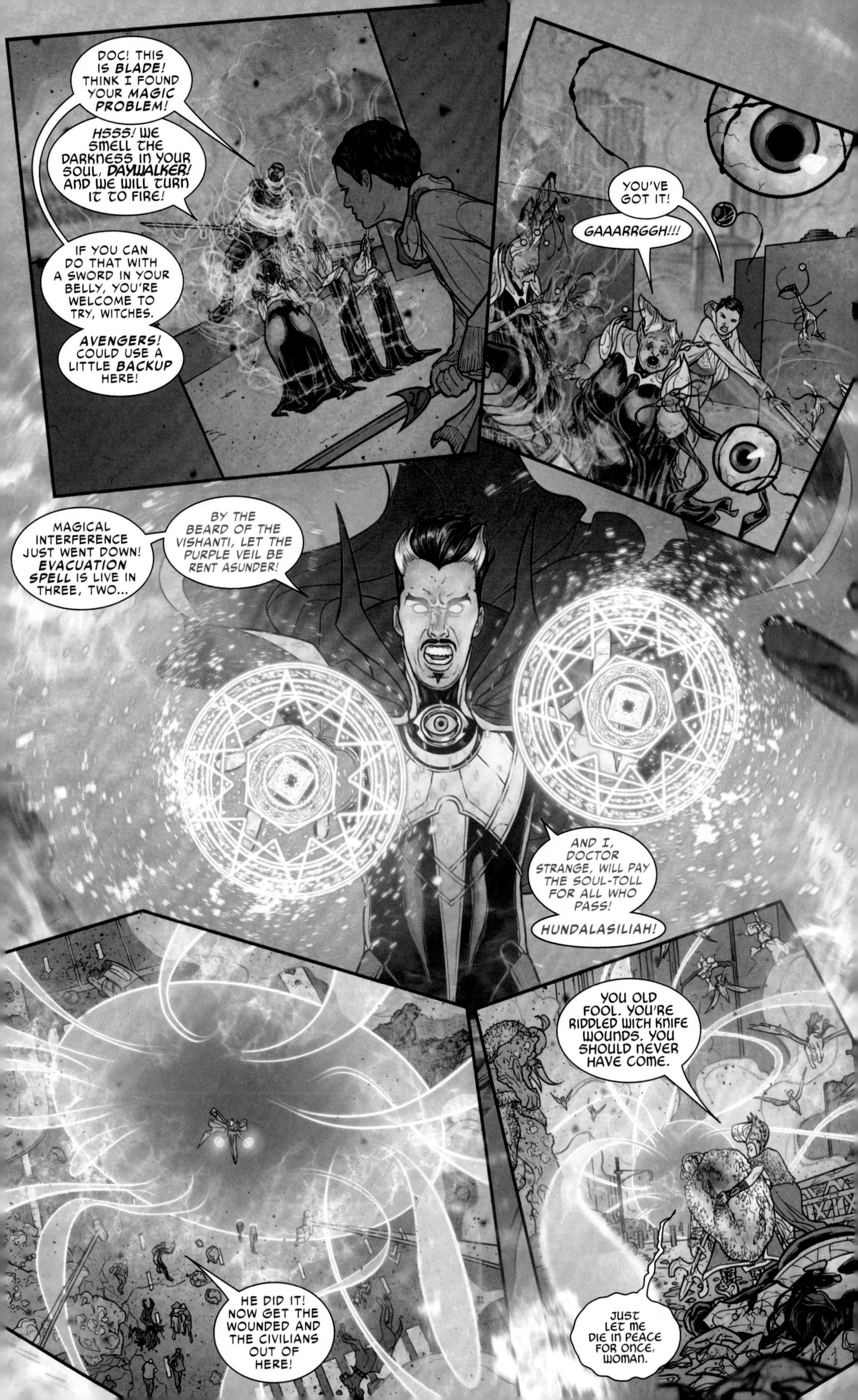

DOC! THIS IS BLADE! THINK I FOUND YOUR MAGIC PROBLEM!
HSSS! WE SMELL THE DARKNESS IN YOUR SOUL, DAYWALKER! AND WE WILL TURN IT TO FIRE!
IF YOU CAN DO THAT WITH A SWORD IN YOUR BELLY, YOU'RE WELCOME TO TRY, WITCHES.
AVENGERS! COULD USE A LITTLE BACKUP HERE!
YOU'VE GOT IT!
GAAARRGGH!!!
MAGICAL INTERFERENCE JUST WENT DOWN! EVACUATION SPELL IS LIVE IN THREE, TWO...
BY THE BEARD OF THE VISHANTI, LET THE PURPLE VEIL BE RENT ASUNDER!
AND I, DOCTOR STRANGE, WILL PAY THE SOUL-TOLL FOR ALL WHO PASS!
HUNDALASILIAH!
HE DID IT! NOW GET THE WOUNDED AND THE CIVILIANS OUT OF HERE!
YOU OLD FOOL. YOU'RE RIDDLED WITH KNIFE WOUNDS. YOU SHOULD NEVER HAVE COME.
JUST LET ME DIE IN PEACE FOR ONCE, WOMAN.

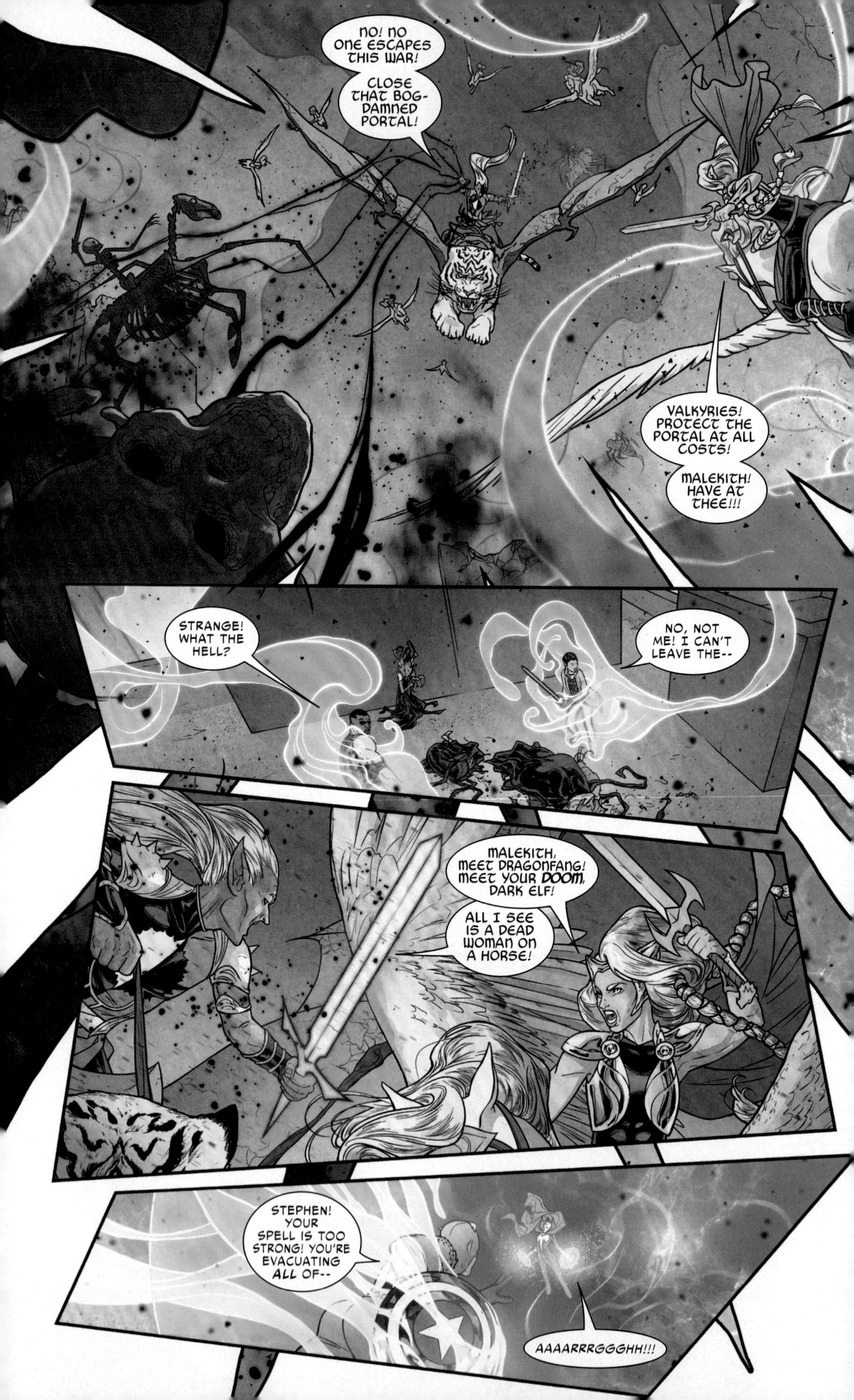
NO! NO ONE ESCAPES THIS WAR!
CLOSE THAT BOG-DAMNED PORTAL!
VALKYRIES! PROTECT THE PORTAL AT ALL COSTS!
MALEKITH! HAVE AT THEE!!!
STRANGE! WHAT THE HELL?
NO, NOT ME! I CAN'T LEAVE THE--
MALEKITH, MEET DRAGONFANG! MEET YOUR DOOM, DARK ELF!
ALL I SEE IS A DEAD WOMAN ON A HORSE!
STEPHEN! YOUR SPELL IS TOO STRONG! YOU'RE EVACUATING ALL OF--
AAAARRRGGGHH!!!

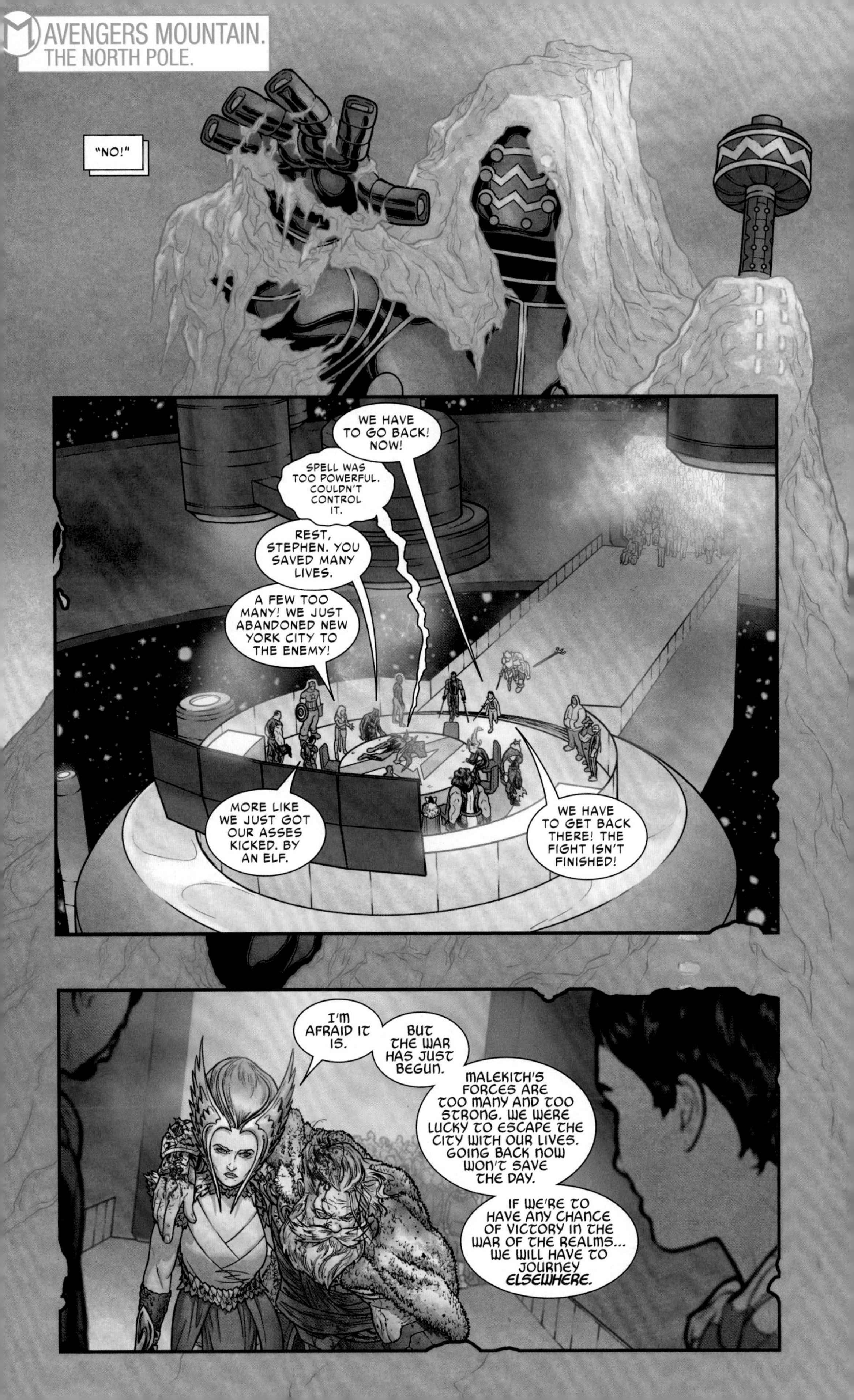
AVENGERS MOUNTAIN.
THE NORTH POLE.
"NO!"
WE HAVE TO GO BACK! NOW!
SPELL WAS TOO POWERFUL. COULDN'T CONTROL IT.
REST, STEPHEN. YOU SAVED MANY LIVES.
A FEW TOO MANY! WE JUST ABANDONED NEW YORK CITY TO THE ENEMY!
MORE LIKE WE JUST GOT OUR ASSES KICKED. BY AN ELF.
WE HAVE TO GET BACK THERE! THE FIGHT ISN'T FINISHED!
I'M AFRAID IT IS.
BUT THE WAR HAS JUST BEGUN.
MALEKITH'S FORCES ARE TOO MANY AND TOO STRONG. WE WERE LUCKY TO ESCAPE THE CITY WITH OUR LIVES. GOING BACK NOW WON'T SAVE THE DAY.
IF WE'RE TO HAVE ANY CHANCE OF VICTORY IN THE WAR OF THE REALMS... WE WILL HAVE TO JOURNEY ELSEWHERE.

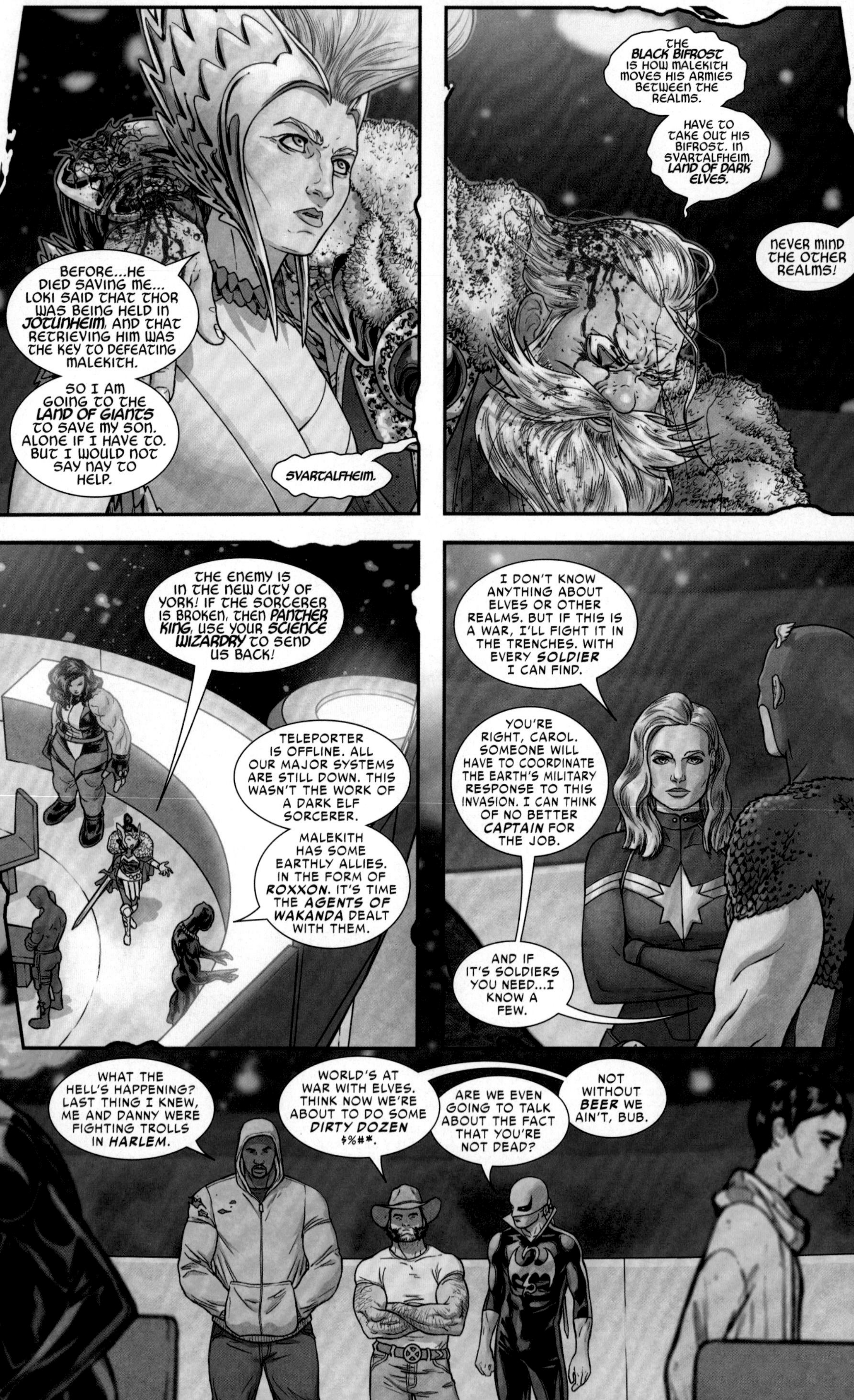
BEFORE...HE DIED SAVING ME... LOKI SAID THAT THOR WAS BEING HELD IN JOTUNHEIM, AND THAT RETRIEVING HIM WAS THE KEY TO DEFEATING MALEKITH.
SO I AM GOING TO THE LAND OF GIANTS TO SAVE MY SON. ALONE IF I HAVE TO. BUT I WOULD NOT SAY NAY TO HELP.
SVARTALFHEIM.
THE BLACK BIFROST IS HOW MALEKITH MOVES HIS ARMIES BETWEEN THE REALMS.
HAVE TO TAKE OUT HIS BIFROST. IN SVARTALFHEIM. LAND OF DARK ELVES.
NEVER MIND THE OTHER REALMS!
THE ENEMY IS IN THE NEW CITY OF YORK! IF THE SORCERER IS BROKEN, THEN PANTHER KING, USE YOUR SCIENCE WIZARDRY TO SEND US BACK!
TELEPORTER IS OFFLINE. ALL OUR MAJOR SYSTEMS ARE STILL DOWN. THIS WASN'T THE WORK OF A DARK ELF SORCERER.
MALEKITH HAS SOME EARTHLY ALLIES. IN THE FORM OF ROXXON. IT'S TIME THE AGENTS OF WAKANDA DEALT WITH THEM.
I DON'T KNOW ANYTHING ABOUT ELVES OR OTHER REALMS. BUT IF THIS IS A WAR, I'LL FIGHT IT IN THE TRENCHES. WITH EVERY SOLDIER I CAN FIND.
YOU'RE RIGHT, CAROL. SOMEONE WILL HAVE TO COORDINATE THE EARTH'S MILITARY RESPONSE TO THIS INVASION. I CAN THINK OF NO BETTER CAPTAIN FOR THE JOB.
AND IF IT'S SOLDIERS YOU NEED...I KNOW A FEW.
WHAT THE HELL'S HAPPENING? LAST THING I KNEW, ME AND DANNY WERE FIGHTING TROLLS IN HARLEM.
WORLD'S AT WAR WITH ELVES. THINK NOW WE'RE ABOUT TO DO SOME DIRTY DOZEN $%#*.
ARE WE EVEN GOING TO TALK ABOUT THE FACT THAT YOU'RE NOT DEAD?
NOT WITHOUT BEER WE AIN'T, BUB.

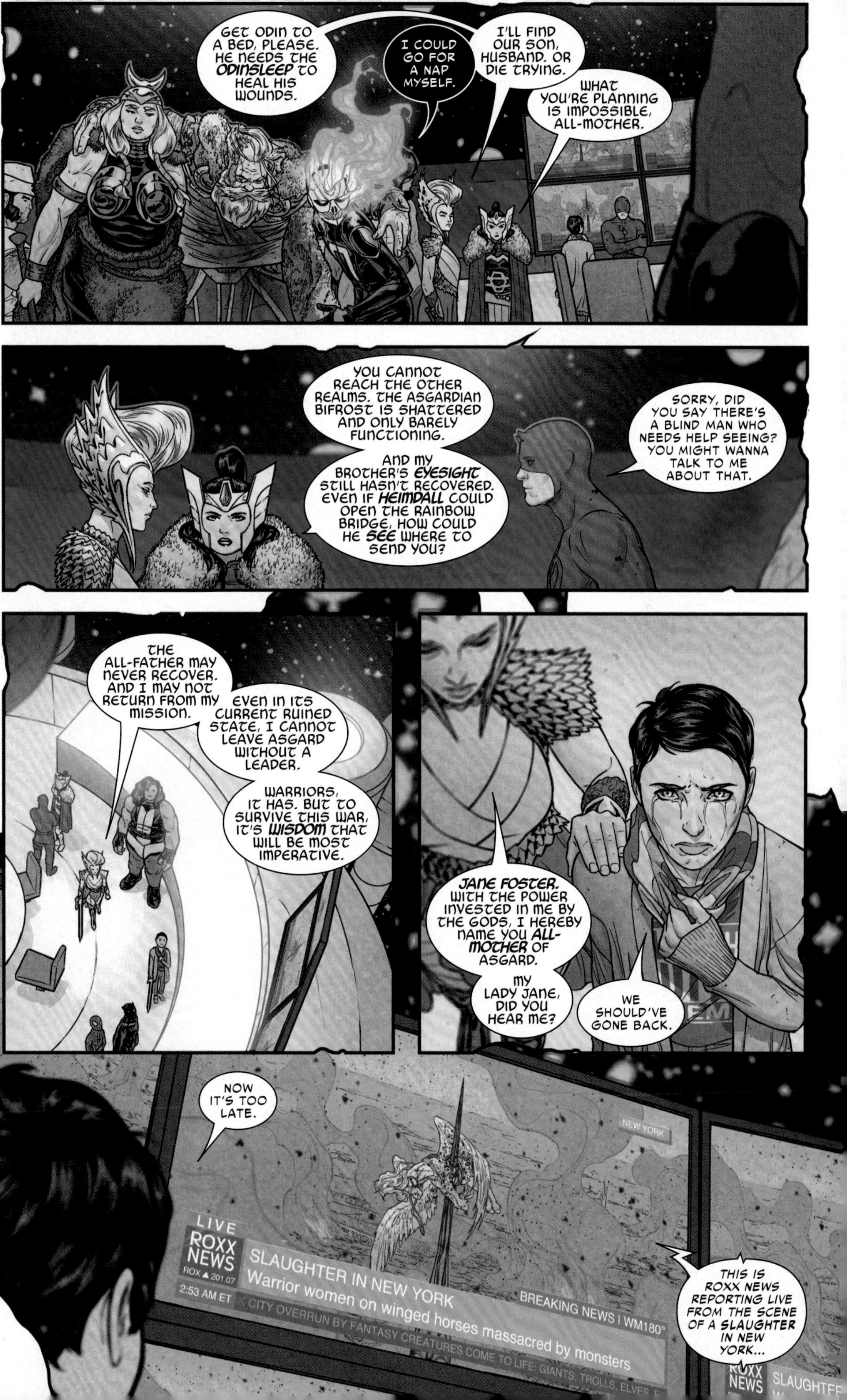
GET ODIN TO A BED, PLEASE. HE NEEDS THE ODINSLEEP TO HEAL HIS WOUNDS.
I COULD GO FOR A NAP MYSELF.
I'LL FIND OUR SON, HUSBAND. OR DIE TRYING.
WHAT YOU'RE PLANNING IS IMPOSSIBLE, ALL-MOTHER.
YOU CANNOT REACH THE OTHER REALMS. THE ASGARDIAN BIFROST IS SHATTERED AND ONLY BARELY FUNCTIONING.
AND MY BROTHER'S EYESIGHT STILL HASN'T RECOVERED. EVEN IF HEIMDALL COULD OPEN THE RAINBOW BRIDGE, HOW COULD HE SEE WHERE TO SEND YOU?
SORRY, DID YOU SAY THERE'S A BLIND MAN WHO NEEDS HELP SEEING? YOU MIGHT WANNA TALK TO ME ABOUT THAT.
THE ALL-FATHER MAY NEVER RECOVER. AND I MAY NOT RETURN FROM MY MISSION.
EVEN IN ITS CURRENT RUINED STATE, I CANNOT LEAVE ASGARD WITHOUT A LEADER.
WARRIORS, IT HAS. BUT TO SURVIVE THIS WAR, IT'S WISDOM THAT WILL BE MOST IMPERATIVE.
JANE FOSTER. WITH THE POWER INVESTED IN ME BY THE GODS, I HEREBY NAME YOU ALL-MOTHER OF ASGARD.
MY LADY JANE, DID YOU HEAR ME?
WE SHOULD'VE GONE BACK.
NOW IT'S TOO LATE.
NEW YORK
LIVE
ROXX NEWS
ROX ▲ 201.07
2:53 AM ET
SLAUGHTER IN NEW YORK
BREAKING NEWS | WM180°
Warrior women on winged horses massacred by monsters
CITY OVERRUN BY FANTASY CREATURES COME TO LIFE: GIANTS, TROLLS, ELVES...
THIS IS ROXX NEWS REPORTING LIVE FROM THE SCENE OF A SLAUGHTER IN NEW YORK...

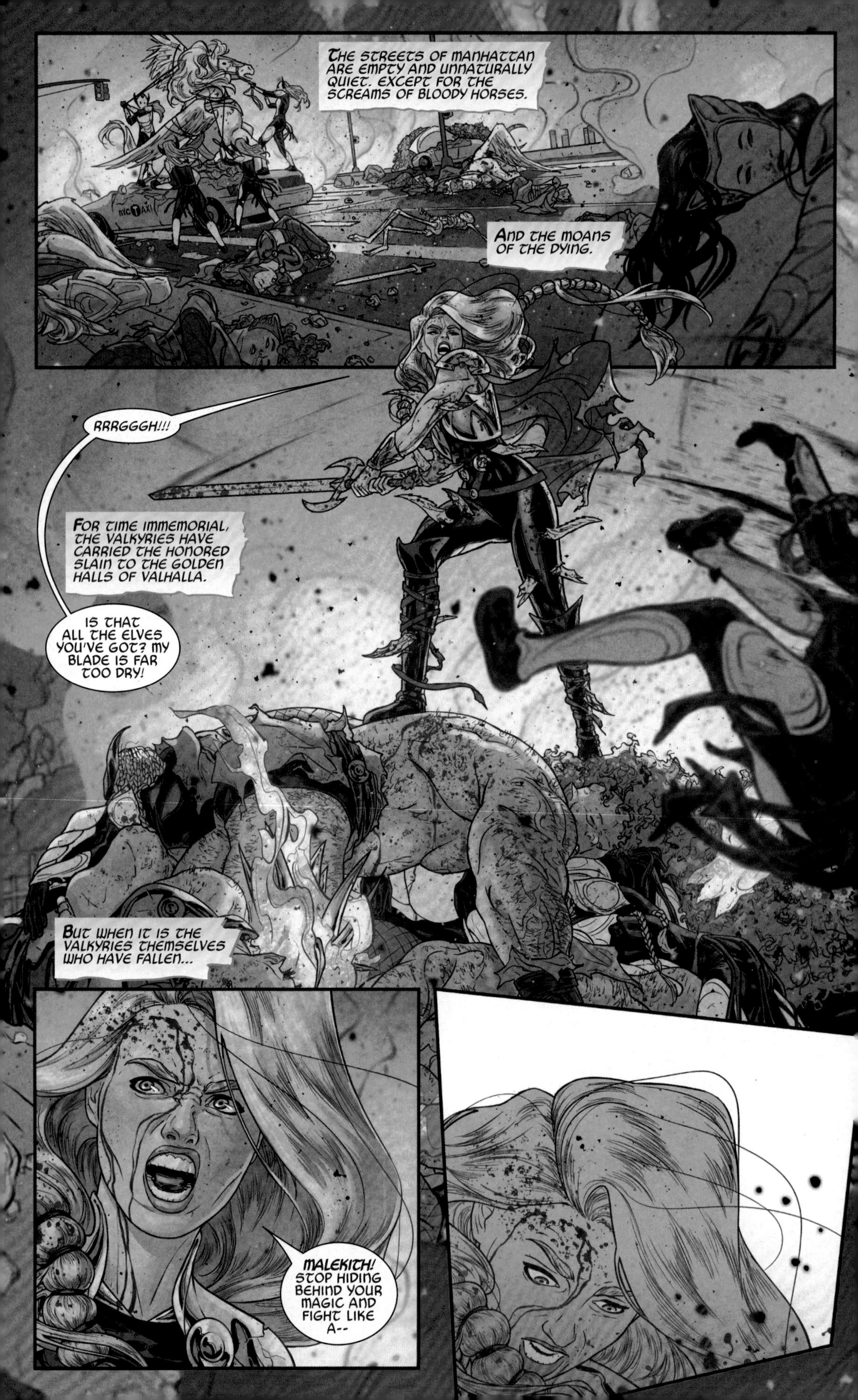
THE STREETS OF MANHATTAN ARE EMPTY AND UNNATURALLY QUIET. EXCEPT FOR THE SCREAMS OF BLOODY HORSES.
AND THE MOANS OF THE DYING.
NYC TAXI
RRRGGGH!!!
FOR TIME IMMEMORIAL, THE VALKYRIES HAVE CARRIED THE HONORED SLAIN TO THE GOLDEN HALLS OF VALHALLA.
IS THAT ALL THE ELVES YOU'VE GOT? MY BLADE IS FAR TOO DRY!
BUT WHEN IT IS THE VALKYRIES THEMSELVES WHO HAVE FALLEN...
MALEKITH! STOP HIDING BEHIND YOUR MAGIC AND FIGHT LIKE A--

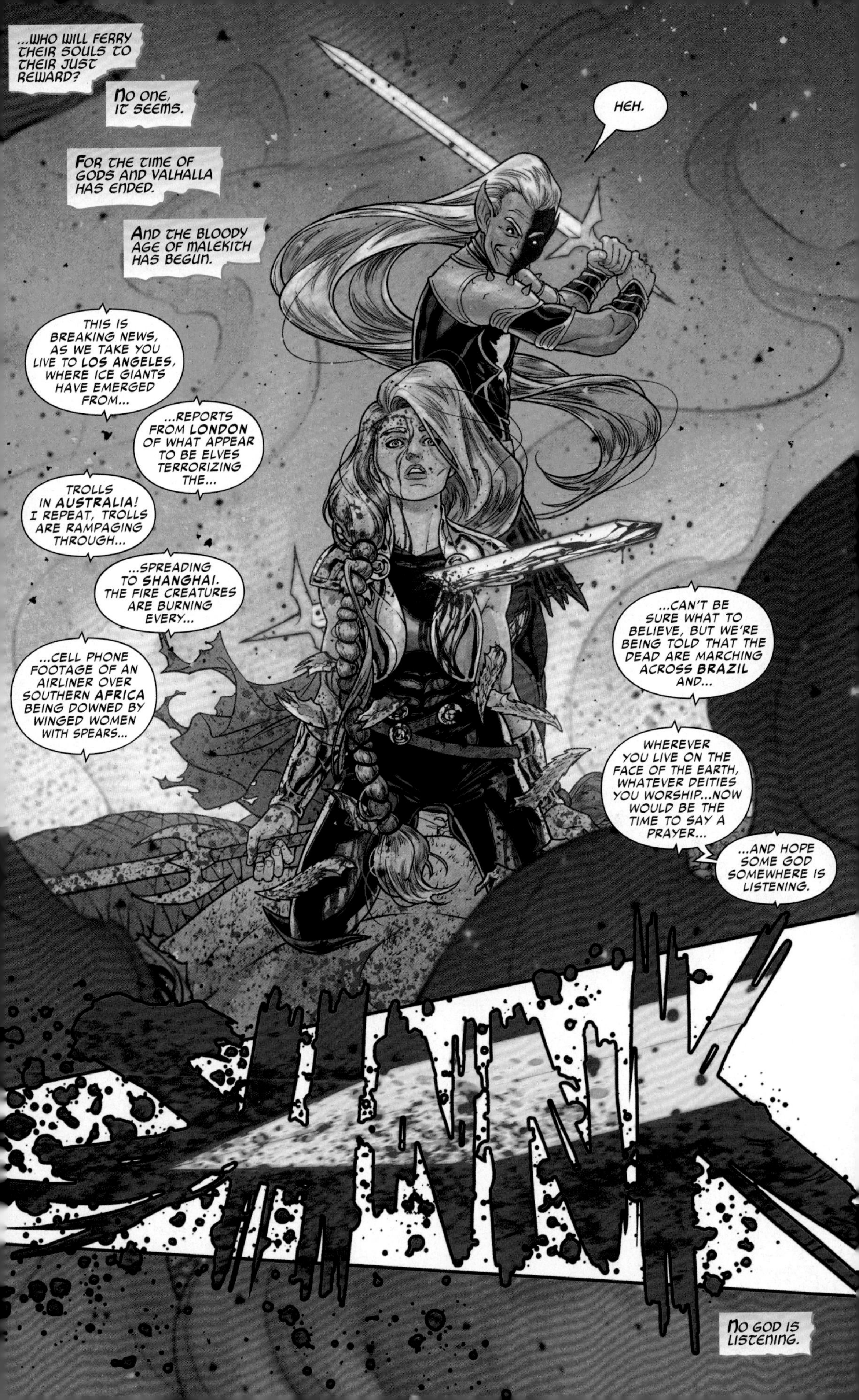
...WHO WILL FERRY THEIR SOULS TO THEIR JUST REWARD?
NO ONE, IT SEEMS.
HEH.
FOR THE TIME OF GODS AND VALHALLA HAS ENDED.
AND THE BLOODY AGE OF MALEKITH HAS BEGUN.
THIS IS BREAKING NEWS, AS WE TAKE YOU LIVE TO LOS ANGELES, WHERE ICE GIANTS HAVE EMERGED FROM...
...REPORTS FROM LONDON OF WHAT APPEAR TO BE ELVES TERRORIZING THE...
TROLLS IN AUSTRALIA! I REPEAT, TROLLS ARE RAMPAGING THROUGH...
...SPREADING TO SHANGHAI. THE FIRE CREATURES ARE BURNING EVERY...
...CELL PHONE FOOTAGE OF AN AIRLINER OVER SOUTHERN AFRICA BEING DOWNED BY WINGED WOMEN WITH SPEARS...
...CAN'T BE SURE WHAT TO BELIEVE, BUT WE'RE BEING TOLD THAT THE DEAD ARE MARCHING ACROSS BRAZIL AND...
WHEREVER YOU LIVE ON THE FACE OF THE EARTH, WHATEVER DEITIES YOU WORSHIP...NOW WOULD BE THE TIME TO SAY A PRAYER...
...AND HOPE SOME GOD SOMEWHERE IS LISTENING.
NO GOD IS LISTENING.

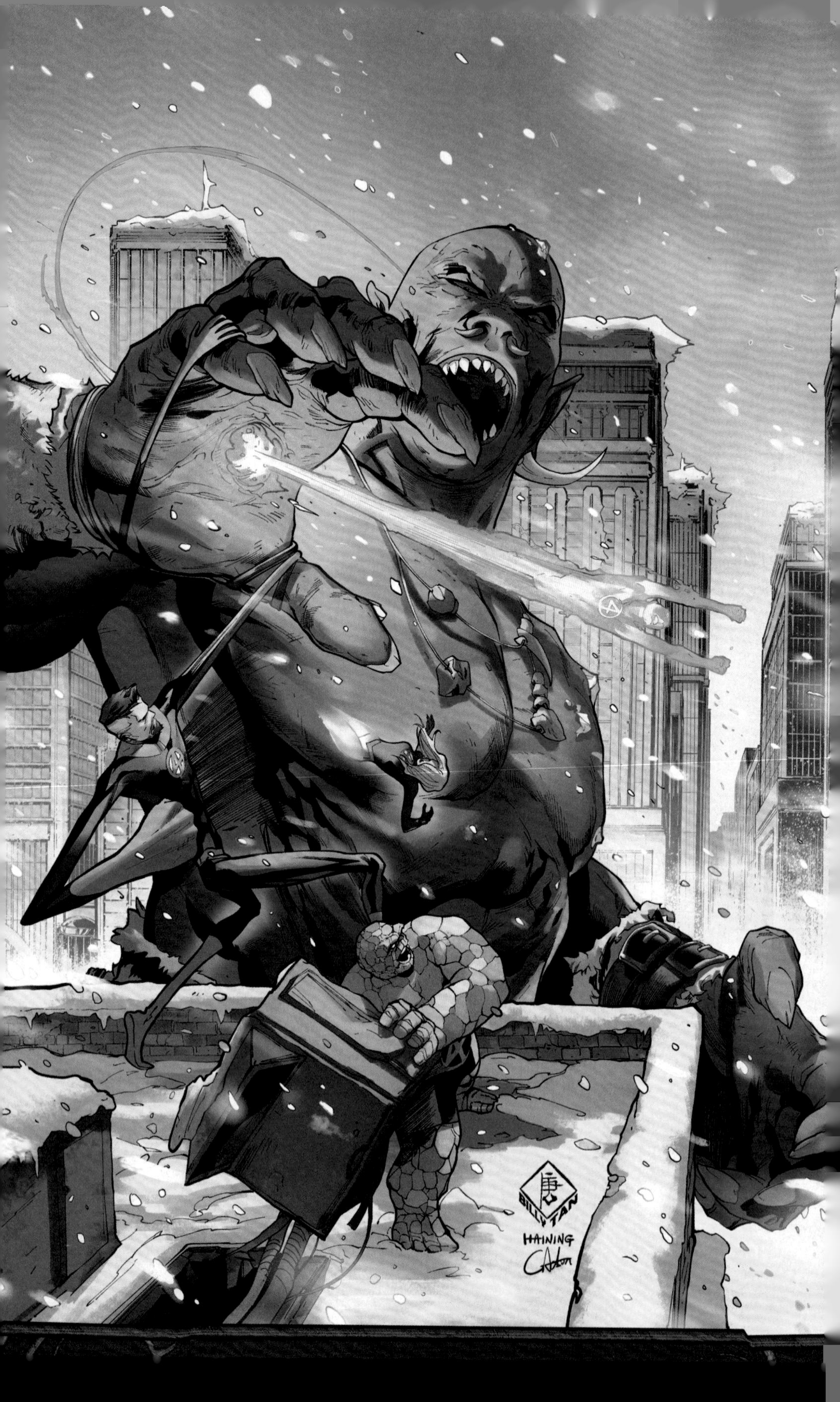
BILLY TAN
HAINING

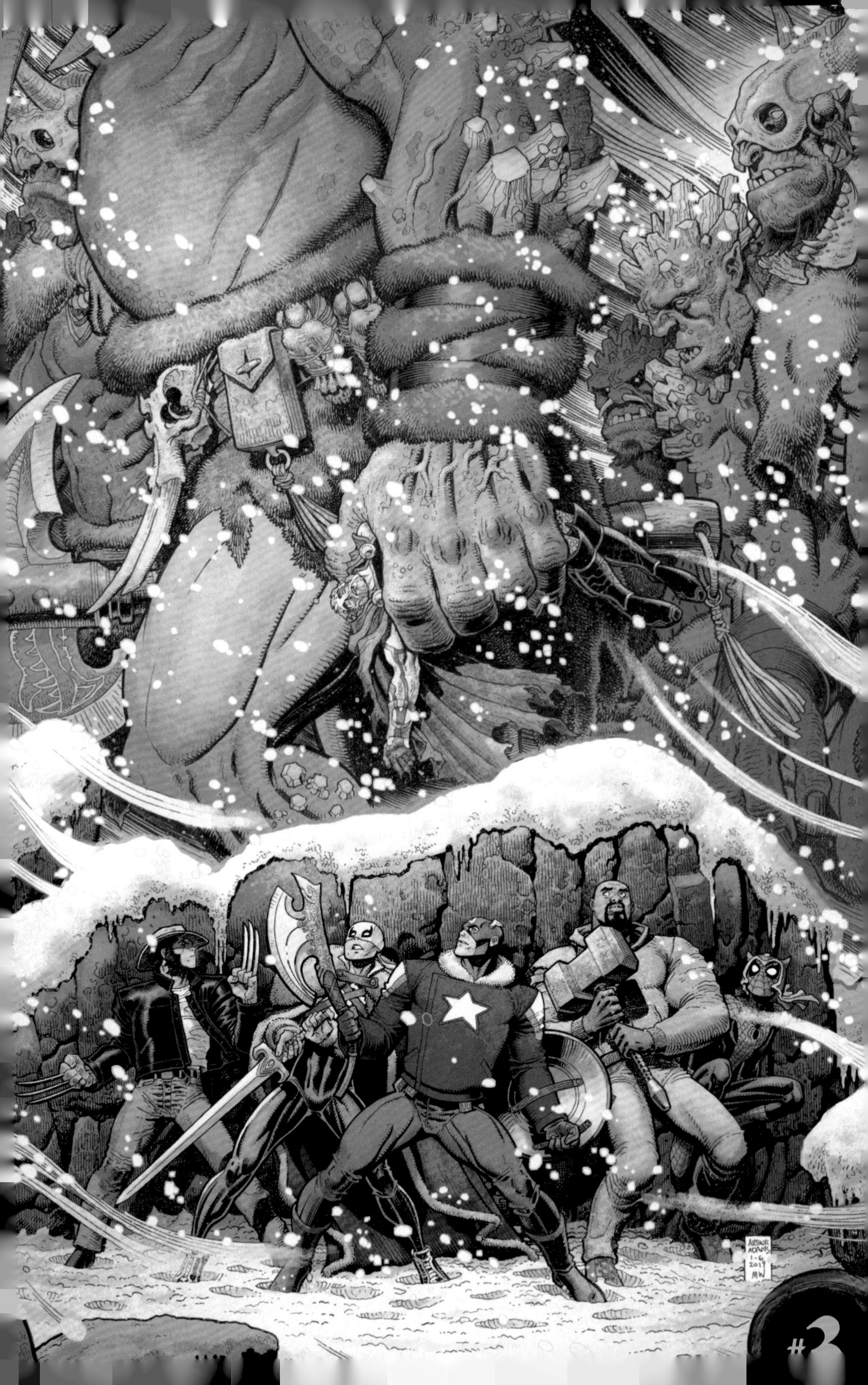
#3

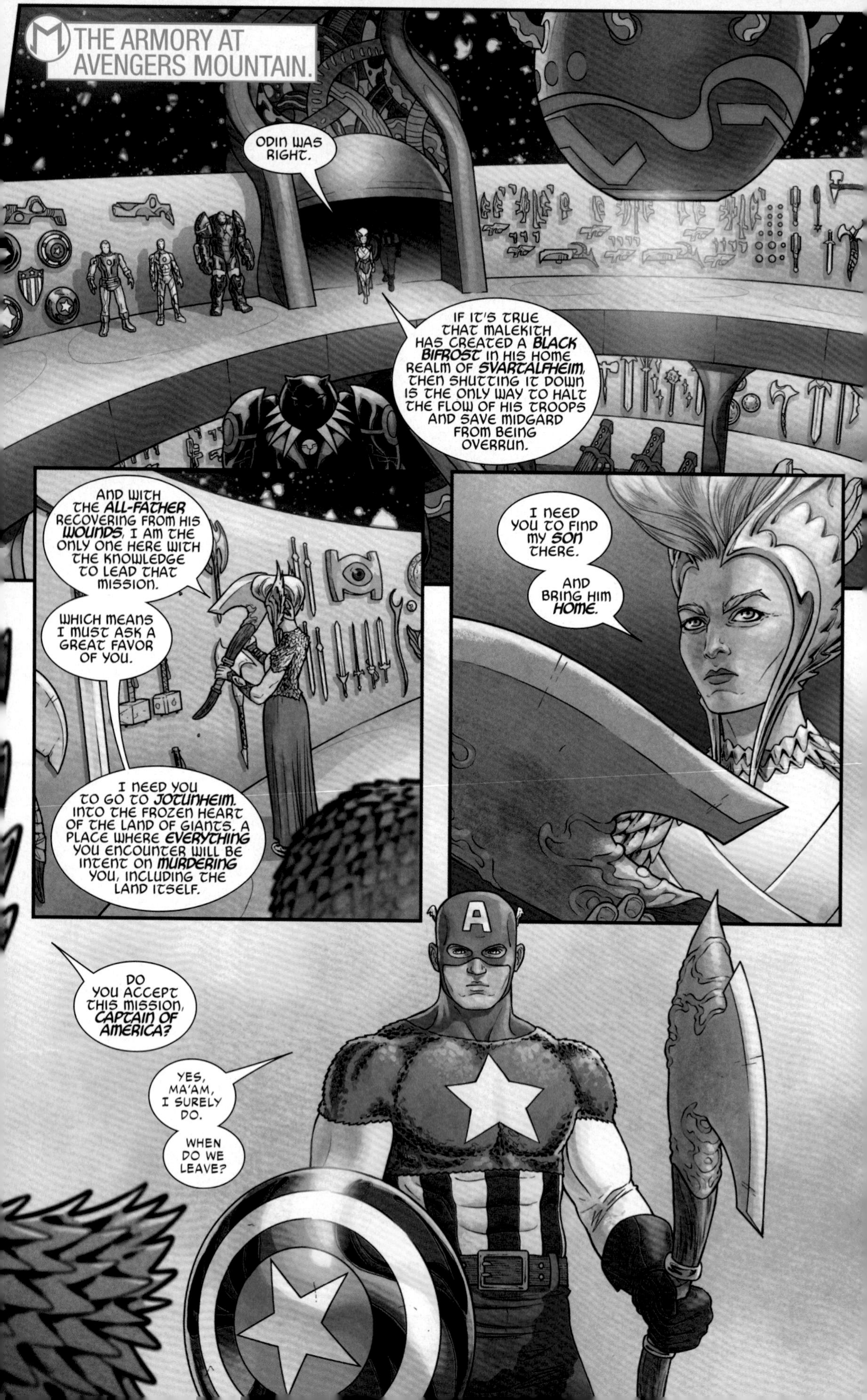
THE ARMORY AT AVENGERS MOUNTAIN.
ODIN WAS RIGHT.
IF IT'S TRUE THAT MALEKITH HAS CREATED A BLACK BIFROST IN HIS HOME REALM OF SVARTALFHEIM, THEN SHUTTING IT DOWN IS THE ONLY WAY TO HALT THE FLOW OF HIS TROOPS AND SAVE MIDGARD FROM BEING OVERRUN.
AND WITH THE ALL-FATHER RECOVERING FROM HIS WOUNDS, I AM THE ONLY ONE HERE WITH THE KNOWLEDGE TO LEAD THAT MISSION.
WHICH MEANS I MUST ASK A GREAT FAVOR OF YOU.
I NEED YOU TO GO TO JOTUNHEIM. INTO THE FROZEN HEART OF THE LAND OF GIANTS. A PLACE WHERE EVERYTHING YOU ENCOUNTER WILL BE INTENT ON MURDERING YOU, INCLUDING THE LAND ITSELF.
I NEED YOU TO FIND MY SON THERE.
AND BRING HIM HOME.
DO YOU ACCEPT THIS MISSION, CAPTAIN OF AMERICA?
YES, MA'AM, I SURELY DO.
WHEN DO WE LEAVE?

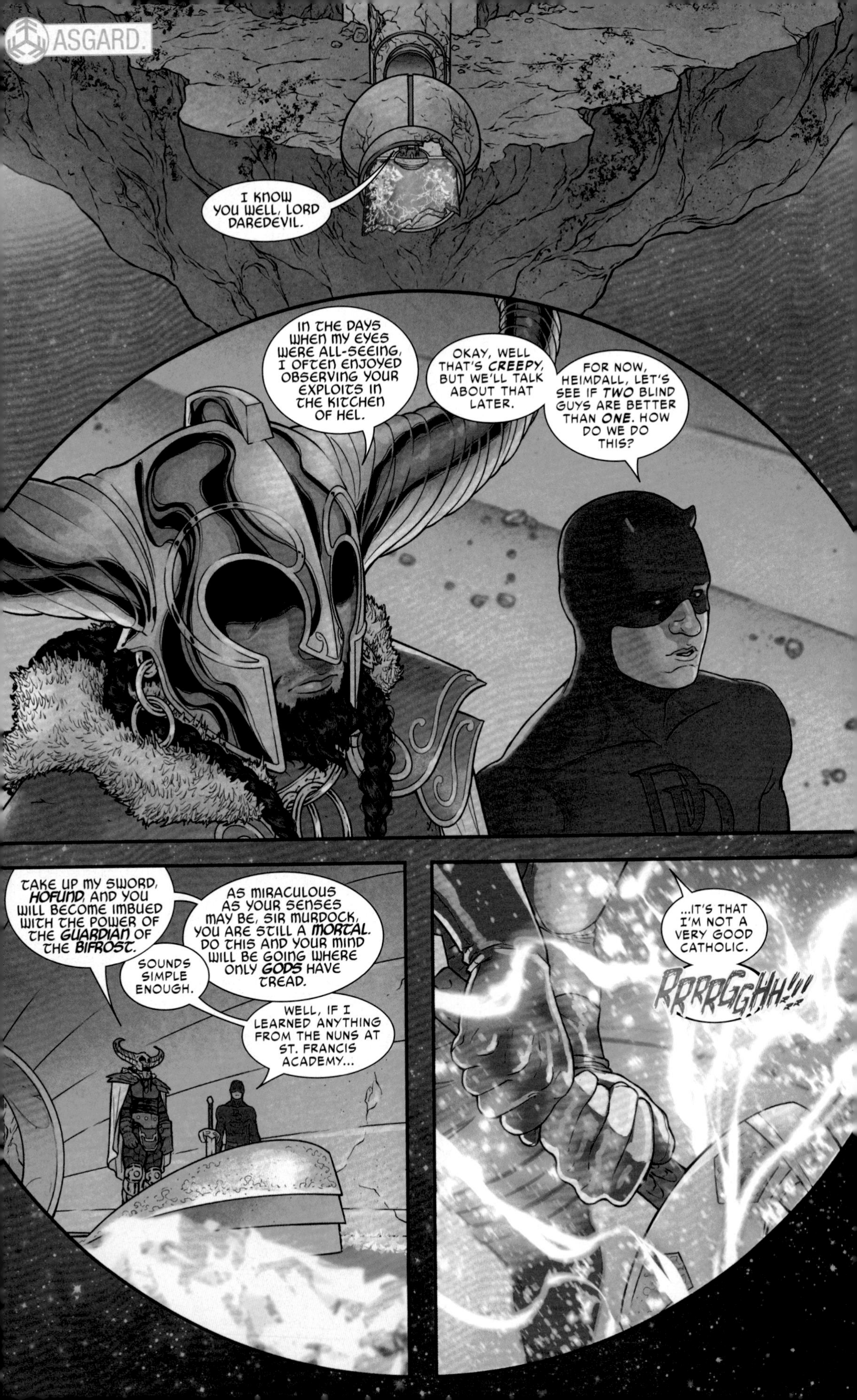
ASGARD.
I KNOW YOU WELL, LORD DAREDEVIL.
IN THE DAYS WHEN MY EYES WERE ALL-SEEING, I OFTEN ENJOYED OBSERVING YOUR EXPLOITS IN THE KITCHEN OF HEL.
OKAY, WELL THAT'S CREEPY, BUT WE'LL TALK ABOUT THAT LATER.
FOR NOW, HEIMDALL, LET'S SEE IF TWO BLIND GUYS ARE BETTER THAN ONE. HOW DO WE DO THIS?
TAKE UP MY SWORD, HOFUND, AND YOU WILL BECOME IMBUED WITH THE POWER OF THE GUARDIAN OF THE BIFROST.
AS MIRACULOUS AS YOUR SENSES MAY BE, SIR MURDOCK, YOU ARE STILL A MORTAL. DO THIS AND YOUR MIND WILL BE GOING WHERE ONLY GODS HAVE TREAD.
SOUNDS SIMPLE ENOUGH.
WELL, IF I LEARNED ANYTHING FROM THE NUNS AT ST. FRANCIS ACADEMY...
...IT'S THAT I'M NOT A VERY GOOD CATHOLIC.
RRRRGGHH!!!

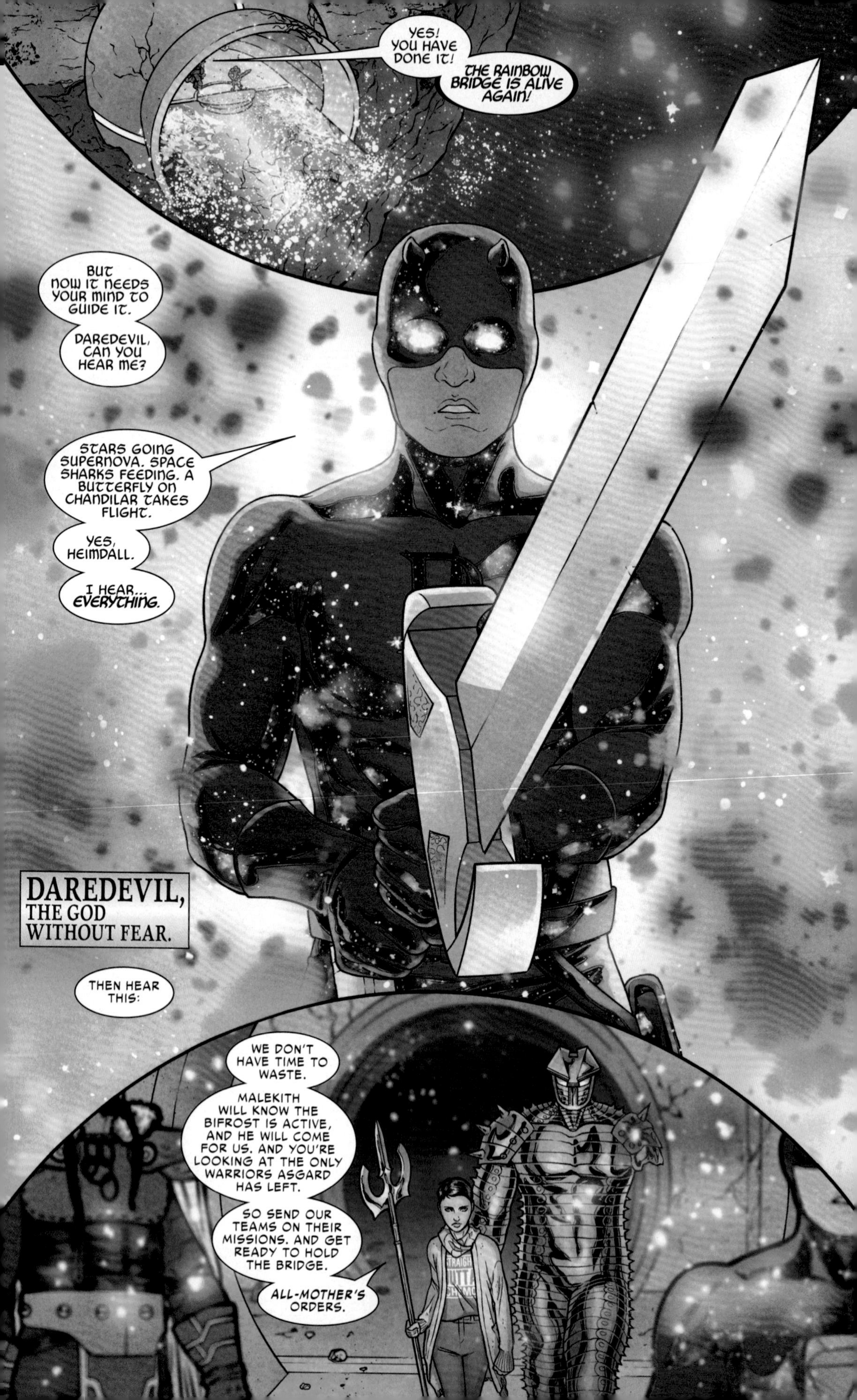

YES! YOU HAVE DONE IT! THE RAINBOW BRIDGE IS ALIVE AGAIN!
BUT NOW IT NEEDS YOUR MIND TO GUIDE IT.
DAREDEVIL, CAN YOU HEAR ME?
STARS GOING SUPERNOVA. SPACE SHARKS FEEDING. A BUTTERFLY ON CHANDILAR TAKES FLIGHT.
YES, HEIMDALL.
I HEAR... EVERYTHING.
DAREDEVIL, THE GOD WITHOUT FEAR.
THEN HEAR THIS:
WE DON'T HAVE TIME TO WASTE.
MALEKITH WILL KNOW THE BIFROST IS ACTIVE, AND HE WILL COME FOR US. AND YOU'RE LOOKING AT THE ONLY WARRIORS ASGARD HAS LEFT.
SO SEND OUR TEAMS ON THEIR MISSIONS. AND GET READY TO HOLD THE BRIDGE.
ALL-MOTHER'S ORDERS.

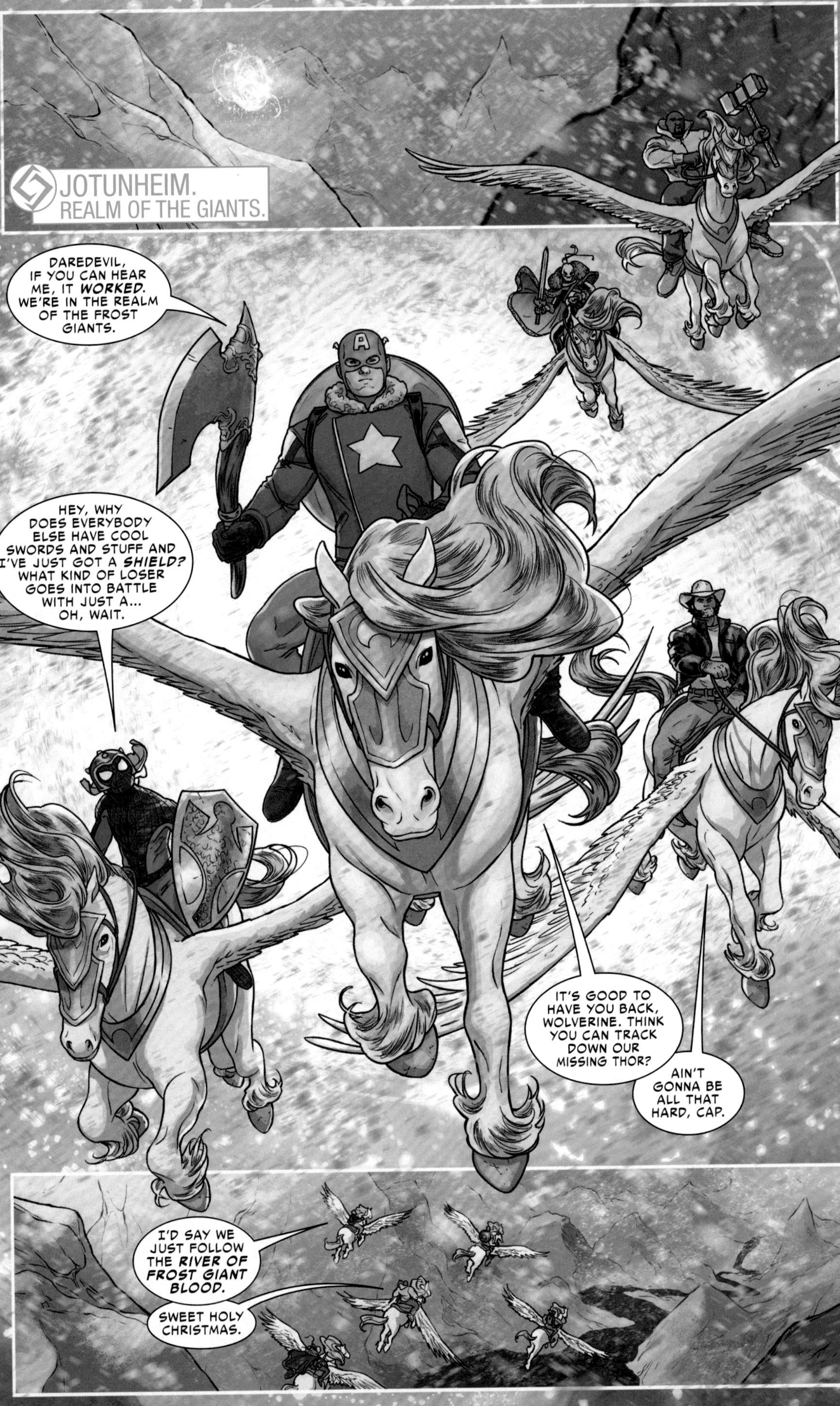
JOTUNHEIM.
REALM OF THE GIANTS.
DAREDEVIL, IF YOU CAN HEAR ME, IT WORKED. WE'RE IN THE REALM OF THE FROST GIANTS.
HEY, WHY DOES EVERYBODY ELSE HAVE COOL SWORDS AND STUFF AND I'VE JUST GOT A SHIELD? WHAT KIND OF LOSER GOES INTO BATTLE WITH JUST A... OH, WAIT.
IT'S GOOD TO HAVE YOU BACK, WOLVERINE. THINK YOU CAN TRACK DOWN OUR MISSING THOR?
AIN'T GONNA BE ALL THAT HARD, CAP.
I'D SAY WE JUST FOLLOW THE RIVER OF FROST GIANT BLOOD.
SWEET HOLY CHRISTMAS.

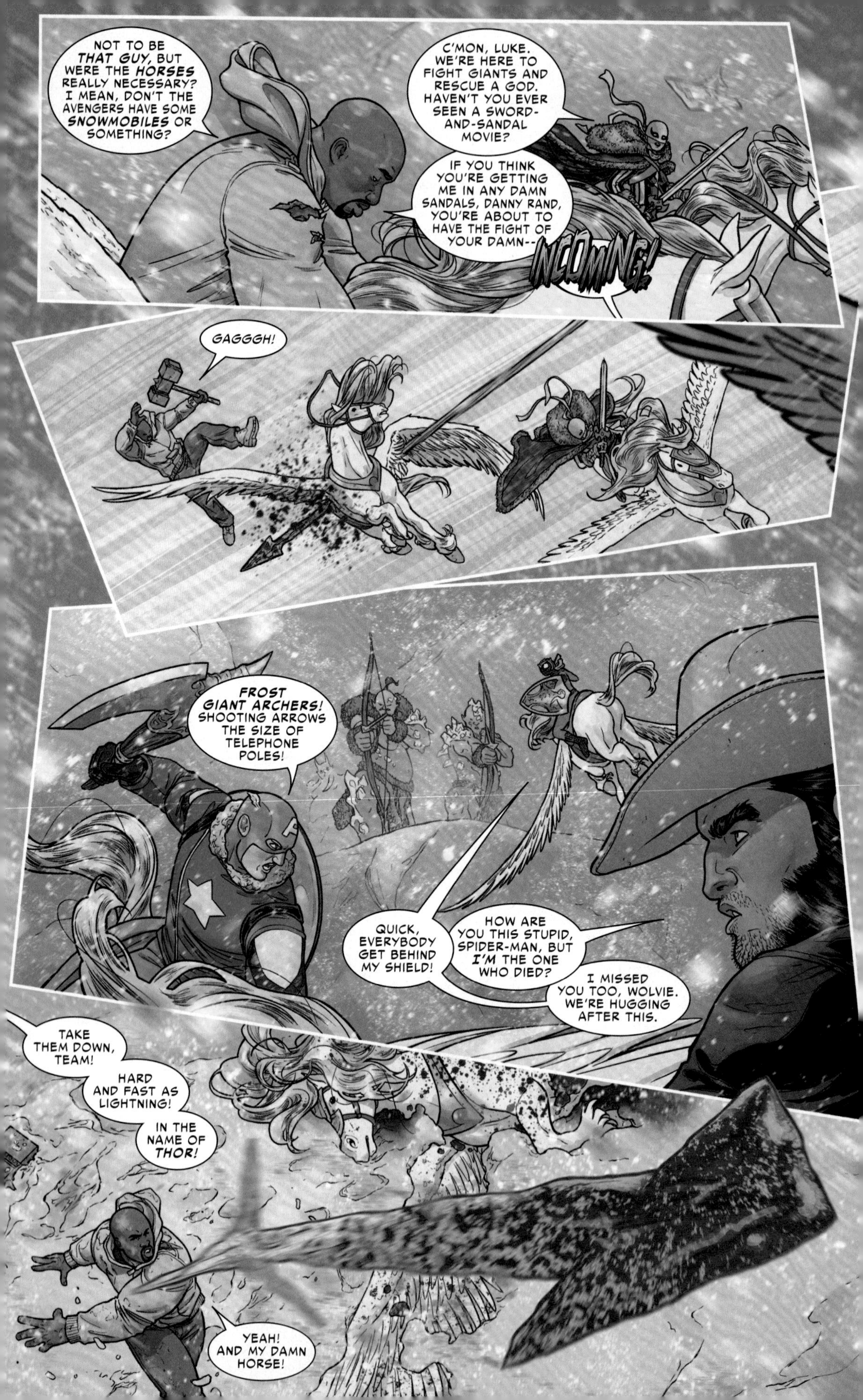
NOT TO BE THAT GUY, BUT WERE THE HORSES REALLY NECESSARY? I MEAN, DON'T THE AVENGERS HAVE SOME SNOWMOBILES OR SOMETHING?
C'MON, LUKE. WE'RE HERE TO FIGHT GIANTS AND RESCUE A GOD. HAVEN'T YOU EVER SEEN A SWORD-AND-SANDAL MOVIE?
IF YOU THINK YOU'RE GETTING ME IN ANY DAMN SANDALS, DANNY RAND, YOU'RE ABOUT TO HAVE THE FIGHT OF YOUR DAMN--
INCOMING!
GAGGGH!
FROST GIANT ARCHERS! SHOOTING ARROWS THE SIZE OF TELEPHONE POLES!
QUICK, EVERYBODY GET BEHIND MY SHIELD!
HOW ARE YOU THIS STUPID, SPIDER-MAN, BUT I'M THE ONE WHO DIED?
I MISSED YOU TOO, WOLVIE. WE'RE HUGGING AFTER THIS.
TAKE THEM DOWN, TEAM!
HARD AND FAST AS LIGHTNING!
IN THE NAME OF THOR!
YEAH! AND MY DAMN HORSE!

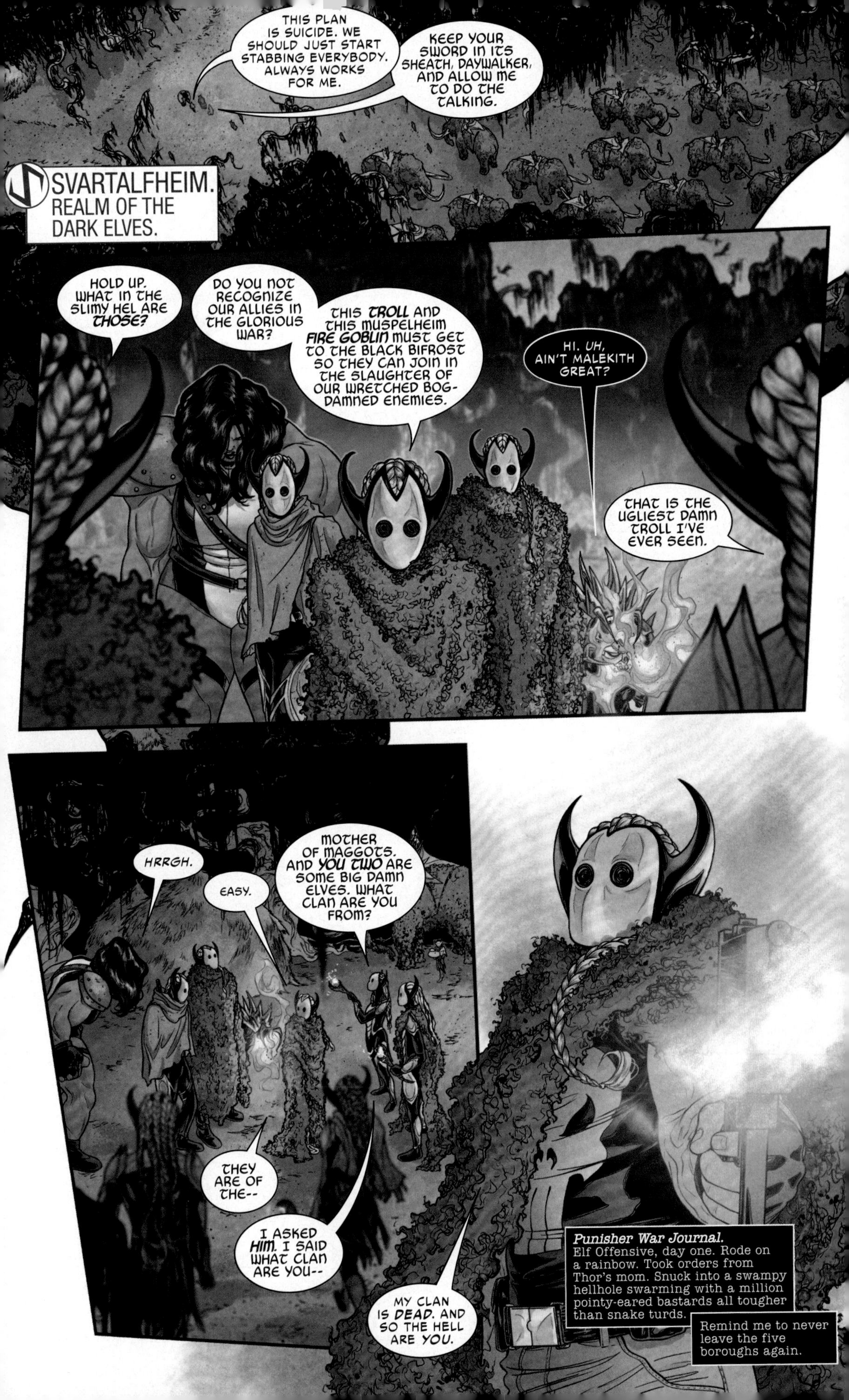
THIS PLAN IS SUICIDE. WE SHOULD JUST START STABBING EVERYBODY. ALWAYS WORKS FOR ME.
KEEP YOUR SWORD IN ITS SHEATH, DAYWALKER, AND ALLOW ME TO DO THE TALKING.
SVARTALFHEIM. REALM OF THE DARK ELVES.
HOLD UP. WHAT IN THE SLIMY HEL ARE THOSE?
DO YOU NOT RECOGNIZE OUR ALLIES IN THE GLORIOUS WAR?
THIS TROLL AND THIS MUSPELHEIM FIRE GOBLIN MUST GET TO THE BLACK BIFROST SO THEY CAN JOIN IN THE SLAUGHTER OF OUR WRETCHED BOG-DAMNED ENEMIES.
HI. UH, AIN'T MALEKITH GREAT?
THAT IS THE UGLIEST DAMN TROLL I'VE EVER SEEN.
HRRGH.
EASY.
MOTHER OF MAGGOTS. AND YOU TWO ARE SOME BIG DAMN ELVES. WHAT CLAN ARE YOU FROM?
THEY ARE OF THE--
I ASKED HIM. I SAID WHAT CLAN ARE YOU--
MY CLAN IS DEAD. AND SO THE HELL ARE YOU.
Punisher War Journal.
Elf Offensive, day one. Rode on a rainbow. Took orders from Thor's mom. Snuck into a swampy hellhole swarming with a million pointy-eared bastards all tougher than snake turds.
Remind me to never leave the five boroughs again.

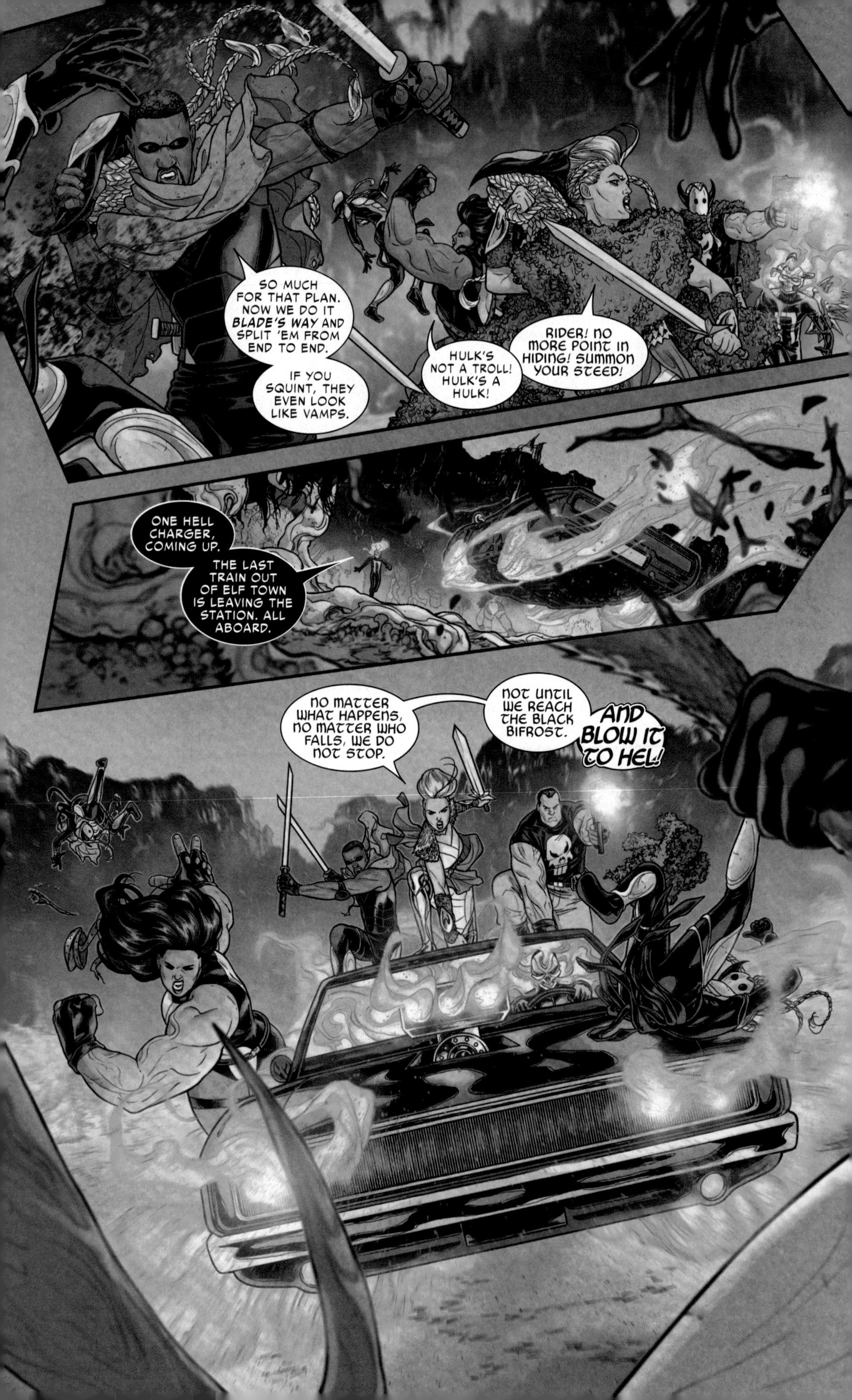
SO MUCH FOR THAT PLAN. NOW WE DO IT BLADE'S WAY AND SPLIT 'EM FROM END TO END.
IF YOU SQUINT, THEY EVEN LOOK LIKE VAMPS.
HULK'S NOT A TROLL! HULK'S A HULK!
RIDER! NO MORE POINT IN HIDING! SUMMON YOUR STEED!
ONE HELL CHARGER, COMING UP.
THE LAST TRAIN OUT OF ELF TOWN IS LEAVING THE STATION. ALL ABOARD.
NO MATTER WHAT HAPPENS, NO MATTER WHO FALLS, WE DO NOT STOP.
NOT UNTIL WE REACH THE BLACK BIFROST.
AND BLOW IT TO HEL!

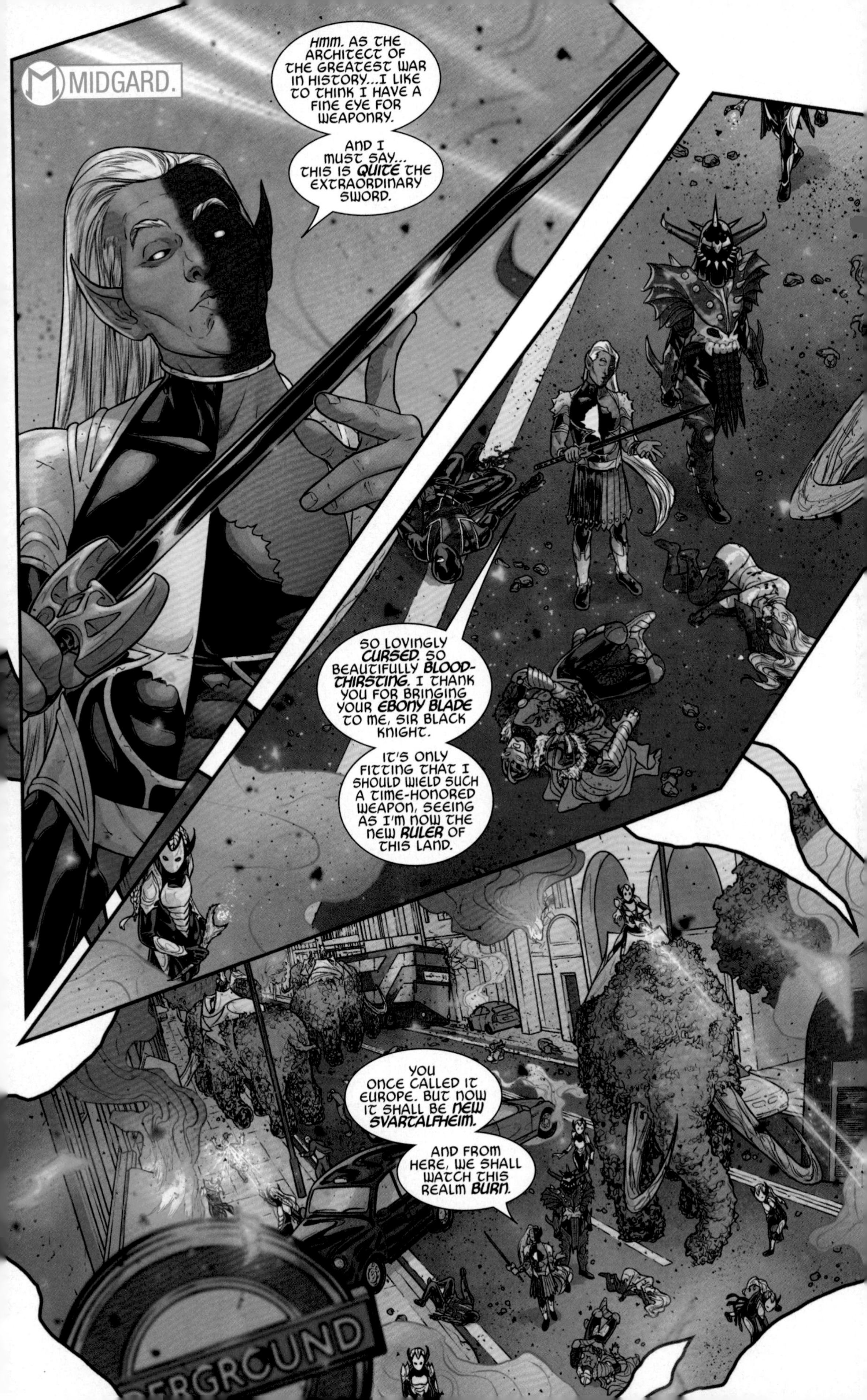
MIDGARD.
HMM. AS THE ARCHITECT OF THE GREATEST WAR IN HISTORY...I LIKE TO THINK I HAVE A FINE EYE FOR WEAPONRY.
AND I MUST SAY... THIS IS QUITE THE EXTRAORDINARY SWORD.
SO LOVINGLY CURSED. SO BEAUTIFULLY BLOOD-THIRSTING. I THANK YOU FOR BRINGING YOUR EBONY BLADE TO ME, SIR BLACK KNIGHT.
IT'S ONLY FITTING THAT I SHOULD WIELD SUCH A TIME-HONORED WEAPON, SEEING AS I'M NOW THE NEW RULER OF THIS LAND.
YOU ONCE CALLED IT EUROPE. BUT NOW IT SHALL BE NEW SVARTALFHEIM.
AND FROM HERE, WE SHALL WATCH THIS REALM BURN.
ERGROUND

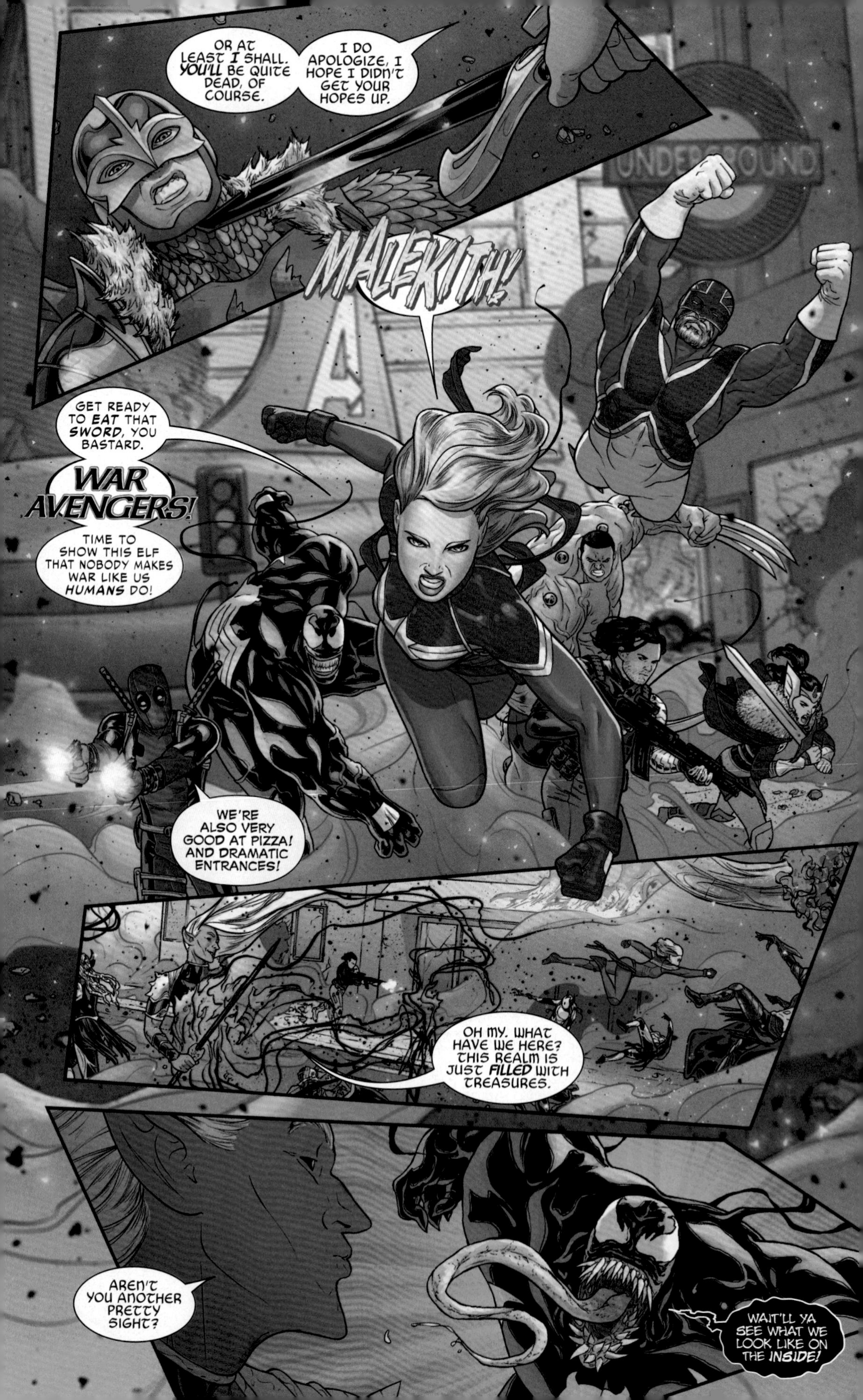
OR AT LEAST I SHALL. YOU'LL BE QUITE DEAD, OF COURSE.
I DO APOLOGIZE, I HOPE I DIDN'T GET YOUR HOPES UP.
MALEKITH!
GET READY TO EAT THAT SWORD, YOU BASTARD.
WAR AVENGERS!
TIME TO SHOW THIS ELF THAT NOBODY MAKES WAR LIKE US HUMANS DO!
WE'RE ALSO VERY GOOD AT PIZZA! AND DRAMATIC ENTRANCES!
OH MY. WHAT HAVE WE HERE? THIS REALM IS JUST FILLED WITH TREASURES.
UNDERGROUND
AREN'T YOU ANOTHER PRETTY SIGHT?
WAIT'LL YA SEE WHAT WE LOOK LIKE ON THE INSIDE!

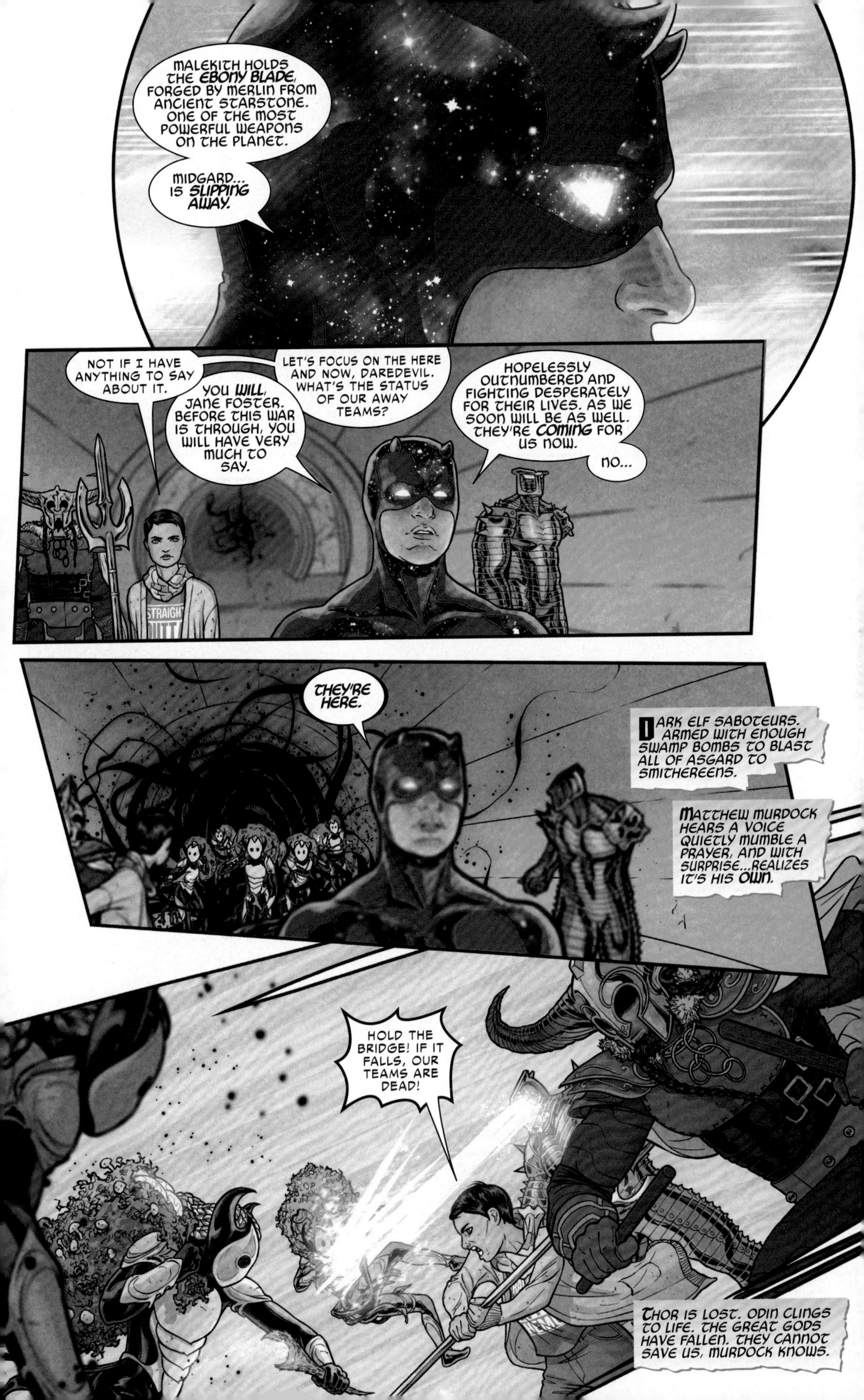
MALEKITH HOLDS THE EBONY BLADE, FORGED BY MERLIN FROM ANCIENT STARSTONE. ONE OF THE MOST POWERFUL WEAPONS ON THE PLANET.
MIDGARD... IS SLIPPING AWAY.
NOT IF I HAVE ANYTHING TO SAY ABOUT IT.
YOU WILL, JANE FOSTER. BEFORE THIS WAR IS THROUGH, YOU WILL HAVE VERY MUCH TO SAY.
LET'S FOCUS ON THE HERE AND NOW, DAREDEVIL. WHAT'S THE STATUS OF OUR AWAY TEAMS?
HOPELESSLY OUTNUMBERED AND FIGHTING DESPERATELY FOR THEIR LIVES. AS WE SOON WILL BE AS WELL. THEY'RE COMING FOR US NOW.
NO...
STRAIGHT
THEY'RE HERE.
DARK ELF SABOTEURS. ARMED WITH ENOUGH SWAMP BOMBS TO BLAST ALL OF ASGARD TO SMITHEREENS.
MATTHEW MURDOCK HEARS A VOICE QUIETLY MUMBLE A PRAYER, AND WITH SURPRISE...REALIZES IT'S HIS OWN.
HOLD THE BRIDGE! IF IT FALLS, OUR TEAMS ARE DEAD!
THOR IS LOST. ODIN CLINGS TO LIFE. THE GREAT GODS HAVE FALLEN. THEY CANNOT SAVE US, MURDOCK KNOWS.

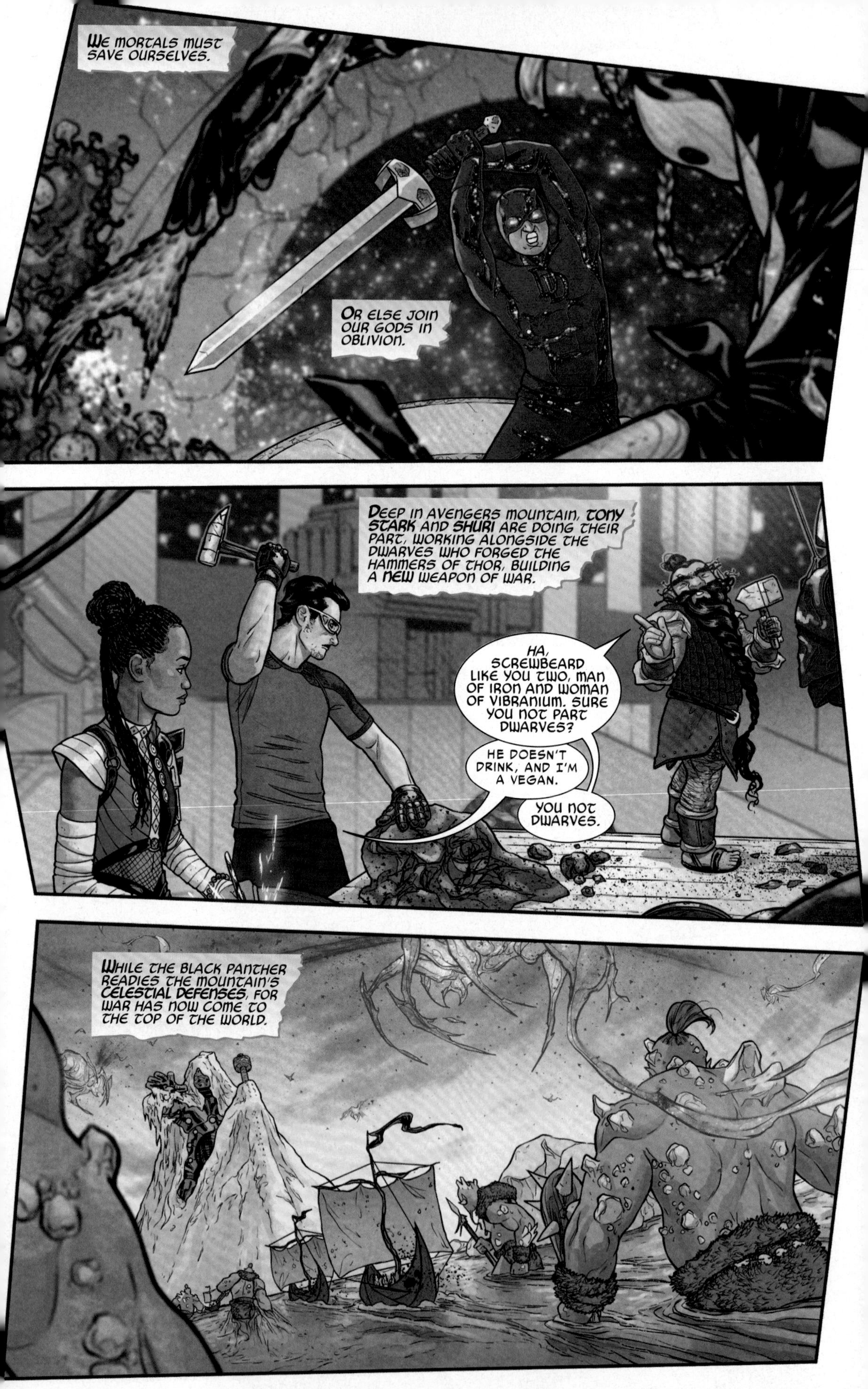
WE MORTALS MUST SAVE OURSELVES.
OR ELSE JOIN OUR GODS IN OBLIVION.
DEEP IN AVENGERS MOUNTAIN, TONY STARK AND SHURI ARE DOING THEIR PART, WORKING ALONGSIDE THE DWARVES WHO FORGED THE HAMMERS OF THOR, BUILDING A NEW WEAPON OF WAR.
HA, SCREWBEARD LIKE YOU TWO, MAN OF IRON AND WOMAN OF VIBRANIUM. SURE YOU NOT PART DWARVES?
HE DOESN'T DRINK, AND I'M A VEGAN.
YOU NOT DWARVES.
WHILE THE BLACK PANTHER READIES THE MOUNTAIN'S CELESTIAL DEFENSES, FOR WAR HAS NOW COME TO THE TOP OF THE WORLD.

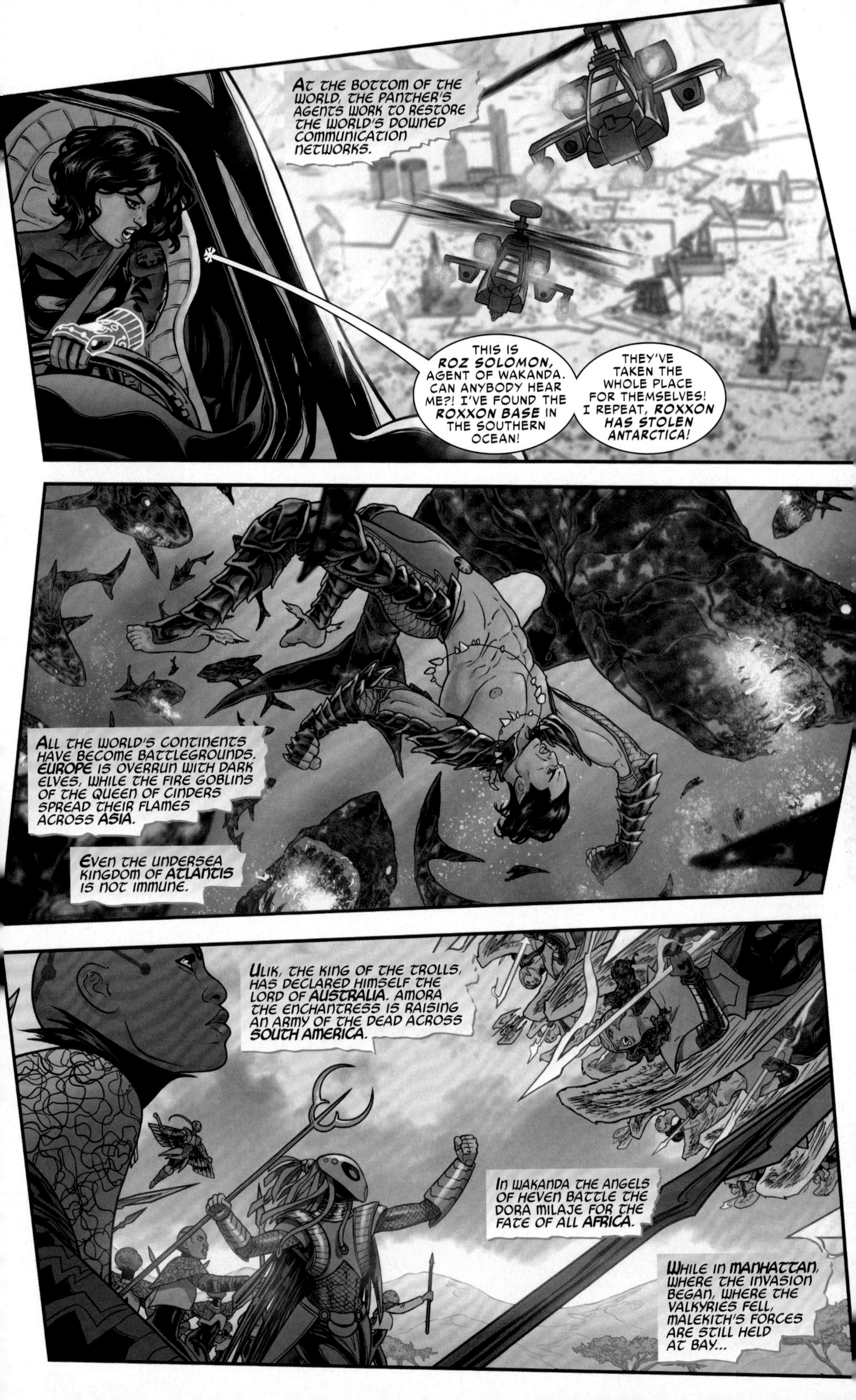
AT THE BOTTOM OF THE WORLD, THE PANTHER'S AGENTS WORK TO RESTORE THE WORLD'S DOWNED COMMUNICATION NETWORKS.
THIS IS ROZ SOLOMON, AGENT OF WAKANDA. CAN ANYBODY HEAR ME?! I'VE FOUND THE ROXXON BASE IN THE SOUTHERN OCEAN!
THEY'VE TAKEN THE WHOLE PLACE FOR THEMSELVES! I REPEAT, ROXXON HAS STOLEN ANTARCTICA!
ALL THE WORLD'S CONTINENTS HAVE BECOME BATTLEGROUNDS. EUROPE IS OVERRUN WITH DARK ELVES, WHILE THE FIRE GOBLINS OF THE QUEEN OF CINDERS SPREAD THEIR FLAMES ACROSS ASIA.
EVEN THE UNDERSEA KINGDOM OF ATLANTIS IS NOT IMMUNE.
ULIK, THE KING OF THE TROLLS, HAS DECLARED HIMSELF THE LORD OF AUSTRALIA. AMORA THE ENCHANTRESS IS RAISING AN ARMY OF THE DEAD ACROSS SOUTH AMERICA.
IN WAKANDA THE ANGELS OF HEVEN BATTLE THE DORA MILAJE FOR THE FATE OF ALL AFRICA.
WHILE IN MANHATTAN, WHERE THE INVASION BEGAN, WHERE THE VALKYRIES FELL, MALEKITH'S FORCES ARE STILL HELD AT BAY...

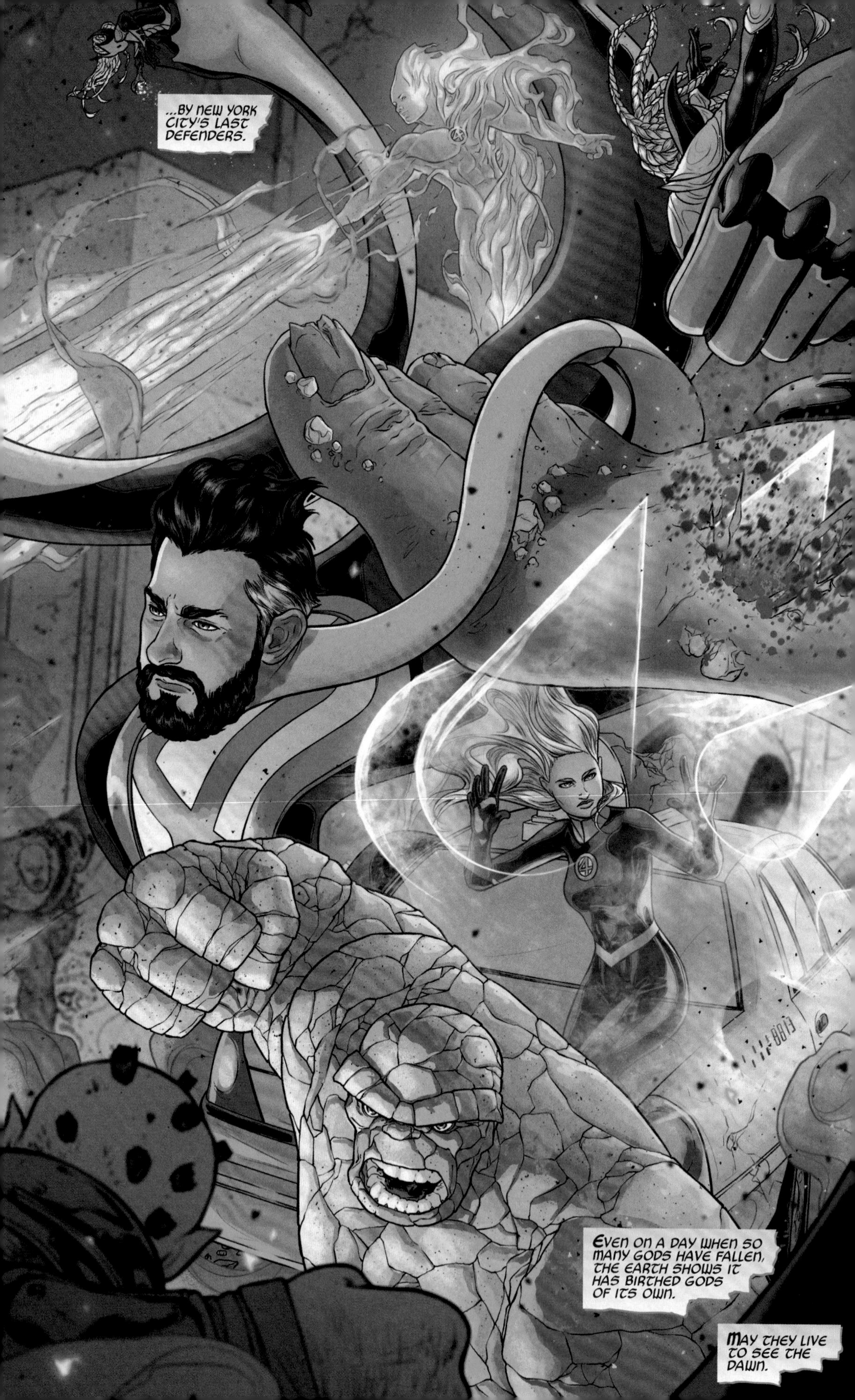
...BY NEW YORK CITY'S LAST DEFENDERS.
EVEN ON A DAY WHEN SO MANY GODS HAVE FALLEN, THE EARTH SHOWS IT HAS BIRTHED GODS OF ITS OWN.
MAY THEY LIVE TO SEE THE DAWN.

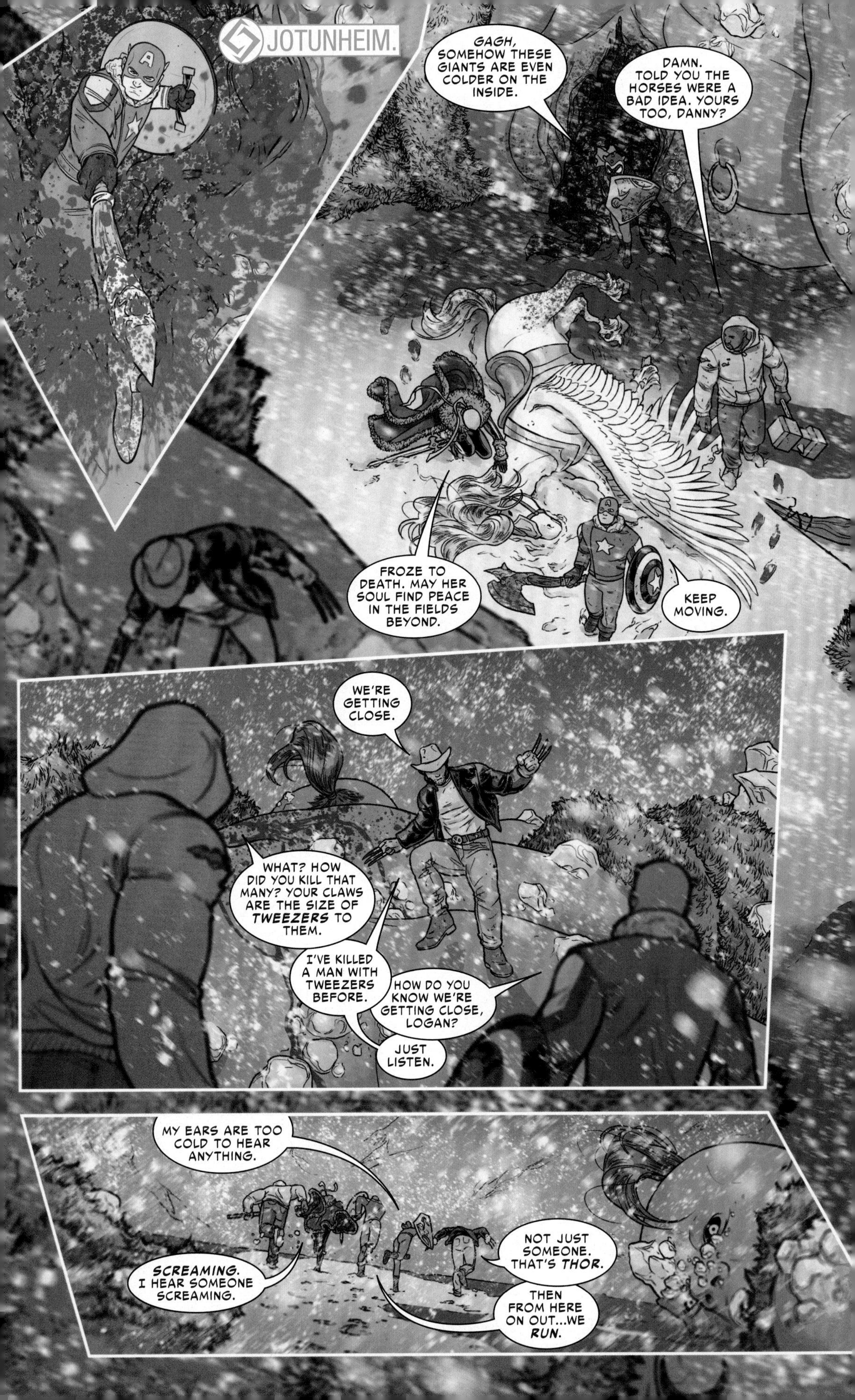
JOTUNHEIM.
GAGH, SOMEHOW THESE GIANTS ARE EVEN COLDER ON THE INSIDE.
DAMN. TOLD YOU THE HORSES WERE A BAD IDEA. YOURS TOO, DANNY?
FROZE TO DEATH. MAY HER SOUL FIND PEACE IN THE FIELDS BEYOND.
KEEP MOVING.
WE'RE GETTING CLOSE.
WHAT? HOW DID YOU KILL THAT MANY? YOUR CLAWS ARE THE SIZE OF TWEEZERS TO THEM.
I'VE KILLED A MAN WITH TWEEZERS BEFORE.
HOW DO YOU KNOW WE'RE GETTING CLOSE, LOGAN?
JUST LISTEN.
MY EARS ARE TOO COLD TO HEAR ANYTHING.
SCREAMING. I HEAR SOMEONE SCREAMING.
NOT JUST SOMEONE. THAT'S THOR.
THEN FROM HERE ON OUT...WE RUN.

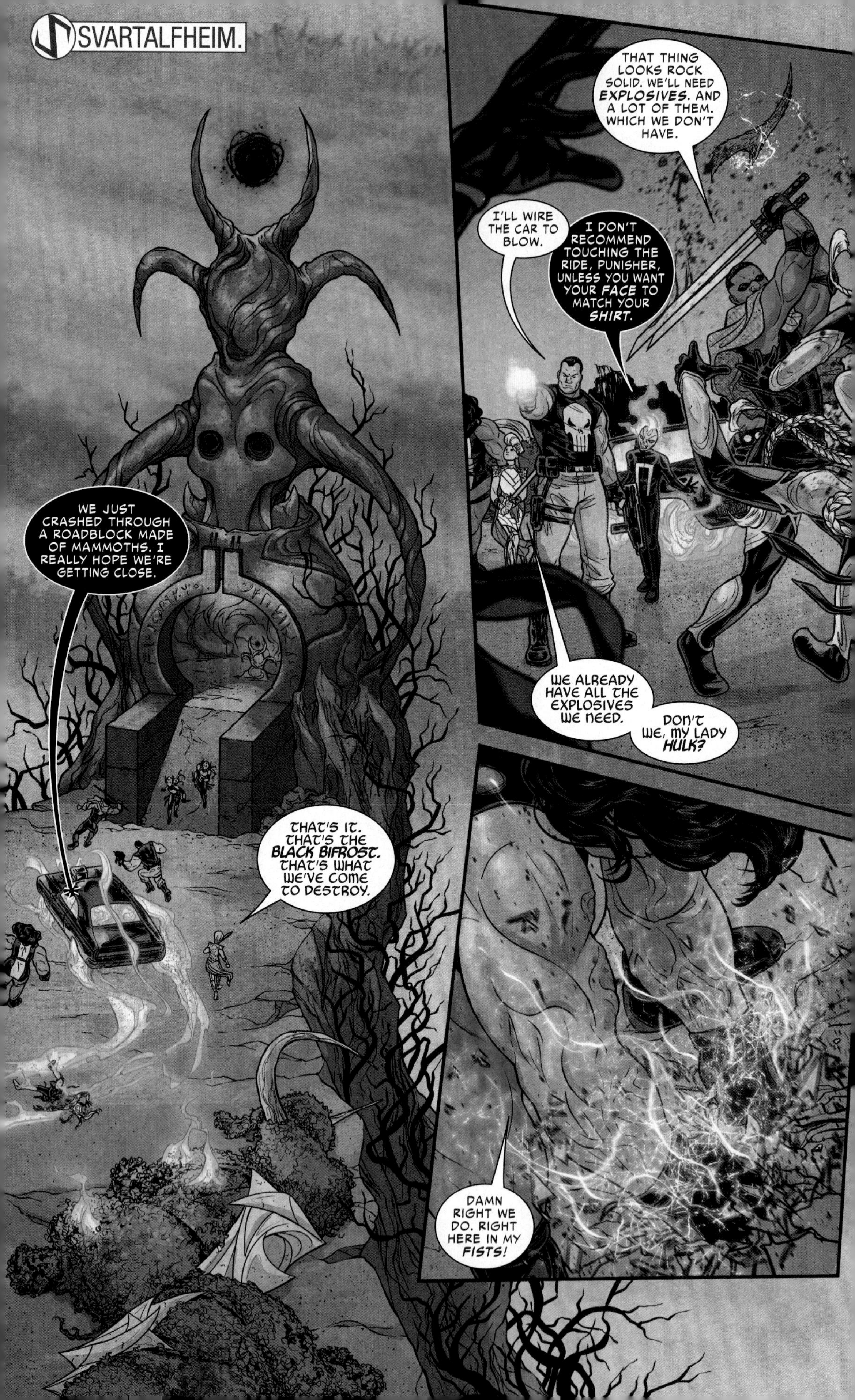
SVARTALFHEIM.
WE JUST CRASHED THROUGH A ROADBLOCK MADE OF MAMMOTHS. I REALLY HOPE WE'RE GETTING CLOSE.
THAT'S IT. THAT'S THE BLACK BIFROST. THAT'S WHAT WE'VE COME TO DESTROY.
THAT THING LOOKS ROCK SOLID. WE'LL NEED EXPLOSIVES. AND A LOT OF THEM. WHICH WE DON'T HAVE.
I'LL WIRE THE CAR TO BLOW.
I DON'T RECOMMEND TOUCHING THE RIDE, PUNISHER, UNLESS YOU WANT YOUR FACE TO MATCH YOUR SHIRT.
WE ALREADY HAVE ALL THE EXPLOSIVES WE NEED.
DON'T WE, MY LADY HULK?
DAMN RIGHT WE DO. RIGHT HERE IN MY FISTS!

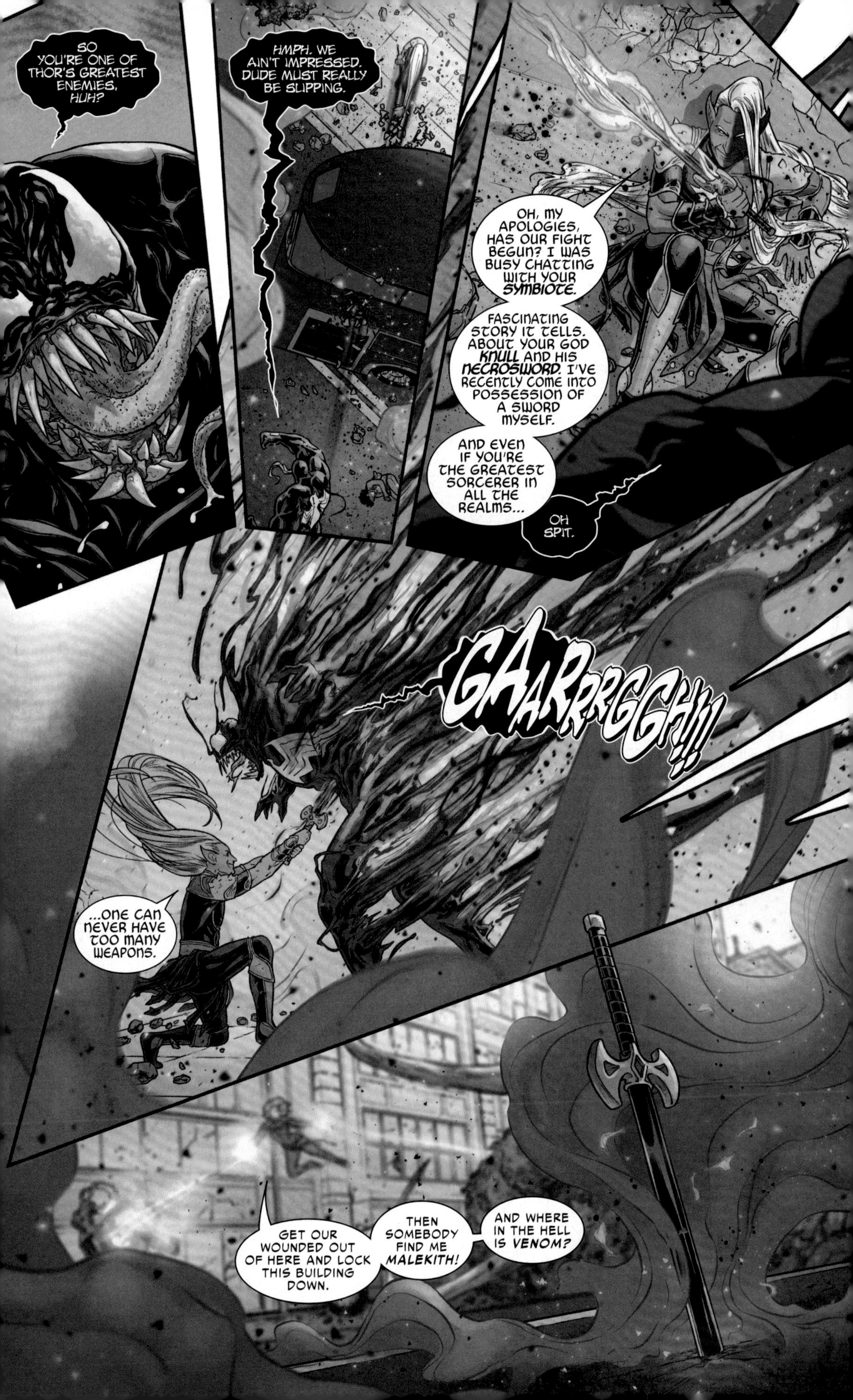
SO YOU'RE ONE OF THOR'S GREATEST ENEMIES, HUH?
HMPH. WE AIN'T IMPRESSED. DUDE MUST REALLY BE SLIPPING.
OH, MY APOLOGIES, HAS OUR FIGHT BEGUN? I WAS BUSY CHATTING WITH YOUR SYMBIOTE.
FASCINATING STORY IT TELLS. ABOUT YOUR GOD KNULL AND HIS NECROSWORD. I'VE RECENTLY COME INTO POSSESSION OF A SWORD MYSELF.
AND EVEN IF YOU'RE THE GREATEST SORCERER IN ALL THE REALMS...
OH SPIT.
GAARRRGGH!!!
...ONE CAN NEVER HAVE TOO MANY WEAPONS.
GET OUR WOUNDED OUT OF HERE AND LOCK THIS BUILDING DOWN.
THEN SOMEBODY FIND ME MALEKITH!
AND WHERE IN THE HELL IS VENOM?

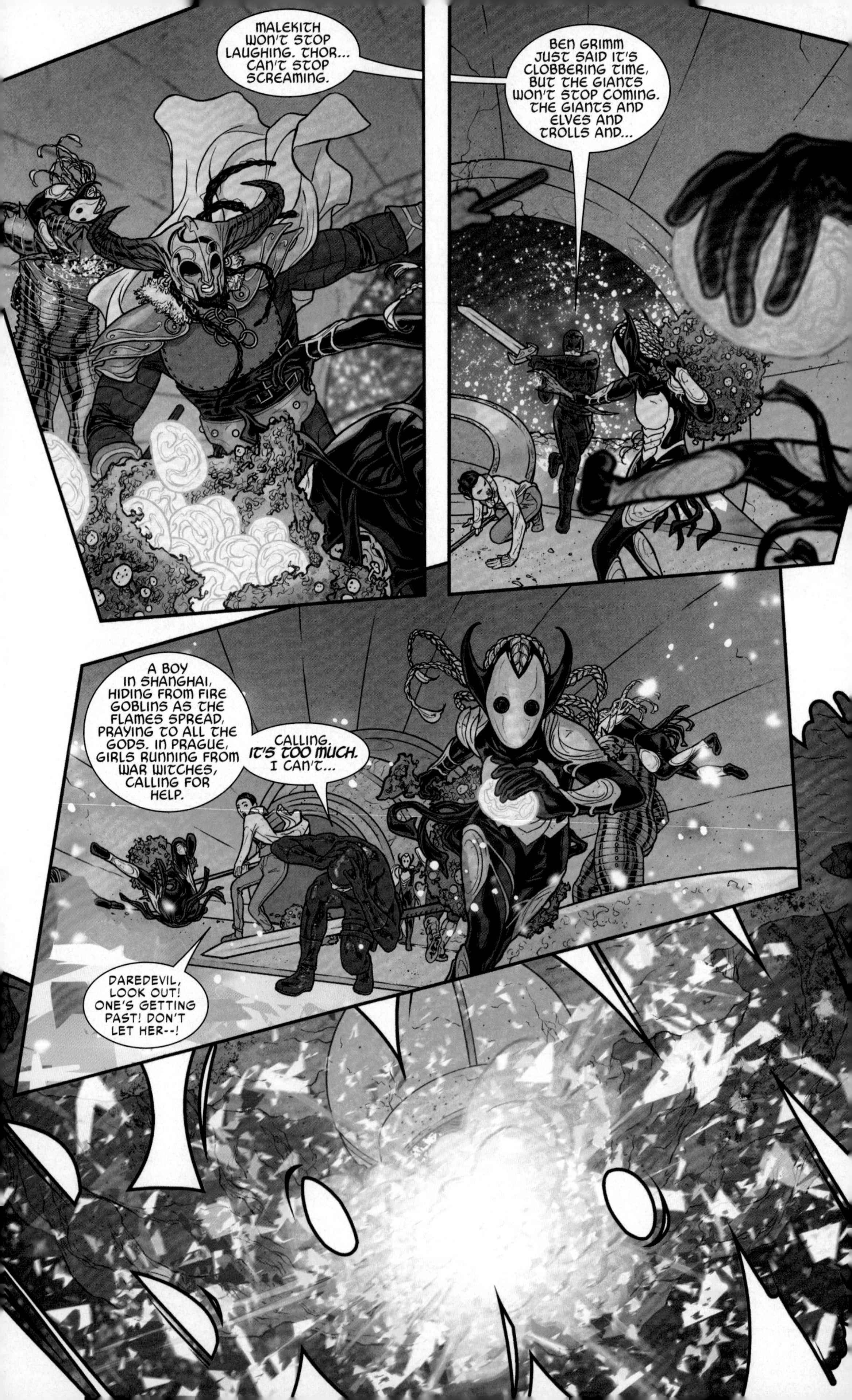
MALEKITH WON'T STOP LAUGHING. THOR... CAN'T STOP SCREAMING.
BEN GRIMM JUST SAID IT'S CLOBBERING TIME, BUT THE GIANTS WON'T STOP COMING. THE GIANTS AND ELVES AND TROLLS AND...
A BOY IN SHANGHAI, HIDING FROM FIRE GOBLINS AS THE FLAMES SPREAD, PRAYING TO ALL THE GODS. IN PRAGUE, GIRLS RUNNING FROM WAR WITCHES, CALLING FOR HELP.
CALLING. IT'S TOO MUCH. I CAN'T...
DAREDEVIL, LOOK OUT! ONE'S GETTING PAST! DON'T LET HER--!

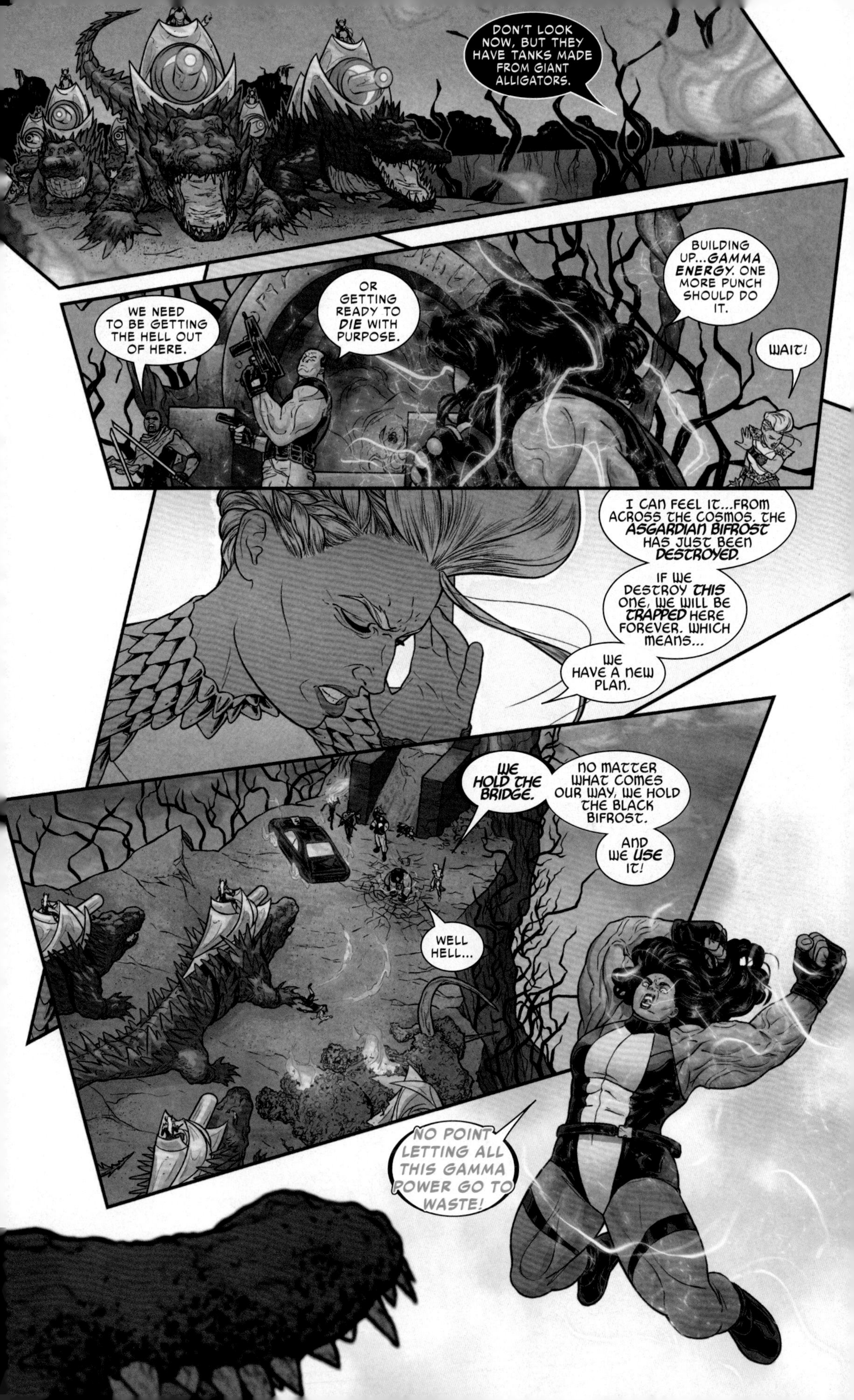

DON'T LOOK NOW, BUT THEY HAVE TANKS MADE FROM GIANT ALLIGATORS.
WE NEED TO BE GETTING THE HELL OUT OF HERE.
OR GETTING READY TO DIE WITH PURPOSE.
BUILDING UP...GAMMA ENERGY. ONE MORE PUNCH SHOULD DO IT.
WAIT!
I CAN FEEL IT...FROM ACROSS THE COSMOS. THE ASGARDIAN BIFROST HAS JUST BEEN DESTROYED.
IF WE DESTROY THIS ONE, WE WILL BE TRAPPED HERE FOREVER. WHICH MEANS...
WE HAVE A NEW PLAN.
WE HOLD THE BRIDGE.
NO MATTER WHAT COMES OUR WAY, WE HOLD THE BLACK BIFROST.
AND WE USE IT!
WELL HELL...
NO POINT LETTING ALL THIS GAMMA POWER GO TO WASTE!

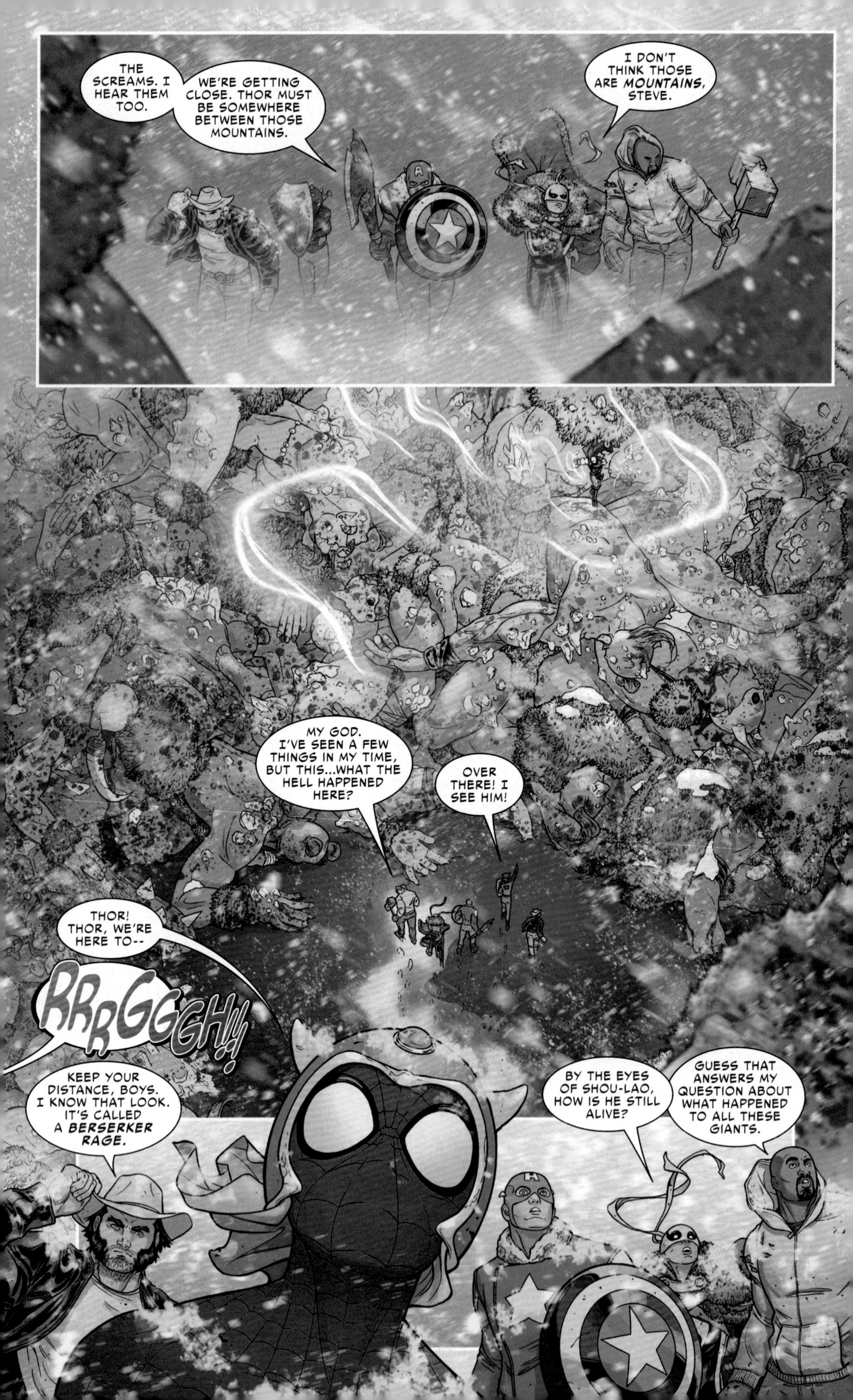
THE SCREAMS. I HEAR THEM TOO.
WE'RE GETTING CLOSE. THOR MUST BE SOMEWHERE BETWEEN THOSE MOUNTAINS.
I DON'T THINK THOSE ARE MOUNTAINS, STEVE.
MY GOD. I'VE SEEN A FEW THINGS IN MY TIME, BUT THIS...WHAT THE HELL HAPPENED HERE?
OVER THERE! I SEE HIM!
THOR! THOR, WE'RE HERE TO--
BRRGGGH!!
KEEP YOUR DISTANCE, BOYS. I KNOW THAT LOOK. IT'S CALLED A BERSERKER RAGE.
BY THE EYES OF SHOU-LAO, HOW IS HE STILL ALIVE?
GUESS THAT ANSWERS MY QUESTION ABOUT WHAT HAPPENED TO ALL THESE GIANTS.

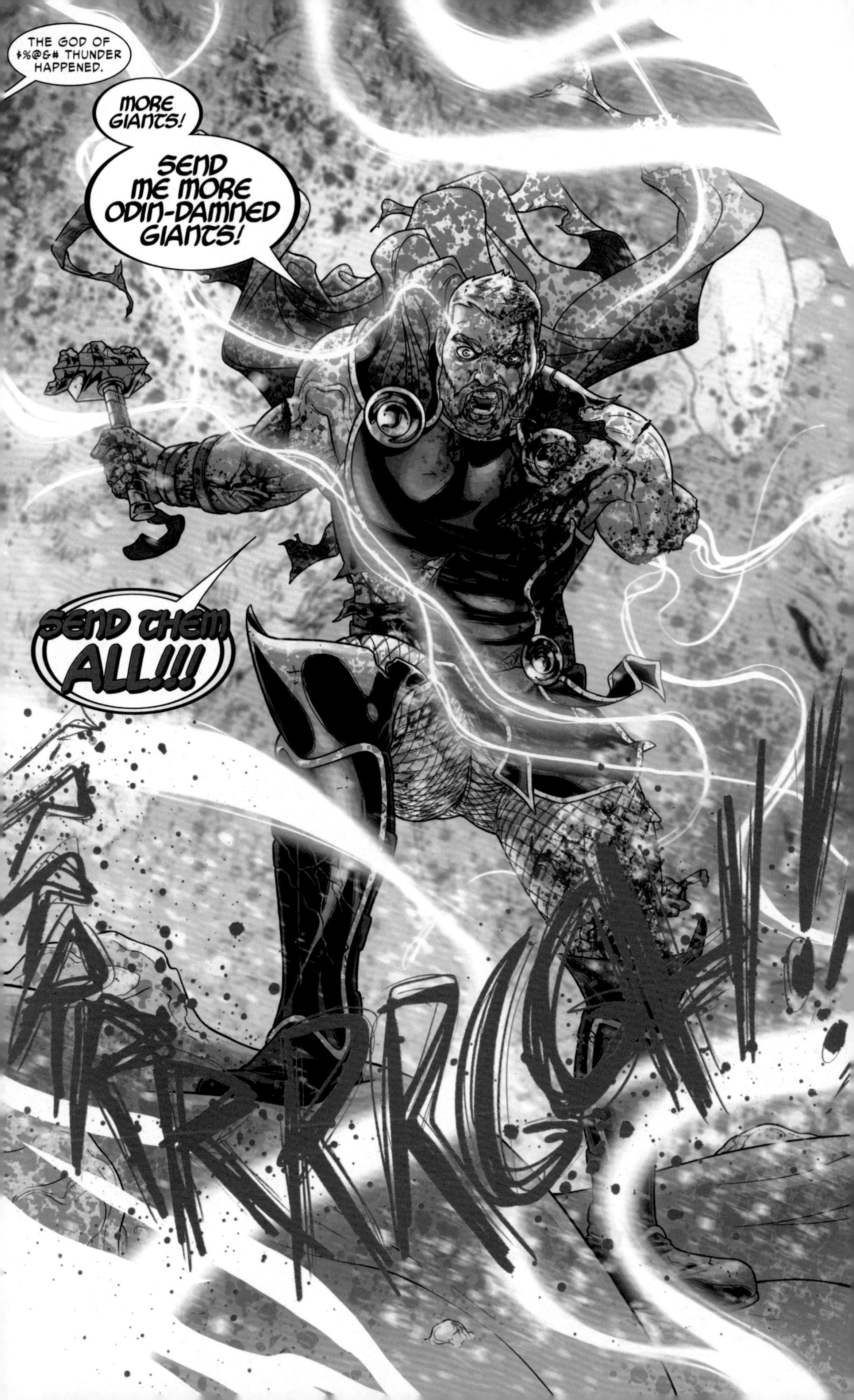
THE GOD OF $%@&# THUNDER HAPPENED.
MORE GIANTS!
SEND ME MORE ODIN-DAMNED GIANTS!
SEND THEM ALL!!!

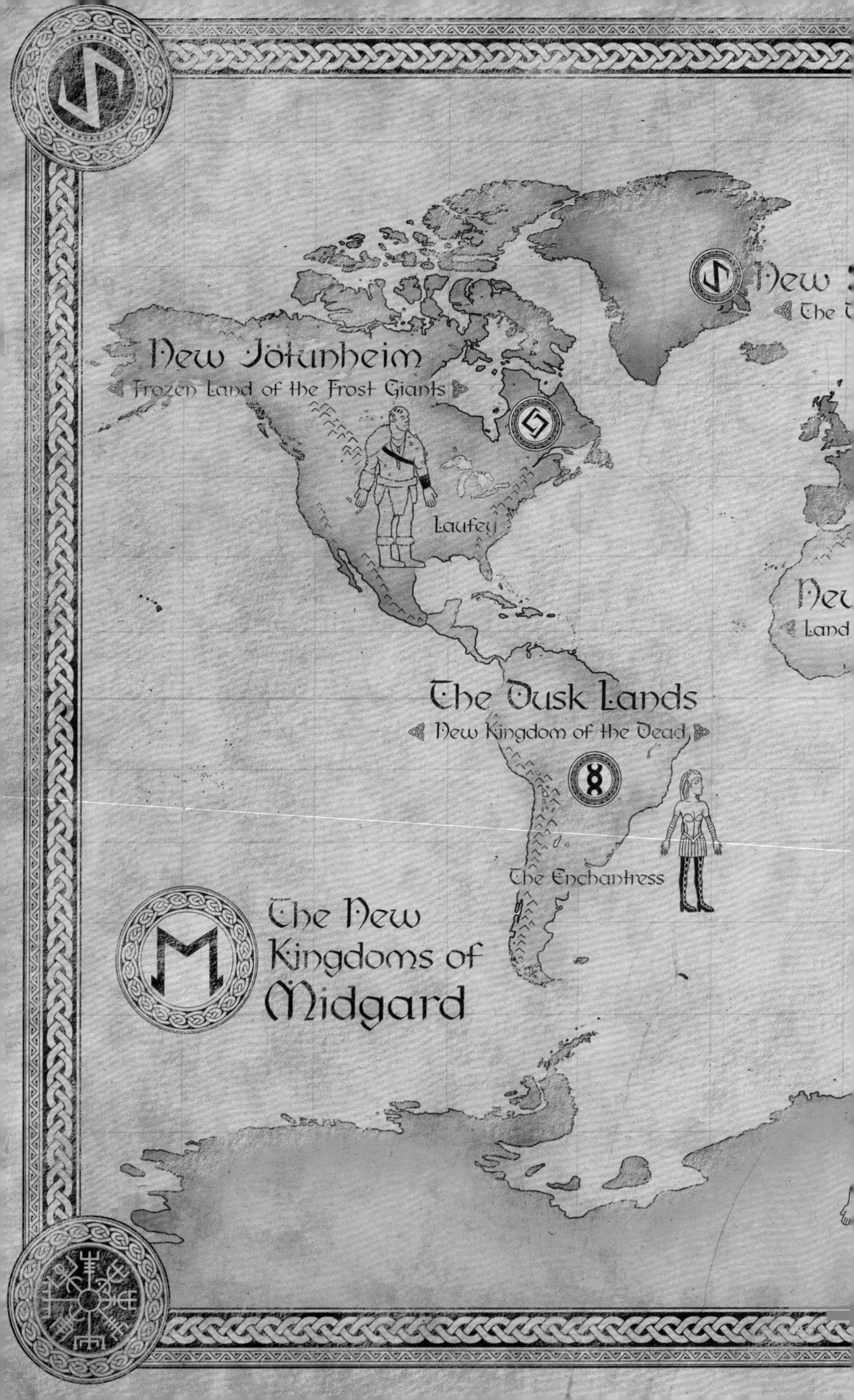
New Jötunheim
Frozen Land of the Frost Giants
Laufey
New
The
New
Land
The Dusk Lands
New Kingdom of the Dead
The Enchantress
The New Kingdoms of Midgard

Halfheim

meric Realm

lekith

New Muspelheim

Land of Fire

The Queen of Cinders

zven

Angels

Queen of Heven

Kingdom of the Trolls

Ulik

The Kingdom of Roxxon Inc

Dario Agger

Map by John Tyler Christopher

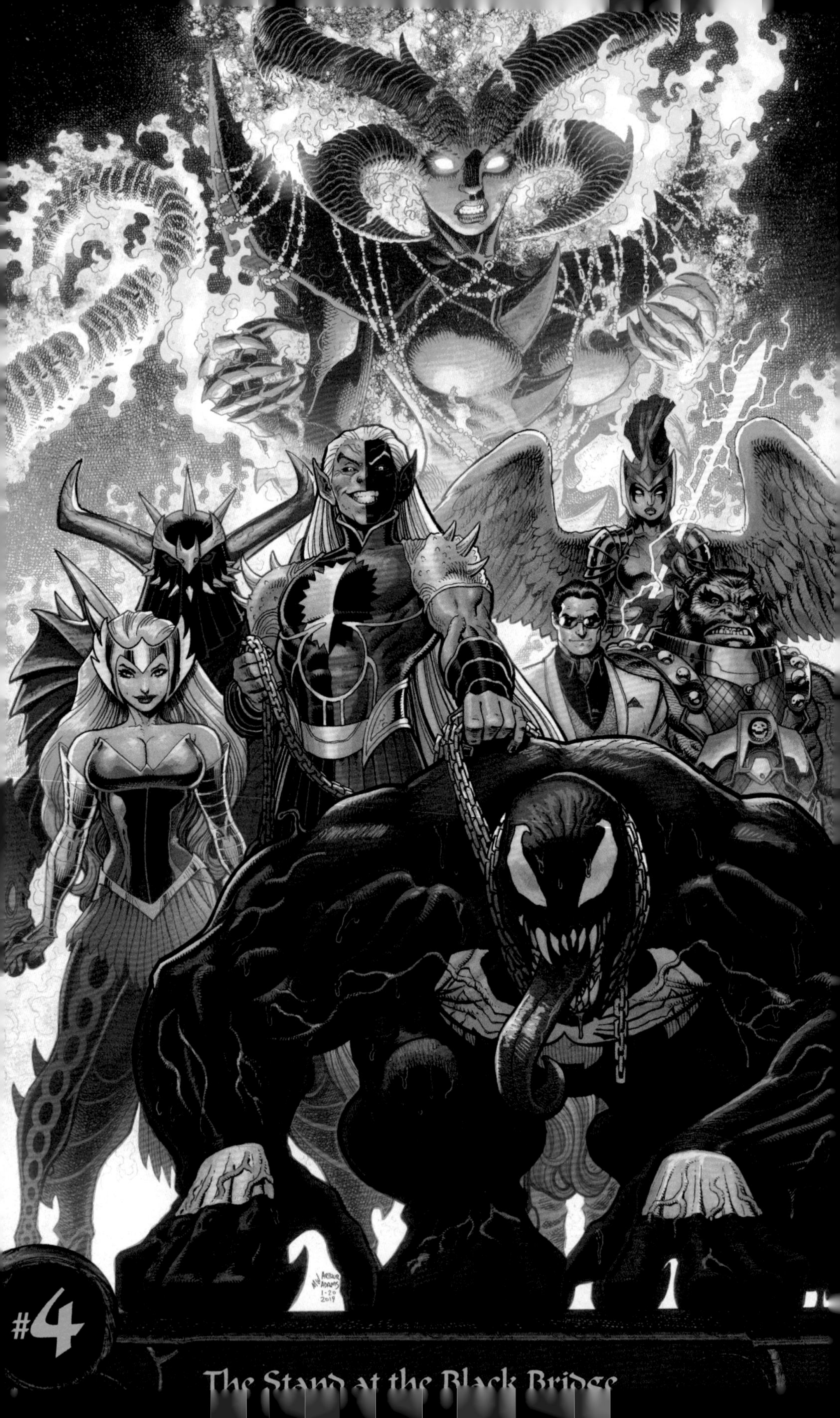

#4
The Stand at the Black Bridge

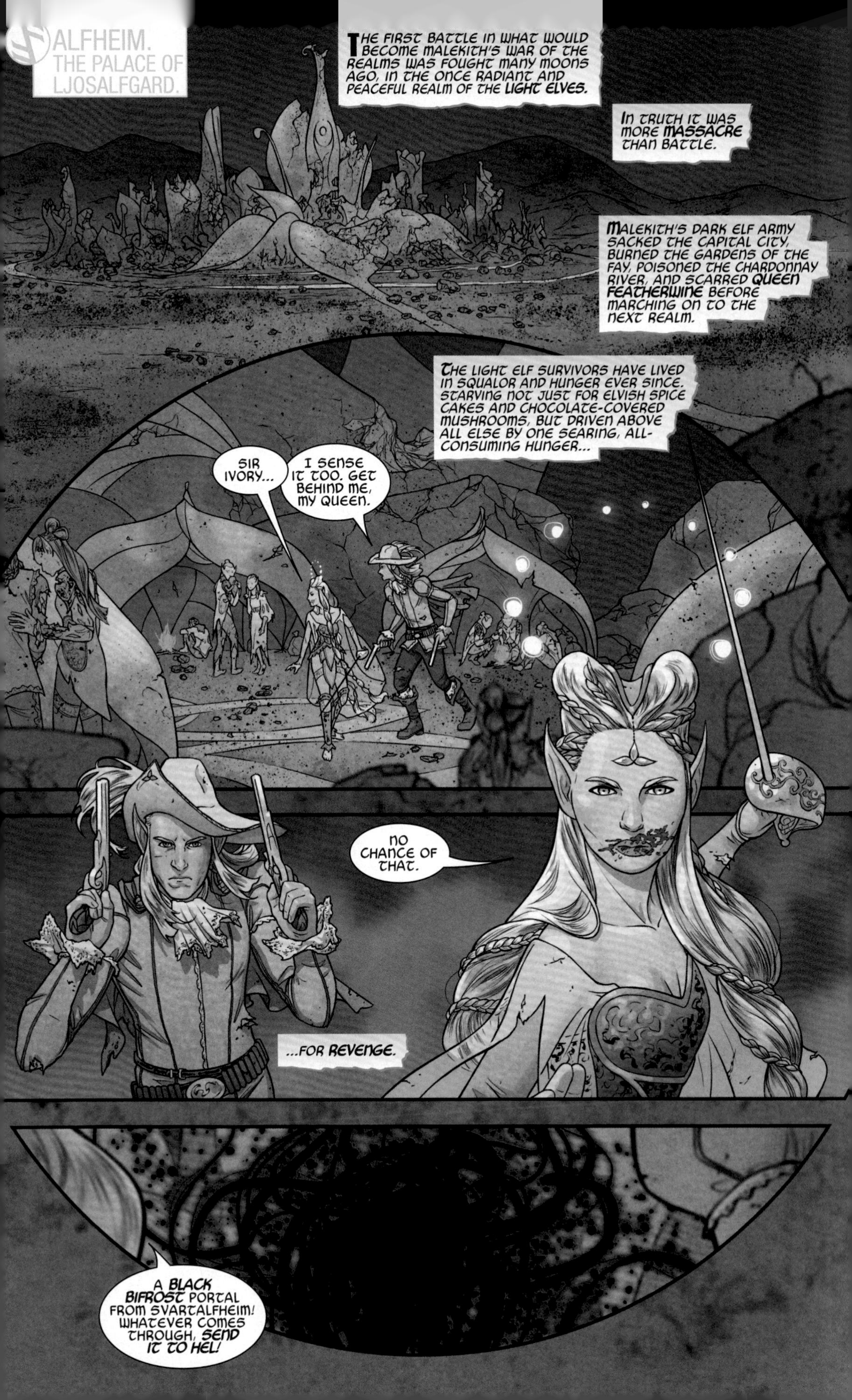
ALFHEIM. THE PALACE OF LJOSALFGARD.
THE FIRST BATTLE IN WHAT WOULD BECOME MALEKITH'S WAR OF THE REALMS WAS FOUGHT MANY MOONS AGO, IN THE ONCE RADIANT AND PEACEFUL REALM OF THE LIGHT ELVES.
IN TRUTH IT WAS MORE MASSACRE THAN BATTLE.
MALEKITH'S DARK ELF ARMY SACKED THE CAPITAL CITY, BURNED THE GARDENS OF THE FAY, POISONED THE CHARDONNAY RIVER, AND SCARRED QUEEN FEATHERWINE BEFORE MARCHING ON TO THE NEXT REALM.
THE LIGHT ELF SURVIVORS HAVE LIVED IN SQUALOR AND HUNGER EVER SINCE. STARVING NOT JUST FOR ELVISH SPICE CAKES AND CHOCOLATE-COVERED MUSHROOMS, BUT DRIVEN ABOVE ALL ELSE BY ONE SEARING, ALL-CONSUMING HUNGER...
SIR IVORY...
I SENSE IT TOO. GET BEHIND ME, MY QUEEN.
NO CHANCE OF THAT.
...FOR REVENGE.
A BLACK BIFROST PORTAL FROM SVARTALFHEIM! WHATEVER COMES THROUGH, SEND IT TO HEL!

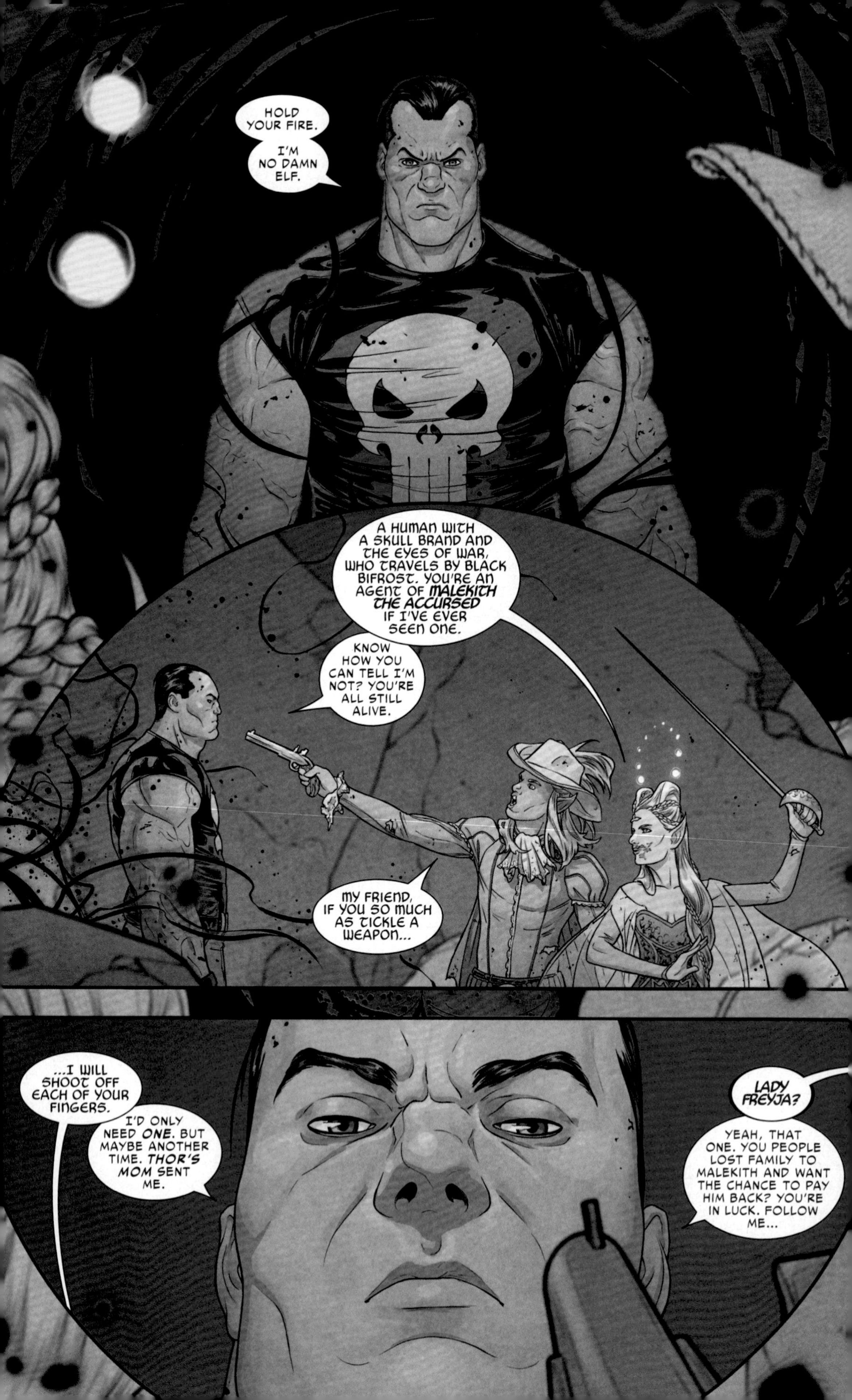
HOLD YOUR FIRE.
I'M NO DAMN ELF.
A HUMAN WITH A SKULL BRAND AND THE EYES OF WAR, WHO TRAVELS BY BLACK BIFROST. YOU'RE AN AGENT OF MALEKITH THE ACCURSED IF I'VE EVER SEEN ONE.
KNOW HOW YOU CAN TELL I'M NOT? YOU'RE ALL STILL ALIVE.
MY FRIEND, IF YOU SO MUCH AS TICKLE A WEAPON...
...I WILL SHOOT OFF EACH OF YOUR FINGERS.
I'D ONLY NEED ONE. BUT MAYBE ANOTHER TIME. THOR'S MOM SENT ME.
LADY FREYJA?
YEAH, THAT ONE. YOU PEOPLE LOST FAMILY TO MALEKITH AND WANT THE CHANCE TO PAY HIM BACK? YOU'RE IN LUCK. FOLLOW ME...

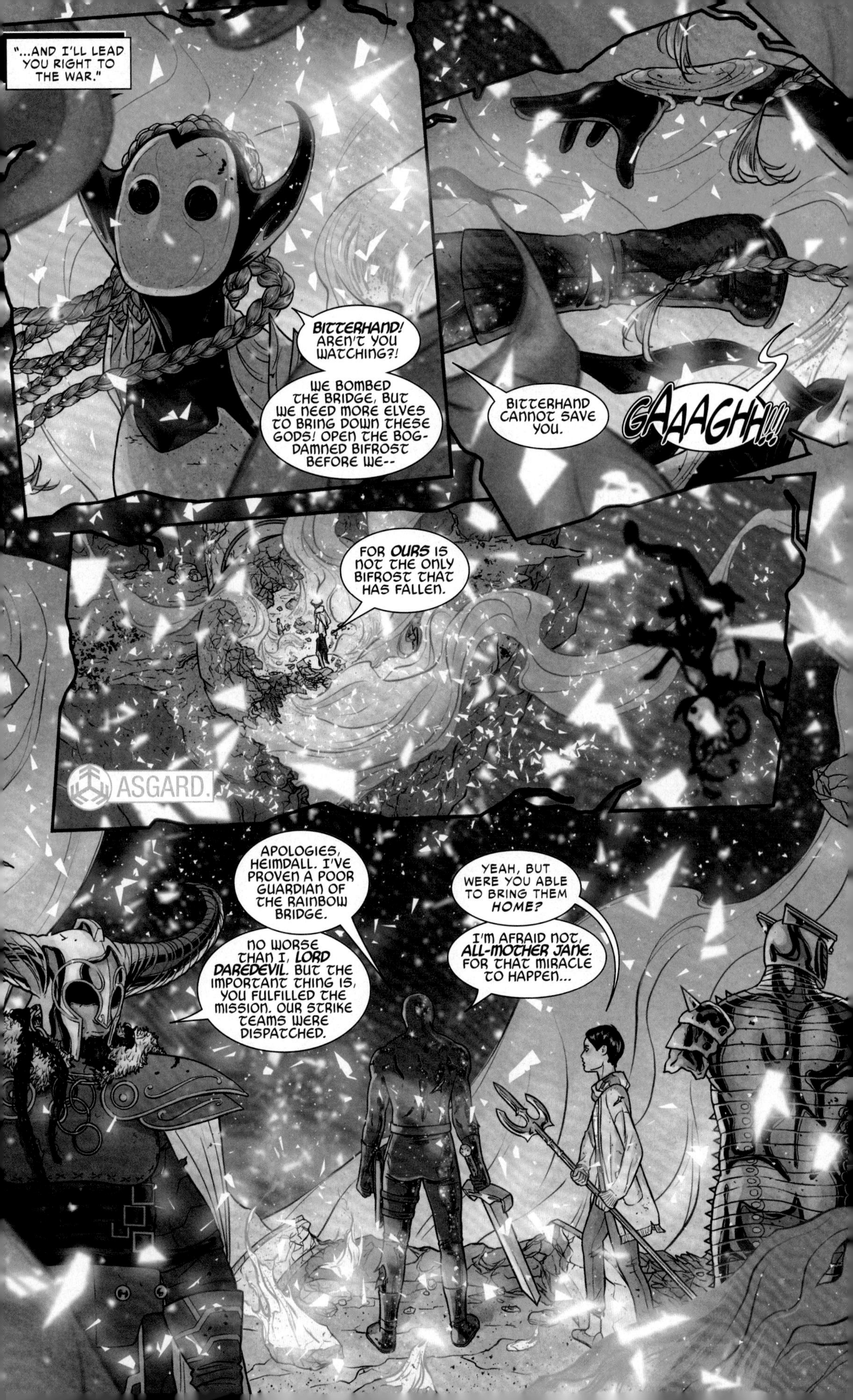
"...AND I'LL LEAD YOU RIGHT TO THE WAR."
BITTERHAND! AREN'T YOU WATCHING?!
WE BOMBED THE BRIDGE, BUT WE NEED MORE ELVES TO BRING DOWN THESE GODS! OPEN THE BOG-DAMNED BIFROST BEFORE WE--
BITTERHAND CANNOT SAVE YOU.
GAAAGHH!!!
FOR OURS IS NOT THE ONLY BIFROST THAT HAS FALLEN.
ASGARD.
APOLOGIES, HEIMDALL. I'VE PROVEN A POOR GUARDIAN OF THE RAINBOW BRIDGE.
NO WORSE THAN I, LORD DAREDEVIL. BUT THE IMPORTANT THING IS, YOU FULFILLED THE MISSION. OUR STRIKE TEAMS WERE DISPATCHED.
YEAH, BUT WERE YOU ABLE TO BRING THEM HOME?
I'M AFRAID NOT, ALL-MOTHER JANE. FOR THAT MIRACLE TO HAPPEN...

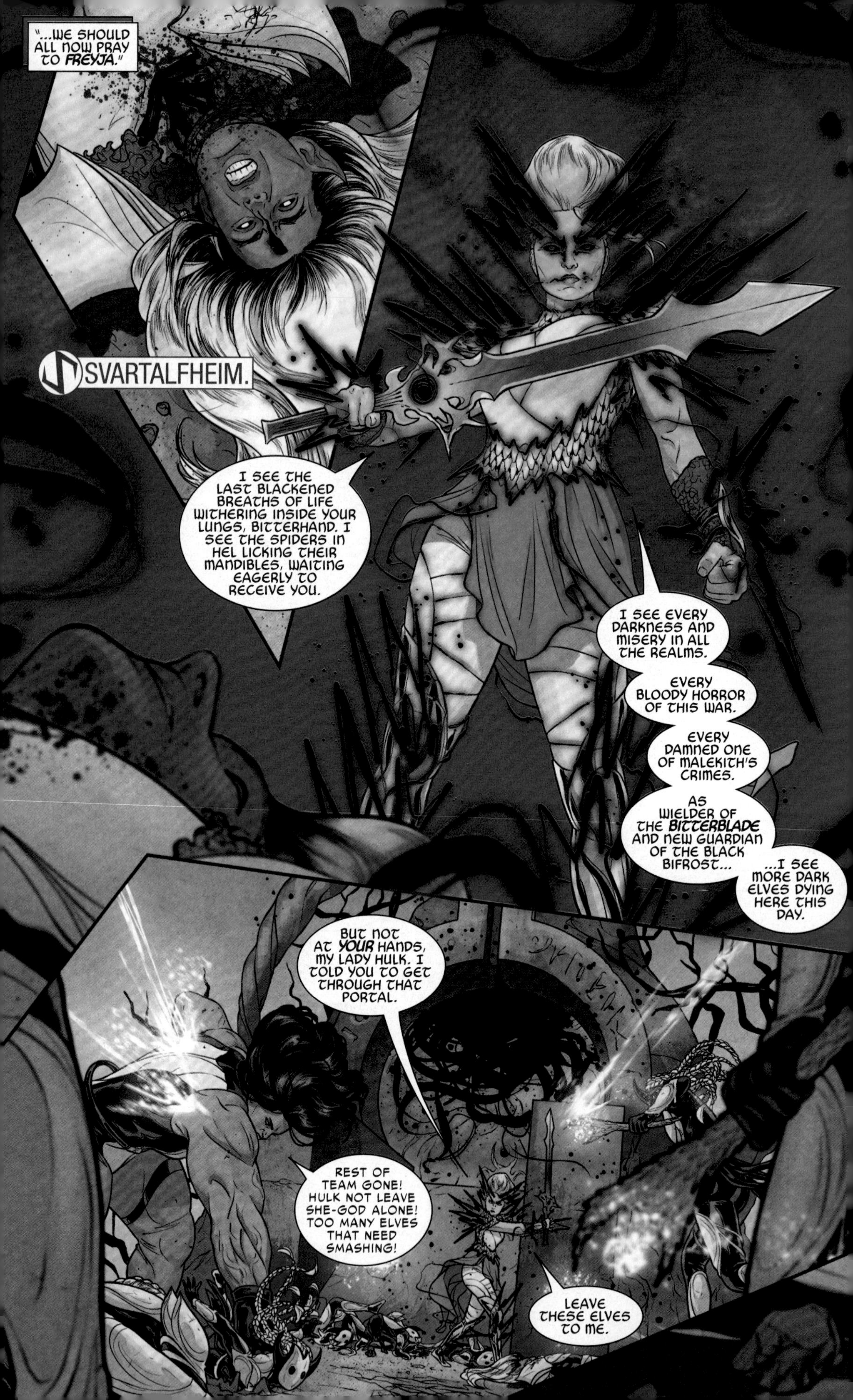
"...WE SHOULD ALL NOW PRAY TO FREYJA."
SVARTALFHEIM.
I SEE THE LAST BLACKENED BREATHS OF LIFE WITHERING INSIDE YOUR LUNGS, BITTERHAND. I SEE THE SPIDERS IN HEL LICKING THEIR MANDIBLES, WAITING EAGERLY TO RECEIVE YOU.
I SEE EVERY DARKNESS AND MISERY IN ALL THE REALMS.
EVERY BLOODY HORROR OF THIS WAR.
EVERY DAMNED ONE OF MALEKITH'S CRIMES.
AS WIELDER OF THE BITTERBLADE AND NEW GUARDIAN OF THE BLACK BIFROST...
...I SEE MORE DARK ELVES DYING HERE THIS DAY.
BUT NOT AT YOUR HANDS, MY LADY HULK. I TOLD YOU TO GET THROUGH THAT PORTAL.
REST OF TEAM GONE! HULK NOT LEAVE SHE-GOD ALONE! TOO MANY ELVES THAT NEED SMASHING!
LEAVE THESE ELVES TO ME.

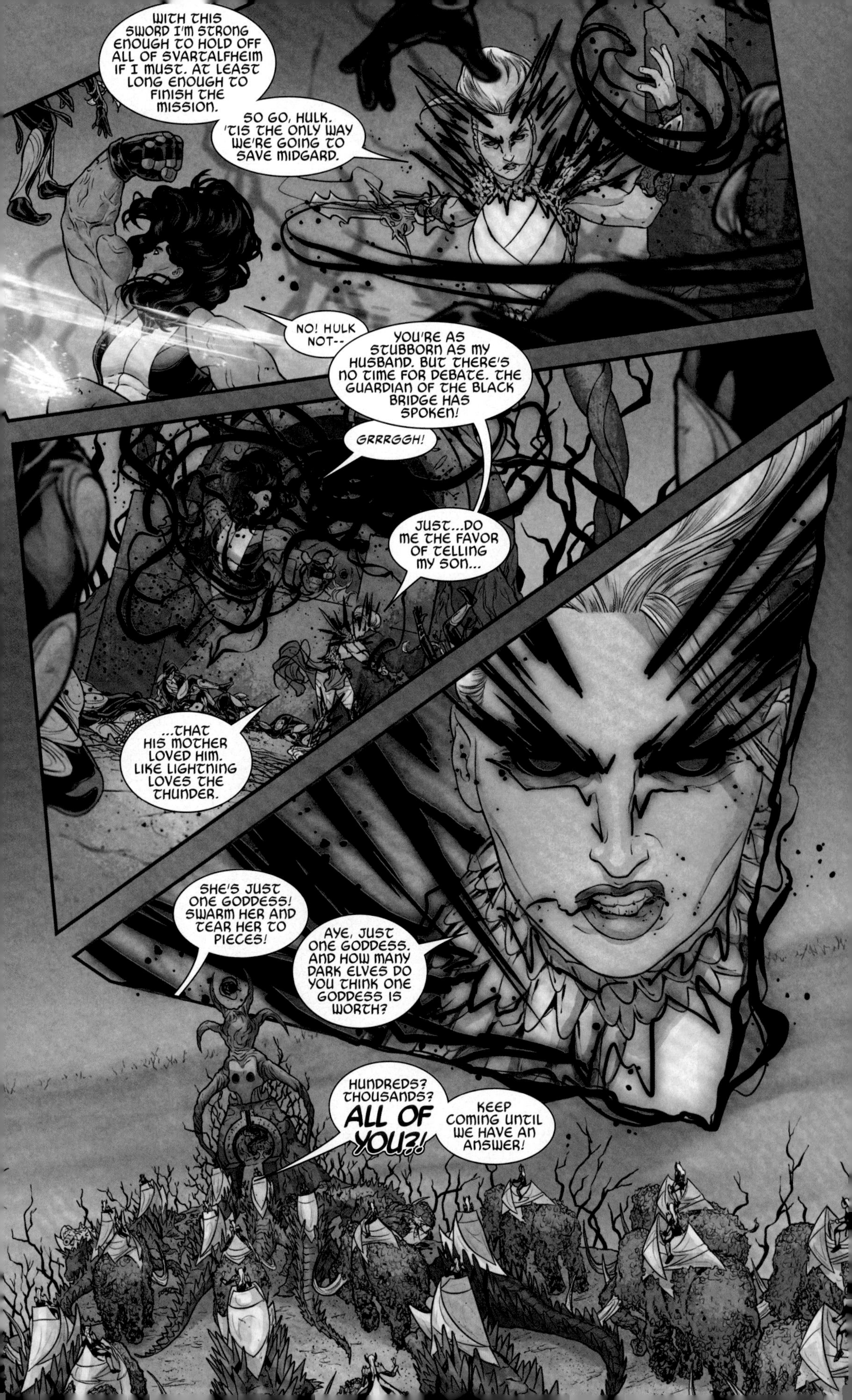

WITH THIS SWORD I'M STRONG ENOUGH TO HOLD OFF ALL OF SVARTALFHEIM IF I MUST. AT LEAST LONG ENOUGH TO FINISH THE MISSION.
SO GO, HULK. 'TIS THE ONLY WAY WE'RE GOING TO SAVE MIDGARD.
NO! HULK NOT--
YOU'RE AS STUBBORN AS MY HUSBAND. BUT THERE'S NO TIME FOR DEBATE. THE GUARDIAN OF THE BLACK BRIDGE HAS SPOKEN!
GRRRGGH!
JUST...DO ME THE FAVOR OF TELLING MY SON...
...THAT HIS MOTHER LOVED HIM. LIKE LIGHTNING LOVES THE THUNDER.
SHE'S JUST ONE GODDESS! SWARM HER AND TEAR HER TO PIECES!
AYE, JUST ONE GODDESS. AND HOW MANY DARK ELVES DO YOU THINK ONE GODDESS IS WORTH?
HUNDREDS? THOUSANDS? ALL OF YOU?!
KEEP COMING UNTIL WE HAVE AN ANSWER!

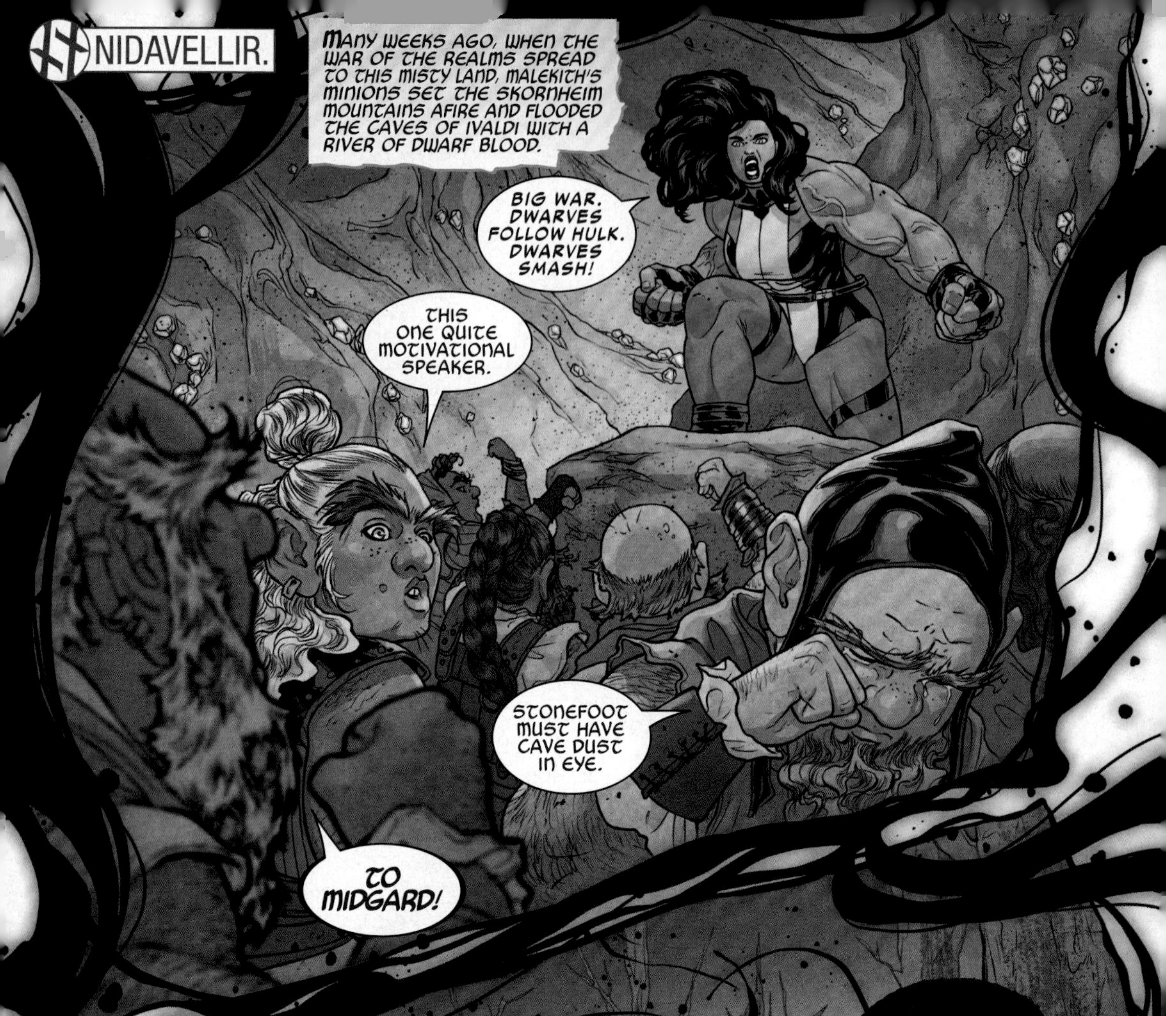
NIDAVELLIR.
MANY WEEKS AGO, WHEN THE WAR OF THE REALMS SPREAD TO THIS MISTY LAND, MALEKITH'S MINIONS SET THE SKORNHEIM MOUNTAINS AFIRE AND FLOODED THE CAVES OF IVALDI WITH A RIVER OF DWARF BLOOD.
BIG WAR. DWARVES FOLLOW HULK. DWARVES SMASH!
THIS ONE QUITE MOTIVATIONAL SPEAKER.
STONEFOOT MUST HAVE CAVE DUST IN EYE.
TO MIDGARD!

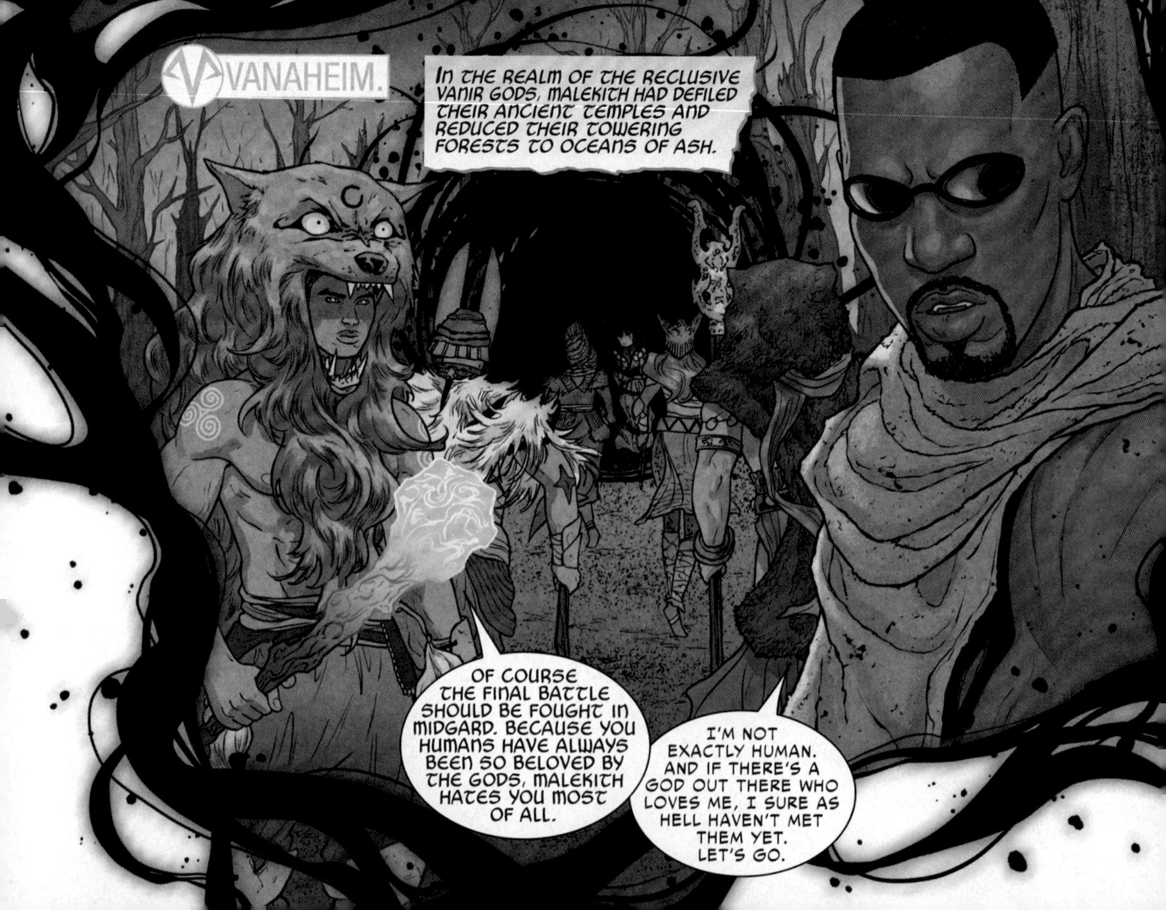
VANAHEIM.
IN THE REALM OF THE RECLUSIVE VANIR GODS, MALEKITH HAD DEFILED THEIR ANCIENT TEMPLES AND REDUCED THEIR TOWERING FORESTS TO OCEANS OF ASH.
OF COURSE THE FINAL BATTLE SHOULD BE FOUGHT IN MIDGARD. BECAUSE YOU HUMANS HAVE ALWAYS BEEN SO BELOVED BY THE GODS, MALEKITH HATES YOU MOST OF ALL.
I'M NOT EXACTLY HUMAN. AND IF THERE'S A GOD OUT THERE WHO LOVES ME, I SURE AS HELL HAVEN'T MET THEM YET. LET'S GO.

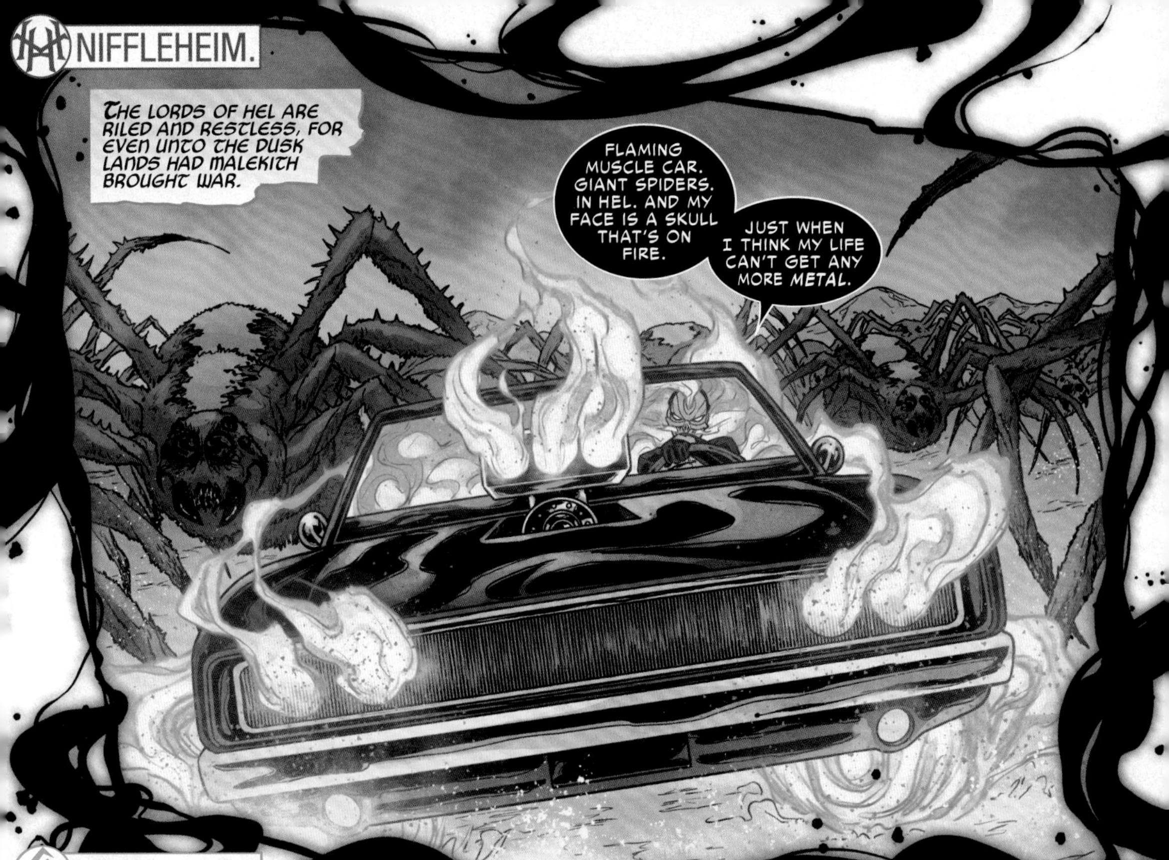
NIFFLEHEIM.
THE LORDS OF HEL ARE RILED AND RESTLESS, FOR EVEN UNTO THE DUSK LANDS HAD MALEKITH BROUGHT WAR.
FLAMING MUSCLE CAR. GIANT SPIDERS. IN HEL. AND MY FACE IS A SKULL THAT'S ON FIRE.
JUST WHEN I THINK MY LIFE CAN'T GET ANY MORE METAL.

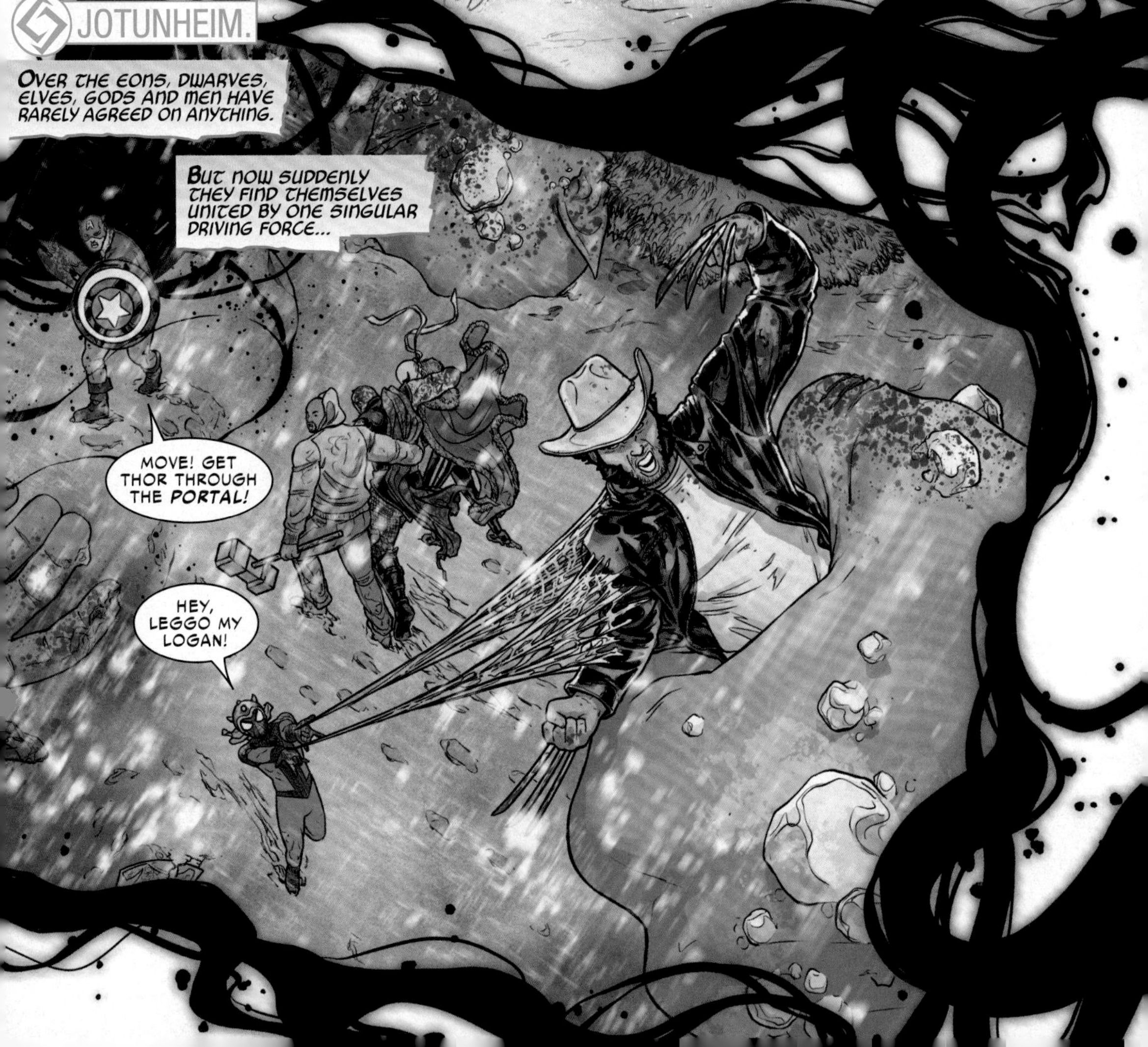
JOTUNHEIM.
OVER THE EONS, DWARVES, ELVES, GODS AND MEN HAVE RARELY AGREED ON ANYTHING.
BUT NOW SUDDENLY THEY FIND THEMSELVES UNITED BY ONE SINGULAR DRIVING FORCE...
MOVE! GET THOR THROUGH THE PORTAL!
HEY, LEGGO MY LOGAN!

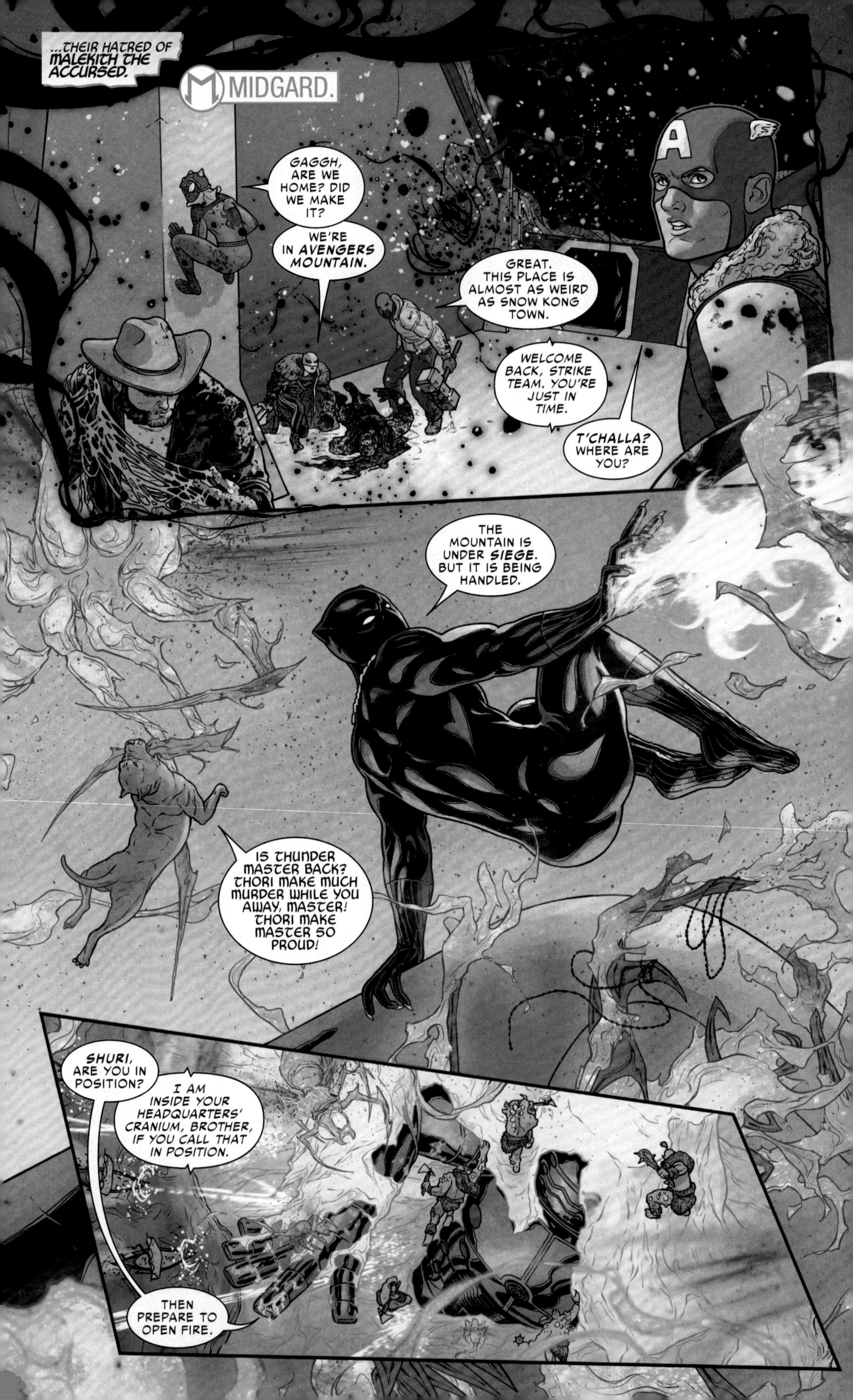
...THEIR HATRED OF MALEKITH THE ACCURSED.
MIDGARD.
GAGGH, ARE WE HOME? DID WE MAKE IT?
WE'RE IN AVENGERS MOUNTAIN.
GREAT. THIS PLACE IS ALMOST AS WEIRD AS SNOW KONG TOWN.
WELCOME BACK, STRIKE TEAM. YOU'RE JUST IN TIME.
T'CHALLA? WHERE ARE YOU?
THE MOUNTAIN IS UNDER SIEGE. BUT IT IS BEING HANDLED.
IS THUNDER MASTER BACK? THORI MAKE MUCH MURDER WHILE YOU AWAY, MASTER! THORI MAKE MASTER SO PROUD!
SHURI, ARE YOU IN POSITION?
I AM INSIDE YOUR HEADQUARTERS' CRANIUM, BROTHER, IF YOU CALL THAT IN POSITION.
THEN PREPARE TO OPEN FIRE.

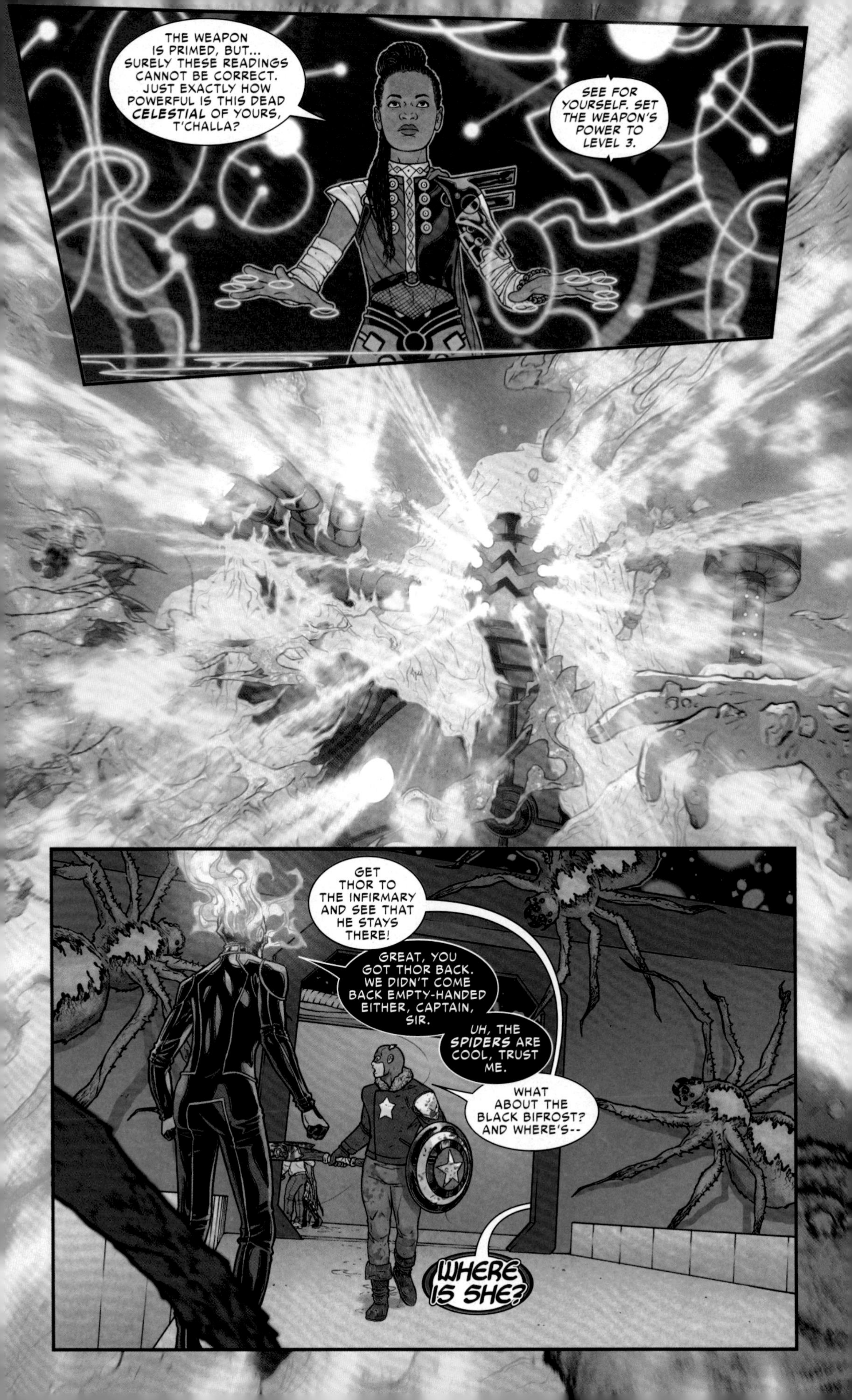
THE WEAPON IS PRIMED, BUT... SURELY THESE READINGS CANNOT BE CORRECT. JUST EXACTLY HOW POWERFUL IS THIS DEAD *CELESTIAL* OF YOURS, T'CHALLA?
SEE FOR YOURSELF. SET THE WEAPON'S POWER TO LEVEL 3.
GET THOR TO THE INFIRMARY AND SEE THAT HE STAYS THERE!
GREAT, YOU GOT THOR BACK. WE DIDN'T COME BACK EMPTY-HANDED EITHER, CAPTAIN, SIR.
UH, THE ***SPIDERS*** ARE COOL, TRUST ME.
WHAT ABOUT THE BLACK BIFROST? AND WHERE'S--
WHERE IS SHE?

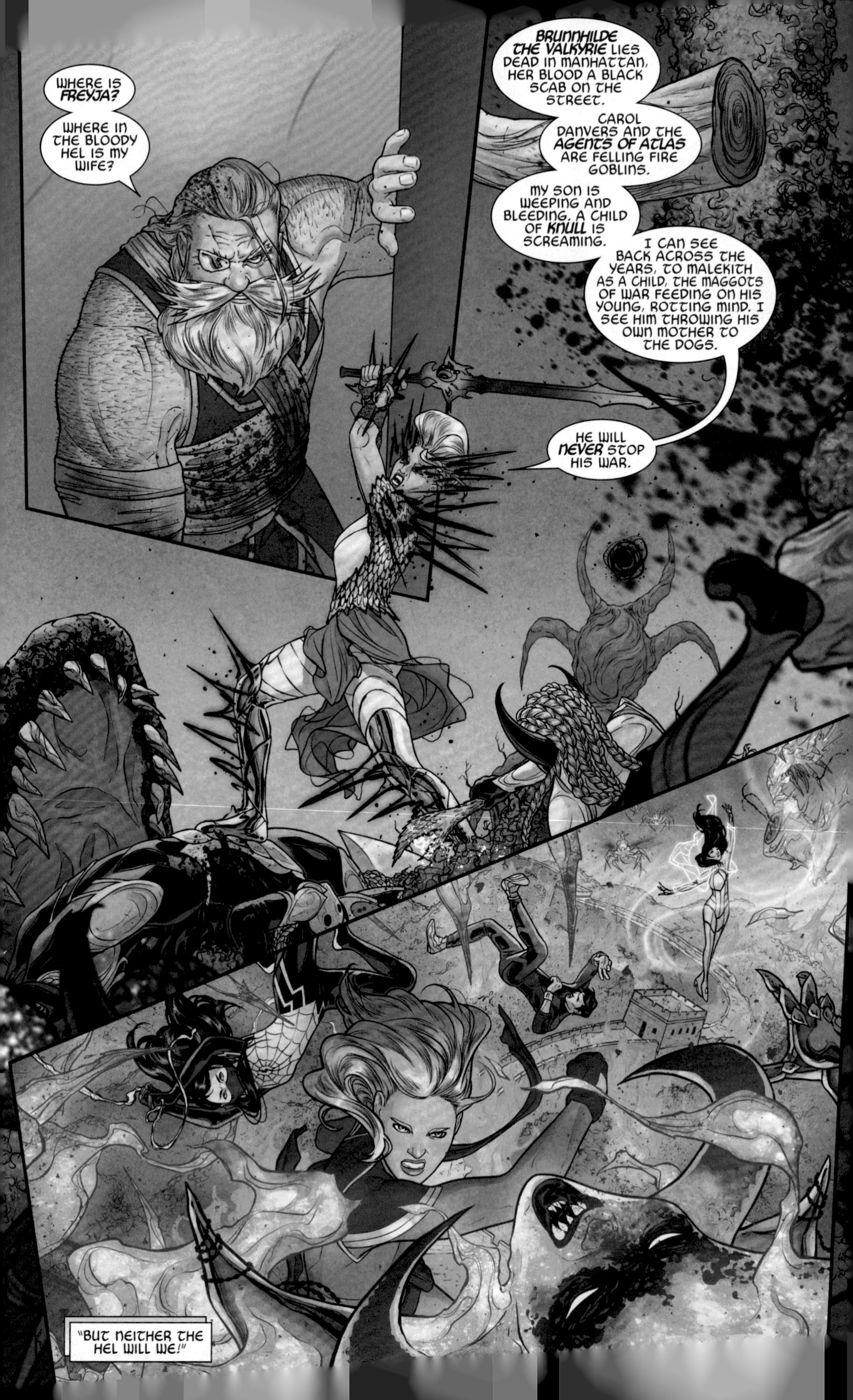
WHERE IS FREYJA?
WHERE IN THE BLOODY HEL IS MY WIFE?
BRUNNHILDE THE VALKYRIE LIES DEAD IN MANHATTAN, HER BLOOD A BLACK SCAB ON THE STREET.
CAROL DANVERS AND THE AGENTS OF ATLAS ARE FELLING FIRE GOBLINS.
MY SON IS WEEPING AND BLEEDING. A CHILD OF KNULL IS SCREAMING.
I CAN SEE BACK ACROSS THE YEARS, TO MALEKITH AS A CHILD, THE MAGGOTS OF WAR FEEDING ON HIS YOUNG, ROTTING MIND. I SEE HIM THROWING HIS OWN MOTHER TO THE DOGS.
HE WILL NEVER STOP HIS WAR.
"BUT NEITHER THE HEL WILL WE!"

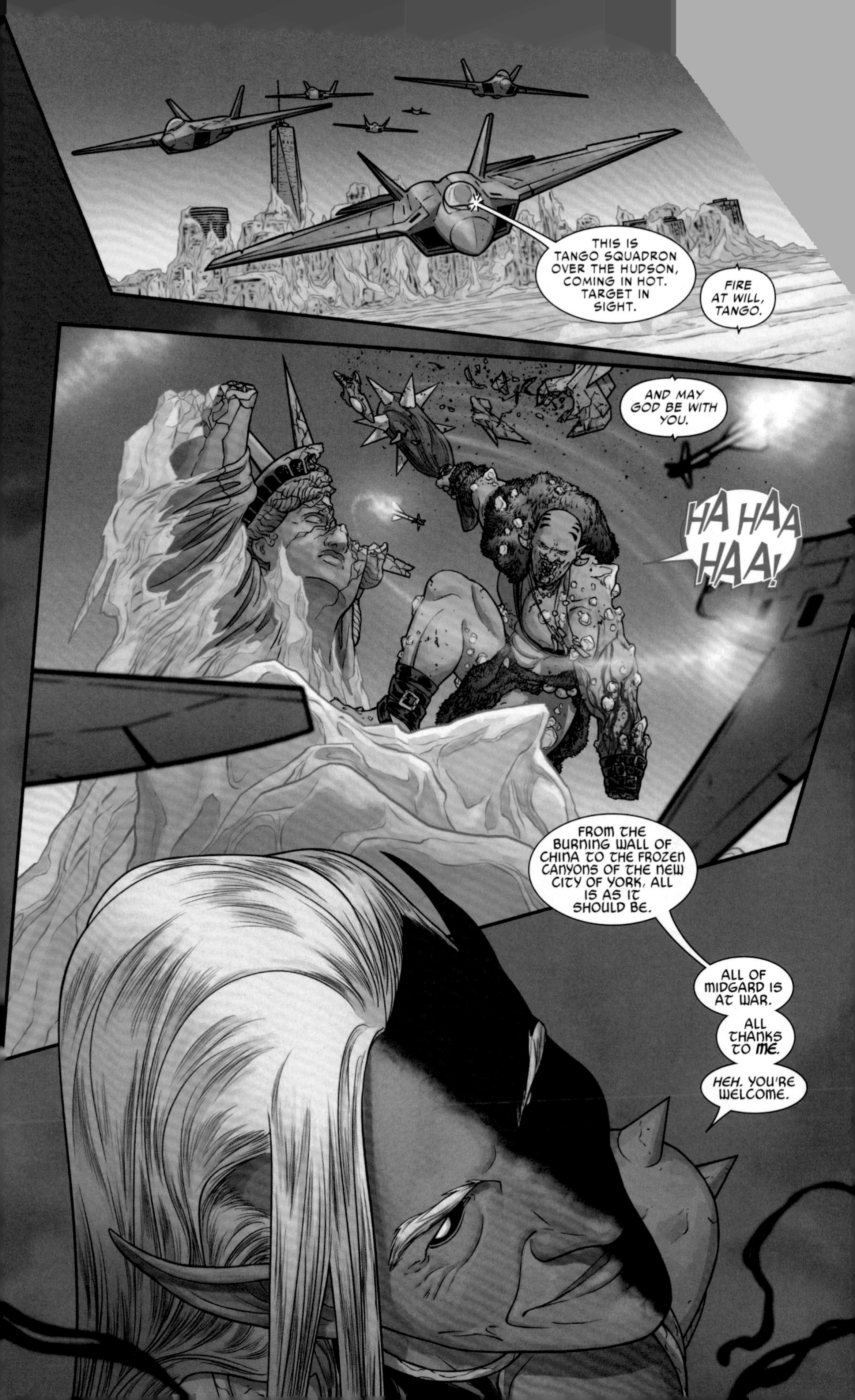

THIS IS TANGO SQUADRON OVER THE HUDSON, COMING IN HOT. TARGET IN SIGHT.
FIRE AT WILL, TANGO.
AND MAY GOD BE WITH YOU.
HA HAA HAA!
FROM THE BURNING WALL OF CHINA TO THE FROZEN CANYONS OF THE NEW CITY OF YORK, ALL IS AS IT SHOULD BE.
ALL OF MIDGARD IS AT WAR.
ALL THANKS TO ME.
HEH. YOU'RE WELCOME.

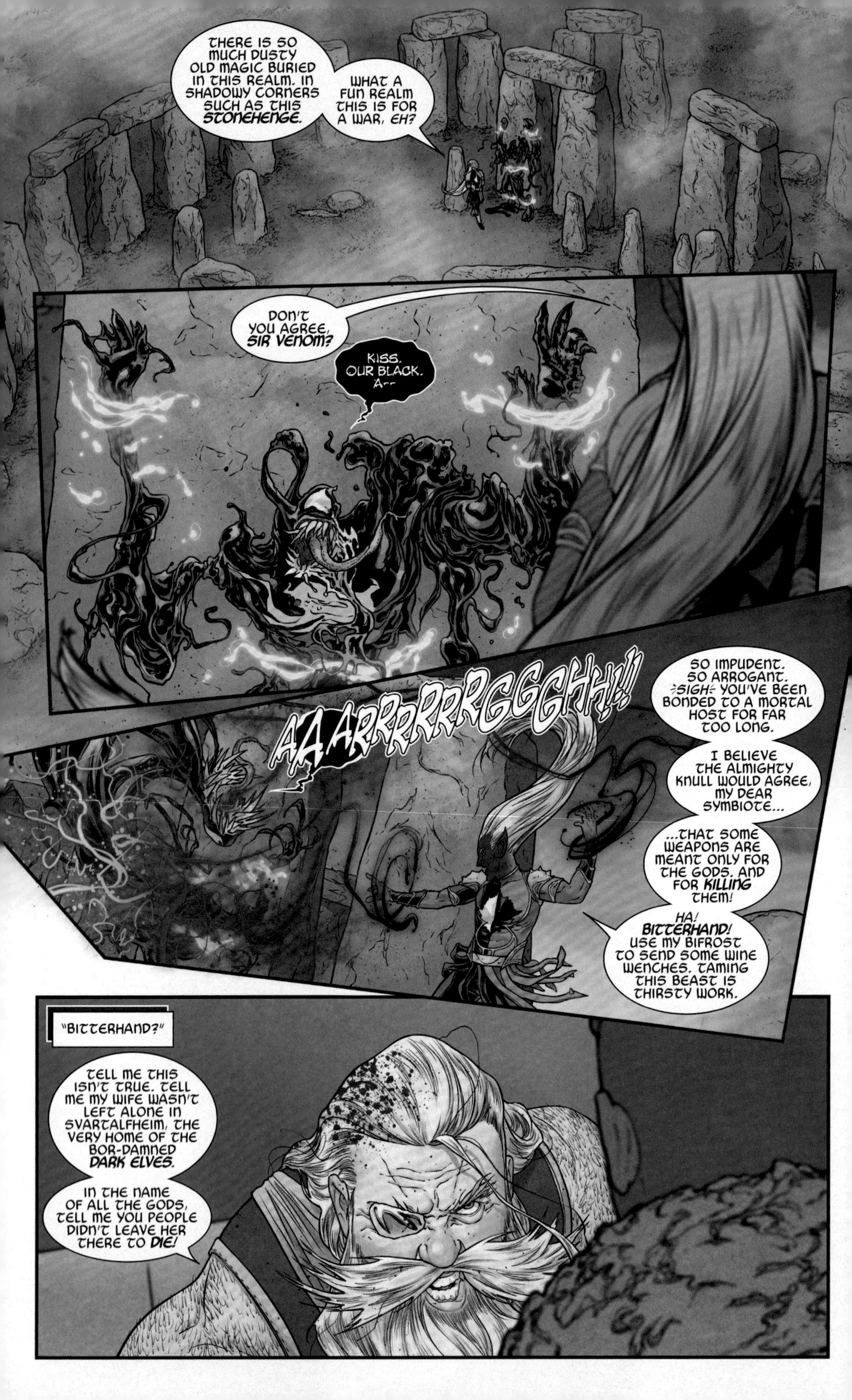
THERE IS SO MUCH DUSTY OLD MAGIC BURIED IN THIS REALM. IN SHADOWY CORNERS SUCH AS THIS STONEHENGE.
WHAT A FUN REALM THIS IS FOR A WAR, EH?
DON'T YOU AGREE, SIR VENOM?
KISS. OUR BLACK. A--
AAARRRRRRGGGGHH!!
SO IMPUDENT. SO ARROGANT. =SIGH= YOU'VE BEEN BONDED TO A MORTAL HOST FOR FAR TOO LONG.
I BELIEVE THE ALMIGHTY KNULL WOULD AGREE, MY DEAR SYMBIOTE...
...THAT SOME WEAPONS ARE MEANT ONLY FOR THE GODS. AND FOR KILLING THEM!
HA! BITTERHAND! USE MY BIFROST TO SEND SOME WINE WENCHES. TAMING THIS BEAST IS THIRSTY WORK.
"BITTERHAND?"
TELL ME THIS ISN'T TRUE. TELL ME MY WIFE WASN'T LEFT ALONE IN SVARTALFHEIM, THE VERY HOME OF THE BOR-DAMNED DARK ELVES.
IN THE NAME OF ALL THE GODS, TELL ME YOU PEOPLE DIDN'T LEAVE HER THERE TO DIE!

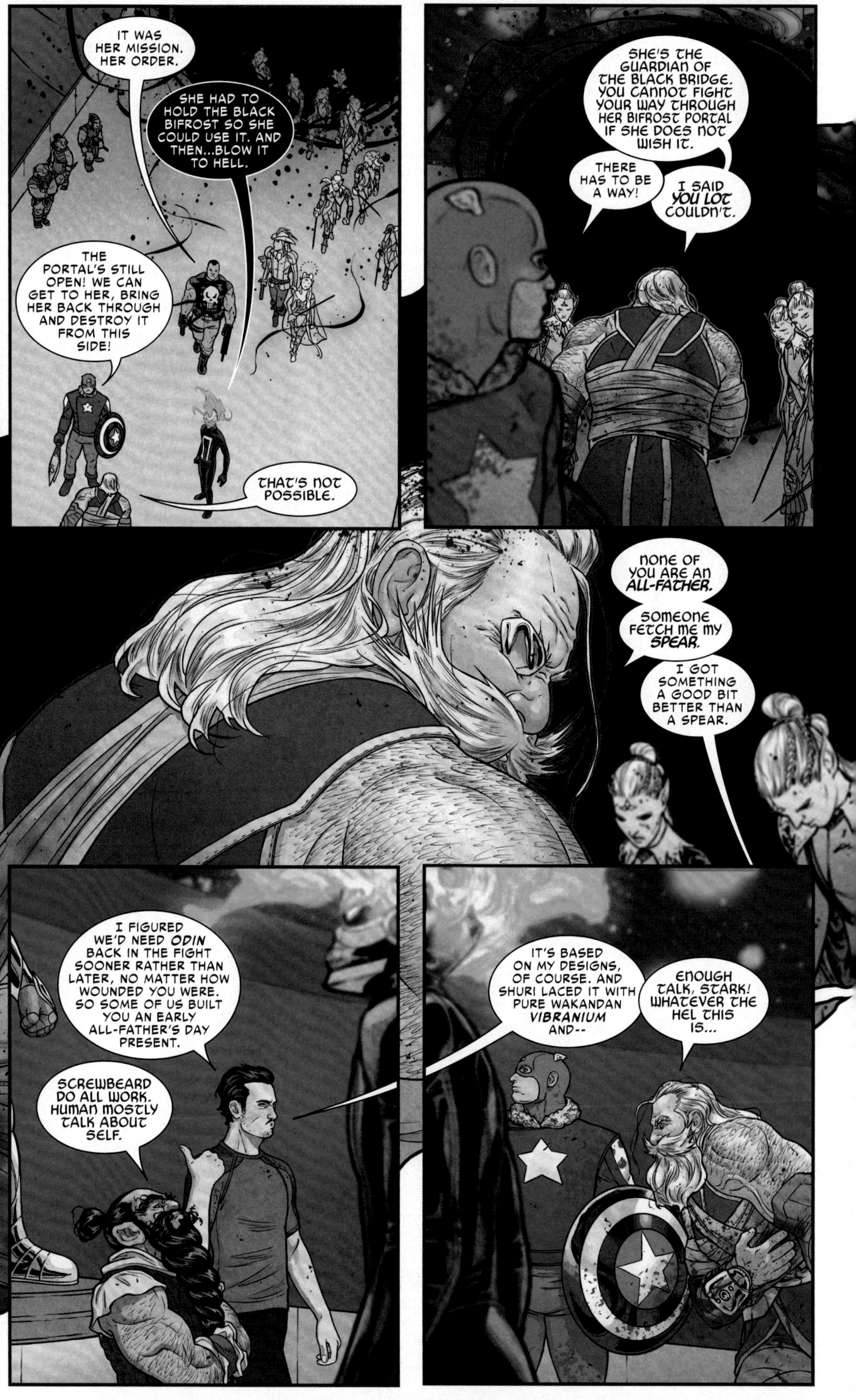
IT WAS HER MISSION. HER ORDER.
SHE HAD TO HOLD THE BLACK BIFROST SO SHE COULD USE IT. AND THEN...BLOW IT TO HELL.
THE PORTAL'S STILL OPEN! WE CAN GET TO HER, BRING HER BACK THROUGH AND DESTROY IT FROM THIS SIDE!
THAT'S NOT POSSIBLE.
SHE'S THE GUARDIAN OF THE BLACK BRIDGE. YOU CANNOT FIGHT YOUR WAY THROUGH HER BIFROST PORTAL IF SHE DOES NOT WISH IT.
THERE HAS TO BE A WAY!
I SAID *YOU LOT* COULDN'T.
NONE OF YOU ARE AN *ALL-FATHER.*
SOMEONE FETCH ME MY *SPEAR.*
I GOT SOMETHING A GOOD BIT BETTER THAN A SPEAR.
I FIGURED WE'D NEED *ODIN* BACK IN THE FIGHT SOONER RATHER THAN LATER, NO MATTER HOW WOUNDED YOU WERE. SO SOME OF US BUILT YOU AN EARLY ALL-FATHER'S DAY PRESENT.
SCREWBEARD DO ALL WORK. HUMAN MOSTLY TALK ABOUT SELF.
IT'S BASED ON MY DESIGNS, OF COURSE. AND SHURI LACED IT WITH PURE WAKANDAN *VIBRANIUM* AND--
ENOUGH TALK, STARK! WHATEVER THE HEL THIS IS...

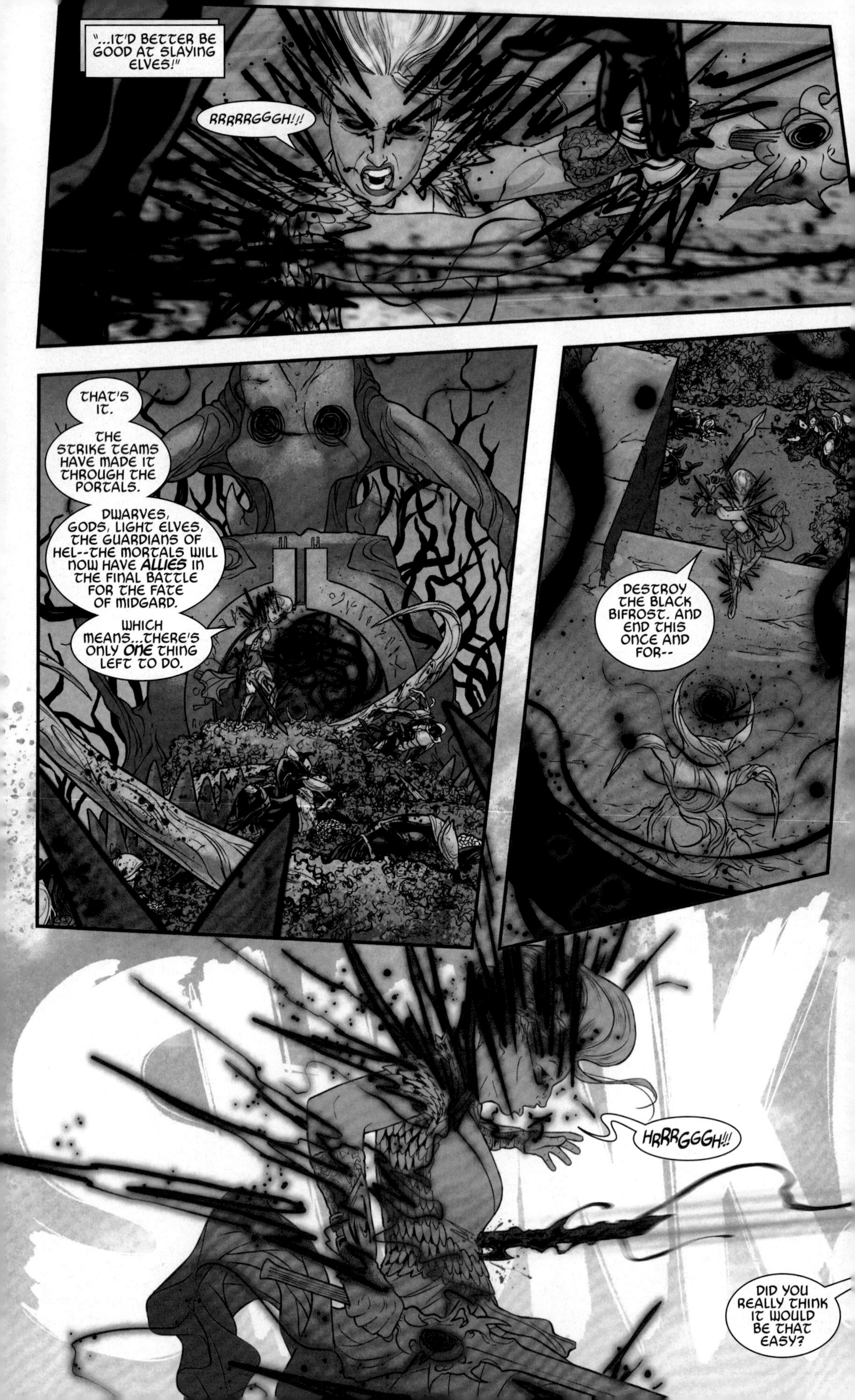
"...IT'D BETTER BE GOOD AT SLAYING ELVES!"
RRRRRGGGH!!!
THAT'S IT.
THE STRIKE TEAMS HAVE MADE IT THROUGH THE PORTALS.
DWARVES, GODS, LIGHT ELVES, THE GUARDIANS OF HEL--THE MORTALS WILL NOW HAVE ALLIES IN THE FINAL BATTLE FOR THE FATE OF MIDGARD.
WHICH MEANS...THERE'S ONLY ONE THING LEFT TO DO.
DESTROY THE BLACK BIFROST. AND END THIS ONCE AND FOR--
HRRRGGGH!!!
DID YOU REALLY THINK IT WOULD BE THAT EASY?

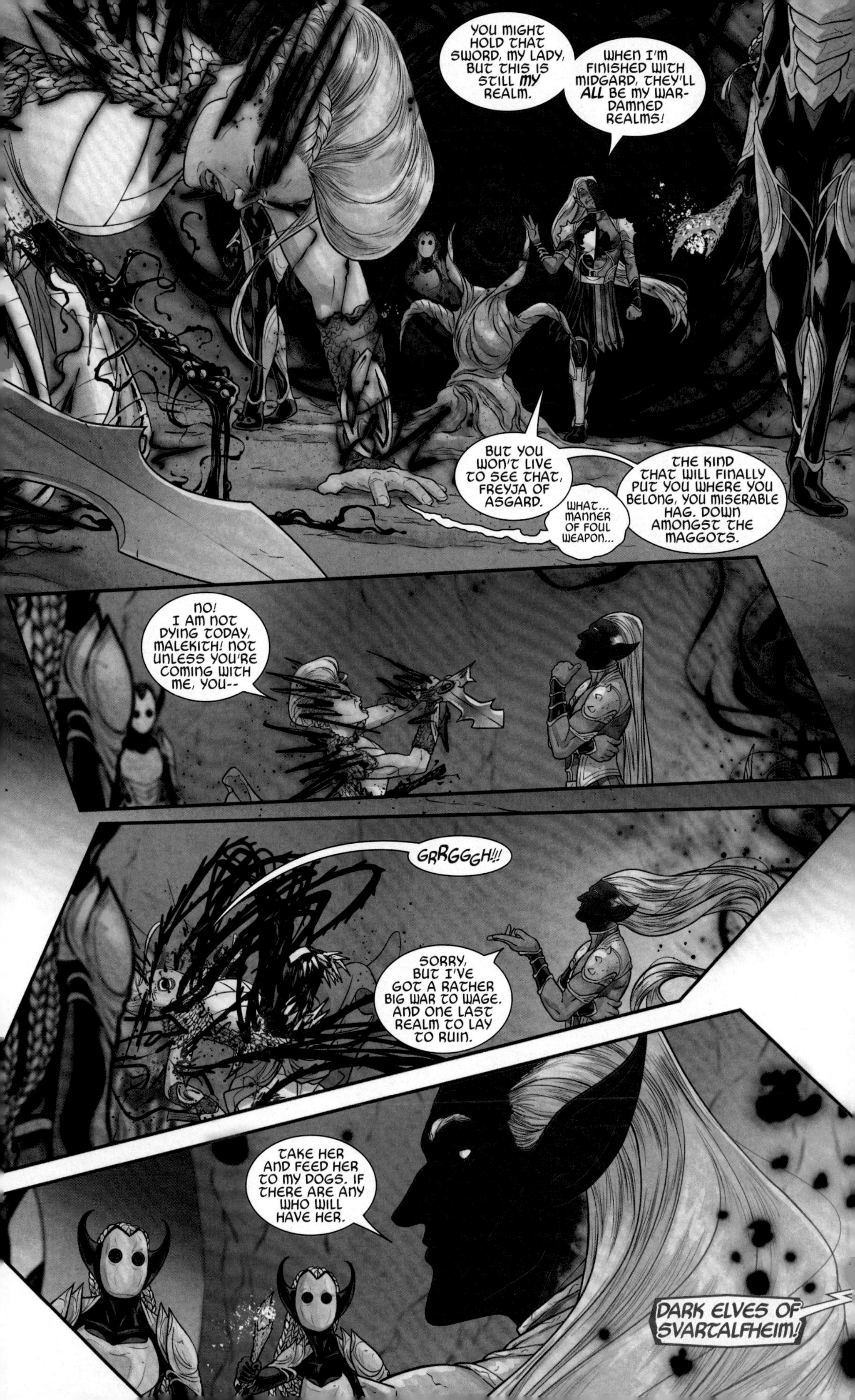

YOU MIGHT HOLD THAT SWORD, MY LADY, BUT THIS IS STILL *MY* REALM.
WHEN I'M FINISHED WITH MIDGARD, THEY'LL **ALL** BE MY WAR-DAMNED REALMS!
BUT YOU WON'T LIVE TO SEE THAT, FREYJA OF ASGARD.
WHAT... MANNER OF FOUL WEAPON...
THE KIND THAT WILL FINALLY PUT YOU WHERE YOU BELONG, YOU MISERABLE HAG. DOWN AMONGST THE MAGGOTS.
NO! I AM NOT DYING TODAY, MALEKITH! NOT UNLESS YOU'RE COMING WITH ME, YOU--
GRRGGGH!!!
SORRY, BUT I'VE GOT A RATHER BIG WAR TO WAGE. AND ONE LAST REALM TO LAY TO RUIN.
TAKE HER AND FEED HER TO MY DOGS. IF THERE ARE ANY WHO WILL HAVE HER.
DARK ELVES OF SVARTALFHEIM!

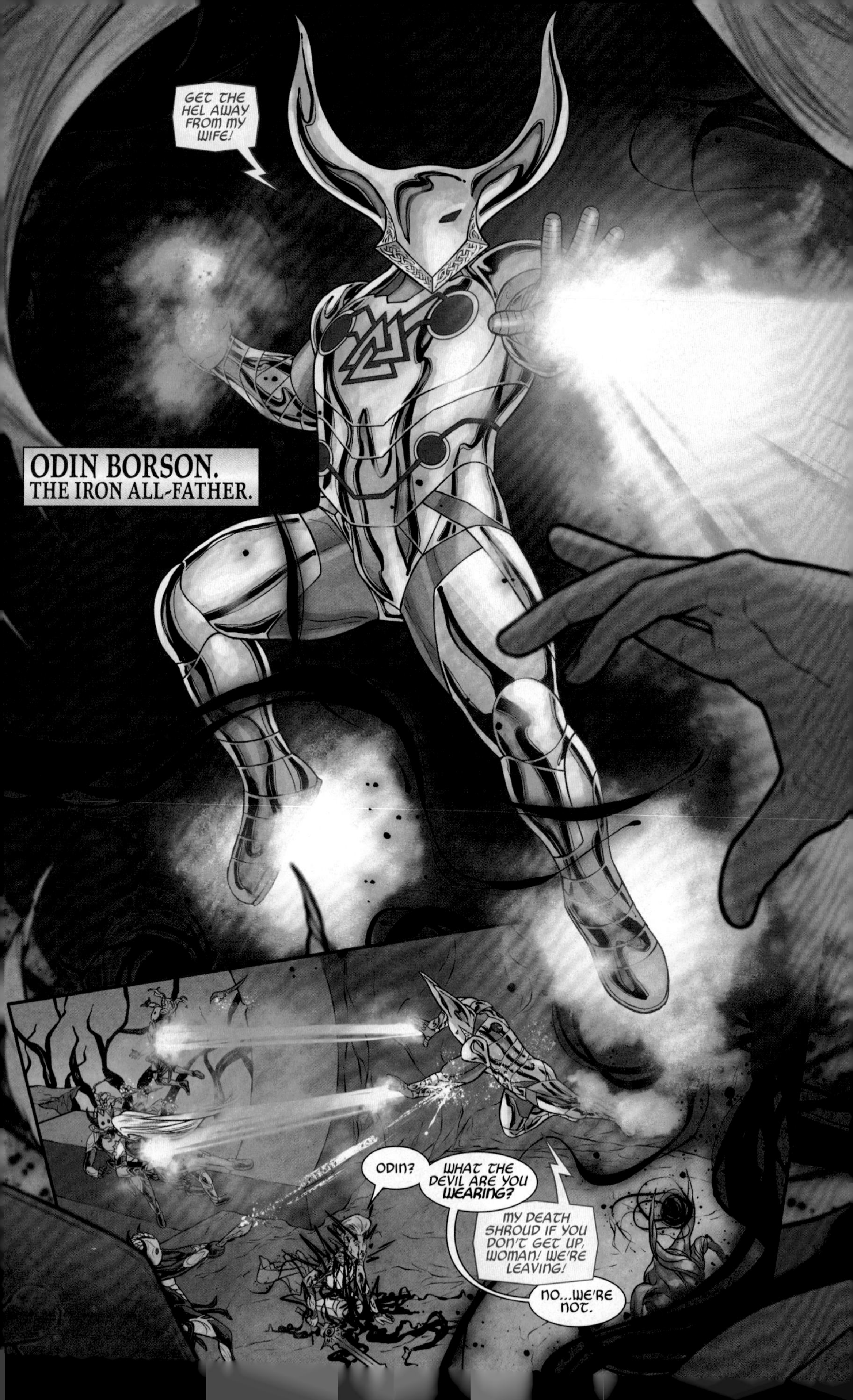
GET THE HEL AWAY FROM MY WIFE!
ODIN BORSON. THE IRON ALL-FATHER.
ODIN?
WHAT THE DEVIL ARE YOU WEARING?
MY DEATH SHROUD IF YOU DON'T GET UP, WOMAN! WE'RE LEAVING!
NO...WE'RE NOT.

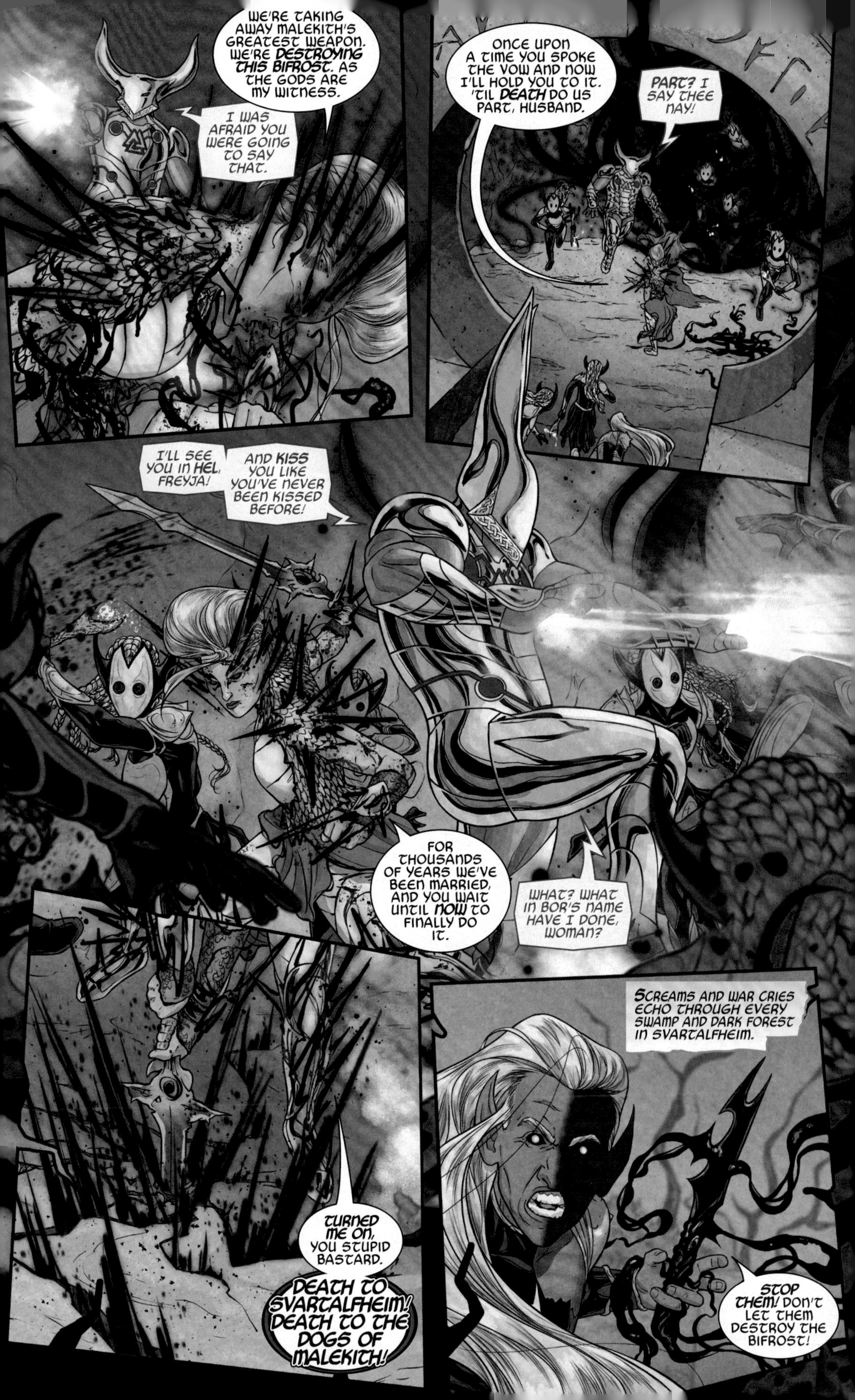
WE'RE TAKING AWAY MALEKITH'S GREATEST WEAPON. WE'RE DESTROYING THIS BIFROST. AS THE GODS ARE MY WITNESS.
I WAS AFRAID YOU WERE GOING TO SAY THAT.
ONCE UPON A TIME YOU SPOKE THE VOW AND NOW I'LL HOLD YOU TO IT. 'TIL DEATH DO US PART, HUSBAND.
PART? I SAY THEE NAY!
I'LL SEE YOU IN HEL, FREYJA!
AND KISS YOU LIKE YOU'VE NEVER BEEN KISSED BEFORE!
FOR THOUSANDS OF YEARS WE'VE BEEN MARRIED, AND YOU WAIT UNTIL NOW TO FINALLY DO IT.
WHAT? WHAT IN BOR'S NAME HAVE I DONE, WOMAN?
TURNED ME ON, YOU STUPID BASTARD.
DEATH TO SVARTALFHEIM! DEATH TO THE DOGS OF MALEKITH!
SCREAMS AND WAR CRIES ECHO THROUGH EVERY SWAMP AND DARK FOREST IN SVARTALFHEIM.
STOP THEM! DON'T LET THEM DESTROY THE BIFROST!

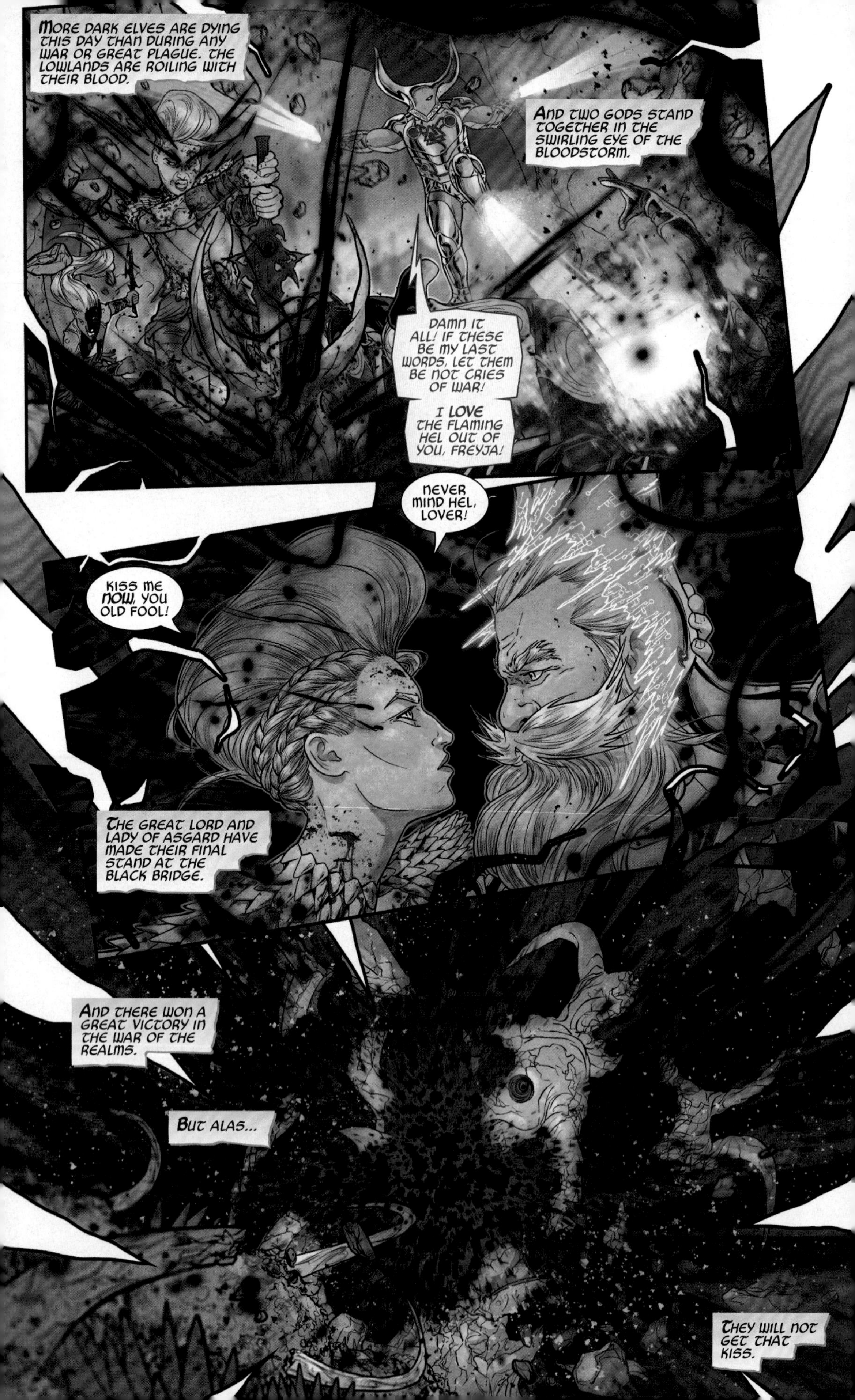

More dark elves are dying this day than during any war or great plague. The lowlands are roiling with their blood.
And two gods stand together in the swirling eye of the bloodstorm.
Damn it all! If these be my last words, let them be not cries of war!
I LOVE the flaming Hel out of you, Freyja!
Never mind Hel, lover!
Kiss me NOW, you old fool!
The great lord and lady of Asgard have made their final stand at the Black Bridge.
And there won a great victory in the War of the Realms.
But alas...
They will not get that kiss.

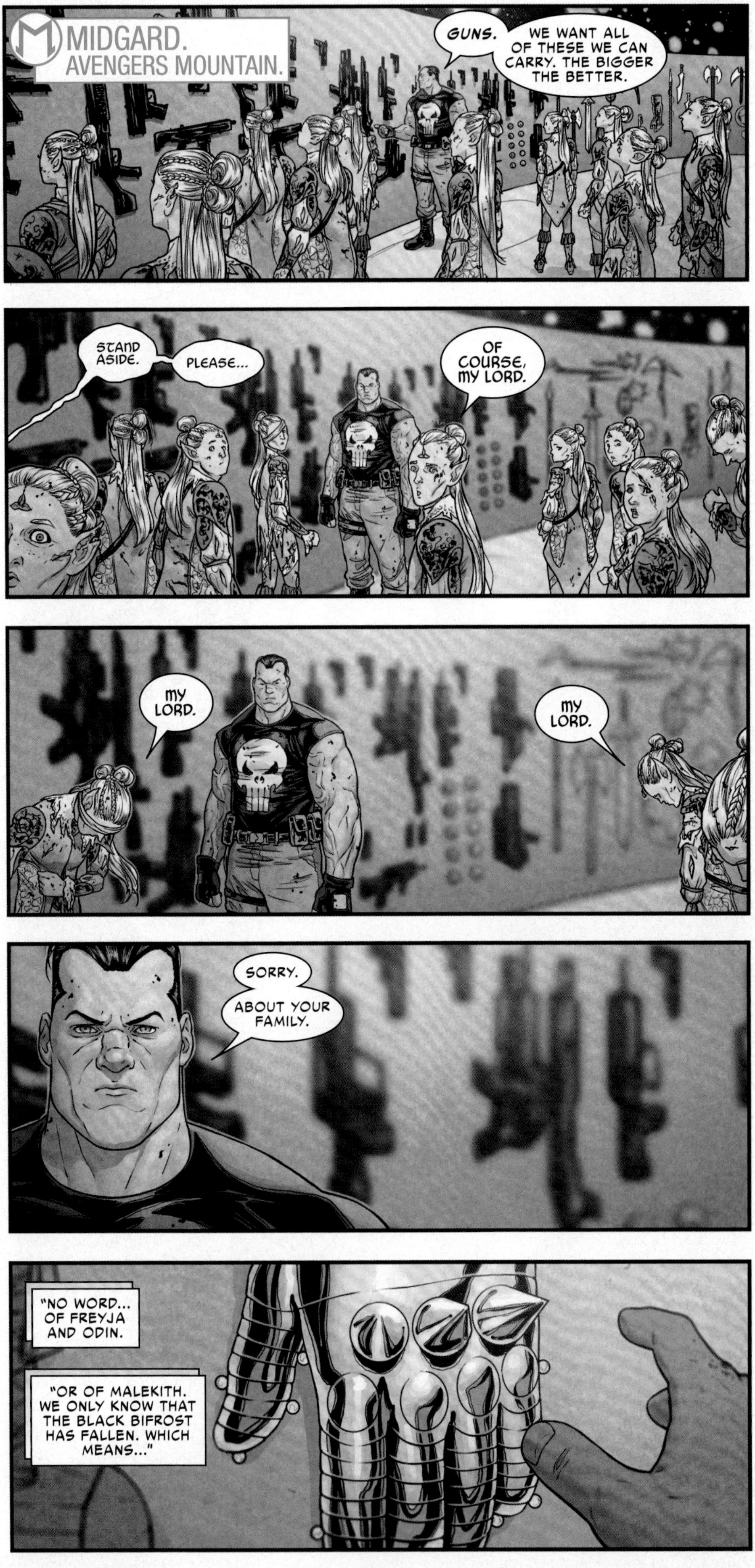
MIDGARD.
AVENGERS MOUNTAIN.
GUNS.
WE WANT ALL OF THESE WE CAN CARRY. THE BIGGER THE BETTER.
STAND ASIDE.
PLEASE...
OF COURSE, MY LORD.
MY LORD.
MY LORD.
SORRY.
ABOUT YOUR FAMILY.
"NO WORD... OF FREYJA AND ODIN.
"OR OF MALEKITH. WE ONLY KNOW THAT THE BLACK BIFROST HAS FALLEN. WHICH MEANS..."

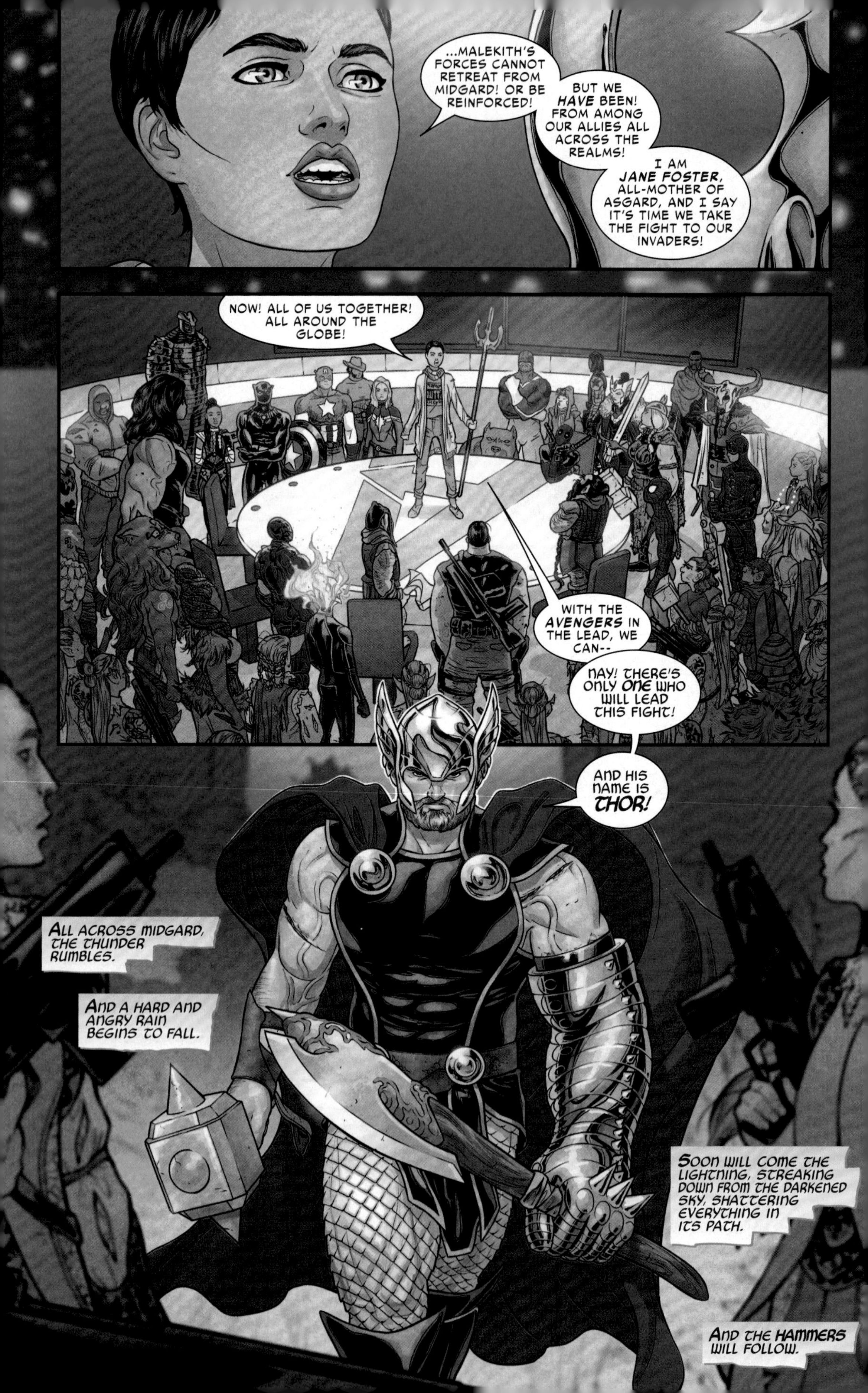
...MALEKITH'S FORCES CANNOT RETREAT FROM MIDGARD! OR BE REINFORCED!
BUT WE HAVE BEEN! FROM AMONG OUR ALLIES ALL ACROSS THE REALMS!
I AM JANE FOSTER, ALL-MOTHER OF ASGARD, AND I SAY IT'S TIME WE TAKE THE FIGHT TO OUR INVADERS!
NOW! ALL OF US TOGETHER! ALL AROUND THE GLOBE!
WITH THE AVENGERS IN THE LEAD, WE CAN--
NAY! THERE'S ONLY ONE WHO WILL LEAD THIS FIGHT!
AND HIS NAME IS THOR!
ALL ACROSS MIDGARD, THE THUNDER RUMBLES.
AND A HARD AND ANGRY RAIN BEGINS TO FALL.
SOON WILL COME THE LIGHTNING, STREAKING DOWN FROM THE DARKENED SKY, SHATTERING EVERYTHING IN ITS PATH.
AND THE HAMMERS WILL FOLLOW.

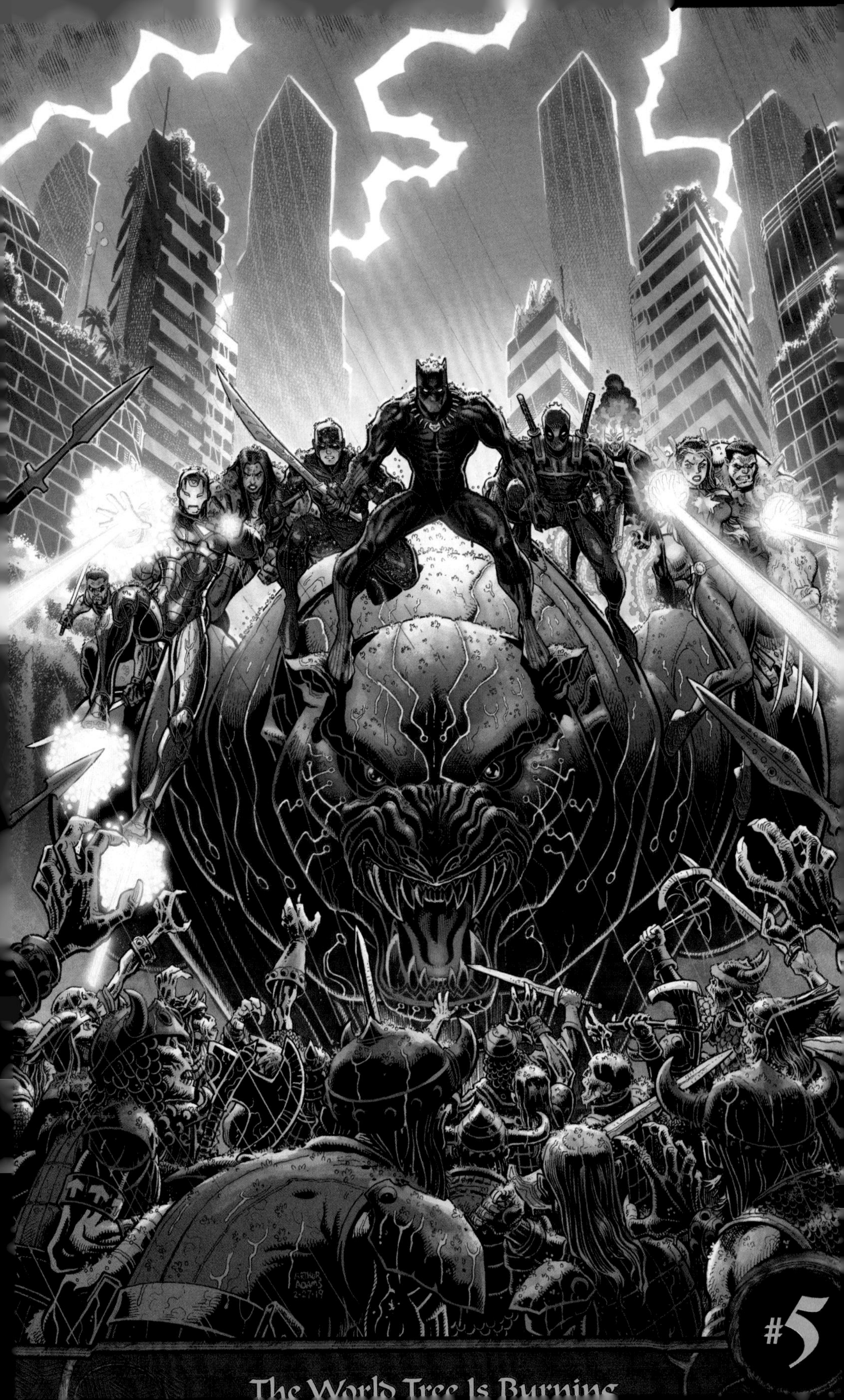
#5

The World Tree Is Burning

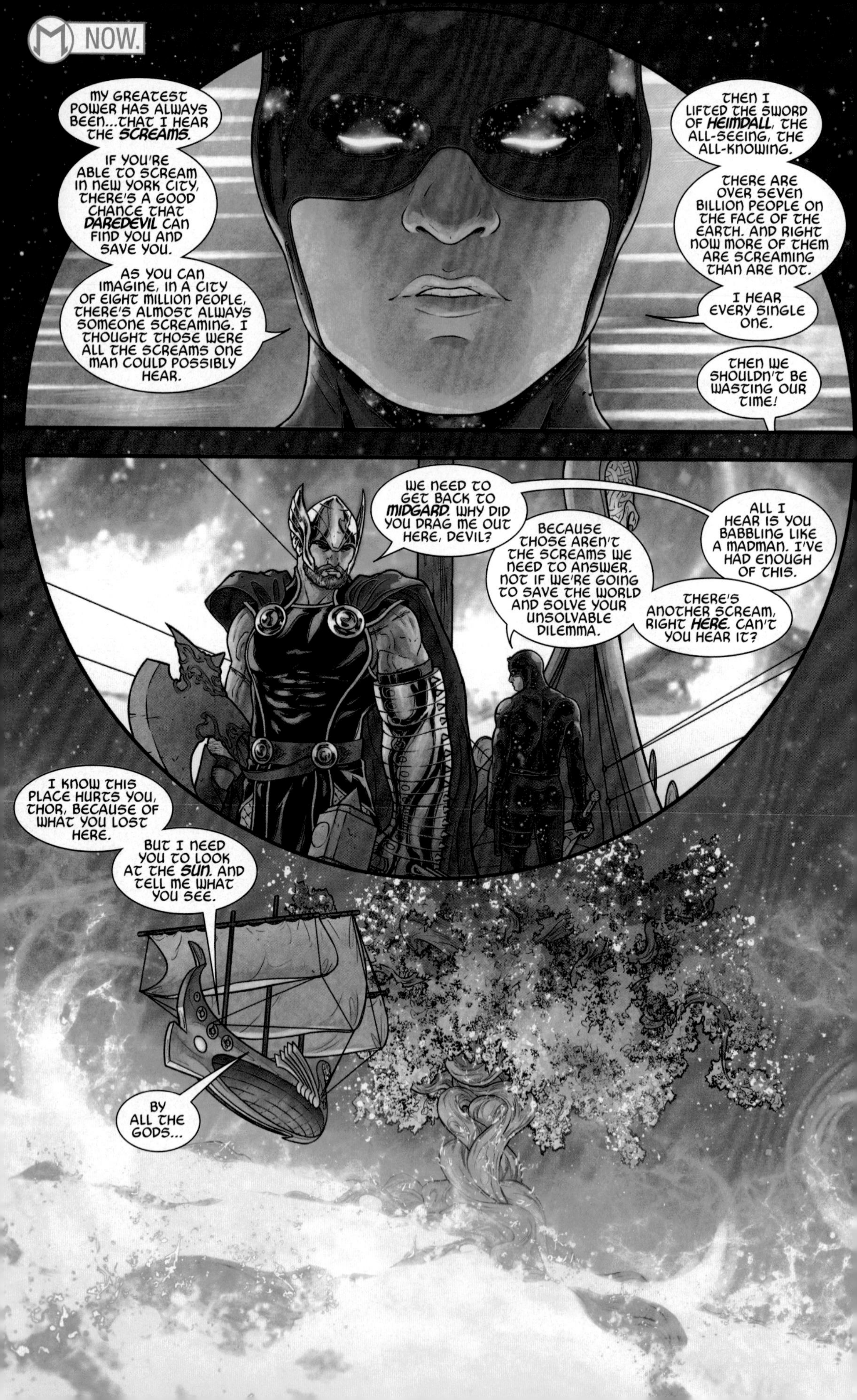
NOW.
MY GREATEST POWER HAS ALWAYS BEEN...THAT I HEAR THE SCREAMS.
IF YOU'RE ABLE TO SCREAM IN NEW YORK CITY, THERE'S A GOOD CHANCE THAT DAREDEVIL CAN FIND YOU AND SAVE YOU.
AS YOU CAN IMAGINE, IN A CITY OF EIGHT MILLION PEOPLE, THERE'S ALMOST ALWAYS SOMEONE SCREAMING. I THOUGHT THOSE WERE ALL THE SCREAMS ONE MAN COULD POSSIBLY HEAR.
THEN I LIFTED THE SWORD OF HEIMDALL, THE ALL-SEEING, THE ALL-KNOWING.
THERE ARE OVER SEVEN BILLION PEOPLE ON THE FACE OF THE EARTH. AND RIGHT NOW MORE OF THEM ARE SCREAMING THAN ARE NOT.
I HEAR EVERY SINGLE ONE.
THEN WE SHOULDN'T BE WASTING OUR TIME!
WE NEED TO GET BACK TO MIDGARD. WHY DID YOU DRAG ME OUT HERE, DEVIL?
BECAUSE THOSE AREN'T THE SCREAMS WE NEED TO ANSWER. NOT IF WE'RE GOING TO SAVE THE WORLD AND SOLVE YOUR UNSOLVABLE DILEMMA.
ALL I HEAR IS YOU BABBLING LIKE A MADMAN. I'VE HAD ENOUGH OF THIS.
THERE'S ANOTHER SCREAM, RIGHT HERE. CAN'T YOU HEAR IT?
I KNOW THIS PLACE HURTS YOU, THOR, BECAUSE OF WHAT YOU LOST HERE.
BUT I NEED YOU TO LOOK AT THE SUN. AND TELL ME WHAT YOU SEE.
BY ALL THE GODS...

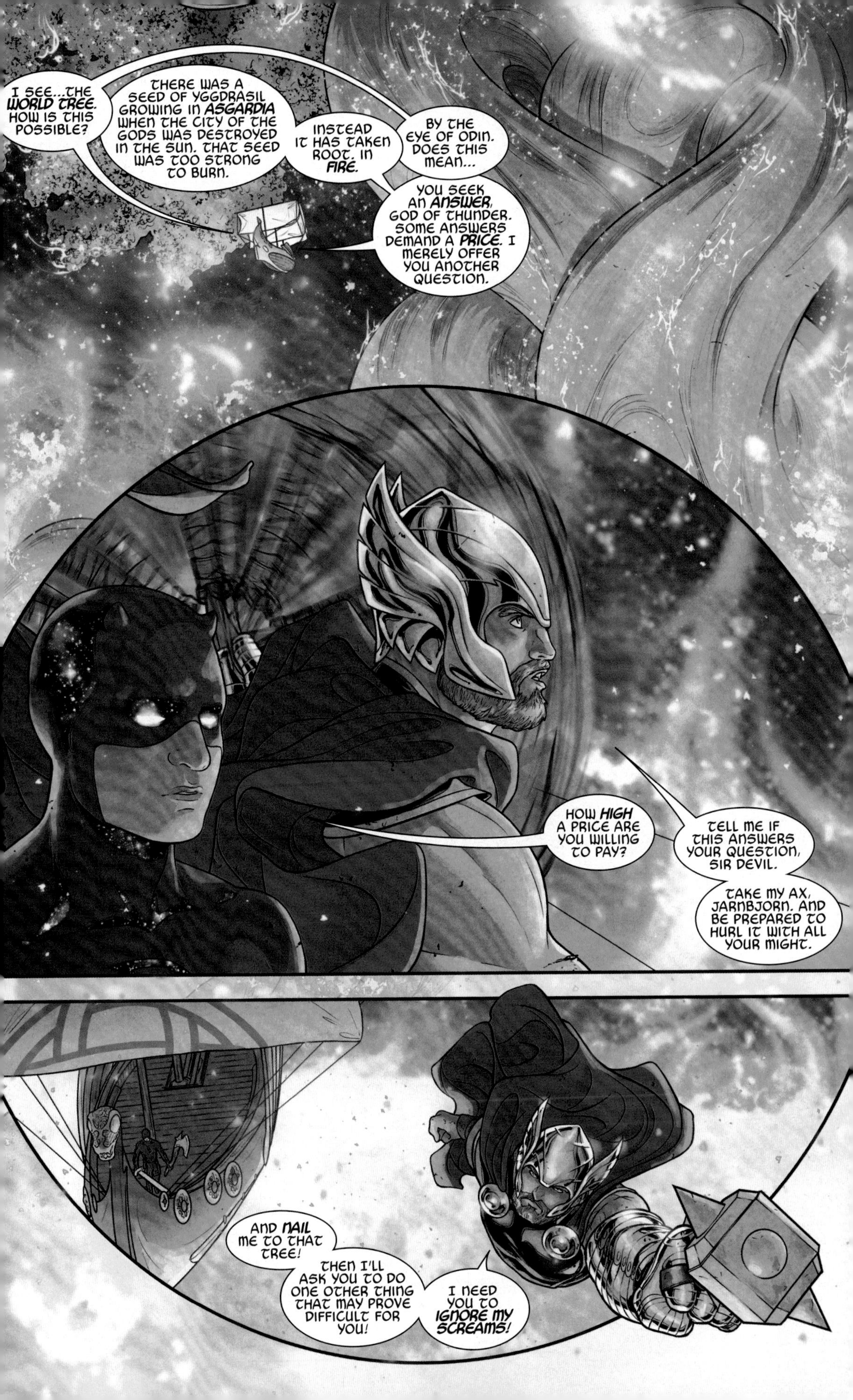

I SEE...THE WORLD TREE. HOW IS THIS POSSIBLE?
THERE WAS A SEED OF YGGDRASIL GROWING IN ASGARDIA WHEN THE CITY OF THE GODS WAS DESTROYED IN THE SUN. THAT SEED WAS TOO STRONG TO BURN.
INSTEAD IT HAS TAKEN ROOT. IN FIRE.
BY THE EYE OF ODIN. DOES THIS MEAN...
YOU SEEK AN ANSWER, GOD OF THUNDER. SOME ANSWERS DEMAND A PRICE. I MERELY OFFER YOU ANOTHER QUESTION.
HOW HIGH A PRICE ARE YOU WILLING TO PAY?
TELL ME IF THIS ANSWERS YOUR QUESTION, SIR DEVIL.
TAKE MY AX, JARNBJORN. AND BE PREPARED TO HURL IT WITH ALL YOUR MIGHT.
AND NAIL ME TO THAT TREE!
THEN I'LL ASK YOU TO DO ONE OTHER THING THAT MAY PROVE DIFFICULT FOR YOU!
I NEED YOU TO IGNORE MY SCREAMS!

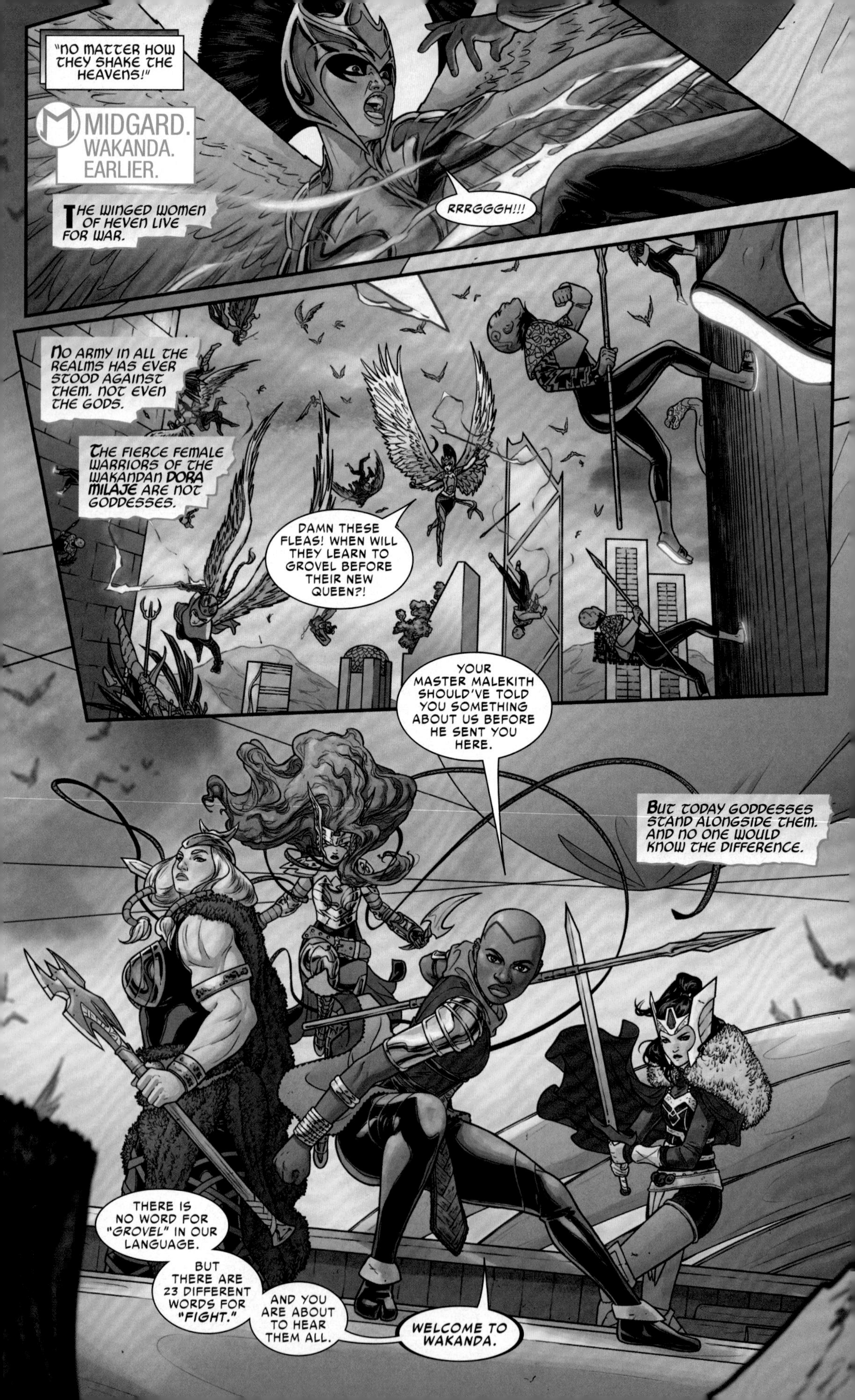
"NO MATTER HOW THEY SHAKE THE HEAVENS!"
MIDGARD. WAKANDA. EARLIER.
THE WINGED WOMEN OF HEVEN LIVE FOR WAR.
RRRGGGH!!!
NO ARMY IN ALL THE REALMS HAS EVER STOOD AGAINST THEM. NOT EVEN THE GODS.
THE FIERCE FEMALE WARRIORS OF THE WAKANDAN DORA MILAJE ARE NOT GODDESSES.
DAMN THESE FLEAS! WHEN WILL THEY LEARN TO GROVEL BEFORE THEIR NEW QUEEN?!
YOUR MASTER MALEKITH SHOULD'VE TOLD YOU SOMETHING ABOUT US BEFORE HE SENT YOU HERE.
BUT TODAY GODDESSES STAND ALONGSIDE THEM. AND NO ONE WOULD KNOW THE DIFFERENCE.
THERE IS NO WORD FOR "GROVEL" IN OUR LANGUAGE.
BUT THERE ARE 23 DIFFERENT WORDS FOR "FIGHT."
AND YOU ARE ABOUT TO HEAR THEM ALL.
WELCOME TO WAKANDA.

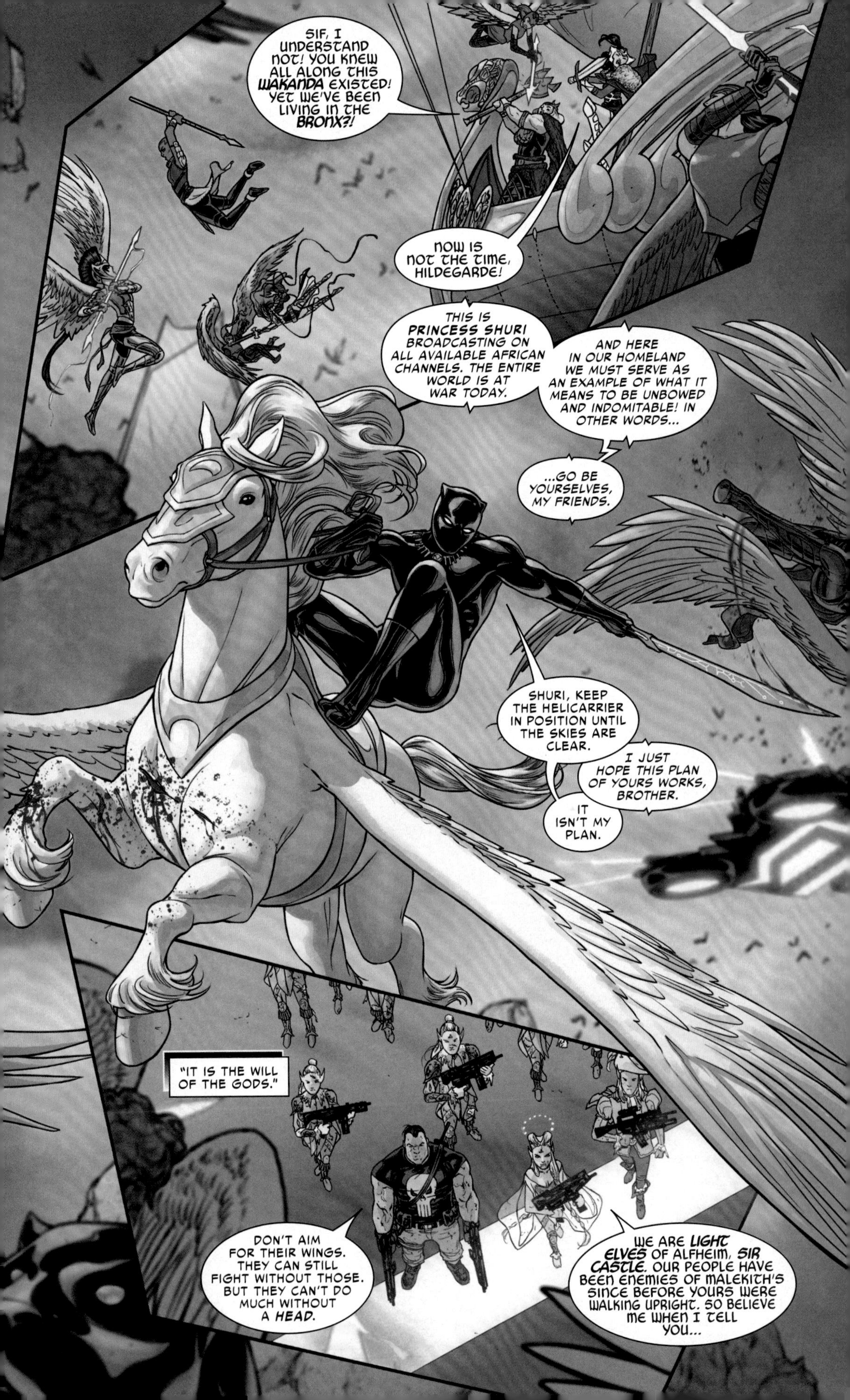
SIF, I UNDERSTAND NOT! YOU KNEW ALL ALONG THIS WAKANDA EXISTED! YET WE'VE BEEN LIVING IN THE BRONX?!
NOW IS NOT THE TIME, HILDEGARDE!
THIS IS PRINCESS SHURI BROADCASTING ON ALL AVAILABLE AFRICAN CHANNELS. THE ENTIRE WORLD IS AT WAR TODAY.
AND HERE IN OUR HOMELAND WE MUST SERVE AS AN EXAMPLE OF WHAT IT MEANS TO BE UNBOWED AND INDOMITABLE! IN OTHER WORDS...
...GO BE YOURSELVES, MY FRIENDS.
SHURI, KEEP THE HELICARRIER IN POSITION UNTIL THE SKIES ARE CLEAR.
I JUST HOPE THIS PLAN OF YOURS WORKS, BROTHER.
IT ISN'T MY PLAN.
"IT IS THE WILL OF THE GODS."
DON'T AIM FOR THEIR WINGS. THEY CAN STILL FIGHT WITHOUT THOSE. BUT THEY CAN'T DO MUCH WITHOUT A HEAD.
WE ARE LIGHT ELVES OF ALFHEIM, SIR CASTLE. OUR PEOPLE HAVE BEEN ENEMIES OF MALEKITH'S SINCE BEFORE YOURS WERE WALKING UPRIGHT. SO BELIEVE ME WHEN I TELL YOU...

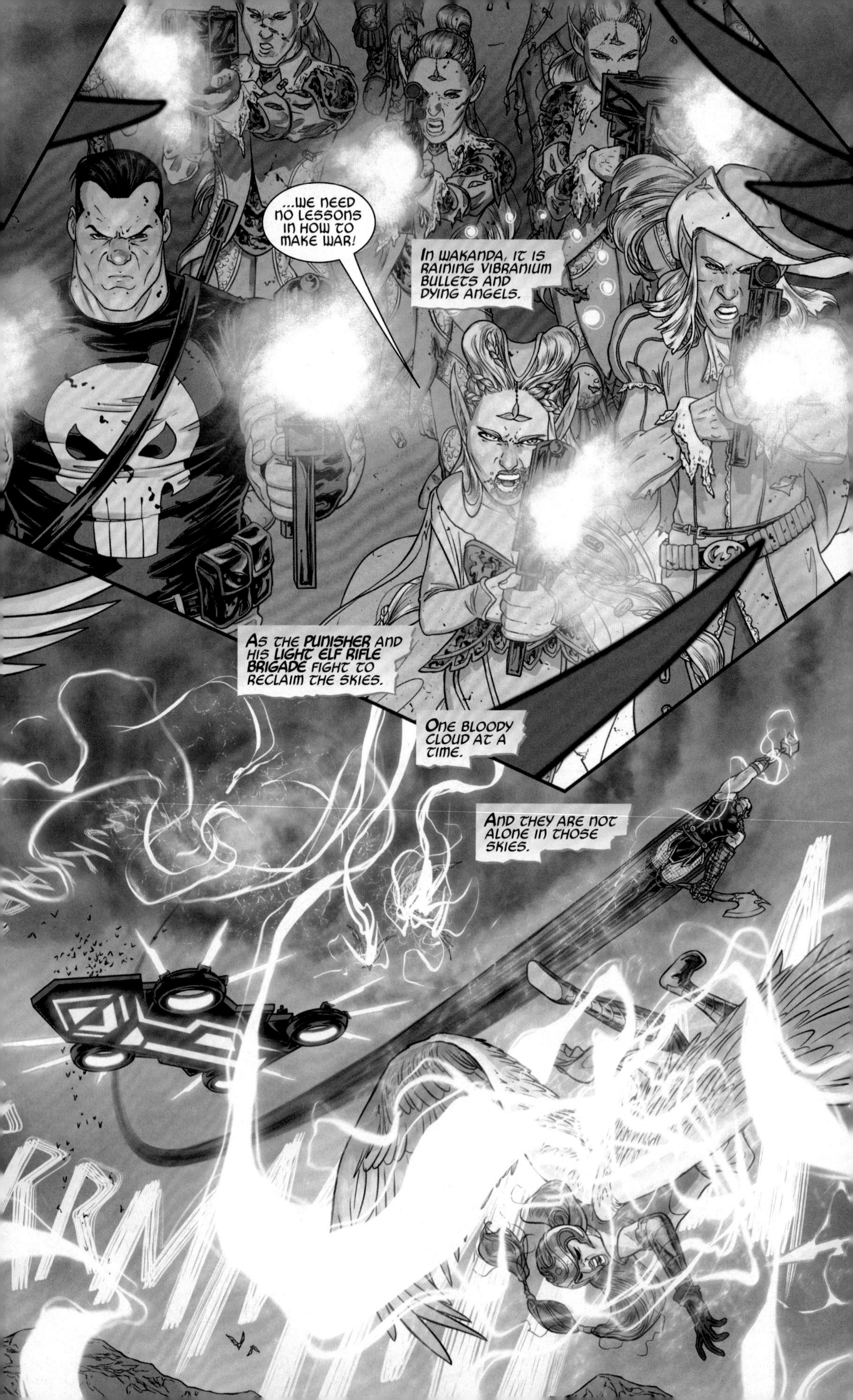

...WE NEED NO LESSONS IN HOW TO MAKE WAR!
IN WAKANDA, IT IS RAINING VIBRANIUM BULLETS AND DYING ANGELS.
AS THE PUNISHER AND HIS LIGHT ELF RIFLE BRIGADE FIGHT TO RECLAIM THE SKIES.
ONE BLOODY CLOUD AT A TIME.
AND THEY ARE NOT ALONE IN THOSE SKIES.

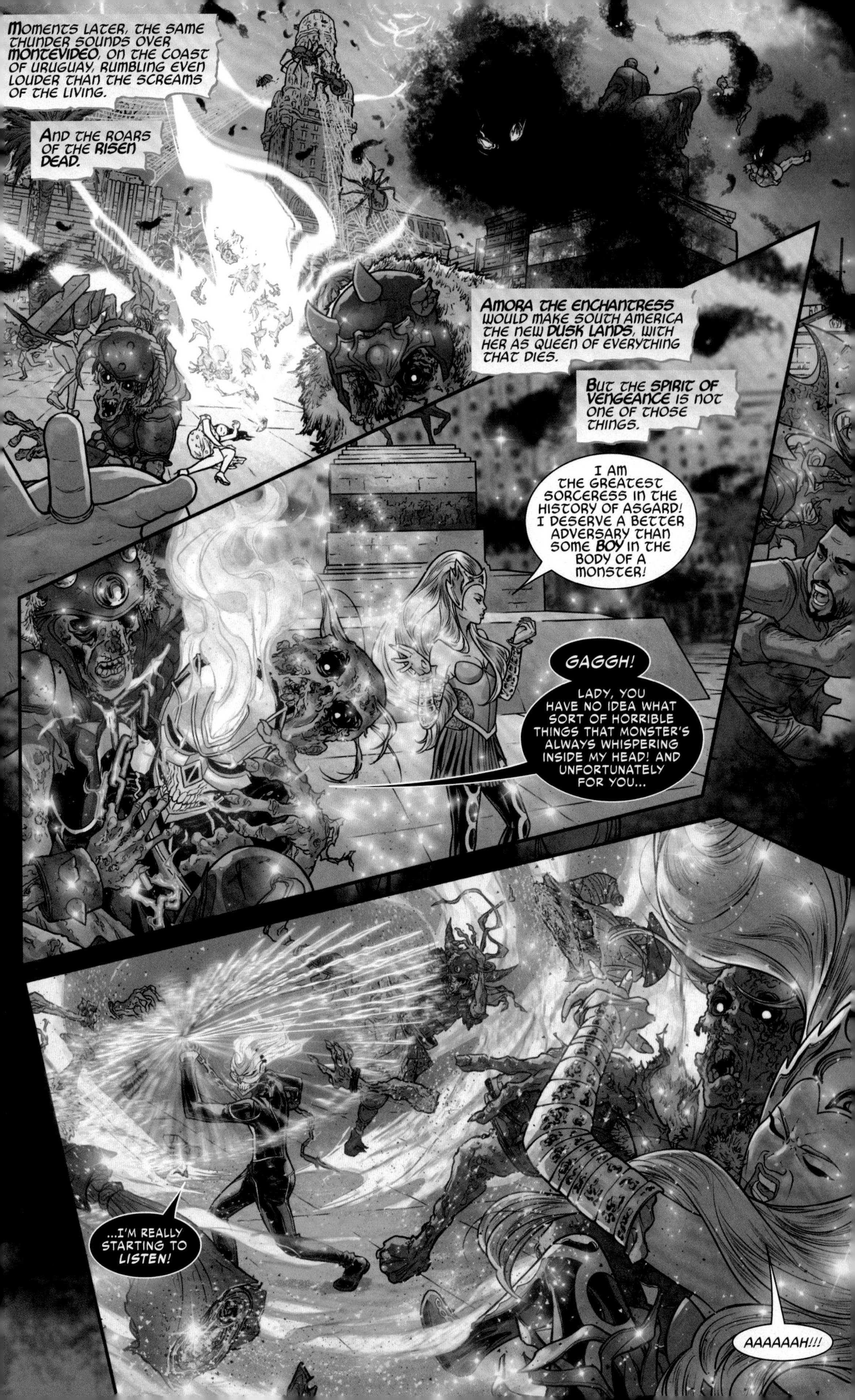
Moments later, the same thunder sounds over Montevideo, on the coast of Uruguay, rumbling even louder than the screams of the living.
And the roars of the risen dead.
Amora the Enchantress would make South America the new Dusk Lands, with her as queen of everything that dies.
But the Spirit of Vengeance is not one of those things.
I am the greatest sorceress in the history of Asgard! I deserve a better adversary than some boy in the body of a monster!
GAGGH!
Lady, you have no idea what sort of horrible things that monster's always whispering inside my head! And unfortunately for you...
...I'm really starting to listen!
AAAAAAH!!!

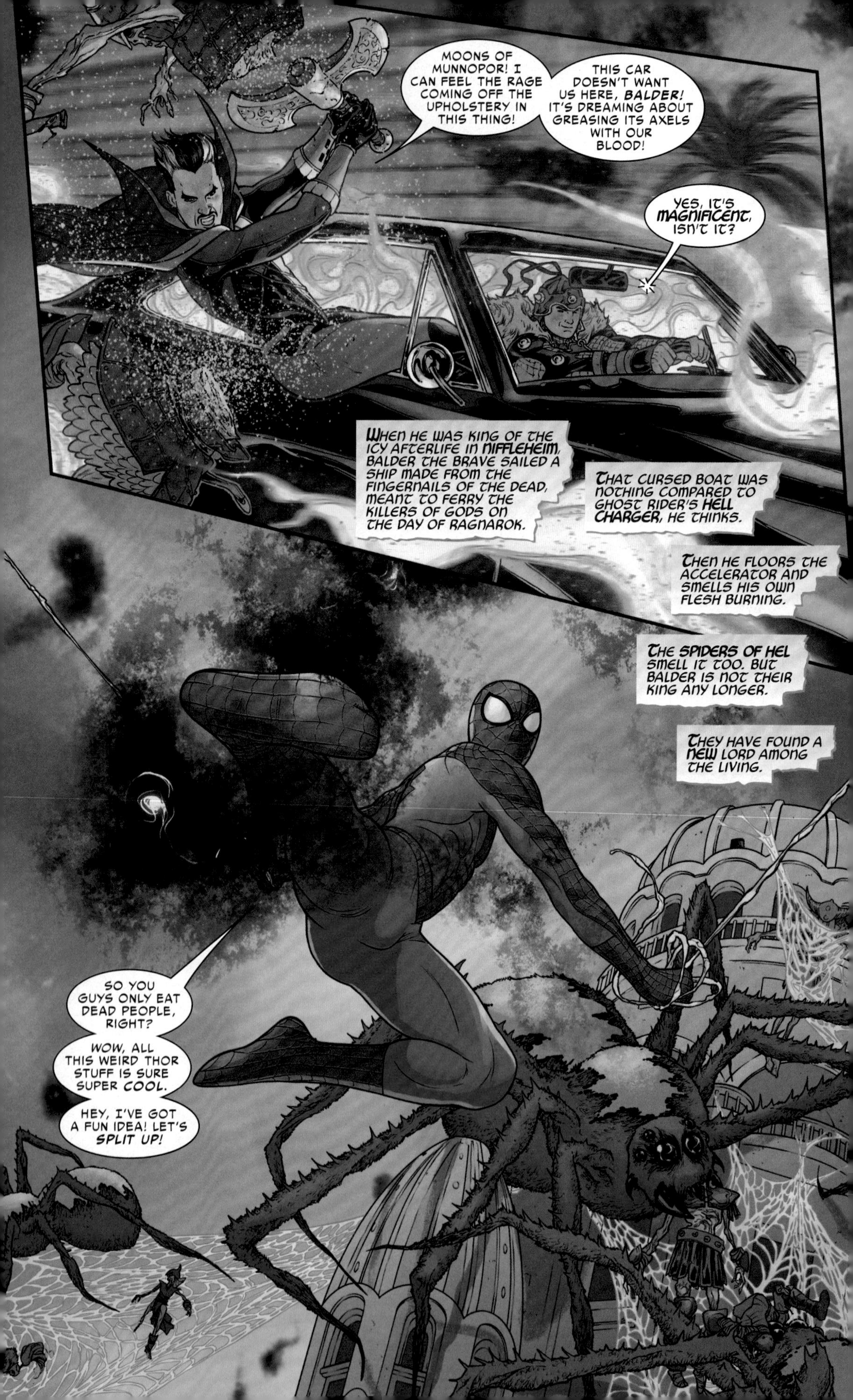

MOONS OF MUNNOPOR! I CAN FEEL THE RAGE COMING OFF THE UPHOLSTERY IN THIS THING!
THIS CAR DOESN'T WANT US HERE, BALDER! IT'S DREAMING ABOUT GREASING ITS AXELS WITH OUR BLOOD!
YES, IT'S MAGNIFICENT, ISN'T IT?
WHEN HE WAS KING OF THE ICY AFTERLIFE IN NIFFLEHEIM, BALDER THE BRAVE SAILED A SHIP MADE FROM THE FINGERNAILS OF THE DEAD, MEANT TO FERRY THE KILLERS OF GODS ON THE DAY OF RAGNAROK.
THAT CURSED BOAT WAS NOTHING COMPARED TO GHOST RIDER'S HELL CHARGER, HE THINKS.
THEN HE FLOORS THE ACCELERATOR AND SMELLS HIS OWN FLESH BURNING.
THE SPIDERS OF HEL SMELL IT TOO. BUT BALDER IS NOT THEIR KING ANY LONGER.
THEY HAVE FOUND A NEW LORD AMONG THE LIVING.
SO YOU GUYS ONLY EAT DEAD PEOPLE, RIGHT?
WOW, ALL THIS WEIRD THOR STUFF IS SURE SUPER COOL.
HEY, I'VE GOT A FUN IDEA! LET'S SPLIT UP!

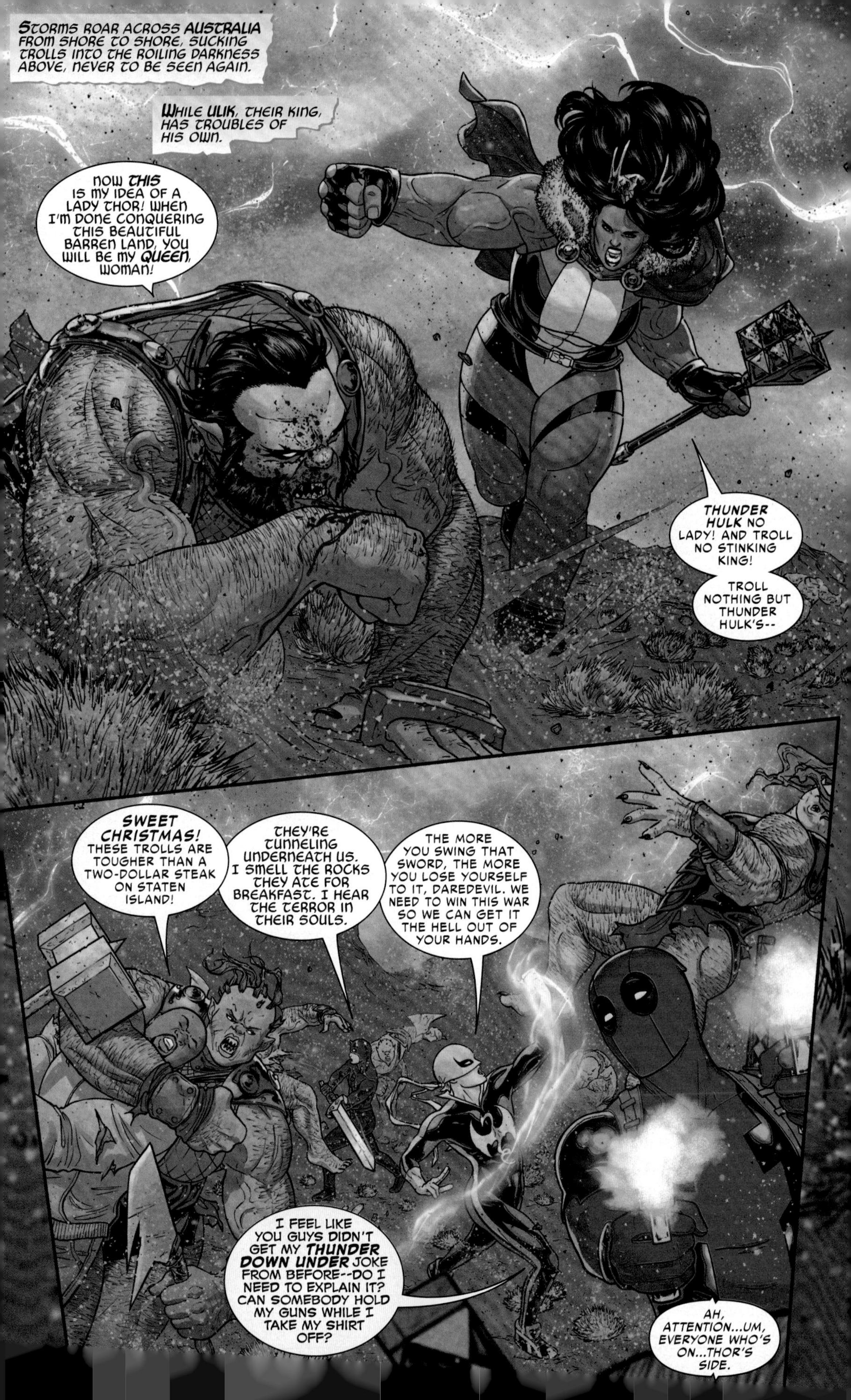

STORMS ROAR ACROSS AUSTRALIA FROM SHORE TO SHORE, SUCKING TROLLS INTO THE ROILING DARKNESS ABOVE, NEVER TO BE SEEN AGAIN.
WHILE ULIK, THEIR KING, HAS TROUBLES OF HIS OWN.
NOW THIS IS MY IDEA OF A LADY THOR! WHEN I'M DONE CONQUERING THIS BEAUTIFUL BARREN LAND, YOU WILL BE MY QUEEN, WOMAN!
THUNDER HULK NO LADY! AND TROLL NO STINKING KING!
TROLL NOTHING BUT THUNDER HULK'S--
SWEET CHRISTMAS! THESE TROLLS ARE TOUGHER THAN A TWO-DOLLAR STEAK ON STATEN ISLAND!
THEY'RE TUNNELING UNDERNEATH US. I SMELL THE ROCKS THEY ATE FOR BREAKFAST. I HEAR THE TERROR IN THEIR SOULS.
THE MORE YOU SWING THAT SWORD, THE MORE YOU LOSE YOURSELF TO IT, DAREDEVIL. WE NEED TO WIN THIS WAR SO WE CAN GET IT THE HELL OUT OF YOUR HANDS.
I FEEL LIKE YOU GUYS DIDN'T GET MY THUNDER DOWN UNDER JOKE FROM BEFORE--DO I NEED TO EXPLAIN IT? CAN SOMEBODY HOLD MY GUNS WHILE I TAKE MY SHIRT OFF?
AH, ATTENTION...UM, EVERYONE WHO'S ON...THOR'S SIDE.

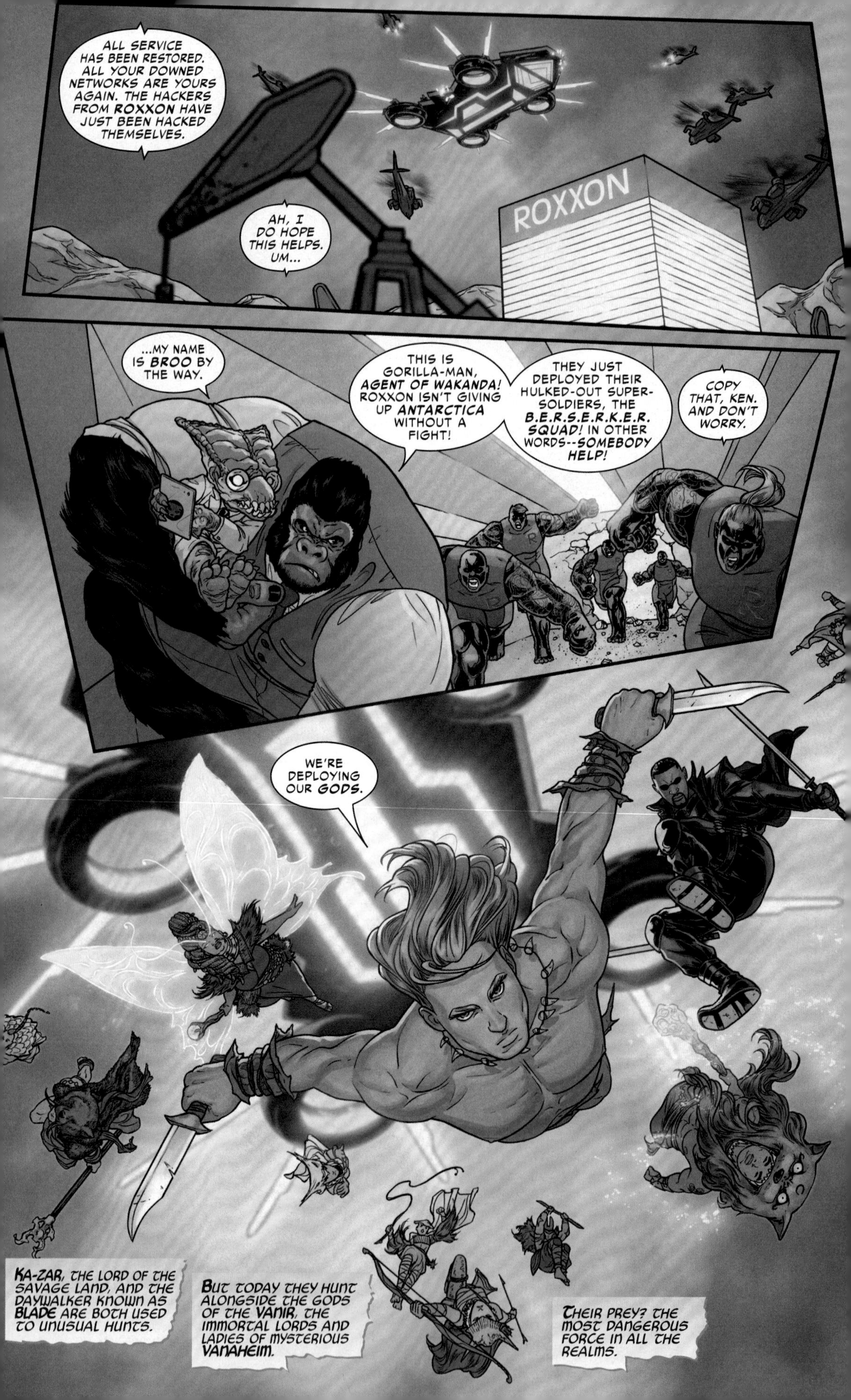
ALL SERVICE HAS BEEN RESTORED. ALL YOUR DOWNED NETWORKS ARE YOURS AGAIN. THE HACKERS FROM ROXXON HAVE JUST BEEN HACKED THEMSELVES.
ROXXON
AH, I DO HOPE THIS HELPS. UM...
...MY NAME IS BROO BY THE WAY.
THIS IS GORILLA-MAN, AGENT OF WAKANDA! ROXXON ISN'T GIVING UP ANTARCTICA WITHOUT A FIGHT!
THEY JUST DEPLOYED THEIR HULKED-OUT SUPER-SOLDIERS, THE B.E.R.S.E.R.K.E.R. SQUAD! IN OTHER WORDS--SOMEBODY HELP!
COPY THAT, KEN. AND DON'T WORRY.
WE'RE DEPLOYING OUR GODS.
KA-ZAR, THE LORD OF THE SAVAGE LAND, AND THE DAYWALKER KNOWN AS BLADE ARE BOTH USED TO UNUSUAL HUNTS.
BUT TODAY THEY HUNT ALONGSIDE THE GODS OF THE VANIR, THE IMMORTAL LORDS AND LADIES OF MYSTERIOUS VANAHEIM.
THEIR PREY? THE MOST DANGEROUS FORCE IN ALL THE REALMS.

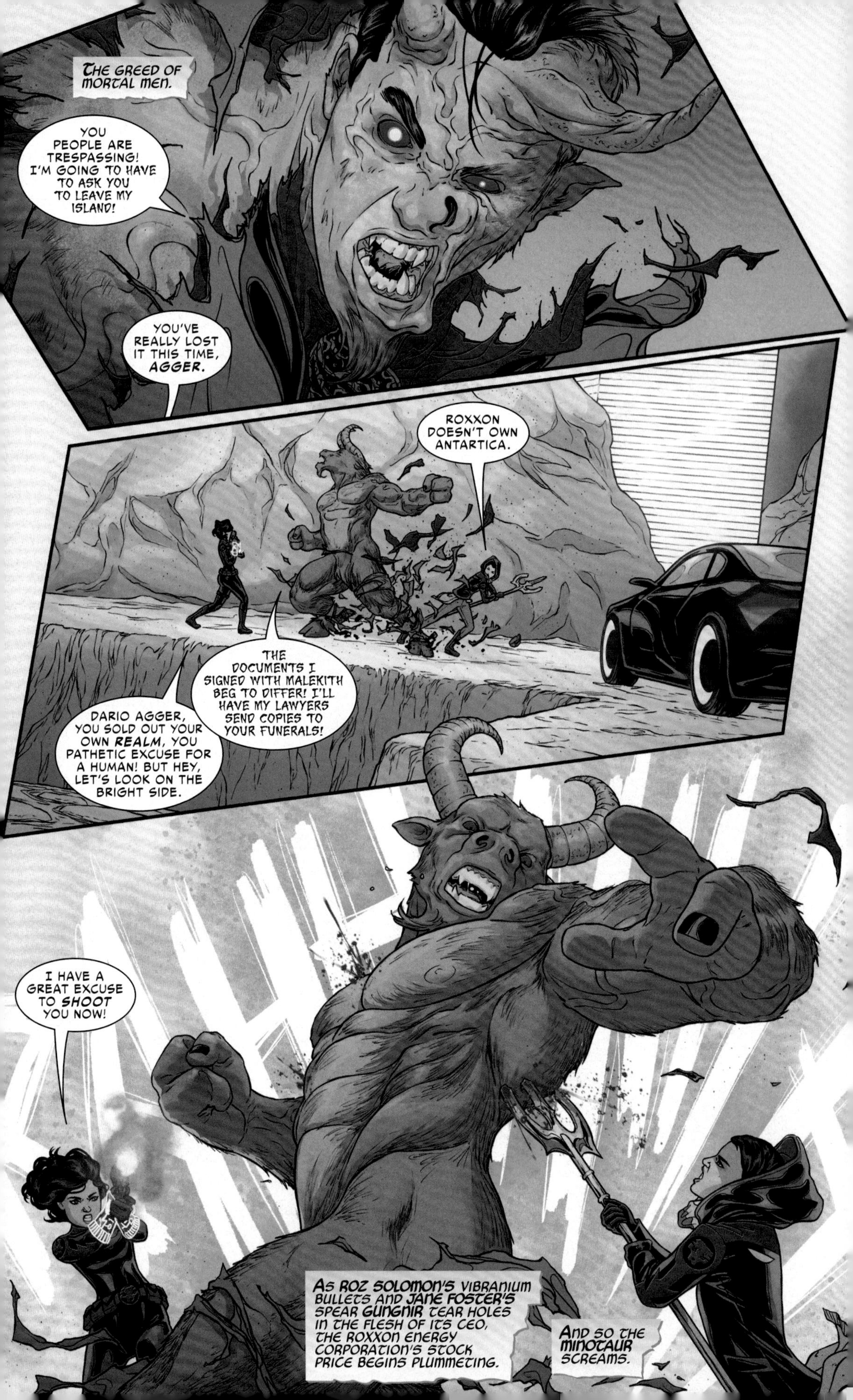
THE GREED OF MORTAL MEN.
YOU PEOPLE ARE TRESPASSING! I'M GOING TO HAVE TO ASK YOU TO LEAVE MY ISLAND!
YOU'VE REALLY LOST IT THIS TIME, AGGER.
ROXXON DOESN'T OWN ANTARTICA.
THE DOCUMENTS I SIGNED WITH MALEKITH BEG TO DIFFER! I'LL HAVE MY LAWYERS SEND COPIES TO YOUR FUNERALS!
DARIO AGGER, YOU SOLD OUT YOUR OWN REALM, YOU PATHETIC EXCUSE FOR A HUMAN! BUT HEY, LET'S LOOK ON THE BRIGHT SIDE.
I HAVE A GREAT EXCUSE TO SHOOT YOU NOW!
AS ROZ SOLOMON'S VIBRANIUM BULLETS AND JANE FOSTER'S SPEAR GUNGNIR TEAR HOLES IN THE FLESH OF ITS CEO, THE ROXXON ENERGY CORPORATION'S STOCK PRICE BEGINS PLUMMETING.
AND SO THE MINOTAUR SCREAMS.

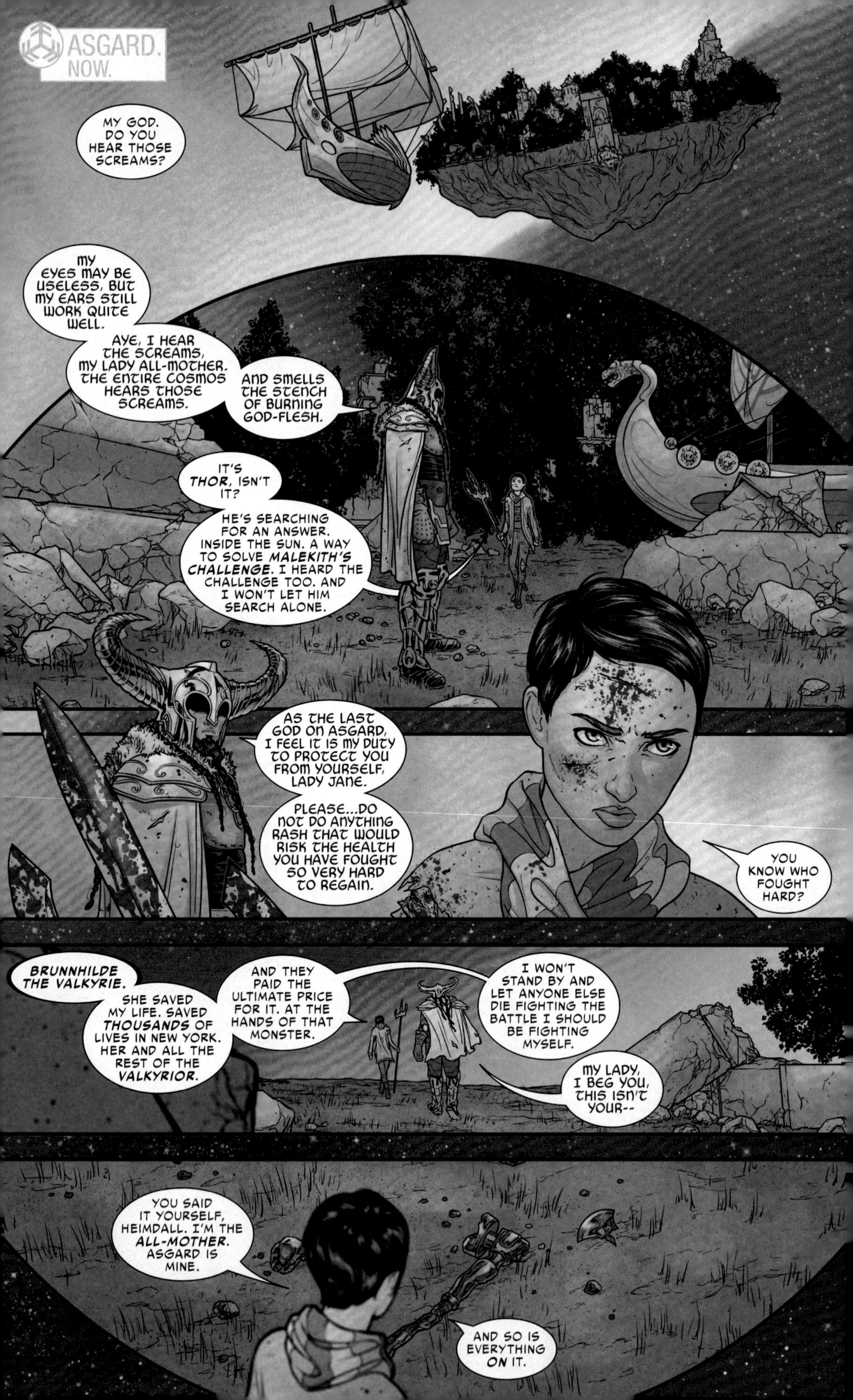
ASGARD. NOW.
MY GOD. DO YOU HEAR THOSE SCREAMS?
MY EYES MAY BE USELESS, BUT MY EARS STILL WORK QUITE WELL.
AYE, I HEAR THE SCREAMS, MY LADY ALL-MOTHER. THE ENTIRE COSMOS HEARS THOSE SCREAMS.
AND SMELLS THE STENCH OF BURNING GOD-FLESH.
IT'S THOR, ISN'T IT?
HE'S SEARCHING FOR AN ANSWER. INSIDE THE SUN. A WAY TO SOLVE MALEKITH'S CHALLENGE. I HEARD THE CHALLENGE TOO. AND I WON'T LET HIM SEARCH ALONE.
AS THE LAST GOD ON ASGARD, I FEEL IT IS MY DUTY TO PROTECT YOU FROM YOURSELF, LADY JANE.
PLEASE...DO NOT DO ANYTHING RASH THAT WOULD RISK THE HEALTH YOU HAVE FOUGHT SO VERY HARD TO REGAIN.
YOU KNOW WHO FOUGHT HARD?
BRUNNHILDE THE VALKYRIE.
SHE SAVED MY LIFE. SAVED THOUSANDS OF LIVES IN NEW YORK. HER AND ALL THE REST OF THE VALKYRIOR.
AND THEY PAID THE ULTIMATE PRICE FOR IT. AT THE HANDS OF THAT MONSTER.
I WON'T STAND BY AND LET ANYONE ELSE DIE FIGHTING THE BATTLE I SHOULD BE FIGHTING MYSELF.
MY LADY, I BEG YOU, THIS ISN'T YOUR--
YOU SAID IT YOURSELF, HEIMDALL. I'M THE ALL-MOTHER. ASGARD IS MINE.
AND SO IS EVERYTHING ON IT.

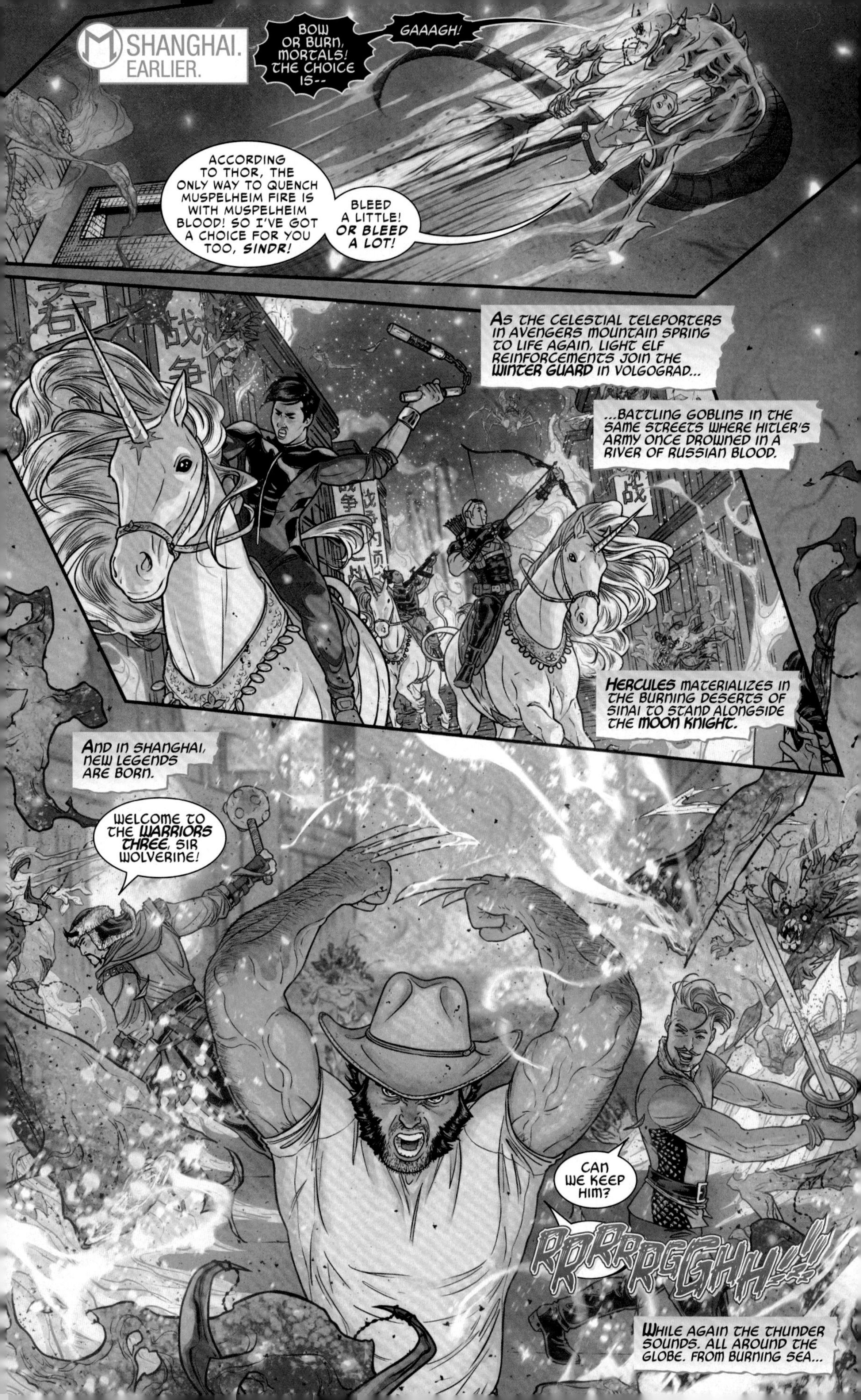
SHANGHAI. EARLIER.
BOW OR BURN, MORTALS! THE CHOICE IS--
GAAAGH!
ACCORDING TO THOR, THE ONLY WAY TO QUENCH MUSPELHEIM FIRE IS WITH MUSPELHEIM BLOOD! SO I'VE GOT A CHOICE FOR YOU TOO, SINDR!
BLEED A LITTLE! OR BLEED A LOT!
AS THE CELESTIAL TELEPORTERS IN AVENGERS MOUNTAIN SPRING TO LIFE AGAIN, LIGHT ELF REINFORCEMENTS JOIN THE WINTER GUARD IN VOLGOGRAD...
...BATTLING GOBLINS IN THE SAME STREETS WHERE HITLER'S ARMY ONCE DROWNED IN A RIVER OF RUSSIAN BLOOD.
HERCULES MATERIALIZES IN THE BURNING DESERTS OF SINAI TO STAND ALONGSIDE THE MOON KNIGHT.
AND IN SHANGHAI, NEW LEGENDS ARE BORN.
WELCOME TO THE WARRIORS THREE, SIR WOLVERINE!
CAN WE KEEP HIM?
RRRRRGHH!!
WHILE AGAIN THE THUNDER SOUNDS. ALL AROUND THE GLOBE. FROM BURNING SEA...

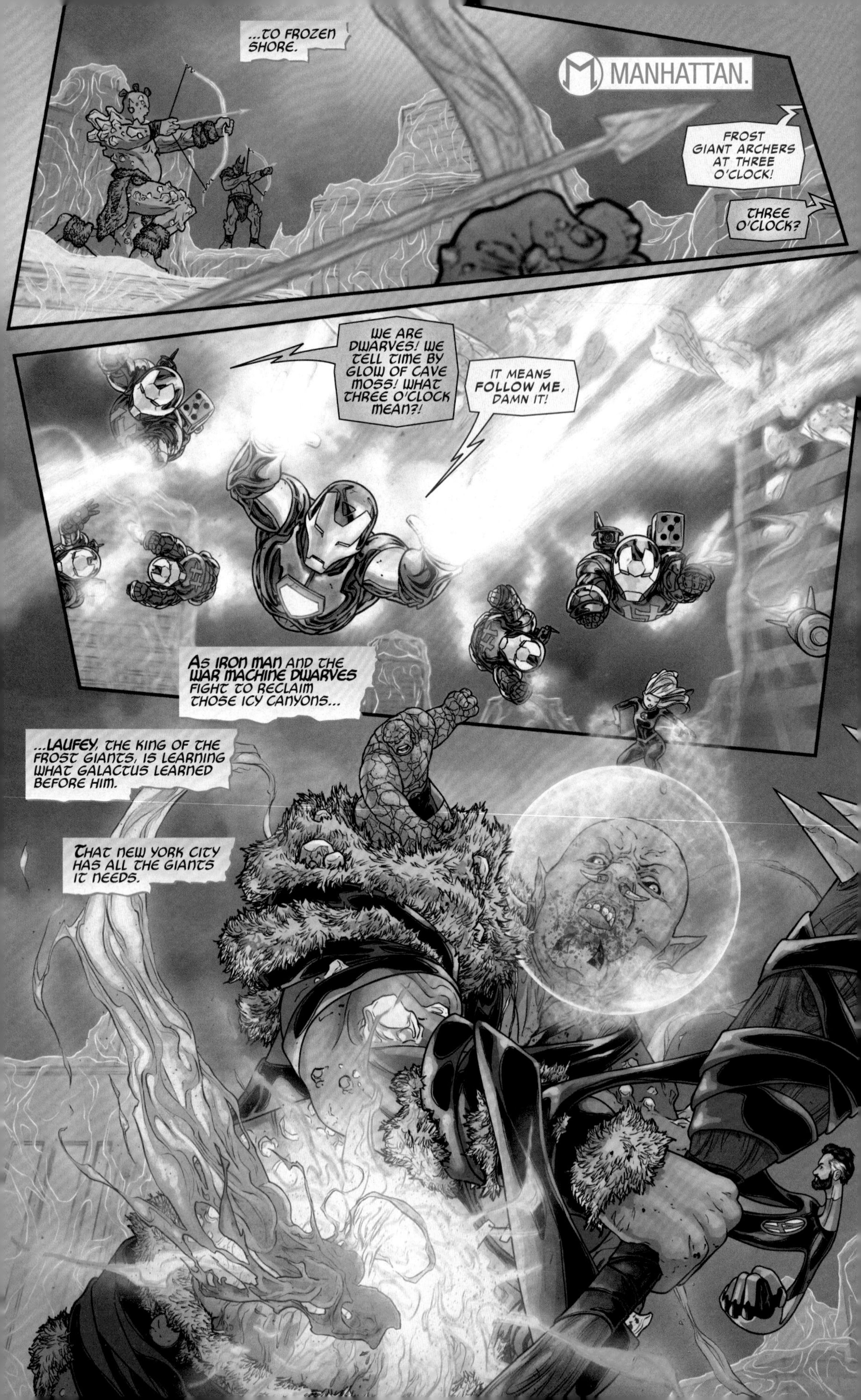
...TO FROZEN SHORE.
MANHATTAN.
FROST GIANT ARCHERS AT THREE O'CLOCK!
THREE O'CLOCK?
WE ARE DWARVES! WE TELL TIME BY GLOW OF CAVE MOSS! WHAT THREE O'CLOCK MEAN?!
IT MEANS FOLLOW ME, DAMN IT!
AS IRON MAN AND THE WAR MACHINE DWARVES FIGHT TO RECLAIM THOSE ICY CANYONS...
...LAUFEY, THE KING OF THE FROST GIANTS, IS LEARNING WHAT GALACTUS LEARNED BEFORE HIM.
THAT NEW YORK CITY HAS ALL THE GIANTS IT NEEDS.

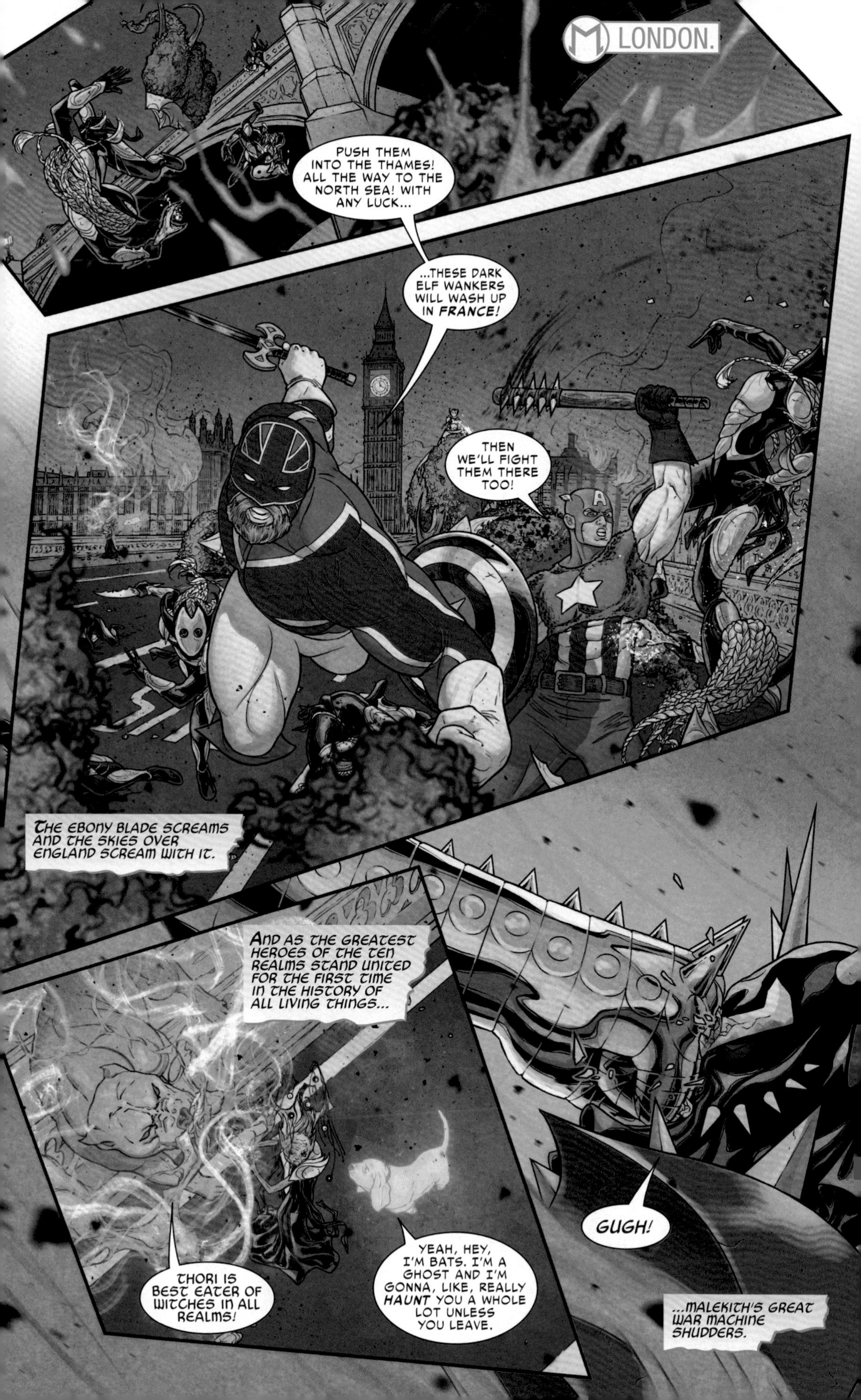
LONDON.
PUSH THEM INTO THE THAMES! ALL THE WAY TO THE NORTH SEA! WITH ANY LUCK...
...THESE DARK ELF WANKERS WILL WASH UP IN FRANCE!
THEN WE'LL FIGHT THEM THERE TOO!
THE EBONY BLADE SCREAMS AND THE SKIES OVER ENGLAND SCREAM WITH IT.
AND AS THE GREATEST HEROES OF THE TEN REALMS STAND UNITED FOR THE FIRST TIME IN THE HISTORY OF ALL LIVING THINGS...
THORI IS BEST EATER OF WITCHES IN ALL REALMS!
YEAH, HEY, I'M BATS. I'M A GHOST AND I'M GONNA, LIKE, REALLY HAUNT YOU A WHOLE LOT UNLESS YOU LEAVE.
GUGH!
...MALEKITH'S GREAT WAR MACHINE SHUDDERS.

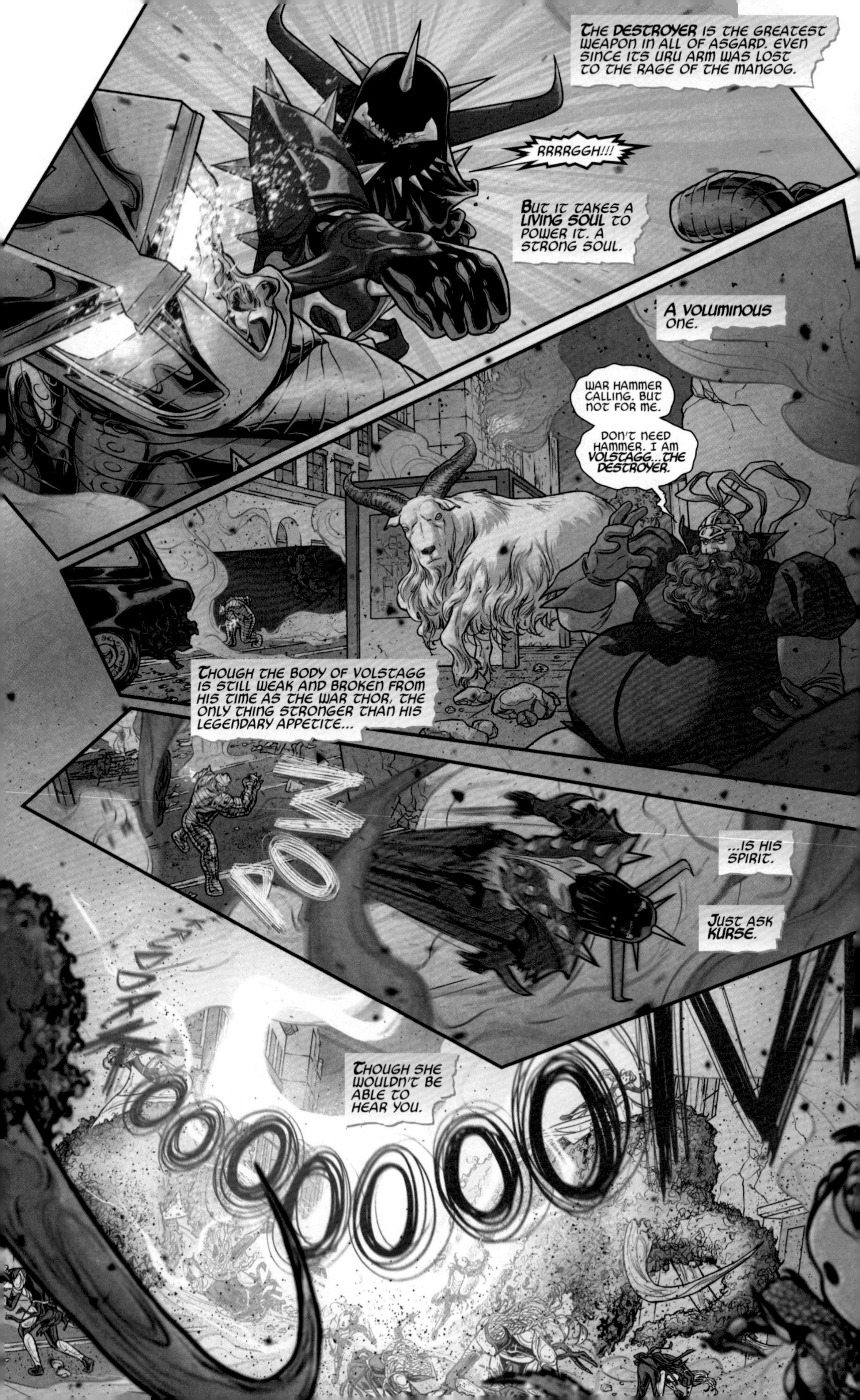
THE DESTROYER IS THE GREATEST WEAPON IN ALL OF ASGARD. EVEN SINCE ITS URU ARM WAS LOST TO THE RAGE OF THE MANGOG.
RRRRGGH!!!
BUT IT TAKES A LIVING SOUL TO POWER IT. A STRONG SOUL.
A VOLUMINOUS ONE.
WAR HAMMER CALLING. BUT NOT FOR ME.
DON'T NEED HAMMER. I AM VOLSTAGG...THE DESTROYER.
THOUGH THE BODY OF VOLSTAGG IS STILL WEAK AND BROKEN FROM HIS TIME AS THE WAR THOR, THE ONLY THING STRONGER THAN HIS LEGENDARY APPETITE...
POW
...IS HIS SPIRIT.
JUST ASK KURSE.
THOUGH SHE WOULDN'T BE ABLE TO HEAR YOU.

IN THE SKIES ABOVE EVERY BATTLEFIELD ALL ACROSS THE WORLD, THE SAME STORM RAGES.

THE SAME SPEARS OF LIGHTNING FALL FROM HEAVEN.

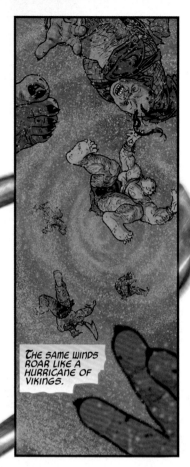

THE SAME WINDS ROAR LIKE A HURRICANE OF VIKINGS.

IT IS A STORM THE SIZE OF A REALM.

WRAPPING MIDGARD IN ITS MIGHTY ARMS.

GOOD TO HAVE YOU BACK, BIG GUY.

A STORM THAT RAINS BLOOD AND URU.

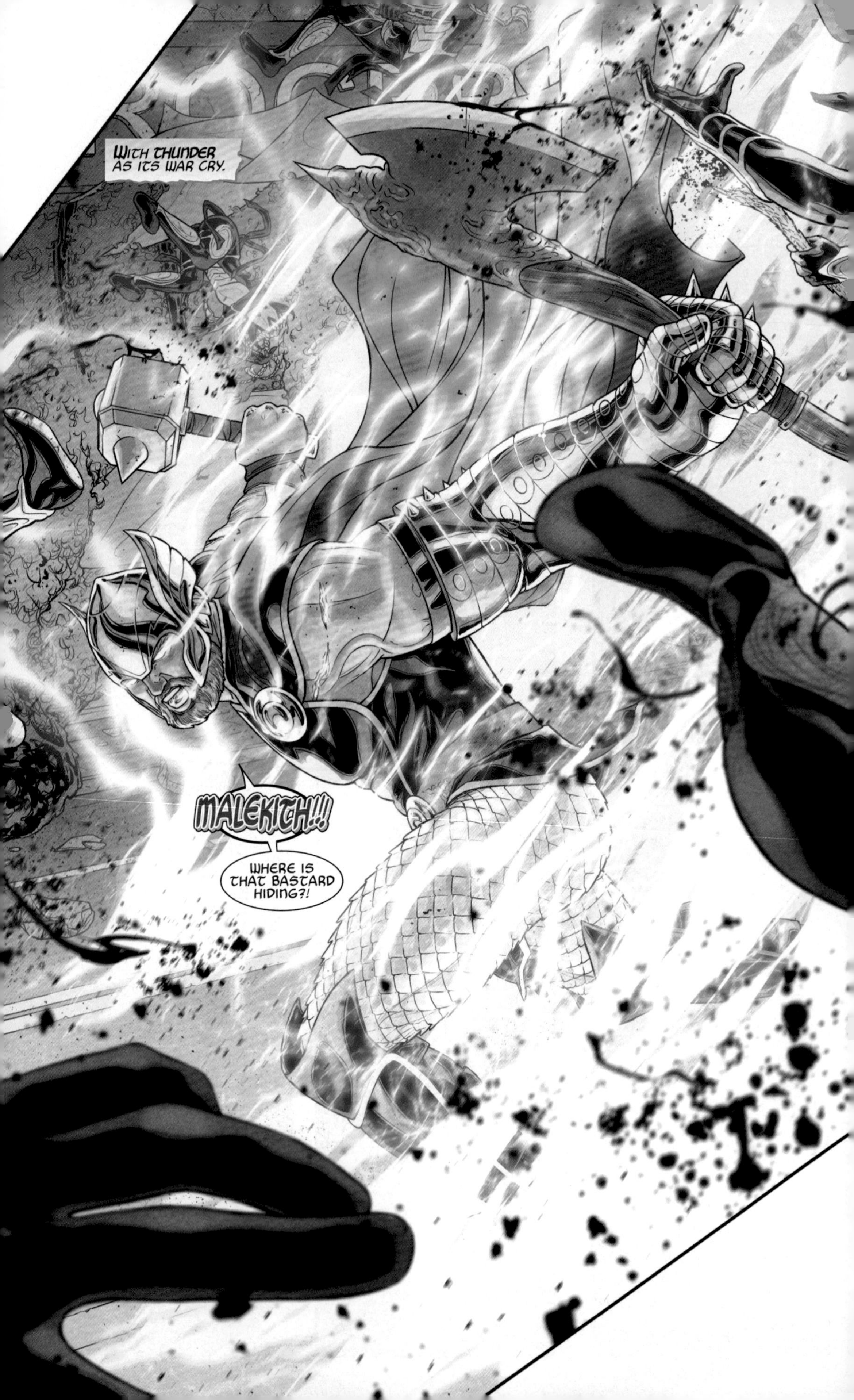
WITH THUNDER AS ITS WAR CRY.
MALEKITH!!!
WHERE IS THAT BASTARD HIDING?!

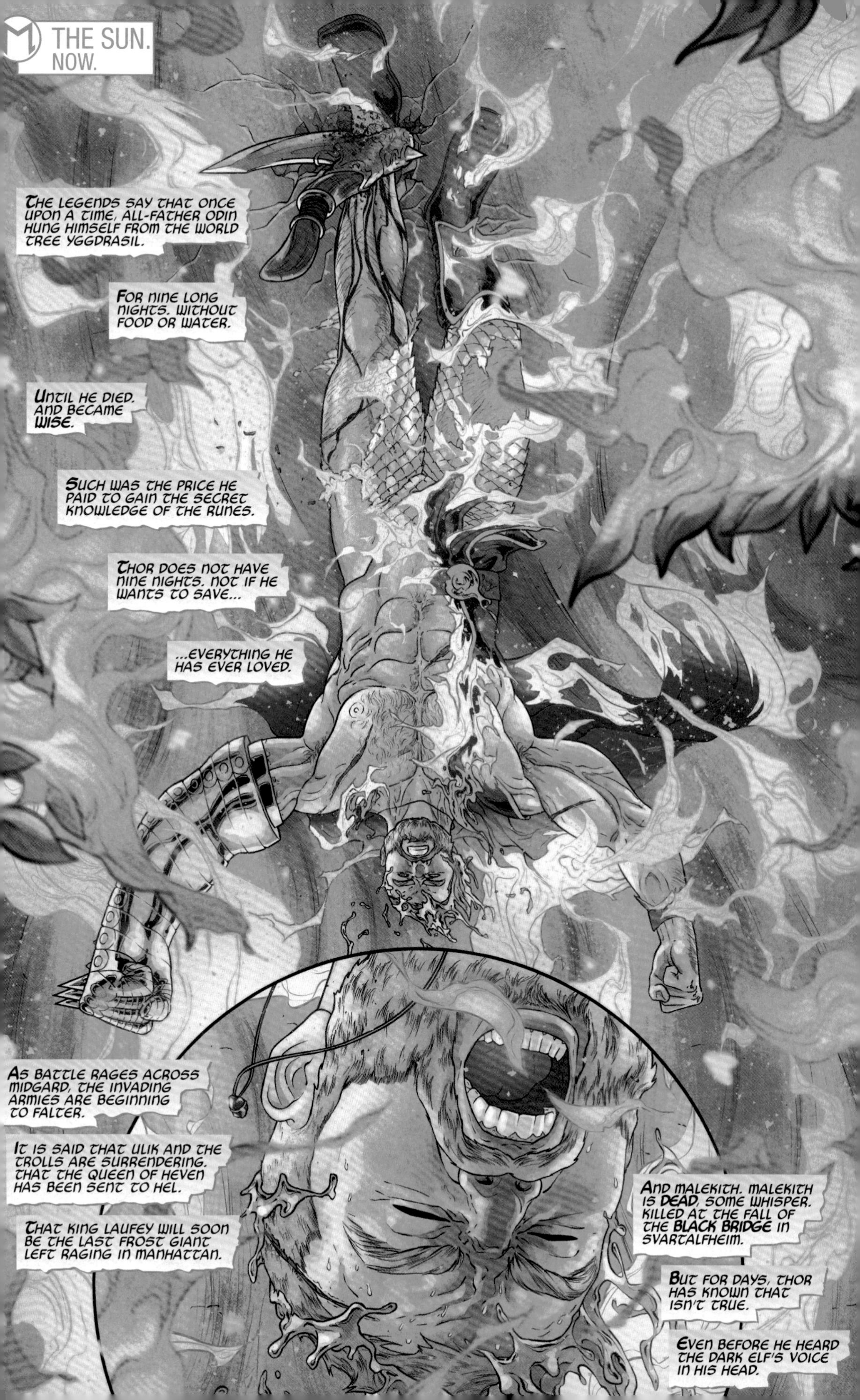

THE SUN. NOW.
THE LEGENDS SAY THAT ONCE UPON A TIME, ALL-FATHER ODIN HUNG HIMSELF FROM THE WORLD TREE YGGDRASIL.
FOR NINE LONG NIGHTS. WITHOUT FOOD OR WATER.
UNTIL HE DIED. AND BECAME WISE.
SUCH WAS THE PRICE HE PAID TO GAIN THE SECRET KNOWLEDGE OF THE RUNES.
THOR DOES NOT HAVE NINE NIGHTS. NOT IF HE WANTS TO SAVE...
...EVERYTHING HE HAS EVER LOVED.
AS BATTLE RAGES ACROSS MIDGARD, THE INVADING ARMIES ARE BEGINNING TO FALTER.
IT IS SAID THAT ULIK AND THE TROLLS ARE SURRENDERING. THAT THE QUEEN OF HEVEN HAS BEEN SENT TO HEL.
THAT KING LAUFEY WILL SOON BE THE LAST FROST GIANT LEFT RAGING IN MANHATTAN.
AND MALEKITH. MALEKITH IS DEAD, SOME WHISPER. KILLED AT THE FALL OF THE BLACK BRIDGE IN SVARTALFHEIM.
BUT FOR DAYS, THOR HAS KNOWN THAT ISN'T TRUE.
EVEN BEFORE HE HEARD THE DARK ELF'S VOICE IN HIS HEAD.

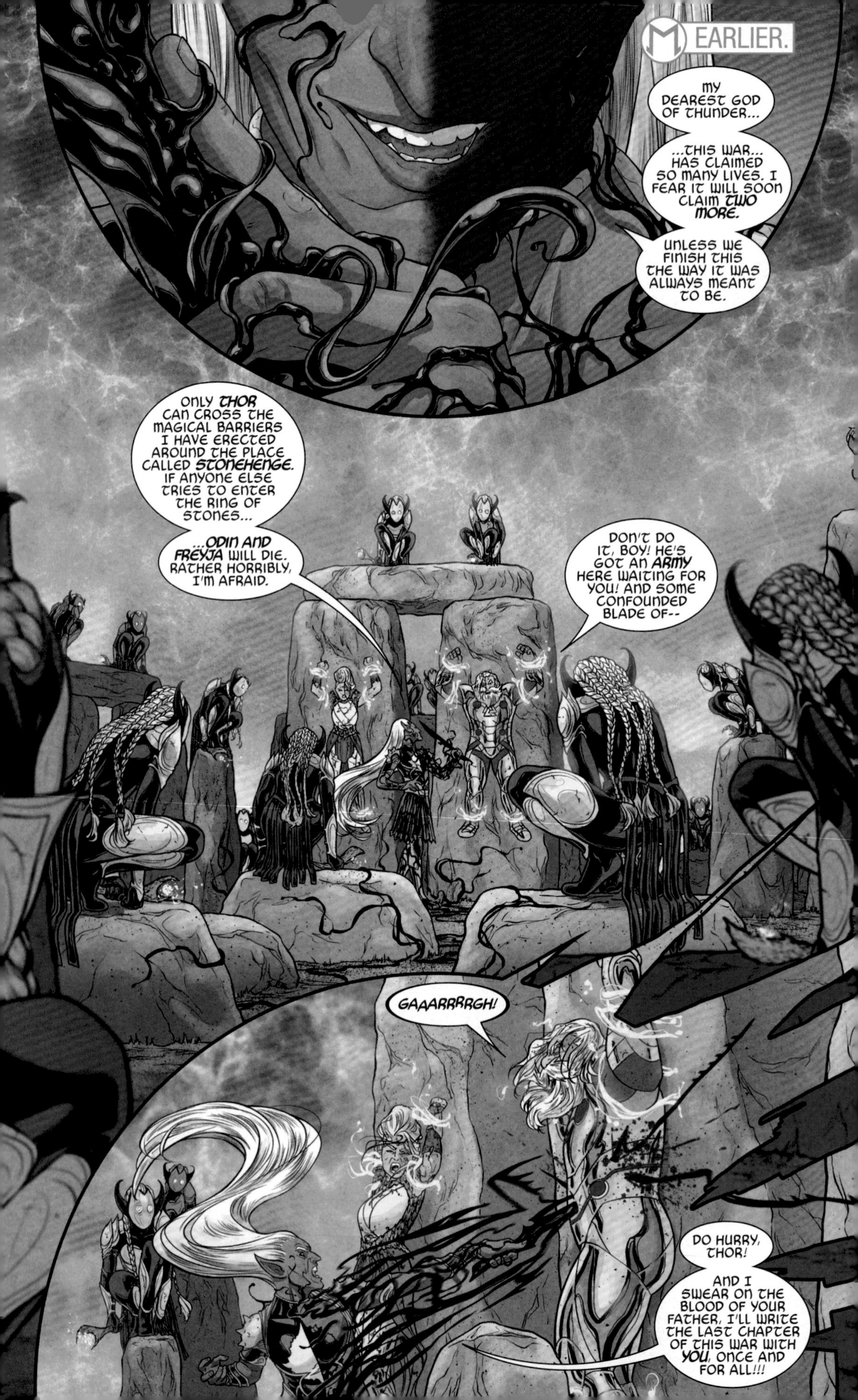
EARLIER.
MY DEAREST GOD OF THUNDER...
...THIS WAR... HAS CLAIMED SO MANY LIVES. I FEAR IT WILL SOON CLAIM TWO MORE.
UNLESS WE FINISH THIS THE WAY IT WAS ALWAYS MEANT TO BE.
ONLY THOR CAN CROSS THE MAGICAL BARRIERS I HAVE ERECTED AROUND THE PLACE CALLED STONEHENGE. IF ANYONE ELSE TRIES TO ENTER THE RING OF STONES...
...ODIN AND FREYJA WILL DIE. RATHER HORRIBLY, I'M AFRAID.
DON'T DO IT, BOY! HE'S GOT AN ARMY HERE WAITING FOR YOU! AND SOME CONFOUNDED BLADE OF--
GAAARRRRGH!
DO HURRY, THOR!
AND I SWEAR ON THE BLOOD OF YOUR FATHER, I'LL WRITE THE LAST CHAPTER OF THIS WAR WITH YOU, ONCE AND FOR ALL!!!

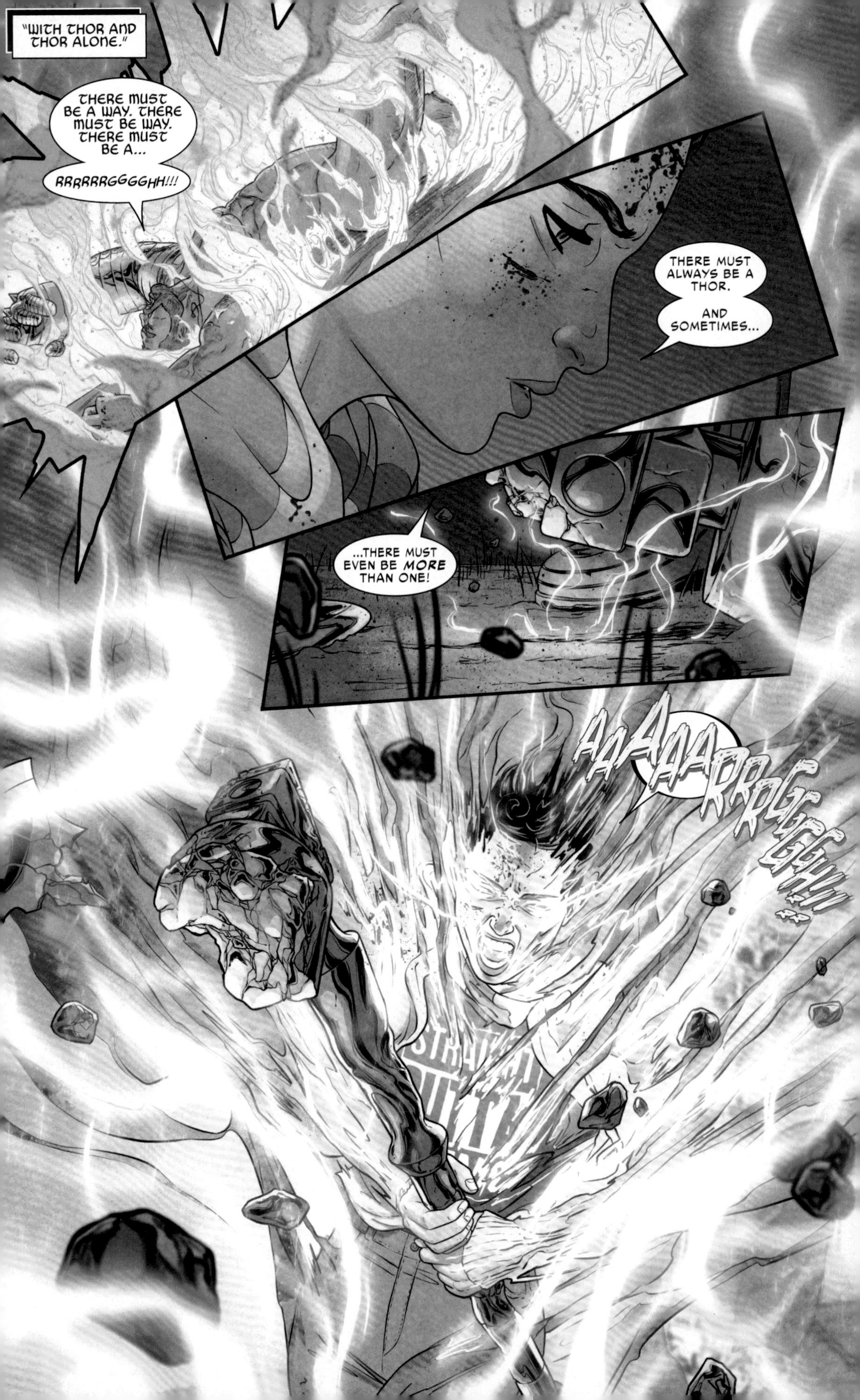
"WITH THOR AND THOR ALONE."
THERE MUST BE A WAY. THERE MUST BE WAY. THERE MUST BE A...
RRRRRRGGGGHH!!!
THERE MUST ALWAYS BE A THOR.
AND SOMETIMES...
...THERE MUST EVEN BE MORE THAN ONE!
AAAAAARRRGGGGGHH!!!

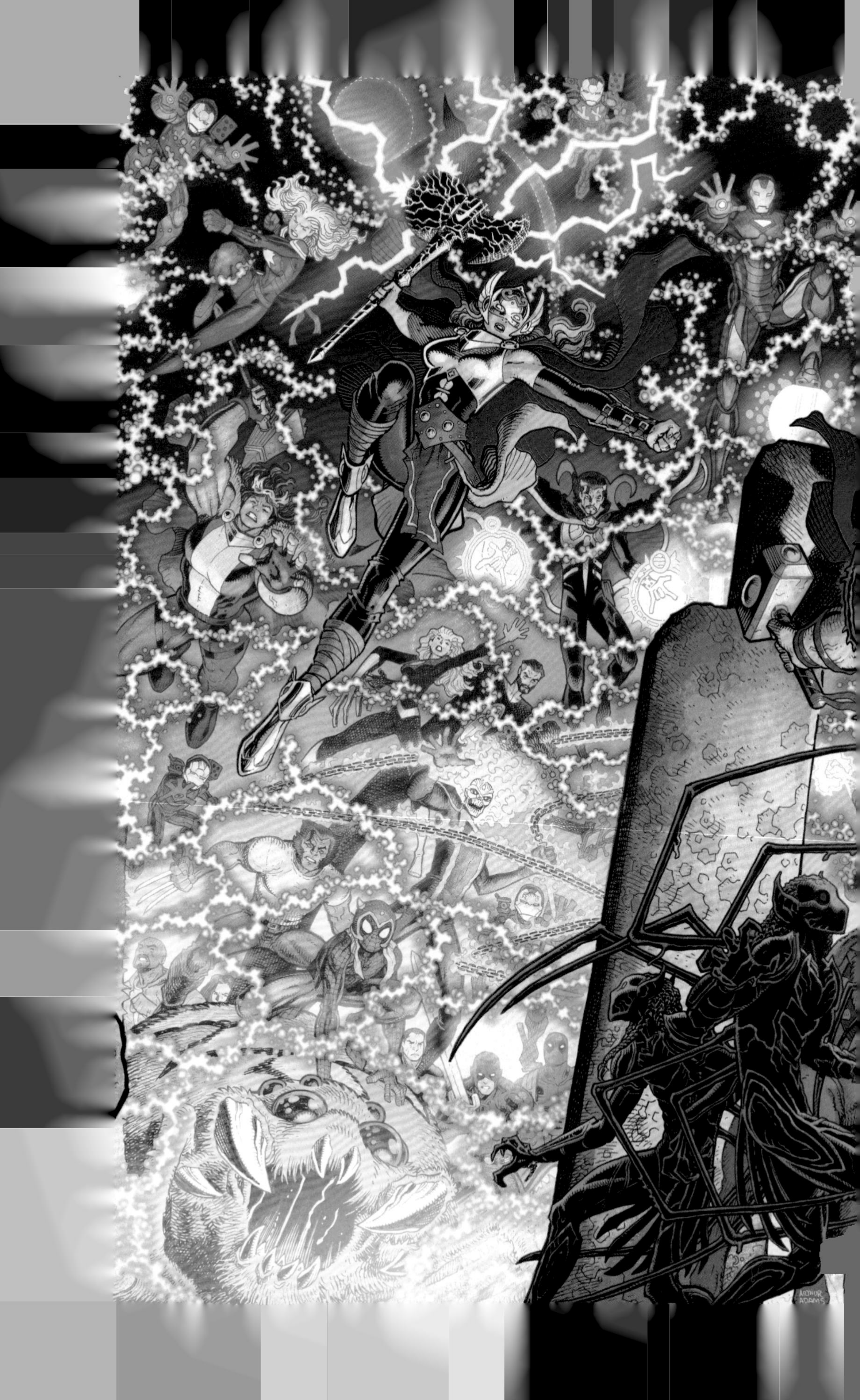

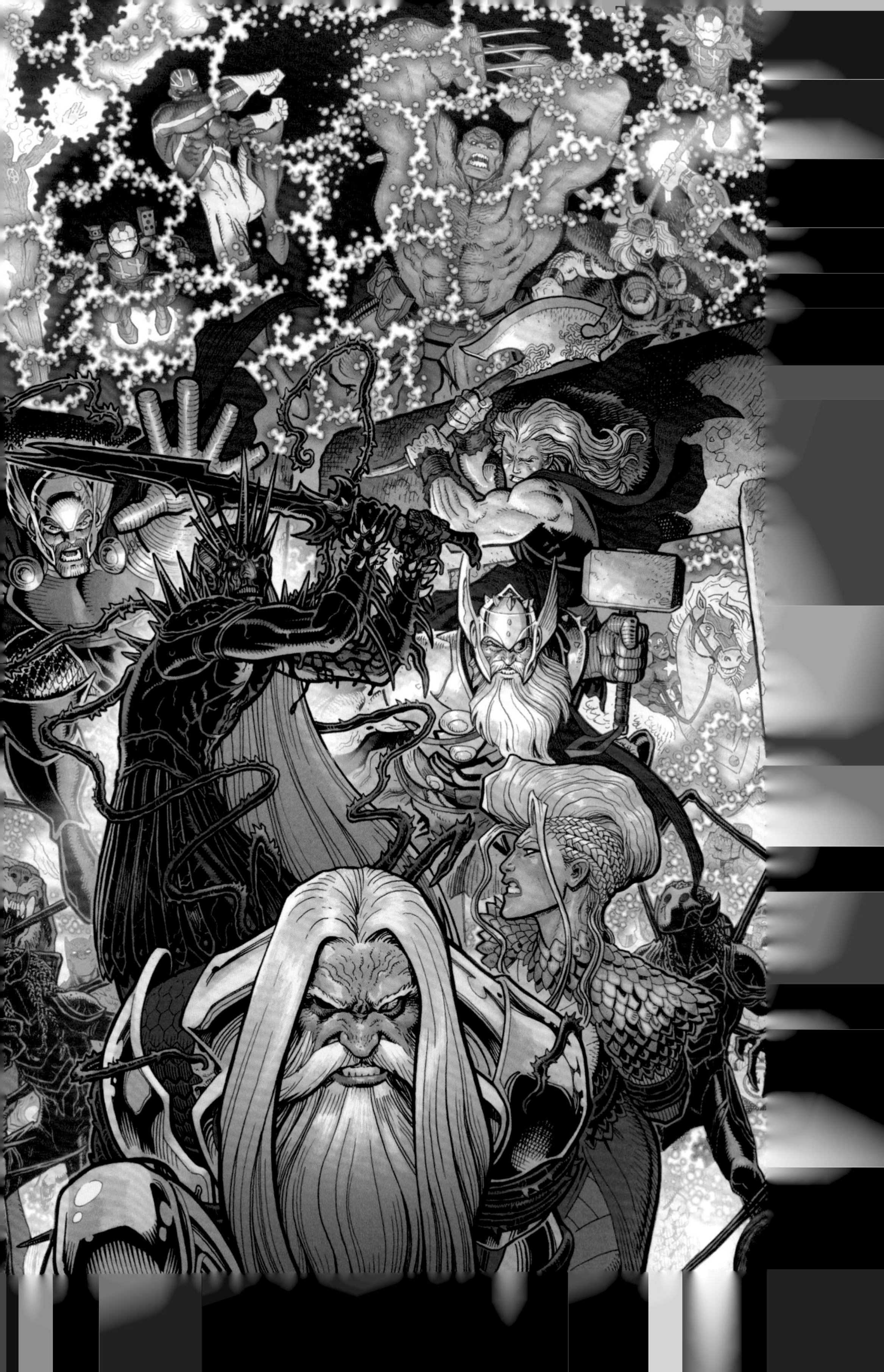

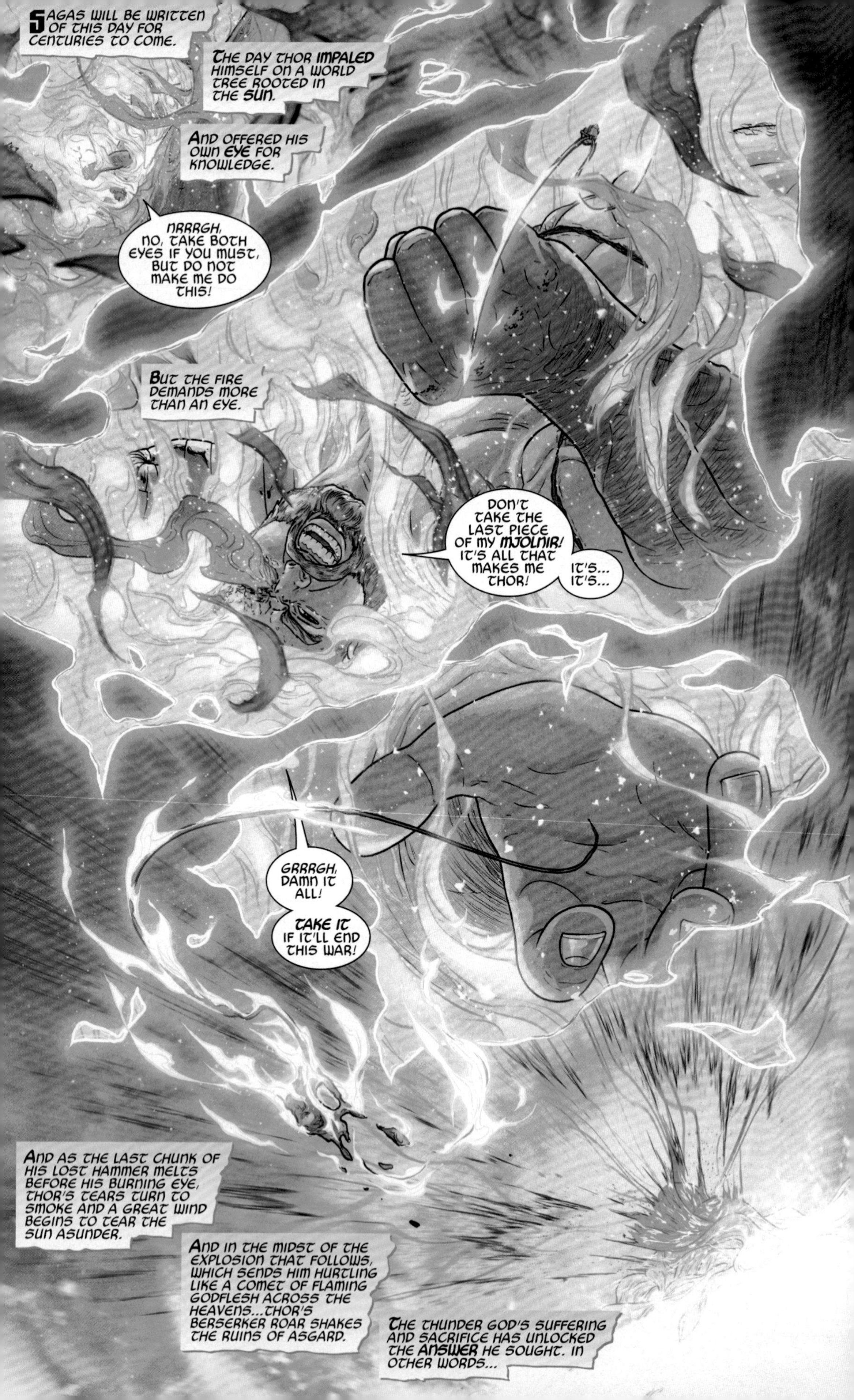

SAGAS WILL BE WRITTEN OF THIS DAY FOR CENTURIES TO COME.
THE DAY THOR IMPALED HIMSELF ON A WORLD TREE ROOTED IN THE SUN.
AND OFFERED HIS OWN EYE FOR KNOWLEDGE.
NRRRGH, NO, TAKE BOTH EYES IF YOU MUST, BUT DO NOT MAKE ME DO THIS!
BUT THE FIRE DEMANDS MORE THAN AN EYE.
DON'T TAKE THE LAST PIECE OF MY MJOLNIR! IT'S ALL THAT MAKES ME THOR!
IT'S... IT'S...
GRRRGH, DAMN IT ALL!
TAKE IT IF IT'LL END THIS WAR!
AND AS THE LAST CHUNK OF HIS LOST HAMMER MELTS BEFORE HIS BURNING EYE, THOR'S TEARS TURN TO SMOKE AND A GREAT WIND BEGINS TO TEAR THE SUN ASUNDER.
AND IN THE MIDST OF THE EXPLOSION THAT FOLLOWS, WHICH SENDS HIM HURTLING LIKE A COMET OF FLAMING GODFLESH ACROSS THE HEAVENS...THOR'S BERSERKER ROAR SHAKES THE RUINS OF ASGARD.
THE THUNDER GOD'S SUFFERING AND SACRIFICE HAS UNLOCKED THE ANSWER HE SOUGHT. IN OTHER WORDS...

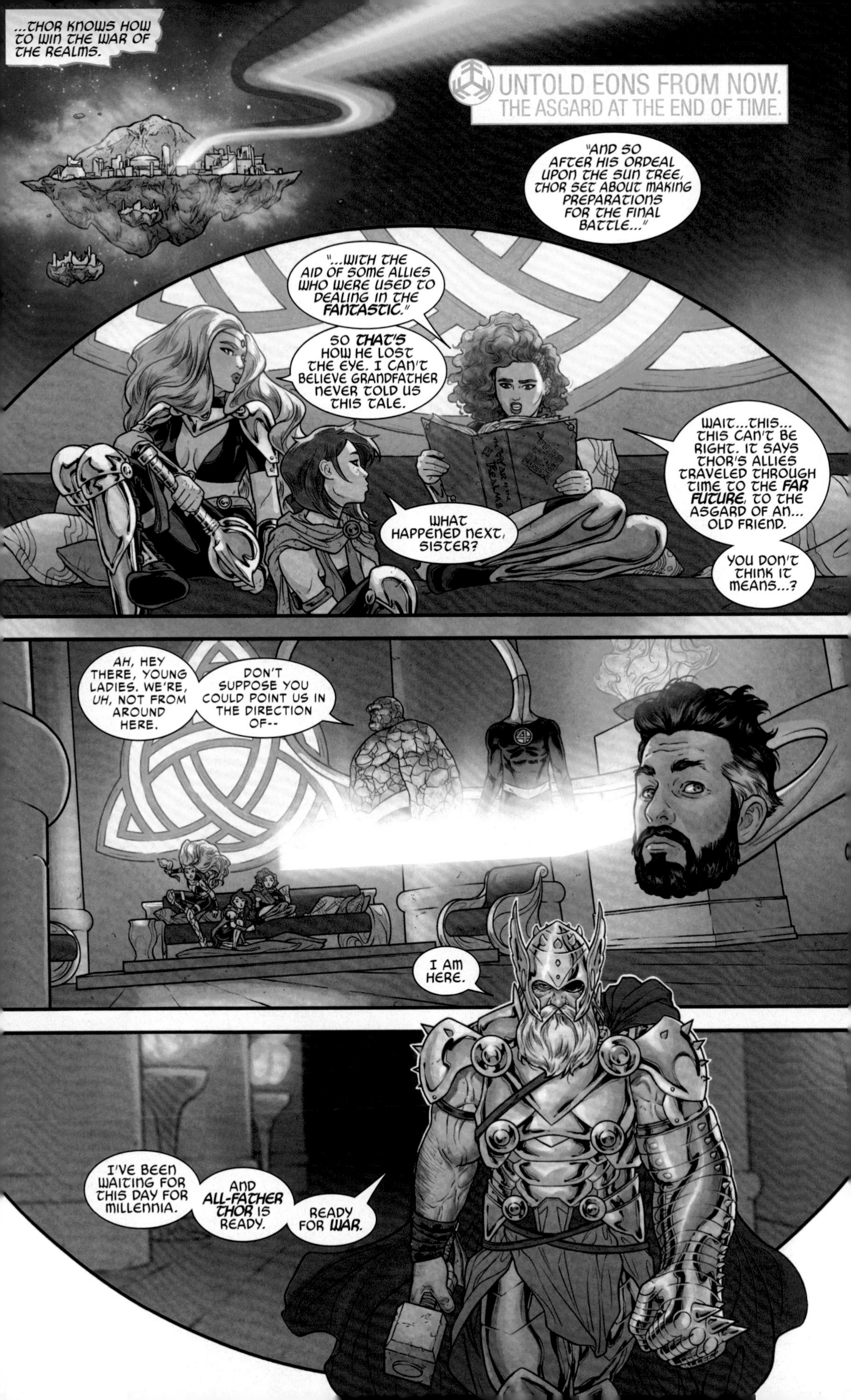
...THOR KNOWS HOW TO WIN THE WAR OF THE REALMS.
UNTOLD EONS FROM NOW.
THE ASGARD AT THE END OF TIME.
"AND SO AFTER HIS ORDEAL UPON THE SUN TREE, THOR SET ABOUT MAKING PREPARATIONS FOR THE FINAL BATTLE..."
"...WITH THE AID OF SOME ALLIES WHO WERE USED TO DEALING IN THE FANTASTIC."
SO THAT'S HOW HE LOST THE EYE. I CAN'T BELIEVE GRANDFATHER NEVER TOLD US THIS TALE.
WHAT HAPPENED NEXT, SISTER?
WAIT...THIS... THIS CAN'T BE RIGHT. IT SAYS THOR'S ALLIES TRAVELED THROUGH TIME TO THE FAR FUTURE, TO THE ASGARD OF AN... OLD FRIEND.
YOU DON'T THINK IT MEANS...?
AH, HEY THERE, YOUNG LADIES. WE'RE, UH, NOT FROM AROUND HERE.
DON'T SUPPOSE YOU COULD POINT US IN THE DIRECTION OF--
I AM HERE.
I'VE BEEN WAITING FOR THIS DAY FOR MILLENNIA.
AND ALL-FATHER THOR IS READY.
READY FOR WAR.

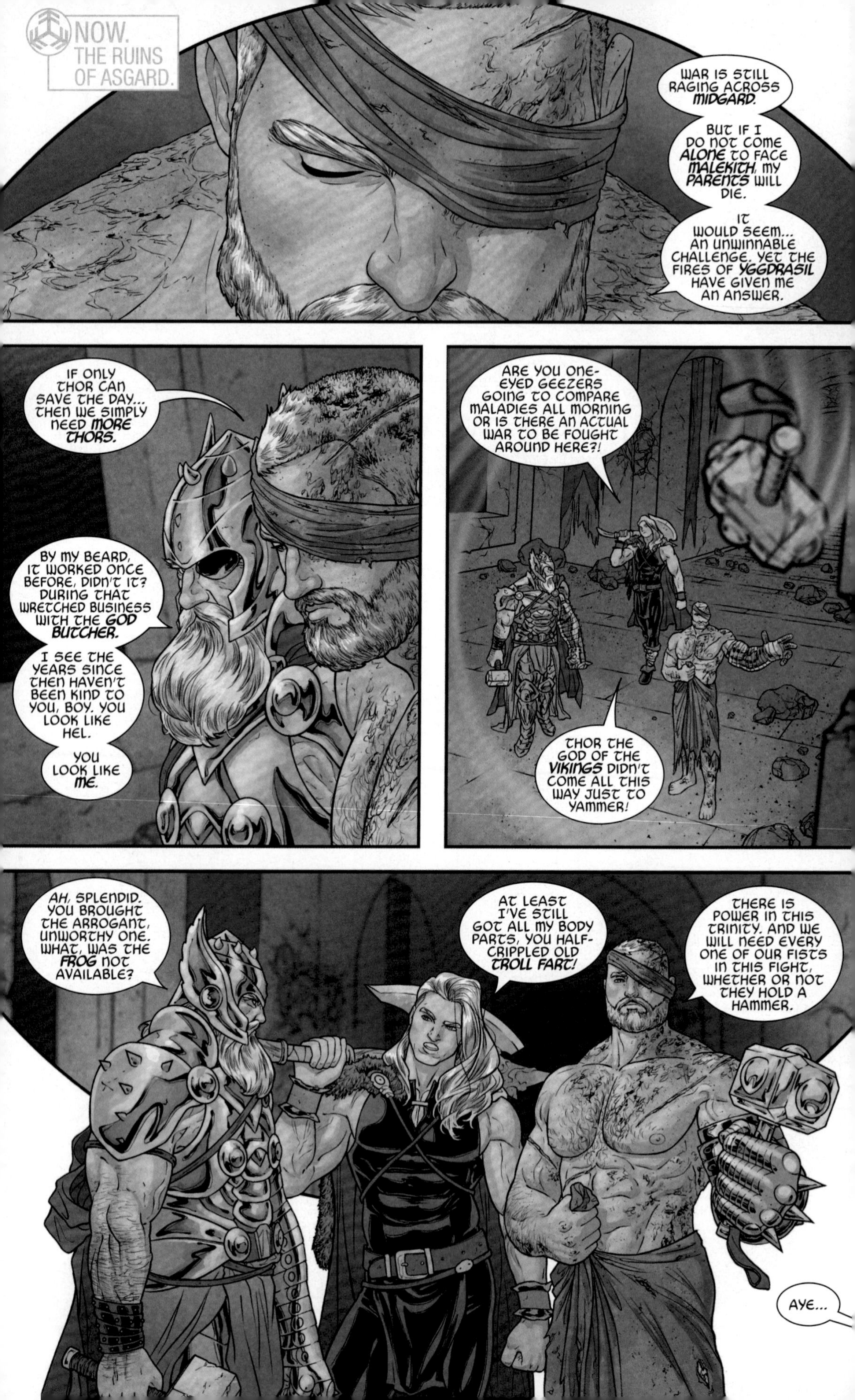
NOW. THE RUINS OF ASGARD.
WAR IS STILL RAGING ACROSS MIDGARD.
BUT IF I DO NOT COME ALONE TO FACE MALEKITH, MY PARENTS WILL DIE.
IT WOULD SEEM... AN UNWINNABLE CHALLENGE. YET THE FIRES OF YGGDRASIL HAVE GIVEN ME AN ANSWER.
IF ONLY THOR CAN SAVE THE DAY... THEN WE SIMPLY NEED MORE THORS.
BY MY BEARD, IT WORKED ONCE BEFORE, DIDN'T IT? DURING THAT WRETCHED BUSINESS WITH THE GOD BUTCHER.
I SEE THE YEARS SINCE THEN HAVEN'T BEEN KIND TO YOU, BOY. YOU LOOK LIKE HEL.
YOU LOOK LIKE ME.
ARE YOU ONE-EYED GEEZERS GOING TO COMPARE MALADIES ALL MORNING OR IS THERE AN ACTUAL WAR TO BE FOUGHT AROUND HERE?!
THOR THE GOD OF THE VIKINGS DIDN'T COME ALL THIS WAY JUST TO YAMMER!
AH, SPLENDID. YOU BROUGHT THE ARROGANT, UNWORTHY ONE. WHAT, WAS THE FROG NOT AVAILABLE?
AT LEAST I'VE STILL GOT ALL MY BODY PARTS, YOU HALF-CRIPPLED OLD TROLL FART!
THERE IS POWER IN THIS TRINITY. AND WE WILL NEED EVERY ONE OF OUR FISTS IN THIS FIGHT, WHETHER OR NOT THEY HOLD A HAMMER.
AYE...

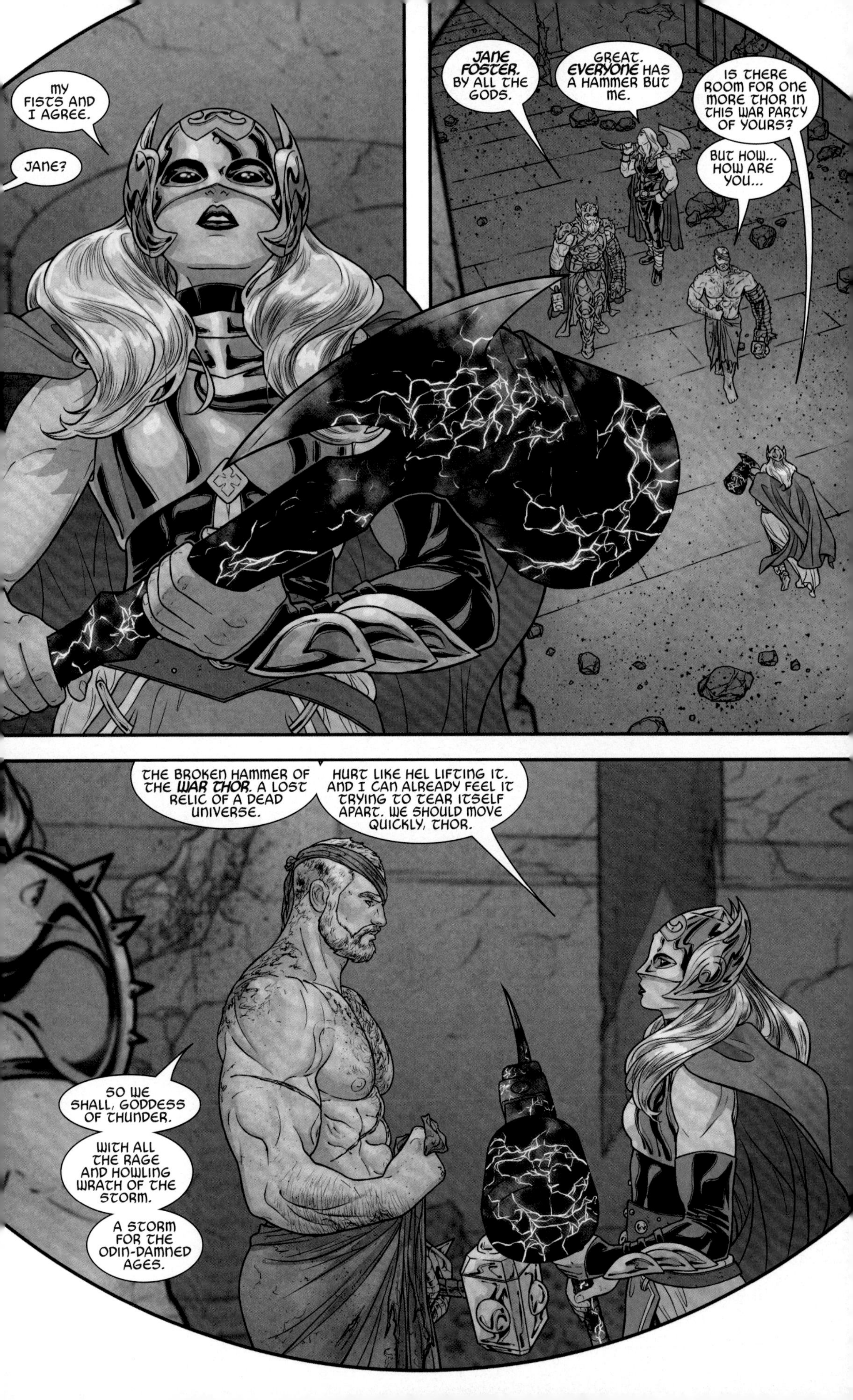

MY FISTS AND I AGREE.
JANE?
JANE FOSTER. BY ALL THE GODS.
GREAT. EVERYONE HAS A HAMMER BUT ME.
IS THERE ROOM FOR ONE MORE THOR IN THIS WAR PARTY OF YOURS?
BUT HOW... HOW ARE YOU...
THE BROKEN HAMMER OF THE WAR THOR. A LOST RELIC OF A DEAD UNIVERSE.
HURT LIKE HEL LIFTING IT. AND I CAN ALREADY FEEL IT TRYING TO TEAR ITSELF APART. WE SHOULD MOVE QUICKLY, THOR.
SO WE SHALL, GODDESS OF THUNDER.
WITH ALL THE RAGE AND HOWLING WRATH OF THE STORM.
A STORM FOR THE ODIN-DAMNED AGES.

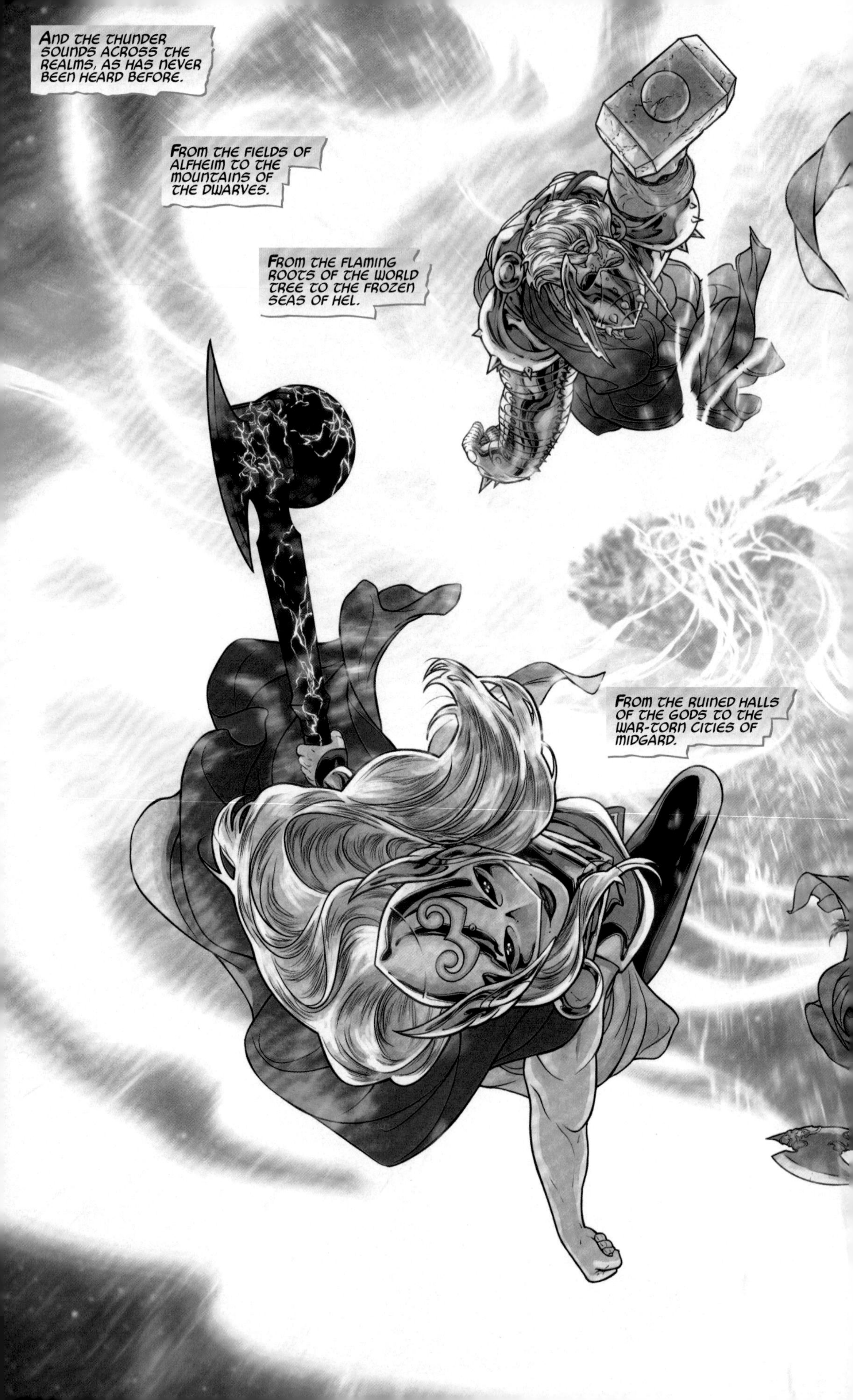
AND THE THUNDER SOUNDS ACROSS THE REALMS, AS HAS NEVER BEEN HEARD BEFORE.
FROM THE FIELDS OF ALFHEIM TO THE MOUNTAINS OF THE DWARVES.
FROM THE FLAMING ROOTS OF THE WORLD TREE TO THE FROZEN SEAS OF HEL.
FROM THE RUINED HALLS OF THE GODS TO THE WAR-TORN CITIES OF MIDGARD.

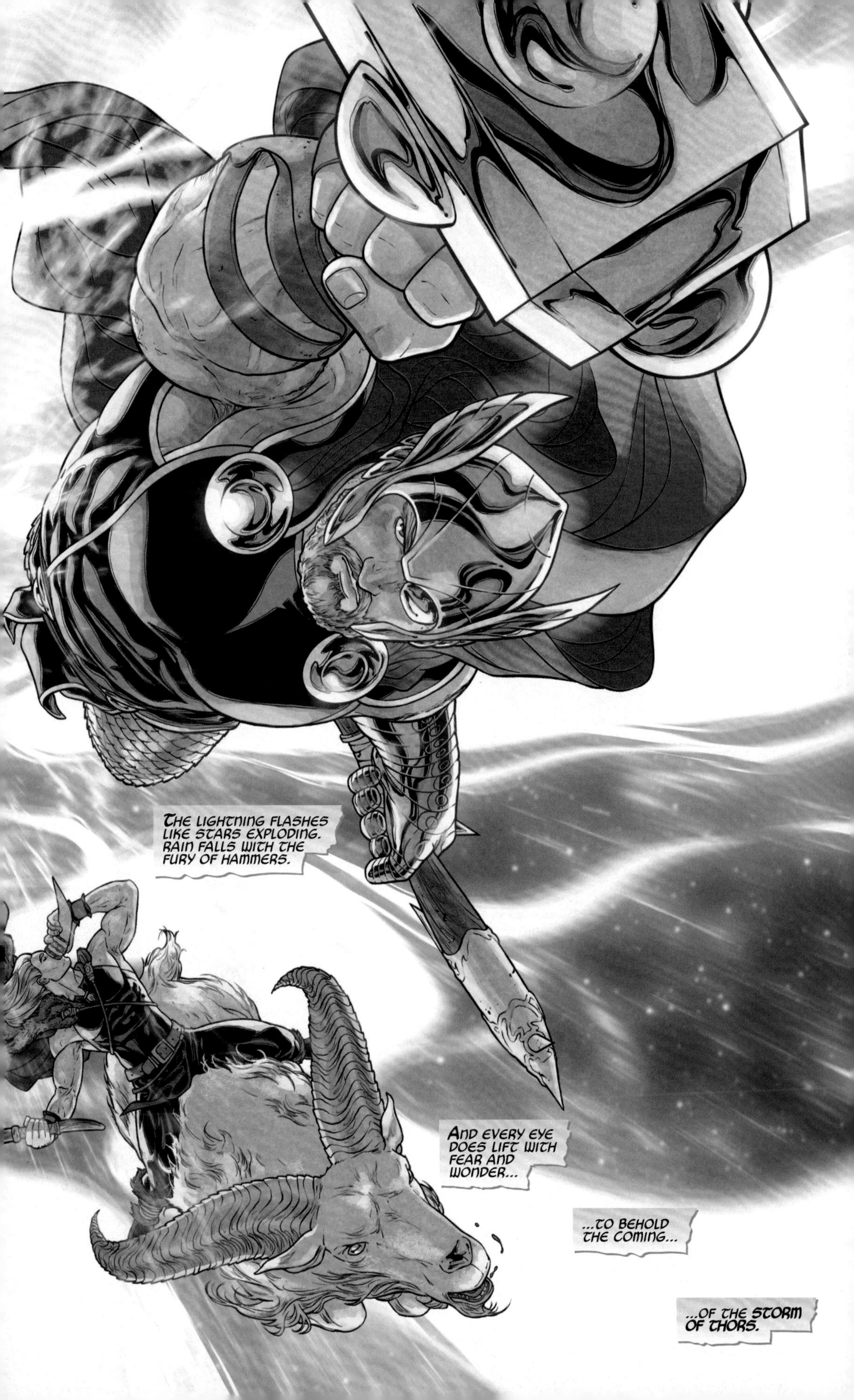

THE LIGHTNING FLASHES LIKE STARS EXPLODING. RAIN FALLS WITH THE FURY OF HAMMERS.
AND EVERY EYE DOES LIFT WITH FEAR AND WONDER...
...TO BEHOLD THE COMING...
...OF THE STORM OF THORS.

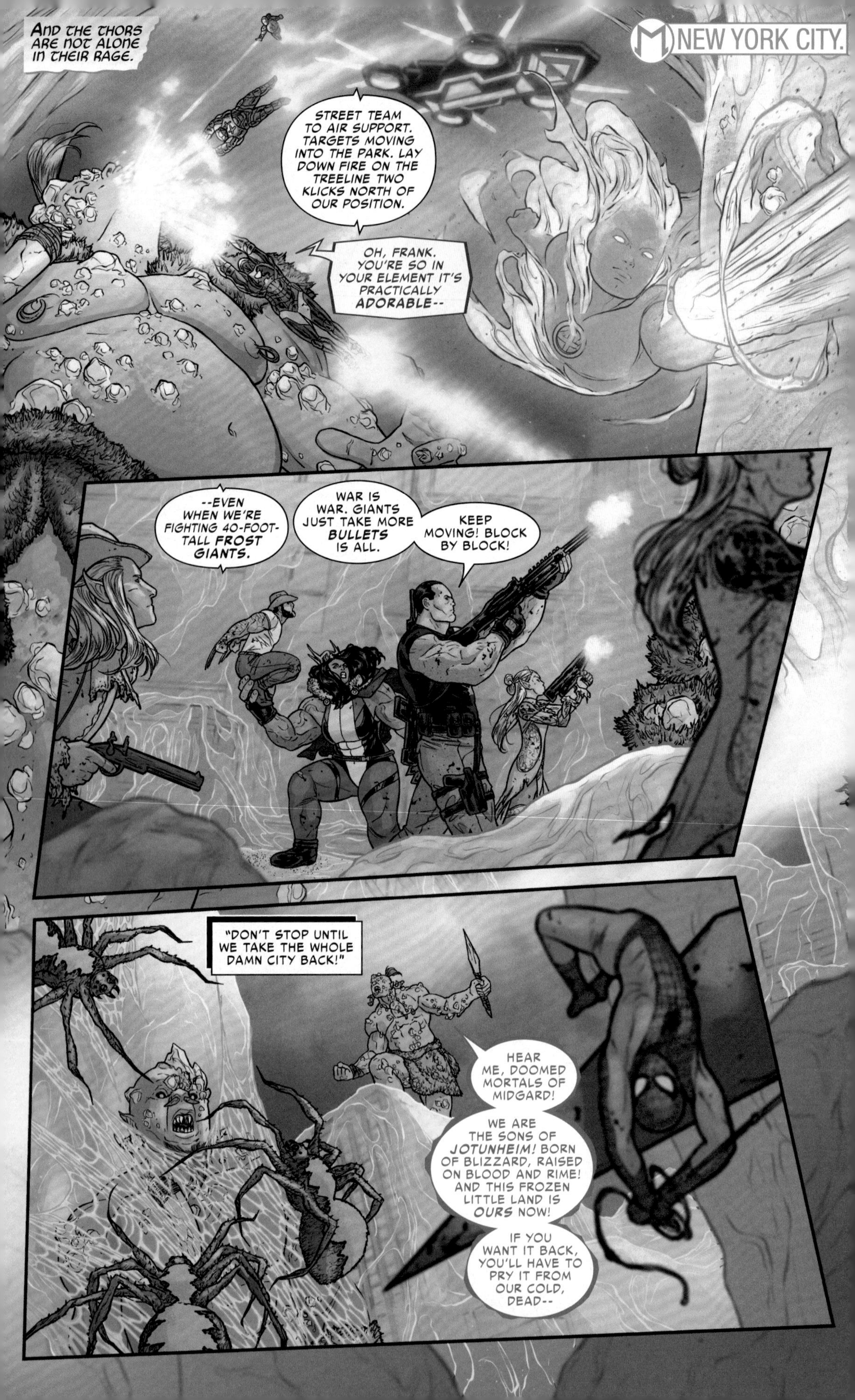

NEW YORK CITY.
AND THE THORS ARE NOT ALONE IN THEIR RAGE.
STREET TEAM TO AIR SUPPORT. TARGETS MOVING INTO THE PARK. LAY DOWN FIRE ON THE TREELINE TWO KLICKS NORTH OF OUR POSITION.
OH, FRANK. YOU'RE SO IN YOUR ELEMENT IT'S PRACTICALLY ADORABLE--
--EVEN WHEN WE'RE FIGHTING 40-FOOT-TALL FROST GIANTS.
WAR IS WAR. GIANTS JUST TAKE MORE BULLETS IS ALL.
KEEP MOVING! BLOCK BY BLOCK!
"DON'T STOP UNTIL WE TAKE THE WHOLE DAMN CITY BACK!"
HEAR ME, DOOMED MORTALS OF MIDGARD!
WE ARE THE SONS OF JOTUNHEIM! BORN OF BLIZZARD, RAISED ON BLOOD AND RIME! AND THIS FROZEN LITTLE LAND IS OURS NOW!
IF YOU WANT IT BACK, YOU'LL HAVE TO PRY IT FROM OUR COLD, DEAD--

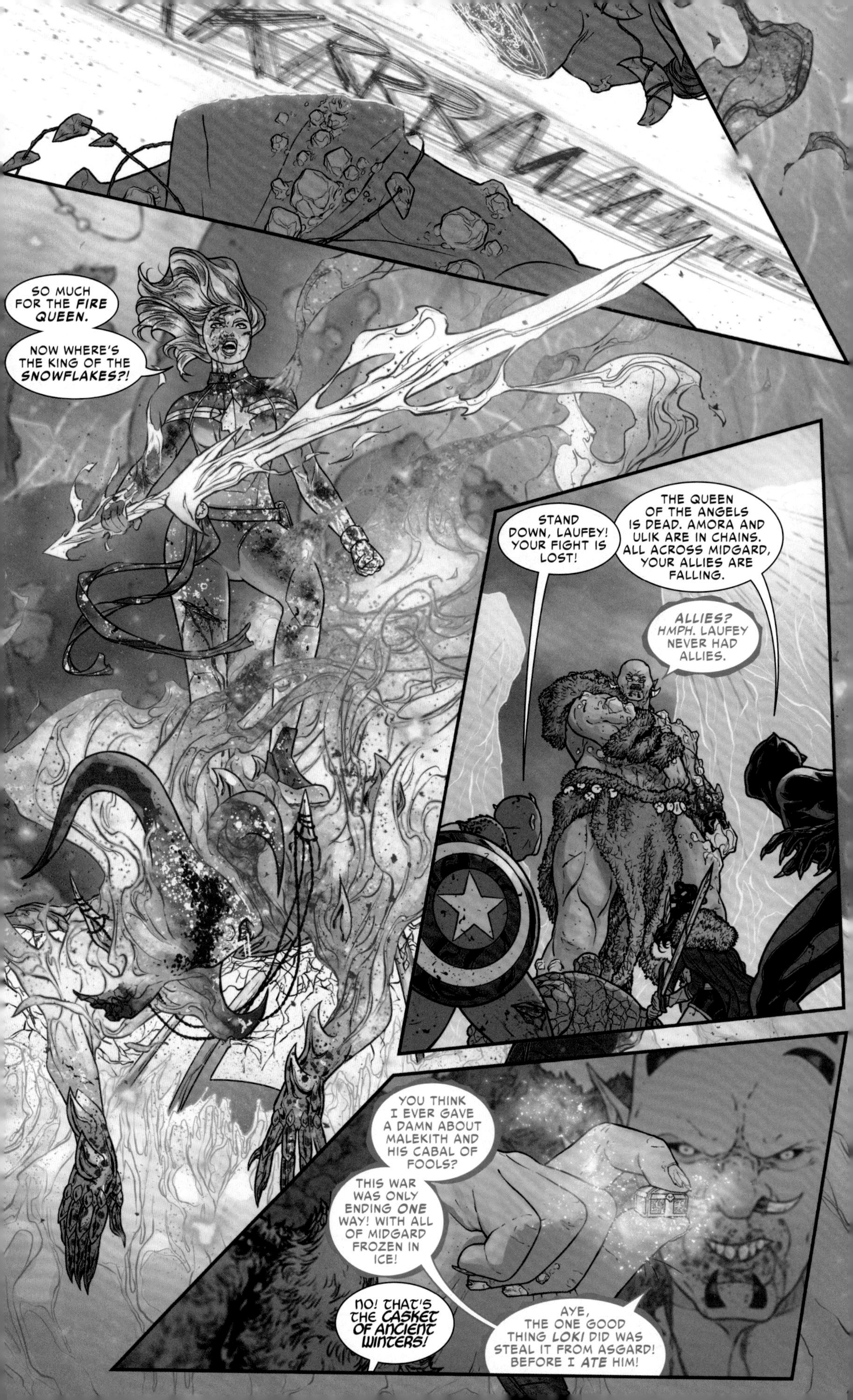

SO MUCH FOR THE *FIRE QUEEN.*
NOW WHERE'S THE KING OF THE *SNOWFLAKES?!*
STAND DOWN, LAUFEY! YOUR FIGHT IS LOST!
THE QUEEN OF THE ANGELS IS DEAD. AMORA AND ULIK ARE IN CHAINS. ALL ACROSS MIDGARD, YOUR ALLIES ARE FALLING.
ALLIES? HMPH. LAUFEY NEVER HAD ALLIES.
YOU THINK I EVER GAVE A DAMN ABOUT MALEKITH AND HIS CABAL OF FOOLS?
THIS WAR WAS ONLY ENDING *ONE* WAY! WITH ALL OF MIDGARD FROZEN IN ICE!
NO! THAT'S THE *CASKET OF ANCIENT WINTERS!*
AYE, THE ONE GOOD THING *LOKI* DID WAS STEAL IT FROM ASGARD! BEFORE I *ATE* HIM!

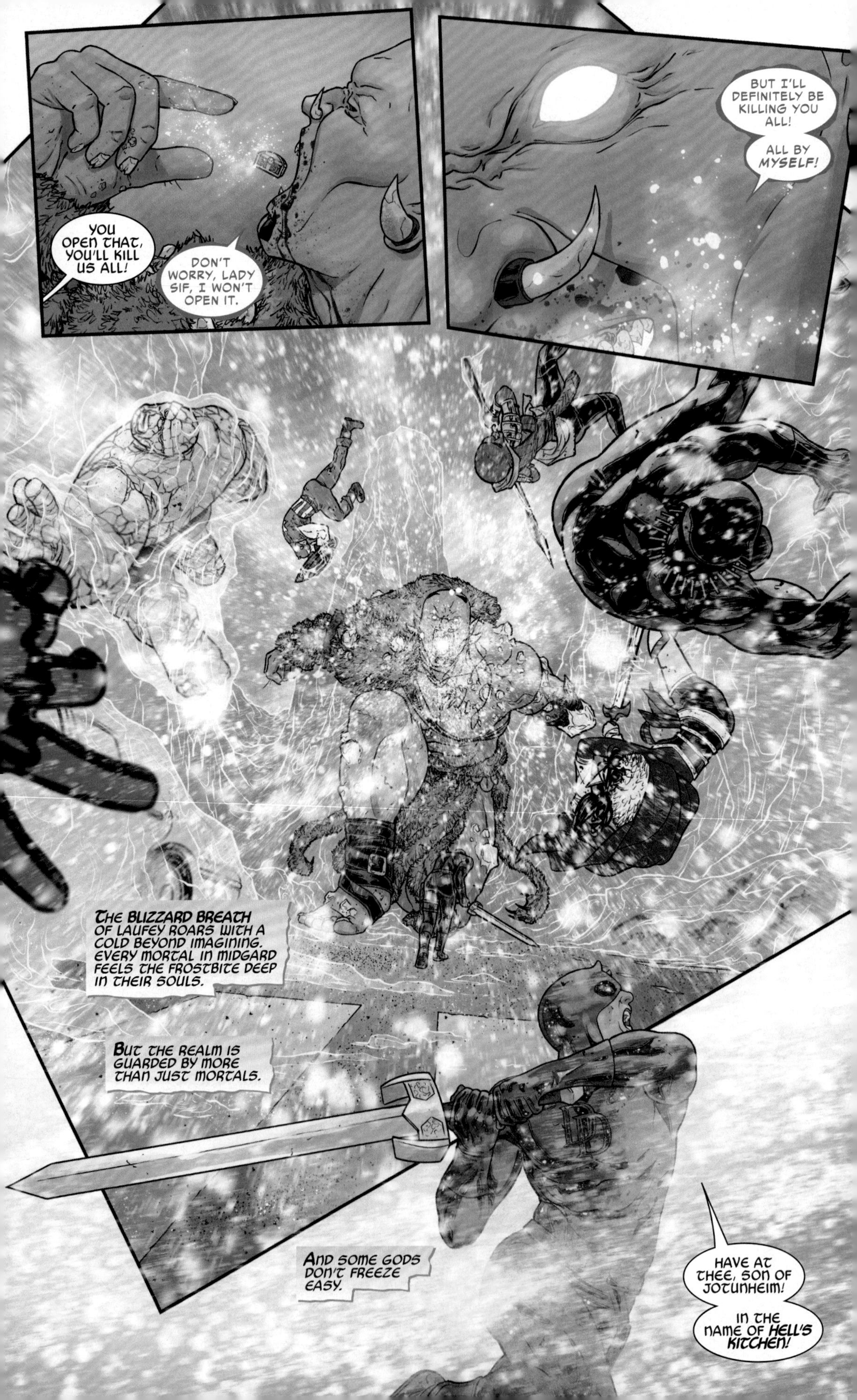
YOU OPEN THAT, YOU'LL KILL US ALL!
DON'T WORRY, LADY SIF, I WON'T OPEN IT.
BUT I'LL DEFINITELY BE KILLING YOU ALL!
ALL BY MYSELF!
THE BLIZZARD BREATH OF LAUFEY ROARS WITH A COLD BEYOND IMAGINING. EVERY MORTAL IN MIDGARD FEELS THE FROSTBITE DEEP IN THEIR SOULS.
BUT THE REALM IS GUARDED BY MORE THAN JUST MORTALS.
AND SOME GODS DON'T FREEZE EASY.
HAVE AT THEE, SON OF JOTUNHEIM!
IN THE NAME OF HELL'S KITCHEN!

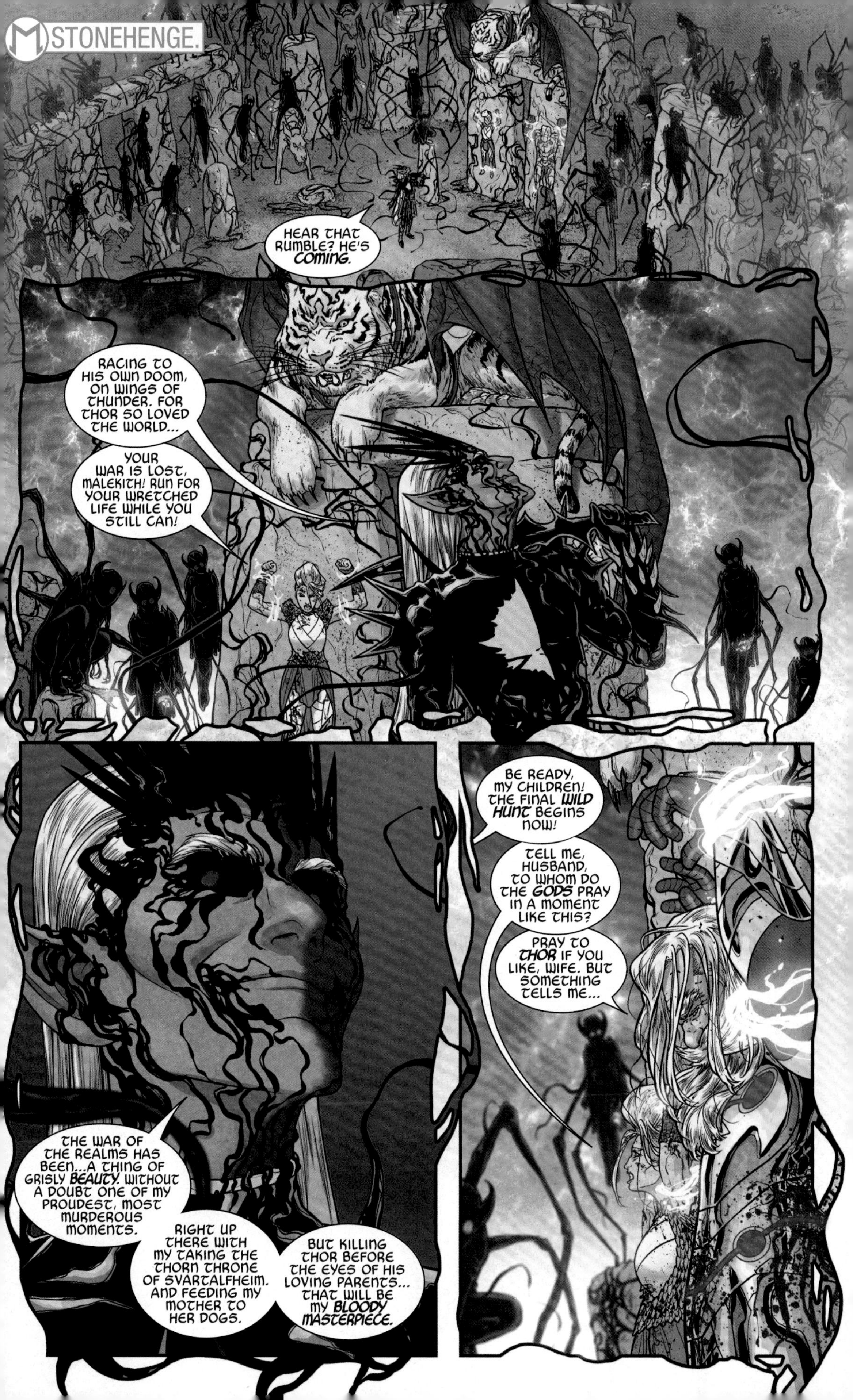
STONEHENGE.
HEAR THAT RUMBLE? HE'S COMING.
RACING TO HIS OWN DOOM, ON WINGS OF THUNDER. FOR THOR SO LOVED THE WORLD...
YOUR WAR IS LOST, MALEKITH! RUN FOR YOUR WRETCHED LIFE WHILE YOU STILL CAN!
THE WAR OF THE REALMS HAS BEEN...A THING OF GRISLY BEAUTY. WITHOUT A DOUBT ONE OF MY PROUDEST, MOST MURDEROUS MOMENTS.
RIGHT UP THERE WITH MY TAKING THE THORN THRONE OF SVARTALFHEIM. AND FEEDING MY MOTHER TO HER DOGS.
BUT KILLING THOR BEFORE THE EYES OF HIS LOVING PARENTS... THAT WILL BE MY BLOODY MASTERPIECE.
BE READY, MY CHILDREN! THE FINAL WILD HUNT BEGINS NOW!
TELL ME, HUSBAND, TO WHOM DO THE GODS PRAY IN A MOMENT LIKE THIS?
PRAY TO THOR IF YOU LIKE, WIFE. BUT SOMETHING TELLS ME...

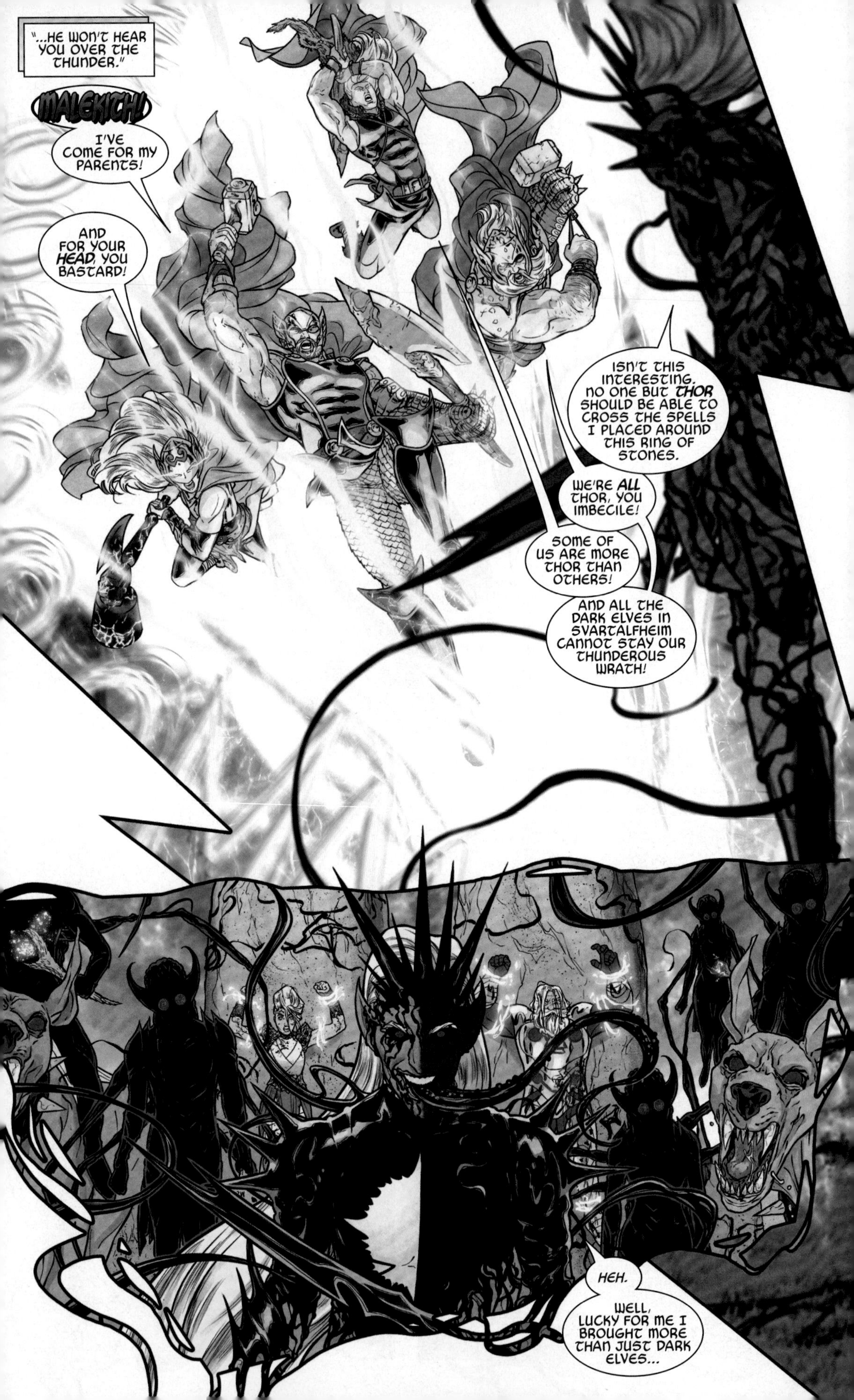
"...HE WON'T HEAR YOU OVER THE THUNDER."
MALEKITH!
I'VE COME FOR MY PARENTS!
AND FOR YOUR HEAD, YOU BASTARD!
ISN'T THIS INTERESTING. NO ONE BUT THOR SHOULD BE ABLE TO CROSS THE SPELLS I PLACED AROUND THIS RING OF STONES.
WE'RE ALL THOR, YOU IMBECILE!
SOME OF US ARE MORE THOR THAN OTHERS!
AND ALL THE DARK ELVES IN SVARTALFHEIM CANNOT STAY OUR THUNDEROUS WRATH!
HEH.
WELL, LUCKY FOR ME I BROUGHT MORE THAN JUST DARK ELVES...

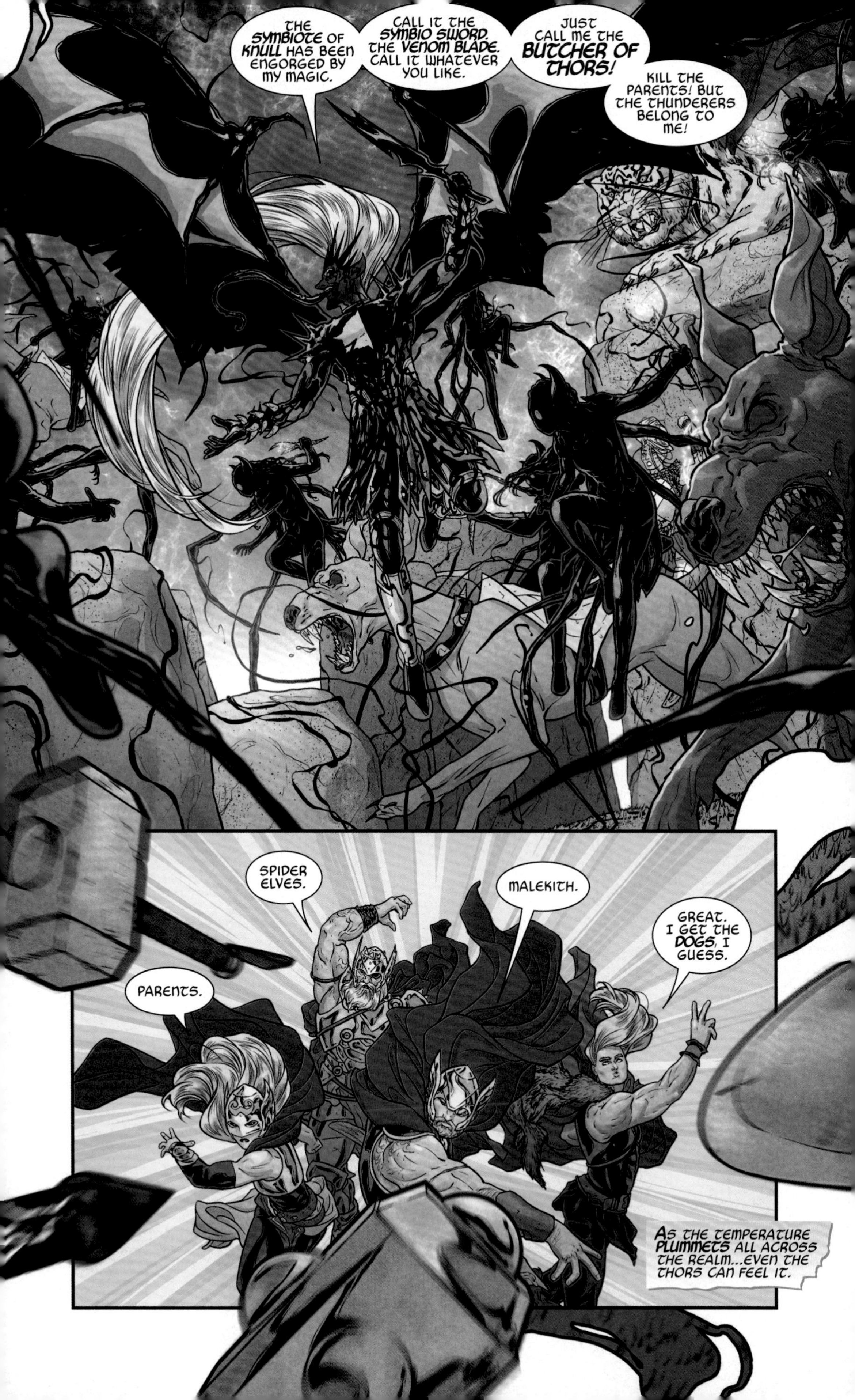
THE SYMBIOTE OF KNULL HAS BEEN ENGORGED BY MY MAGIC.
CALL IT THE SYMBIO SWORD. THE VENOM BLADE. CALL IT WHATEVER YOU LIKE.
JUST CALL ME THE BUTCHER OF THORS!
KILL THE PARENTS! BUT THE THUNDERERS BELONG TO ME!
SPIDER ELVES.
MALEKITH.
GREAT. I GET THE DOGS, I GUESS.
PARENTS.
AS THE TEMPERATURE PLUMMETS ALL ACROSS THE REALM...EVEN THE THORS CAN FEEL IT.

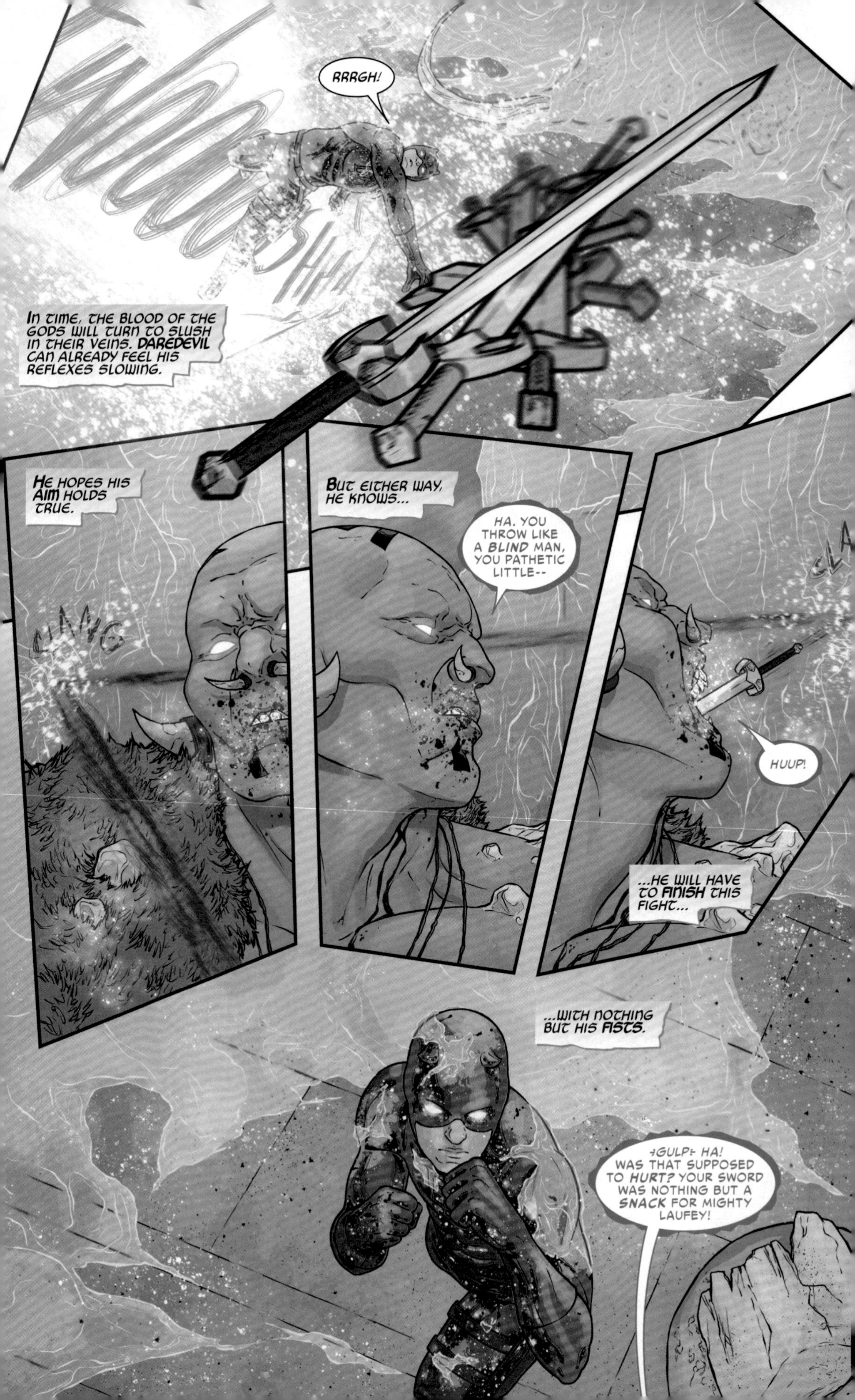
RRRGH!
In time, the blood of the gods will turn to slush in their veins. DAREDEVIL can already feel his reflexes slowing.
He hopes his AIM holds true.
But either way, he knows...
HA. YOU THROW LIKE A BLIND MAN, YOU PATHETIC LITTLE--
HUUP!
...he will have to FINISH this fight...
...with nothing but his FISTS.
+GULP+ HA! WAS THAT SUPPOSED TO HURT? YOUR SWORD WAS NOTHING BUT A SNACK FOR MIGHTY LAUFEY!

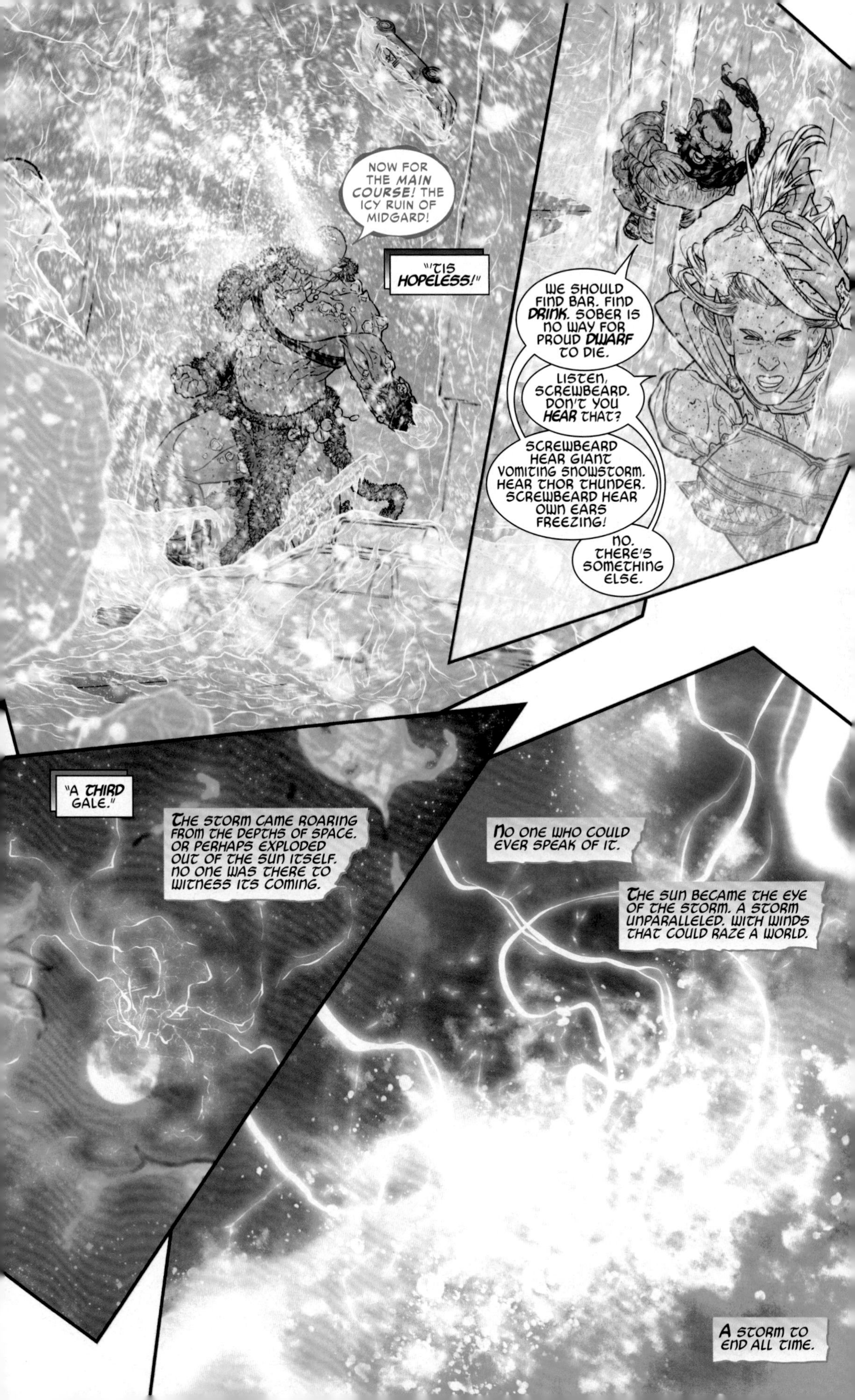

NOW FOR THE *MAIN COURSE!* THE ICY RUIN OF MIDGARD!
"'TIS *HOPELESS!*"
WE SHOULD FIND BAR. FIND *DRINK*. SOBER IS NO WAY FOR PROUD *DWARF* TO DIE.
LISTEN, SCREWBEARD. DON'T YOU *HEAR* THAT?
SCREWBEARD HEAR GIANT VOMITING SNOWSTORM. HEAR THOR THUNDER. SCREWBEARD HEAR OWN EARS FREEZING!
NO. THERE'S SOMETHING ELSE.
"A *THIRD* GALE."
THE STORM CAME ROARING FROM THE DEPTHS OF SPACE. OR PERHAPS EXPLODED OUT OF THE SUN ITSELF. NO ONE WAS THERE TO WITNESS ITS COMING.
NO ONE WHO COULD EVER SPEAK OF IT.
THE SUN BECAME THE EYE OF THE STORM. A STORM UNPARALLELED. WITH WINDS THAT COULD RAZE A WORLD.
A STORM TO END ALL TIME.

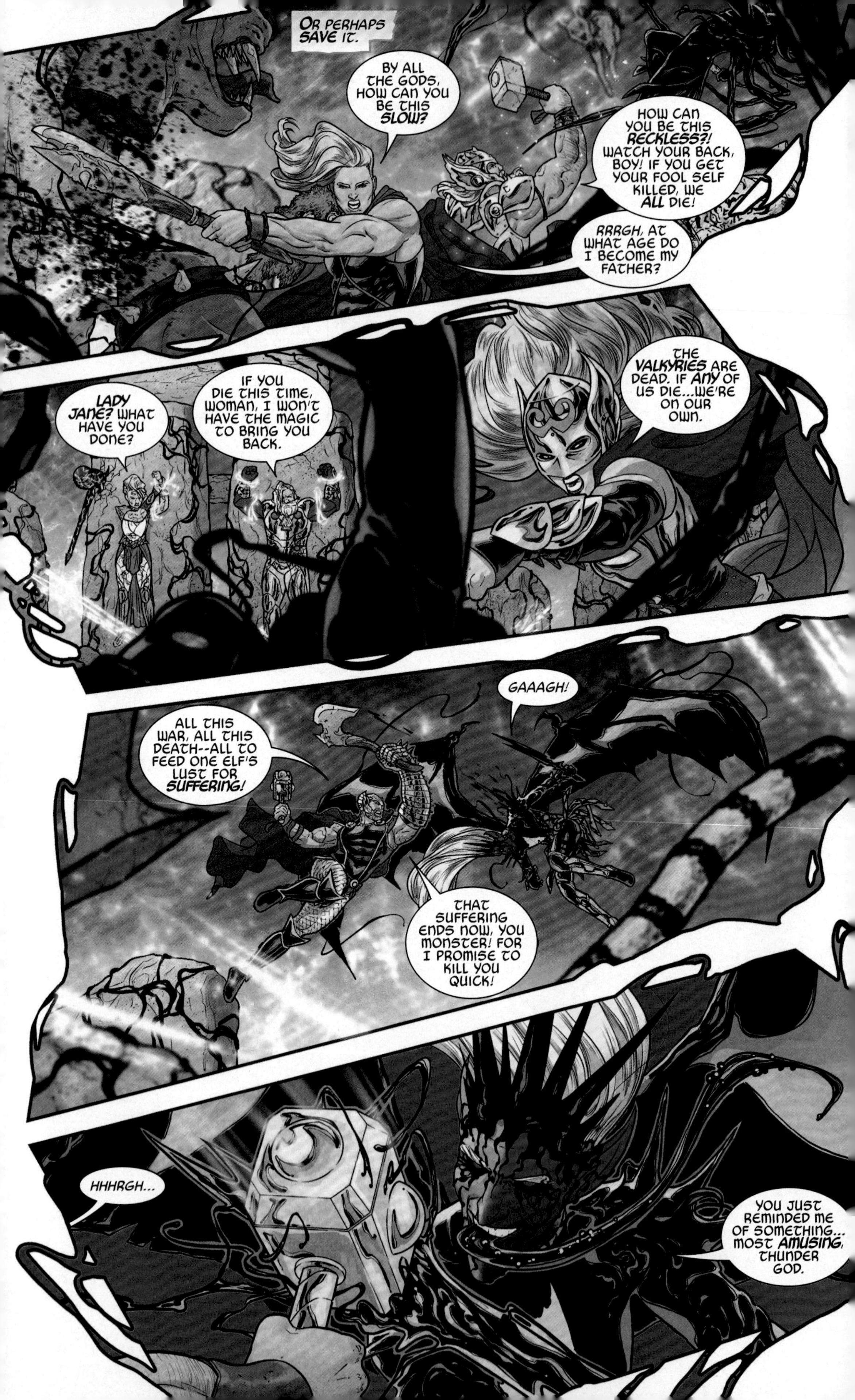
OR PERHAPS SAVE IT.
BY ALL THE GODS, HOW CAN YOU BE THIS SLOW?
HOW CAN YOU BE THIS RECKLESS?! WATCH YOUR BACK, BOY! IF YOU GET YOUR FOOL SELF KILLED, WE ALL DIE!
RRRGH, AT WHAT AGE DO I BECOME MY FATHER?
LADY JANE? WHAT HAVE YOU DONE?
IF YOU DIE THIS TIME, WOMAN, I WON'T HAVE THE MAGIC TO BRING YOU BACK.
THE VALKYRIES ARE DEAD. IF ANY OF US DIE...WE'RE ON OUR OWN.
ALL THIS WAR, ALL THIS DEATH--ALL TO FEED ONE ELF'S LUST FOR SUFFERING!
GAAAGH!
THAT SUFFERING ENDS NOW, YOU MONSTER! FOR I PROMISE TO KILL YOU QUICK!
HHHRGH...
YOU JUST REMINDED ME OF SOMETHING... MOST AMUSING, THUNDER GOD.

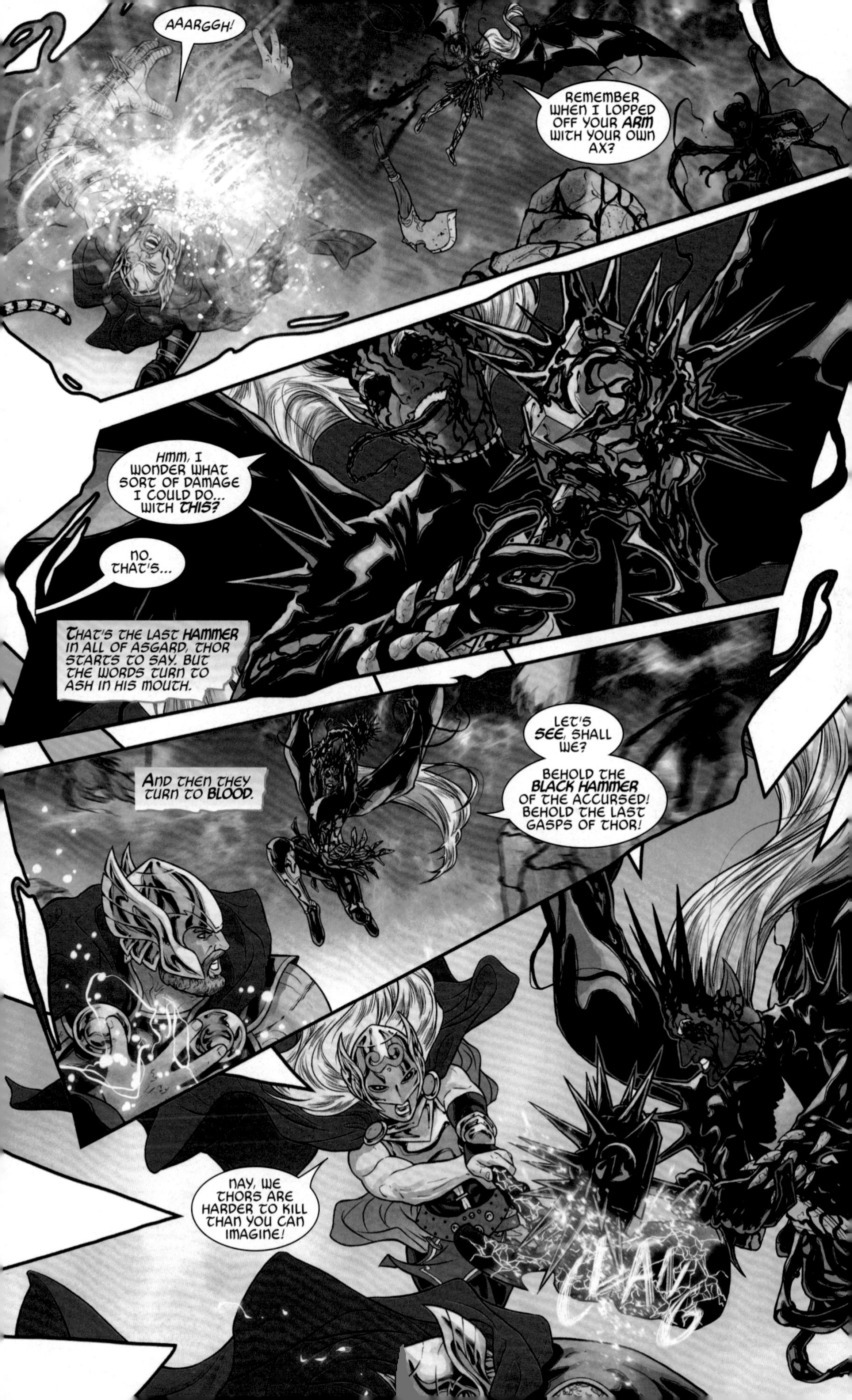
AAARGGH!
REMEMBER WHEN I LOPPED OFF YOUR ARM WITH YOUR OWN AX?
HMM, I WONDER WHAT SORT OF DAMAGE I COULD DO... WITH THIS?
NO. THAT'S...
THAT'S THE LAST HAMMER IN ALL OF ASGARD, THOR STARTS TO SAY. BUT THE WORDS TURN TO ASH IN HIS MOUTH.
AND THEN THEY TURN TO BLOOD.
LET'S SEE, SHALL WE?
BEHOLD THE BLACK HAMMER OF THE ACCURSED! BEHOLD THE LAST GASPS OF THOR!
NAY, WE THORS ARE HARDER TO KILL THAN YOU CAN IMAGINE!

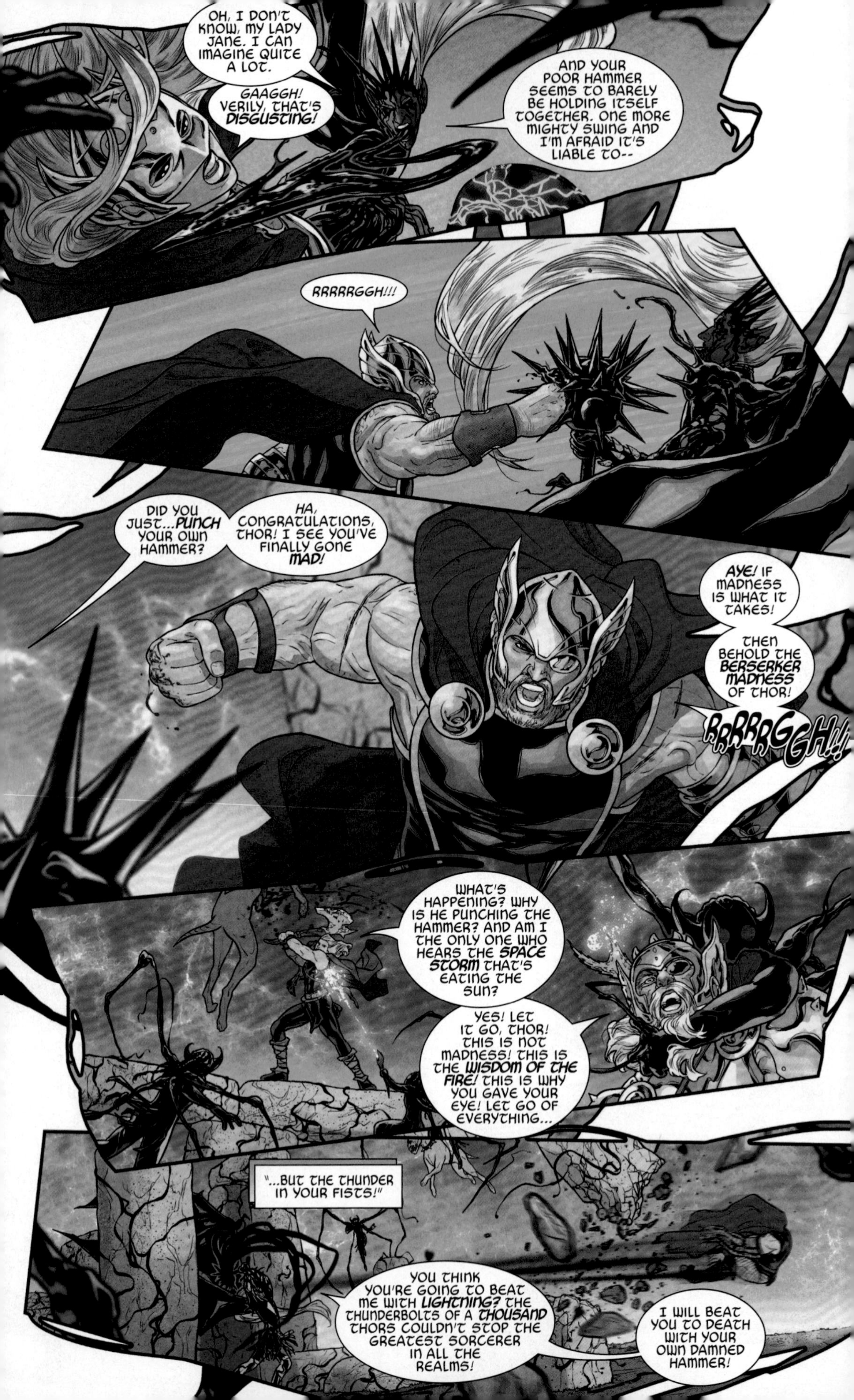
OH, I DON'T KNOW, MY LADY JANE. I CAN IMAGINE QUITE A LOT.
GAAGGH! VERILY, THAT'S DISGUSTING!
AND YOUR POOR HAMMER SEEMS TO BARELY BE HOLDING ITSELF TOGETHER. ONE MORE MIGHTY SWING AND I'M AFRAID IT'S LIABLE TO--
RRRRRGGH!!!
DID YOU JUST...PUNCH YOUR OWN HAMMER?
HA, CONGRATULATIONS, THOR! I SEE YOU'VE FINALLY GONE MAD!
AYE! IF MADNESS IS WHAT IT TAKES!
THEN BEHOLD THE BERSERKER MADNESS OF THOR!
RRRRRGGH!!!
WHAT'S HAPPENING? WHY IS HE PUNCHING THE HAMMER? AND AM I THE ONLY ONE WHO HEARS THE SPACE STORM THAT'S EATING THE SUN?
YES! LET IT GO, THOR! THIS IS NOT MADNESS! THIS IS THE WISDOM OF THE FIRE! THIS IS WHY YOU GAVE YOUR EYE! LET GO OF EVERYTHING...
"...BUT THE THUNDER IN YOUR FISTS!"
YOU THINK YOU'RE GOING TO BEAT ME WITH LIGHTNING? THE THUNDERBOLTS OF A THOUSAND THORS COULDN'T STOP THE GREATEST SORCERER IN ALL THE REALMS!
I WILL BEAT YOU TO DEATH WITH YOUR OWN DAMNED HAMMER!

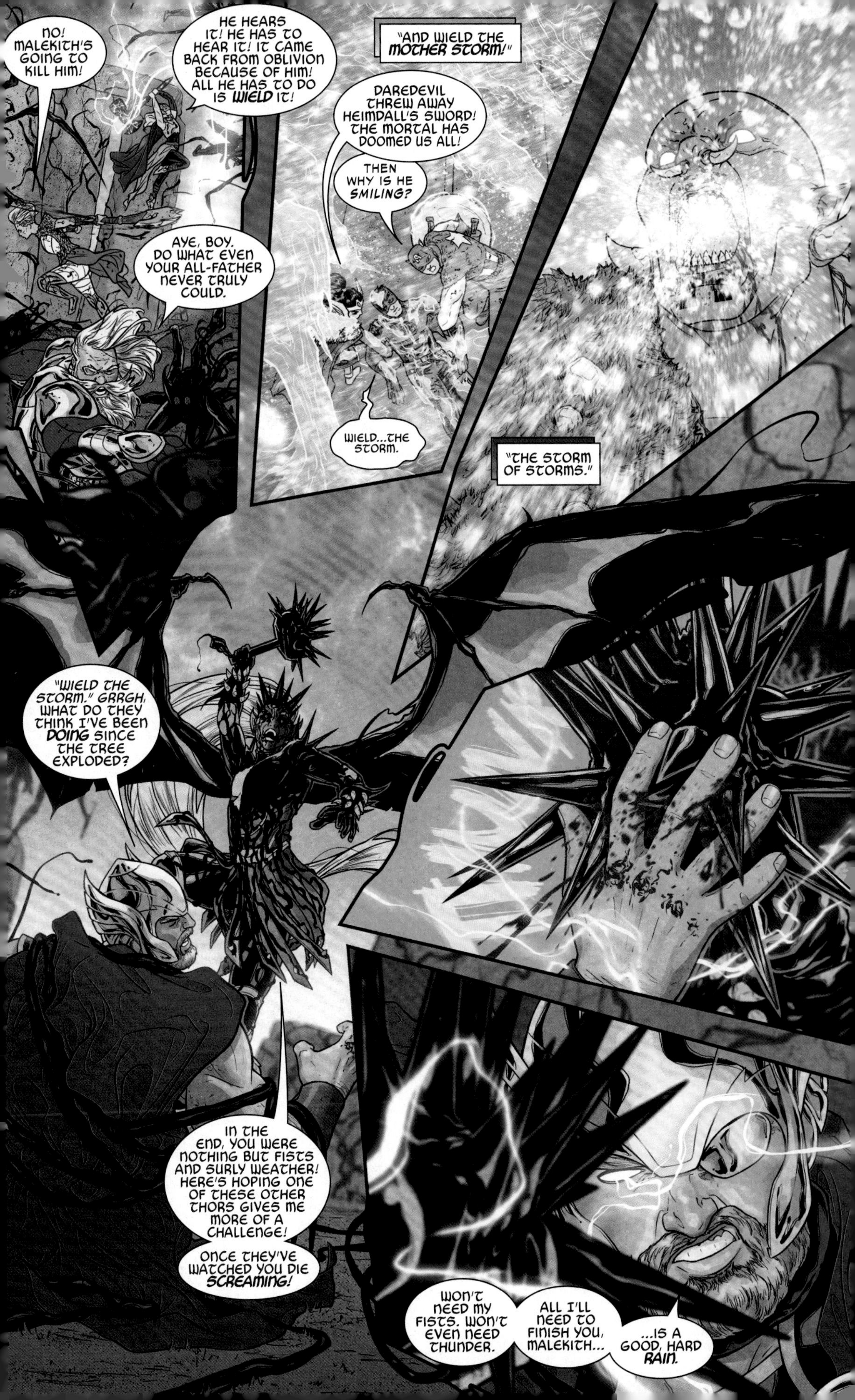
NO! MALEKITH'S GOING TO KILL HIM!
HE HEARS IT! HE HAS TO HEAR IT! IT CAME BACK FROM OBLIVION BECAUSE OF HIM! ALL HE HAS TO DO IS WIELD IT!
"AND WIELD THE MOTHER STORM!"
DAREDEVIL THREW AWAY HEIMDALL'S SWORD! THE MORTAL HAS DOOMED US ALL!
THEN WHY IS HE SMILING?
AYE, BOY. DO WHAT EVEN YOUR ALL-FATHER NEVER TRULY COULD.
WIELD...THE STORM.
"THE STORM OF STORMS."
"WIELD THE STORM." GRRGH, WHAT DO THEY THINK I'VE BEEN DOING SINCE THE TREE EXPLODED?
IN THE END, YOU WERE NOTHING BUT FISTS AND SURLY WEATHER! HERE'S HOPING ONE OF THESE OTHER THORS GIVES ME MORE OF A CHALLENGE!
ONCE THEY'VE WATCHED YOU DIE SCREAMING!
WON'T NEED MY FISTS. WON'T EVEN NEED THUNDER.
ALL I'LL NEED TO FINISH YOU, MALEKITH...
...IS A GOOD, HARD RAIN.

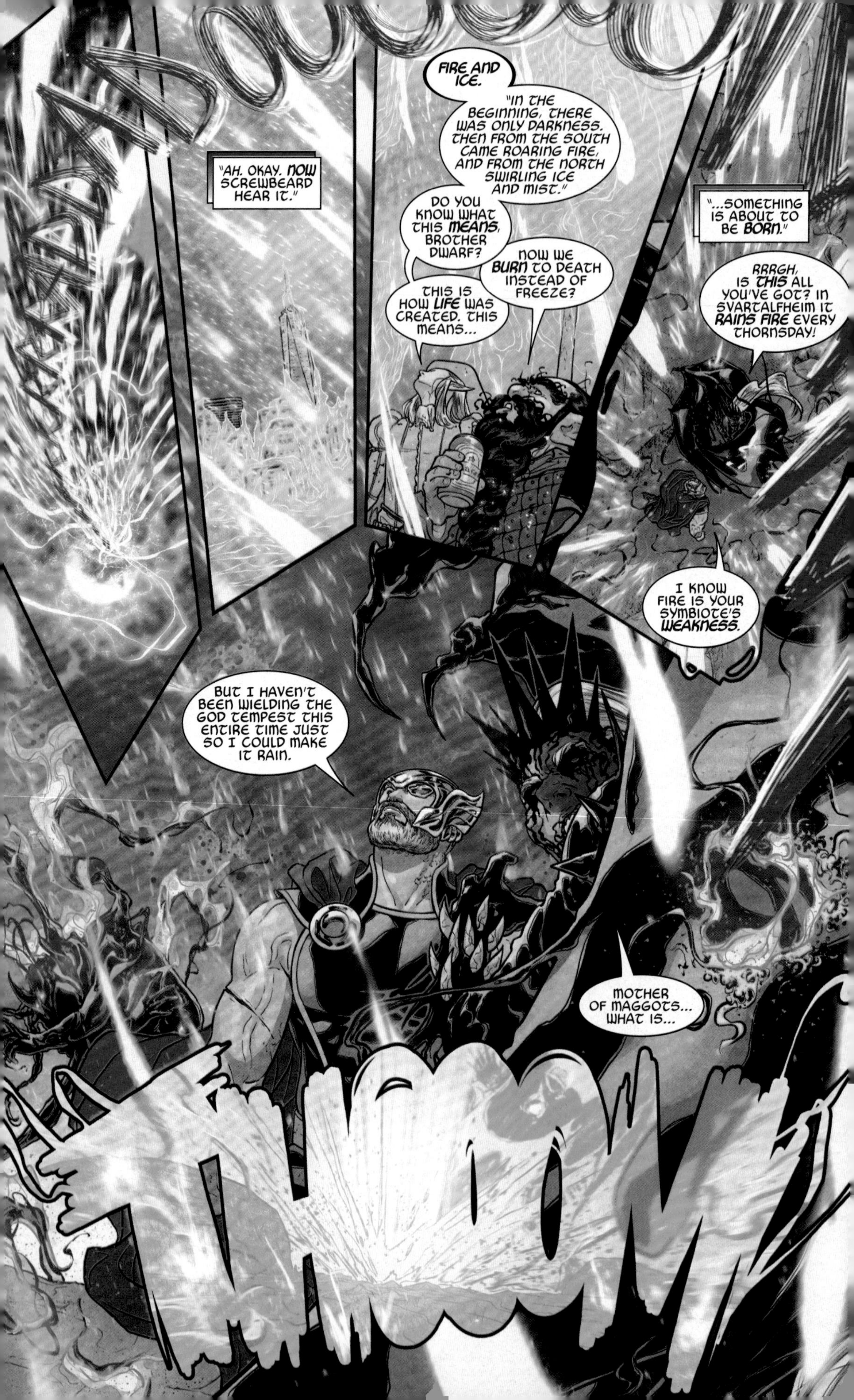
"AH. OKAY. NOW SCREWBEARD HEAR IT."
FIRE AND ICE.
"IN THE BEGINNING, THERE WAS ONLY DARKNESS. THEN FROM THE SOUTH CAME ROARING FIRE, AND FROM THE NORTH SWIRLING ICE AND MIST."
DO YOU KNOW WHAT THIS MEANS, BROTHER DWARF?
NOW WE BURN TO DEATH INSTEAD OF FREEZE?
THIS IS HOW LIFE WAS CREATED. THIS MEANS...
"...SOMETHING IS ABOUT TO BE BORN."
RRRGH, IS THIS ALL YOU'VE GOT? IN SVARTALFHEIM IT RAINS FIRE EVERY THORNSDAY!
I KNOW FIRE IS YOUR SYMBIOTE'S WEAKNESS.
BUT I HAVEN'T BEEN WIELDING THE GOD TEMPEST THIS ENTIRE TIME JUST SO I COULD MAKE IT RAIN.
MOTHER OF MAGGOTS... WHAT IS...

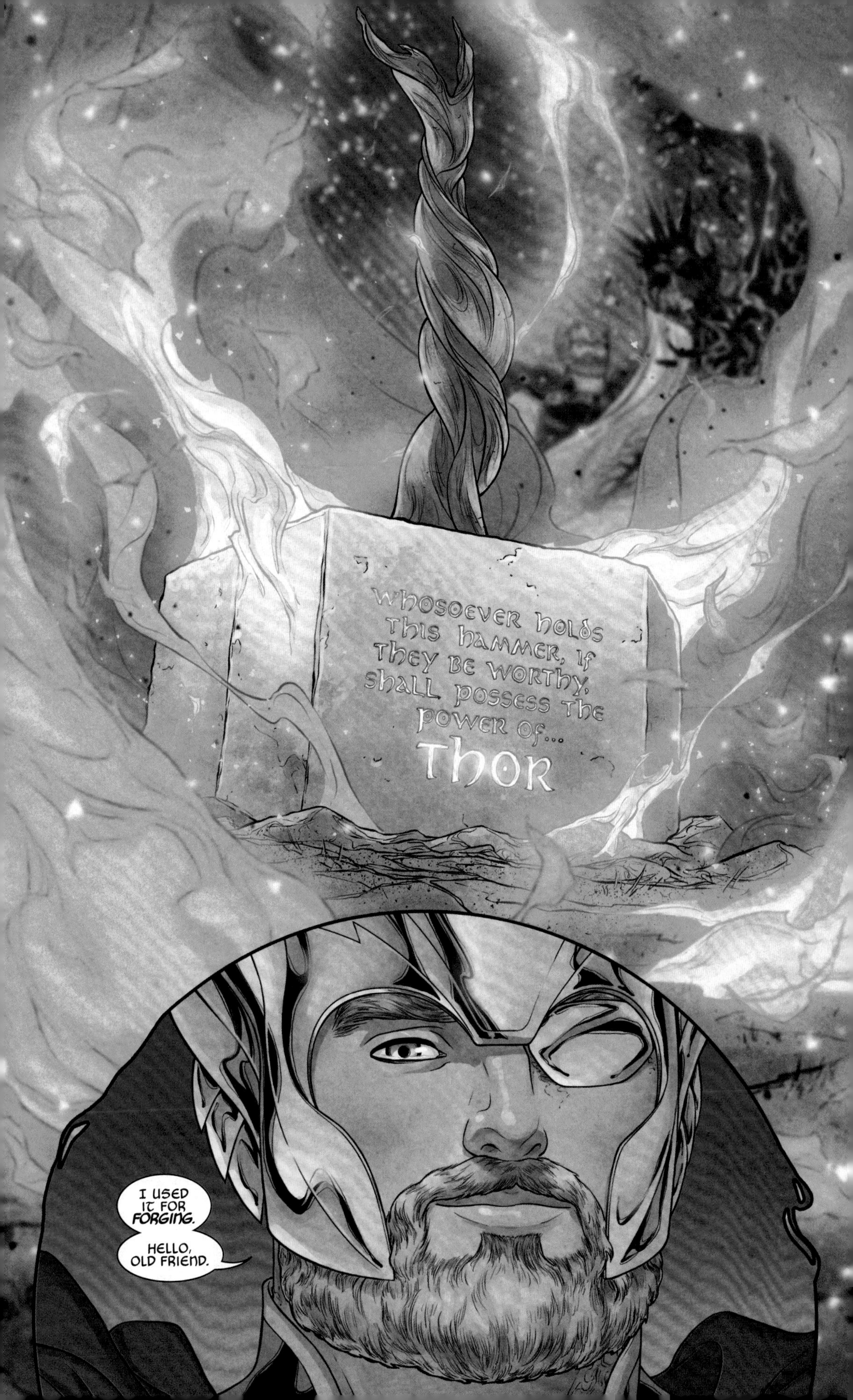

WHOSOEVER HOLDS THIS HAMMER, IF THEY BE WORTHY, SHALL POSSESS THE POWER OF... THOR
I USED IT FOR FORGING.
HELLO, OLD FRIEND.

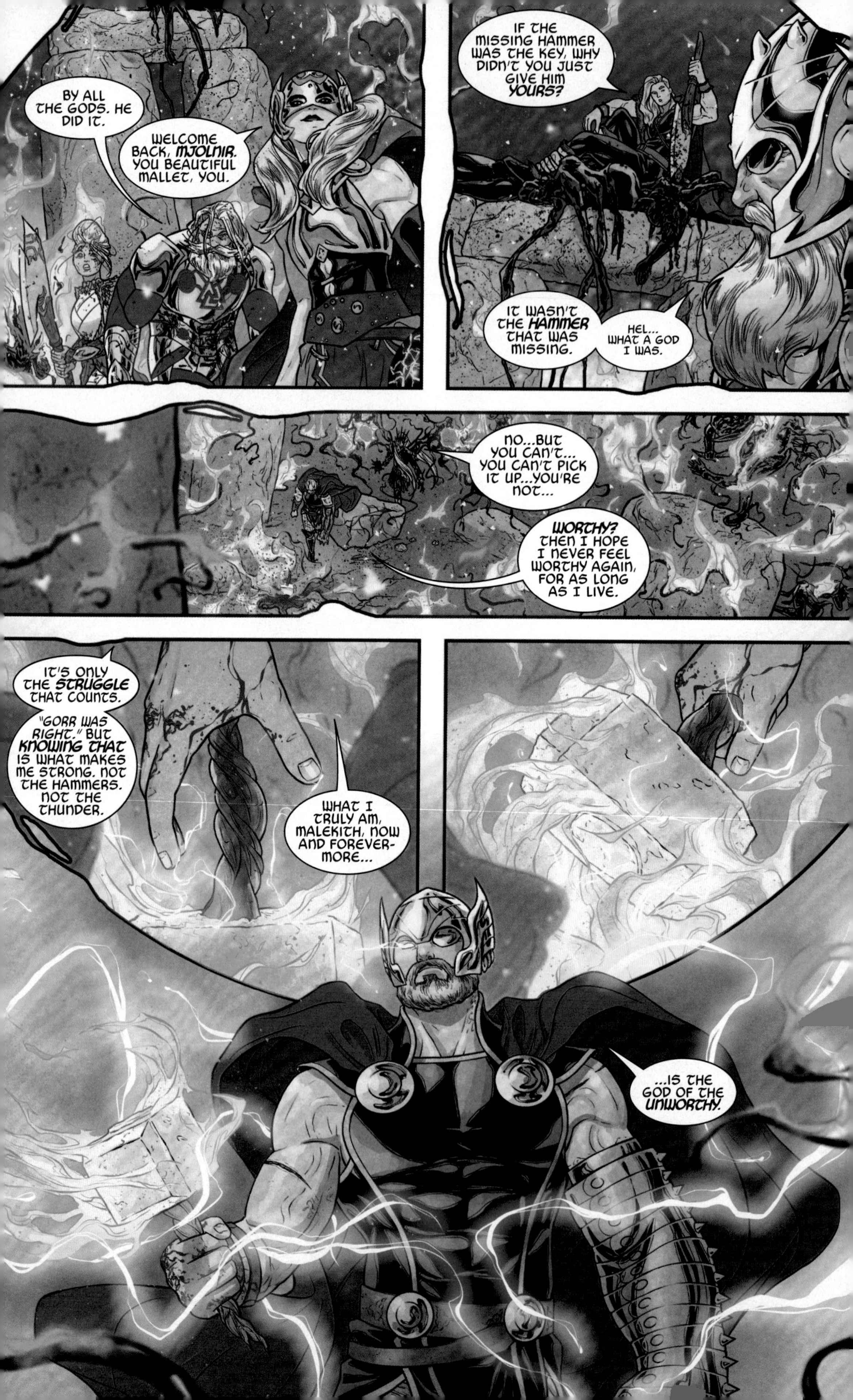
BY ALL THE GODS. HE DID IT.
WELCOME BACK, MJOLNIR. YOU BEAUTIFUL MALLET, YOU.
IF THE MISSING HAMMER WAS THE KEY, WHY DIDN'T YOU JUST GIVE HIM YOURS?
IT WASN'T THE HAMMER THAT WAS MISSING.
HEL... WHAT A GOD I WAS.
NO...BUT YOU CAN'T... YOU CAN'T PICK IT UP...YOU'RE NOT...
WORTHY? THEN I HOPE I NEVER FEEL WORTHY AGAIN, FOR AS LONG AS I LIVE.
IT'S ONLY THE STRUGGLE THAT COUNTS.
"GORR WAS RIGHT." BUT KNOWING THAT IS WHAT MAKES ME STRONG. NOT THE HAMMERS. NOT THE THUNDER.
WHAT I TRULY AM, MALEKITH, NOW AND FOREVER-MORE...
...IS THE GOD OF THE UNWORTHY.

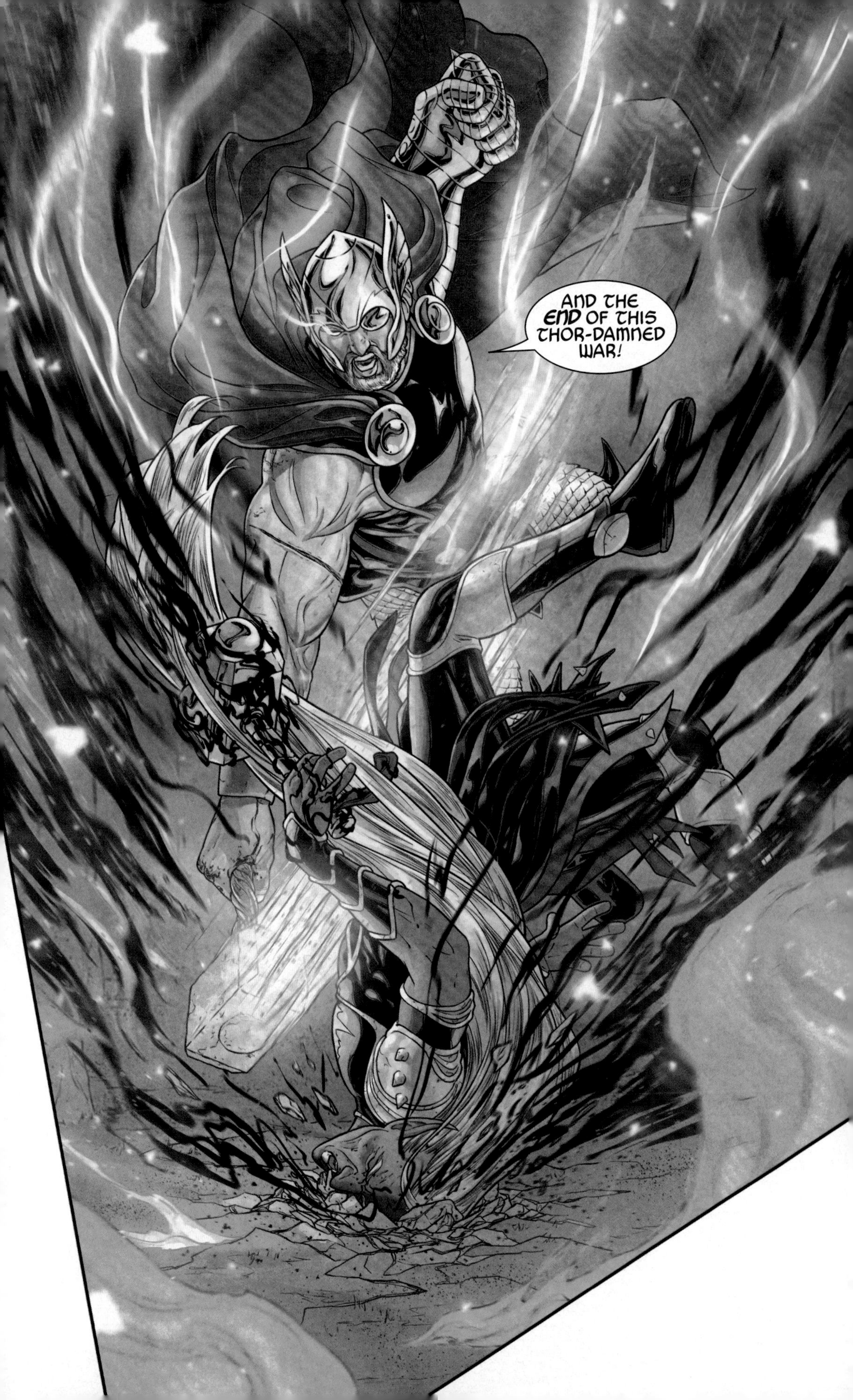
AND THE END OF THIS THOR-DAMNED WAR!

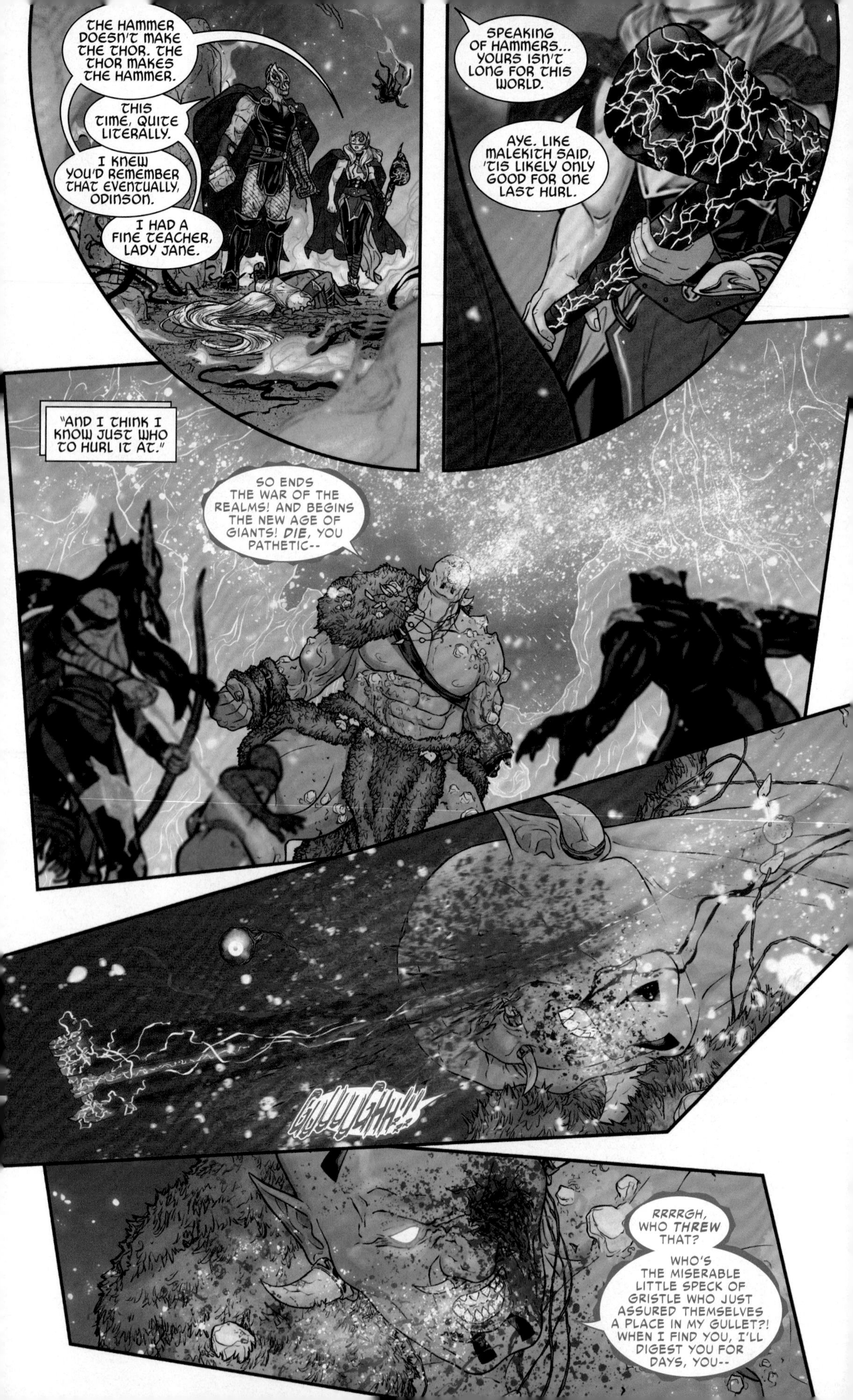
THE HAMMER DOESN'T MAKE THE THOR. THE THOR MAKES THE HAMMER.
THIS TIME, QUITE LITERALLY.
I KNEW YOU'D REMEMBER THAT EVENTUALLY, ODINSON.
I HAD A FINE TEACHER, LADY JANE.
SPEAKING OF HAMMERS... YOURS ISN'T LONG FOR THIS WORLD.
AYE. LIKE MALEKITH SAID, 'TIS LIKELY ONLY GOOD FOR ONE LAST HURL.
"AND I THINK I KNOW JUST WHO TO HURL IT AT."
SO ENDS THE WAR OF THE REALMS! AND BEGINS THE NEW AGE OF GIANTS! *DIE*, YOU PATHETIC--
GOUUUGHH!!
RRRRGH, WHO *THREW* THAT?
WHO'S THE MISERABLE LITTLE SPECK OF GRISTLE WHO JUST ASSURED THEMSELVES A PLACE IN MY GULLET?! WHEN I FIND YOU, I'LL DIGEST YOU FOR DAYS, YOU--

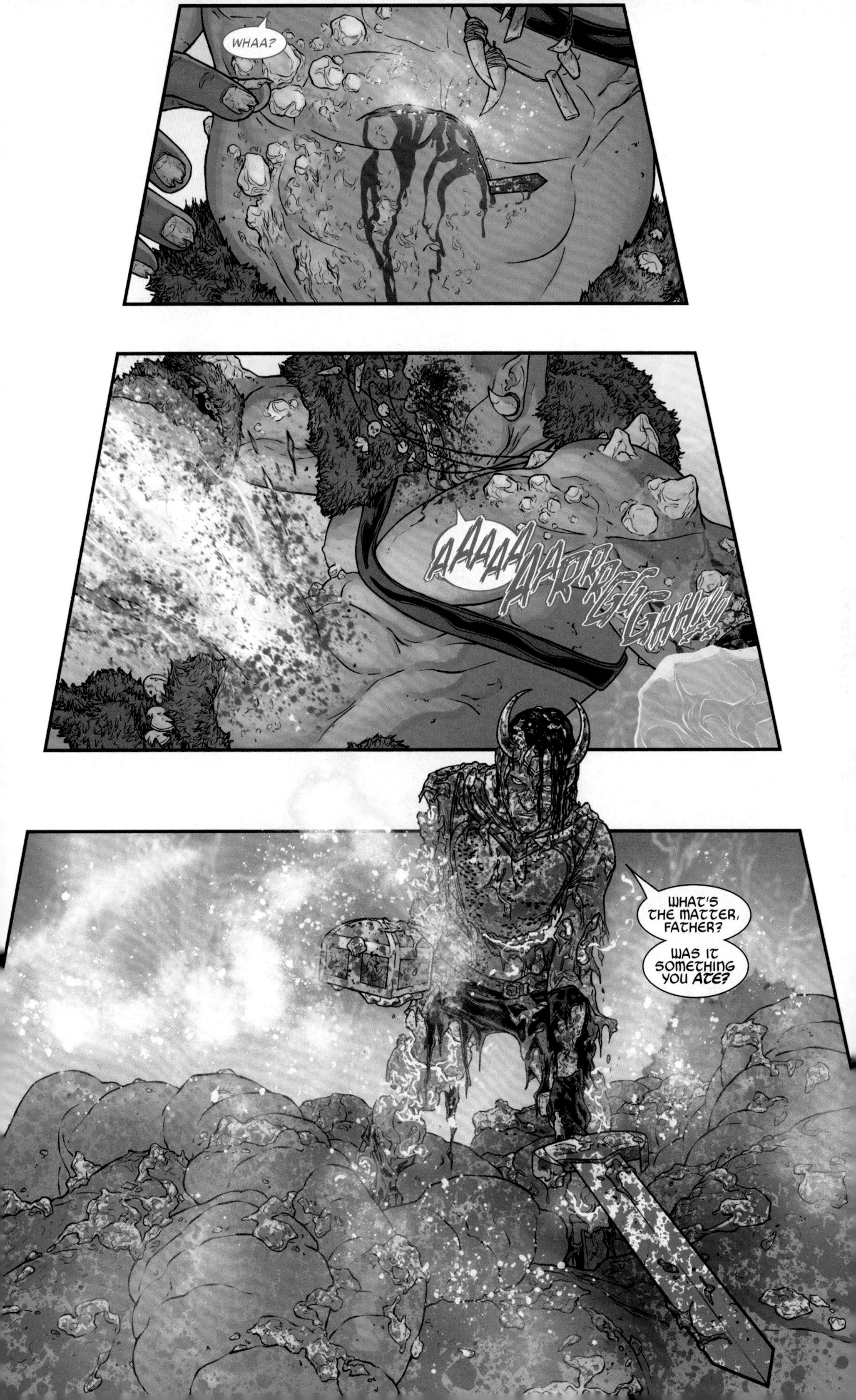
WHAA?
AAAAAAARRGGGHHH!!
WHAT'S THE MATTER, FATHER?
WAS IT SOMETHING YOU ATE?

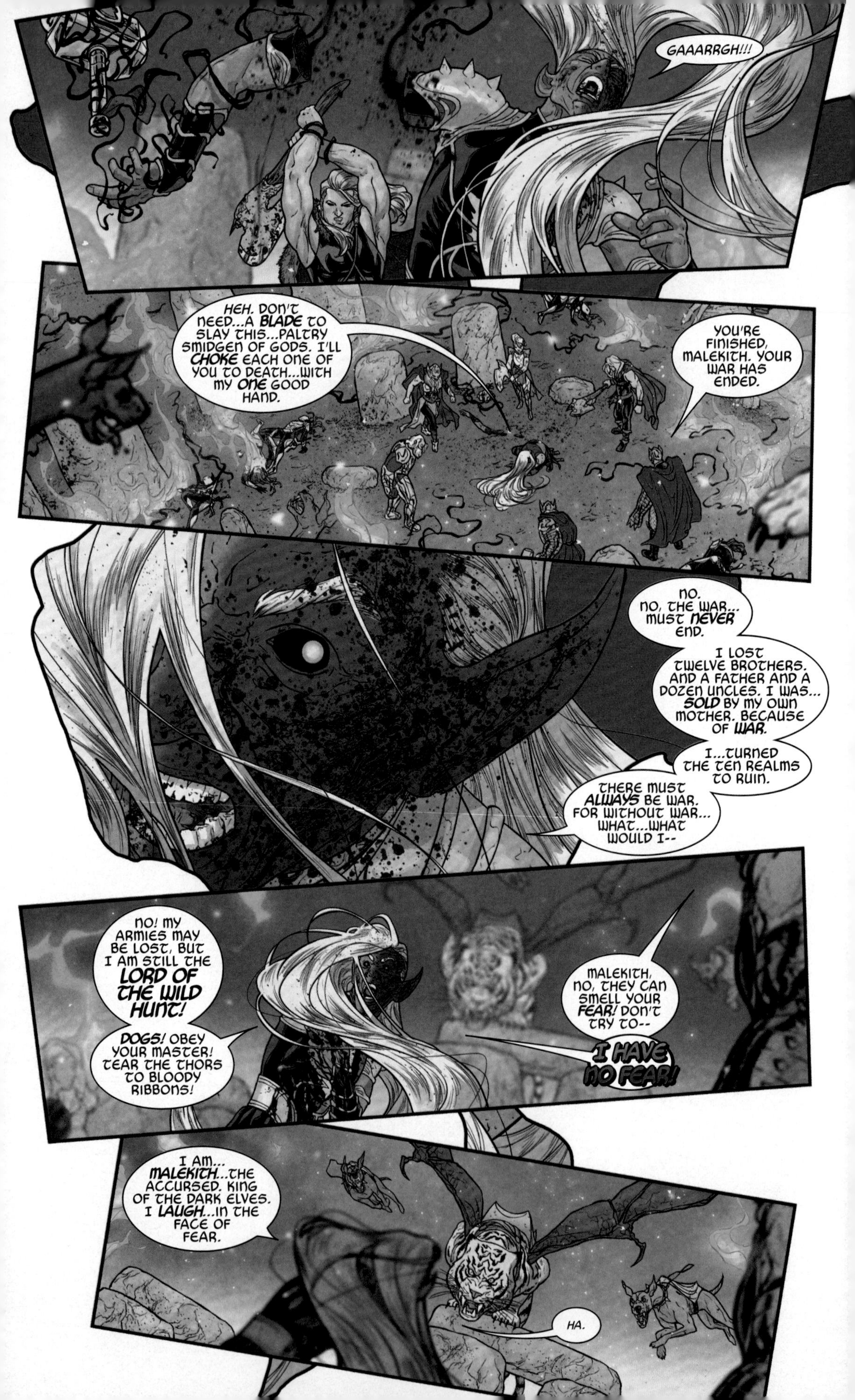
GAAAARRGH!!!
HEH. DON'T NEED...A BLADE TO SLAY THIS...PALTRY SMIDGEN OF GODS. I'LL CHOKE EACH ONE OF YOU TO DEATH...WITH MY ONE GOOD HAND.
YOU'RE FINISHED, MALEKITH. YOUR WAR HAS ENDED.
NO. NO, THE WAR... MUST NEVER END.
I LOST TWELVE BROTHERS. AND A FATHER AND A DOZEN UNCLES. I WAS... SOLD BY MY OWN MOTHER. BECAUSE OF WAR.
I...TURNED THE TEN REALMS TO RUIN.
THERE MUST ALWAYS BE WAR. FOR WITHOUT WAR... WHAT...WHAT WOULD I--
NO! MY ARMIES MAY BE LOST, BUT I AM STILL THE LORD OF THE WILD HUNT!
DOGS! OBEY YOUR MASTER! TEAR THE THORS TO BLOODY RIBBONS!
MALEKITH, NO, THEY CAN SMELL YOUR FEAR! DON'T TRY TO--
I HAVE NO FEAR!
I AM... MALEKITH...THE ACCURSED. KING OF THE DARK ELVES. I LAUGH...IN THE FACE OF FEAR.
HA.

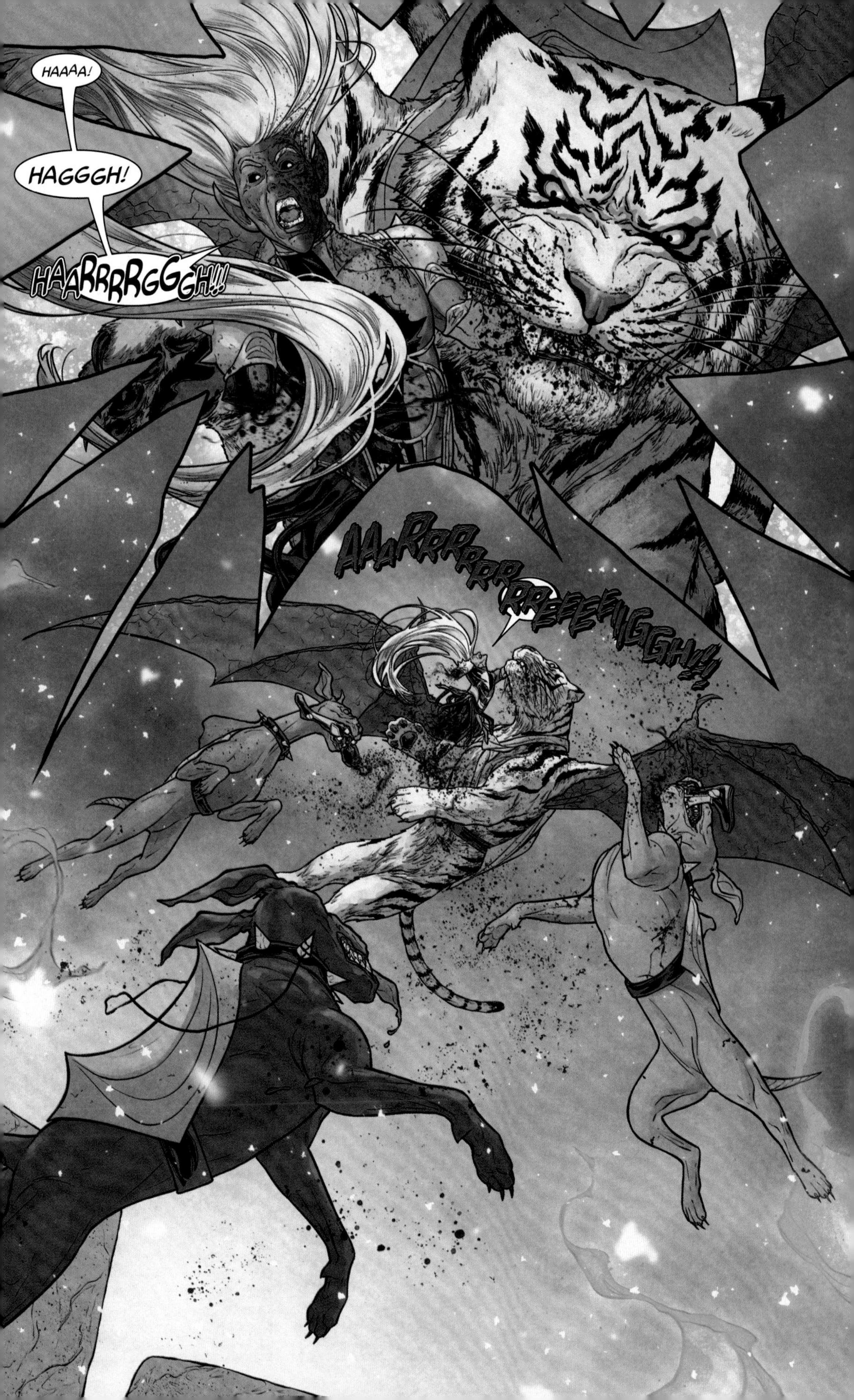
HAAAA!
HAGGGH!
HAARRRRGGGH!!!
AAARRRRRRRREEEEIGGH!!

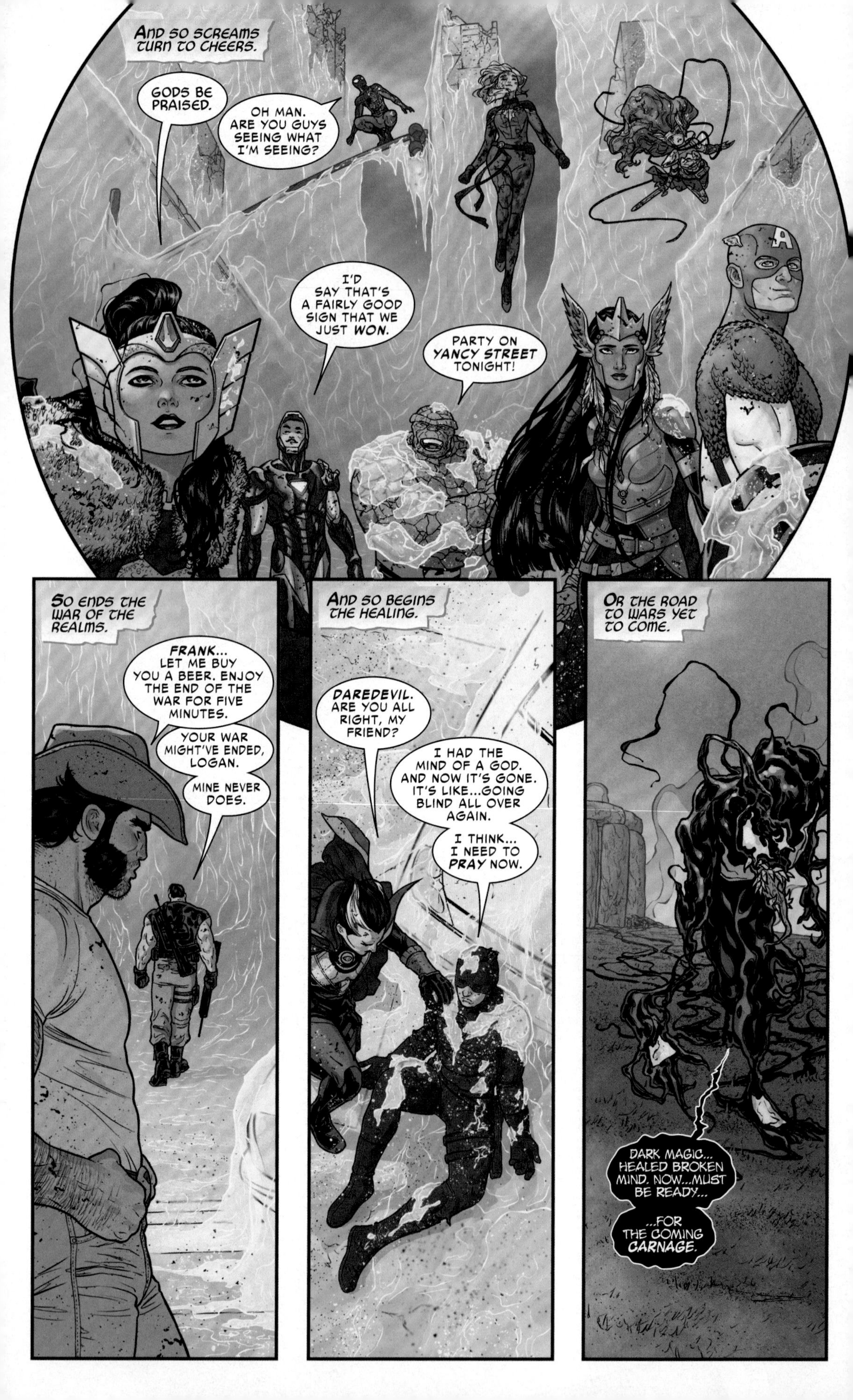
AND SO SCREAMS TURN TO CHEERS.
GODS BE PRAISED.
OH MAN. ARE YOU GUYS SEEING WHAT I'M SEEING?
I'D SAY THAT'S A FAIRLY GOOD SIGN THAT WE JUST WON.
PARTY ON YANCY STREET TONIGHT!
SO ENDS THE WAR OF THE REALMS.
FRANK... LET ME BUY YOU A BEER. ENJOY THE END OF THE WAR FOR FIVE MINUTES.
YOUR WAR MIGHT'VE ENDED, LOGAN.
MINE NEVER DOES.
AND SO BEGINS THE HEALING.
DAREDEVIL. ARE YOU ALL RIGHT, MY FRIEND?
I HAD THE MIND OF A GOD. AND NOW IT'S GONE. IT'S LIKE...GOING BLIND ALL OVER AGAIN.
I THINK... I NEED TO PRAY NOW.
OR THE ROAD TO WARS YET TO COME.
DARK MAGIC... HEALED BROKEN MIND. NOW...MUST BE READY...
...FOR THE COMING CARNAGE.

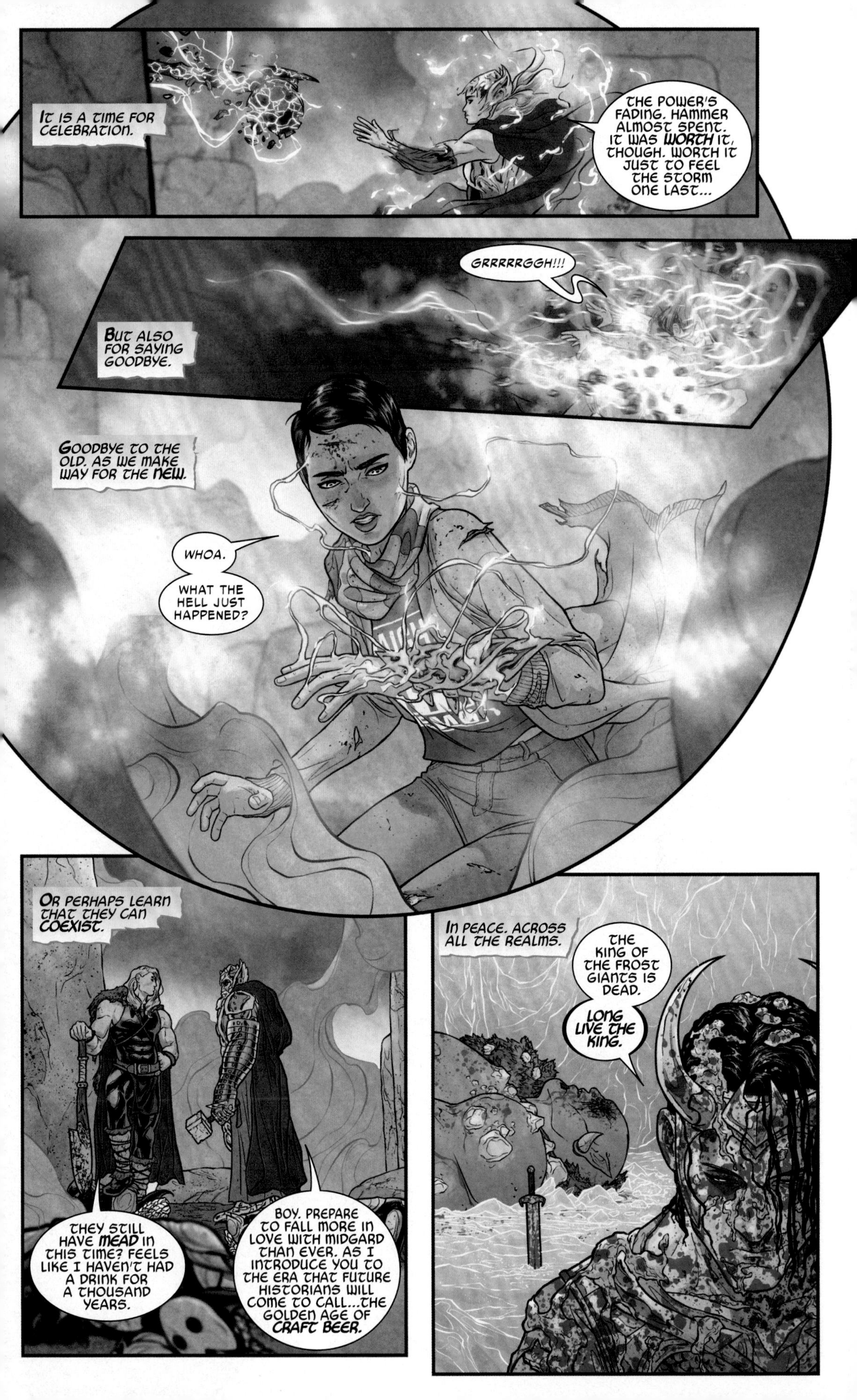
IT IS A TIME FOR CELEBRATION.
THE POWER'S FADING. HAMMER ALMOST SPENT. IT WAS WORTH IT, THOUGH. WORTH IT JUST TO FEEL THE STORM ONE LAST...
GRRRRRGGH!!!
BUT ALSO FOR SAYING GOODBYE.
GOODBYE TO THE OLD. AS WE MAKE WAY FOR THE NEW.
WHOA.
WHAT THE HELL JUST HAPPENED?
OR PERHAPS LEARN THAT THEY CAN COEXIST.
THEY STILL HAVE MEAD IN THIS TIME? FEELS LIKE I HAVEN'T HAD A DRINK FOR A THOUSAND YEARS.
BOY. PREPARE TO FALL MORE IN LOVE WITH MIDGARD THAN EVER. AS I INTRODUCE YOU TO THE ERA THAT FUTURE HISTORIANS WILL COME TO CALL...THE GOLDEN AGE OF CRAFT BEER.
IN PEACE. ACROSS ALL THE REALMS.
THE KING OF THE FROST GIANTS IS DEAD.
LONG LIVE THE KING.

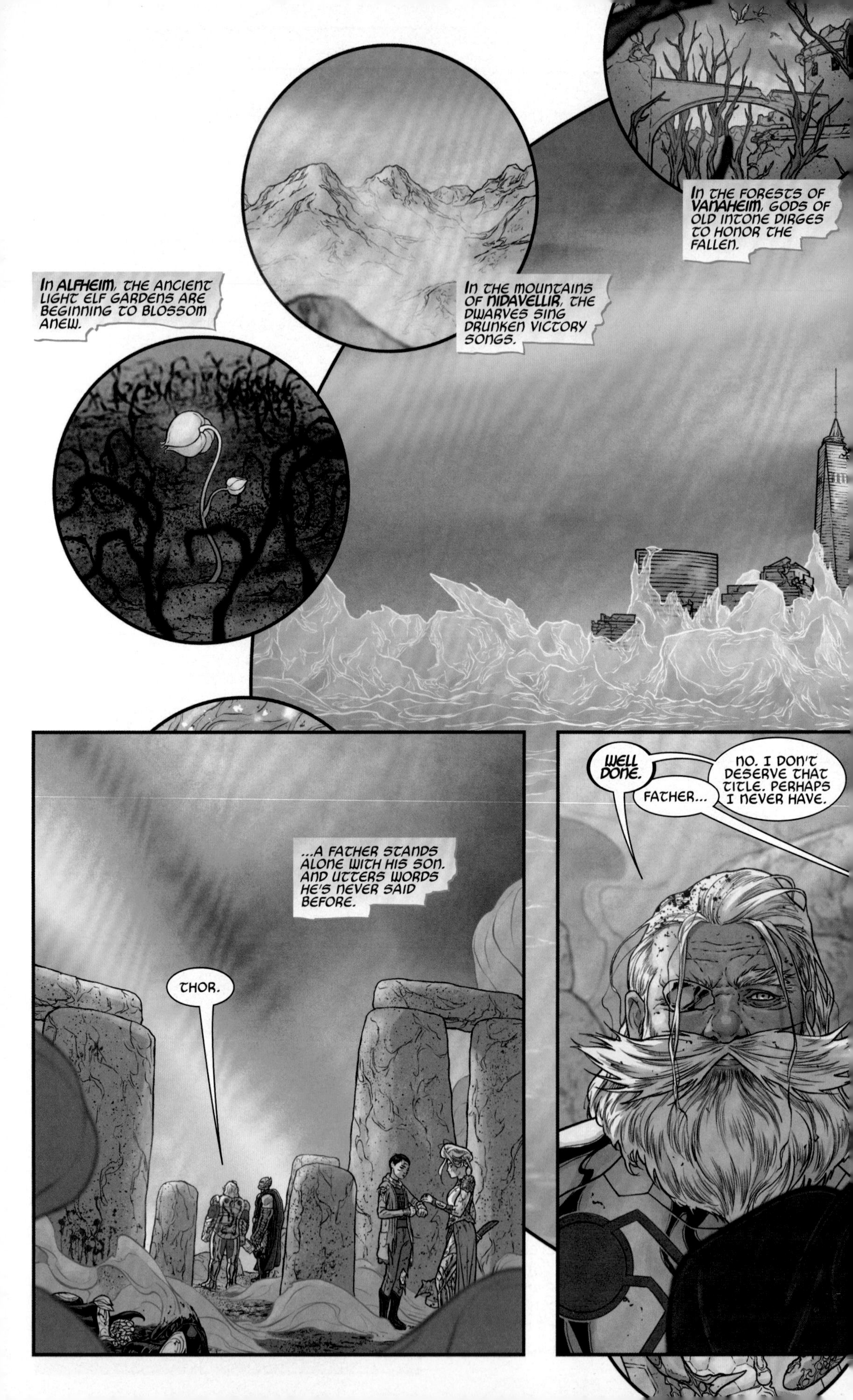
In the forests of Vanaheim, gods of old intone dirges to honor the fallen.
In Alfheim, the ancient light elf gardens are beginning to blossom anew.
In the mountains of Nidavellir, the dwarves sing drunken victory songs.
...A father stands alone with his son. And utters words he's never said before.
THOR.
WELL DONE.
FATHER...
NO. I DON'T DESERVE THAT TITLE. PERHAPS I NEVER HAVE.

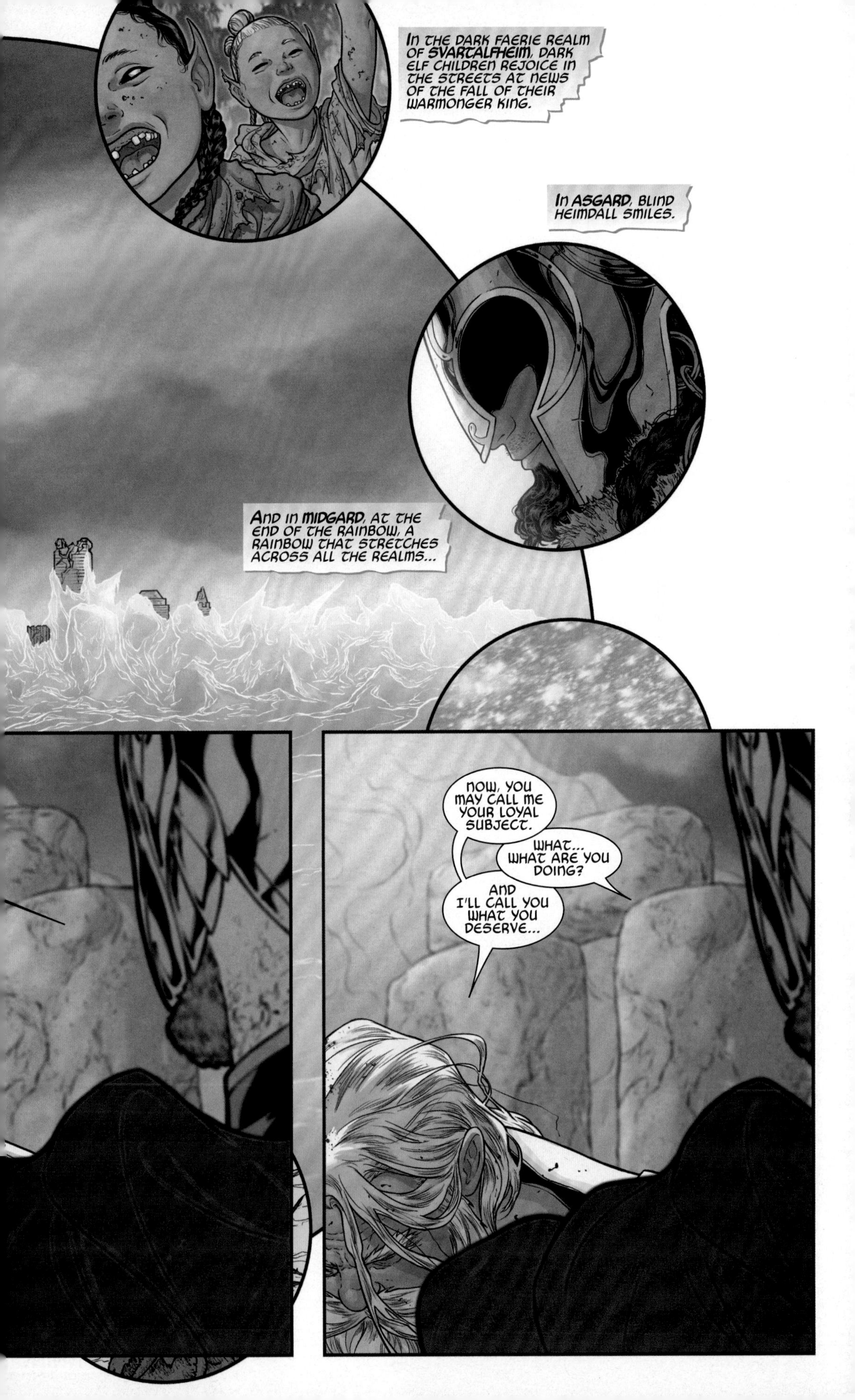
In the dark faerie realm of SVARTALFHEIM, dark elf children rejoice in the streets at news of the fall of their warmonger king.
In ASGARD, blind Heimdall smiles.
And in MIDGARD, at the end of the rainbow, a rainbow that stretches across all the realms...
Now, you may call me your loyal subject.
What... what are you doing?
And I'll call you what you deserve...

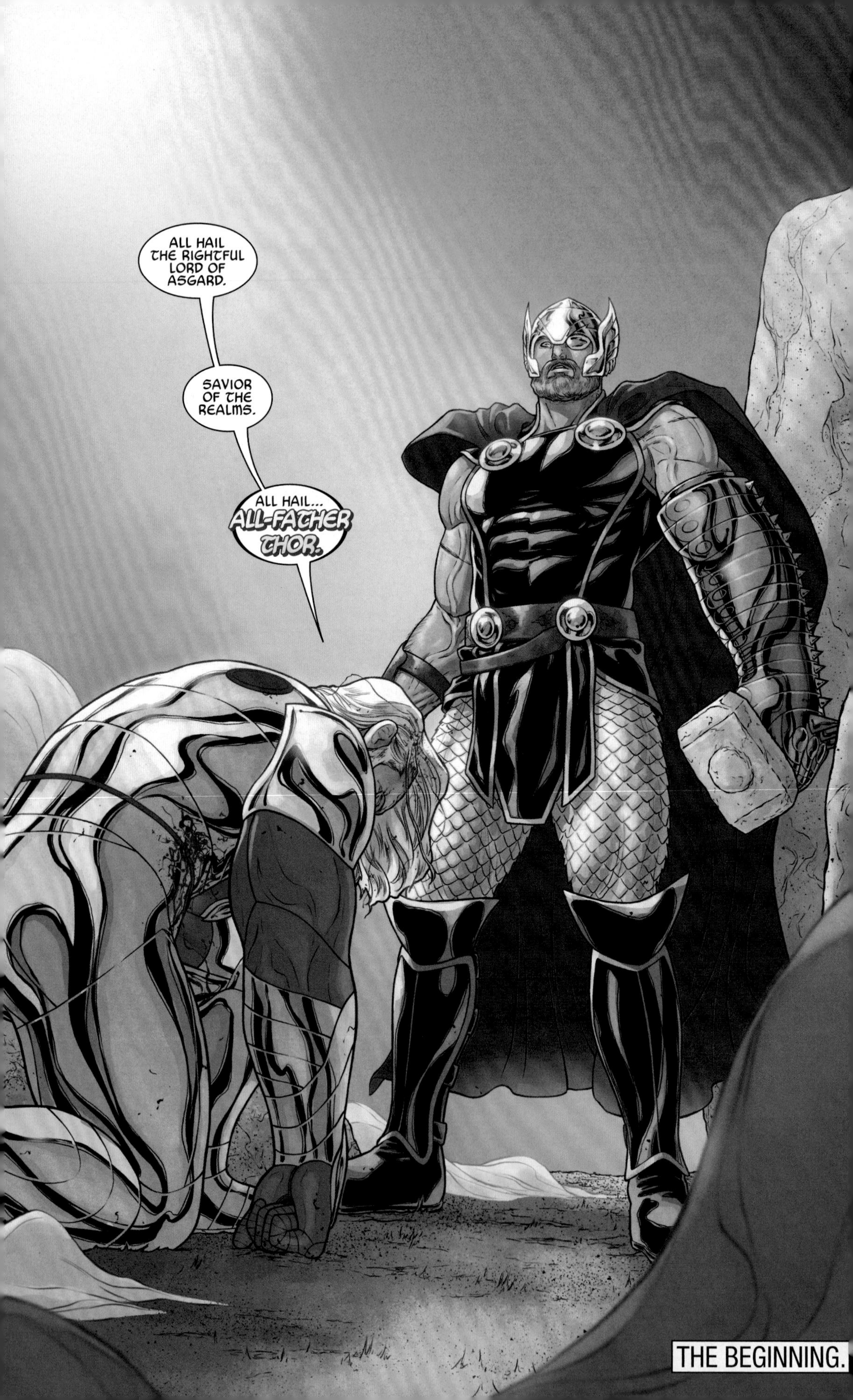
ALL HAIL THE RIGHTFUL LORD OF ASGARD.
SAVIOR OF THE REALMS.
ALL HAIL... ALL-FATHER THOR.
THE BEGINNING.

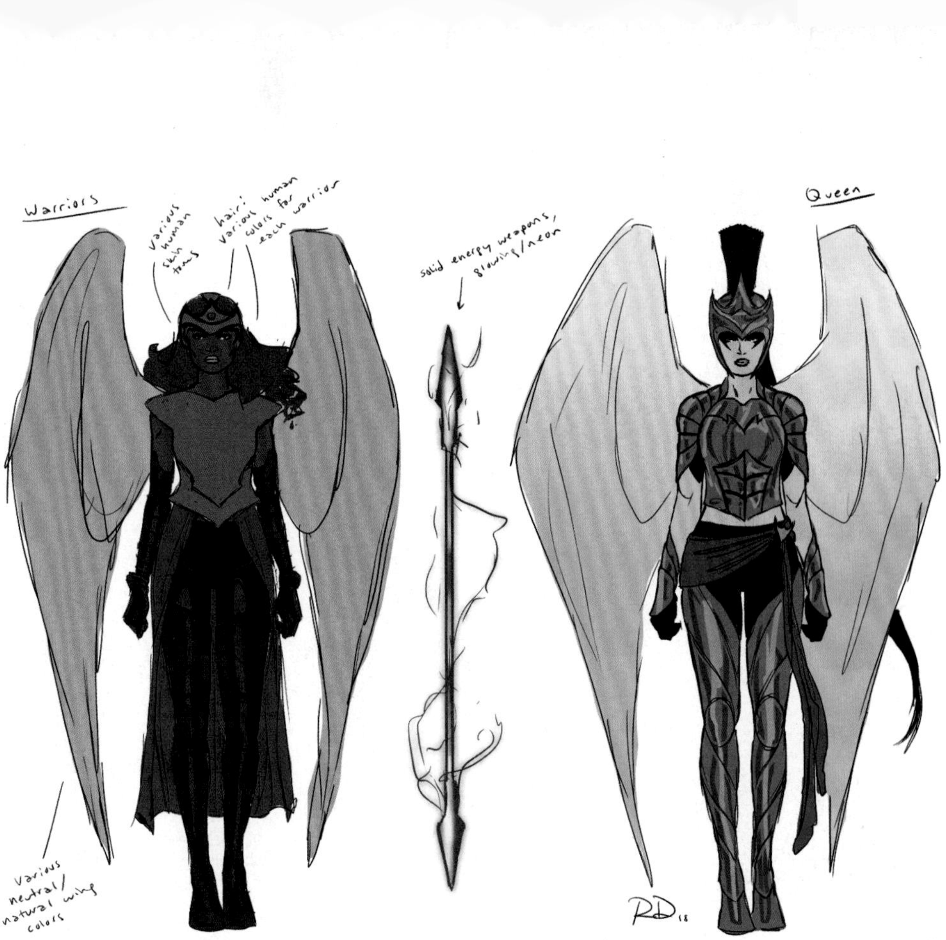

Warriors
various human skin tones
hair: various human colors for each warrior
various neutral/natural wing colors
solid energy weapons, glowing/neon
Queen
RD 18

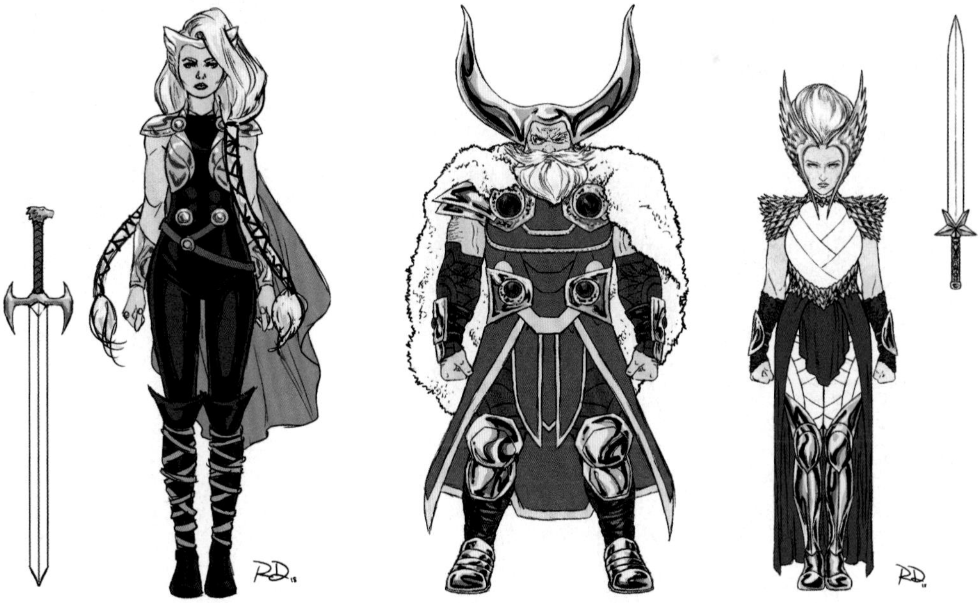

man

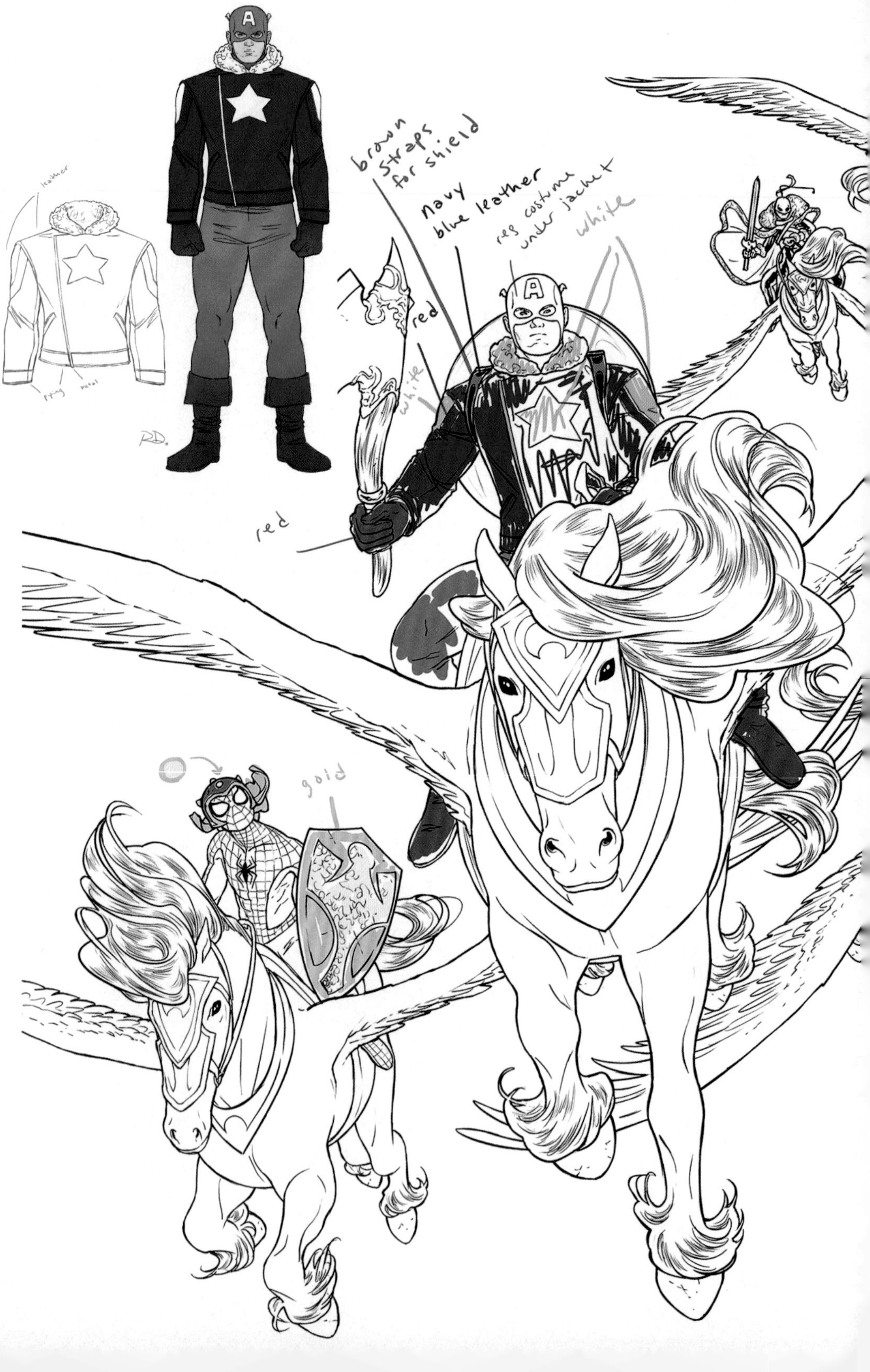
leather
piping
metal
RD.
brown straps for shield
navy blue leather
reg costume under jacket
white
red
white
red
gold

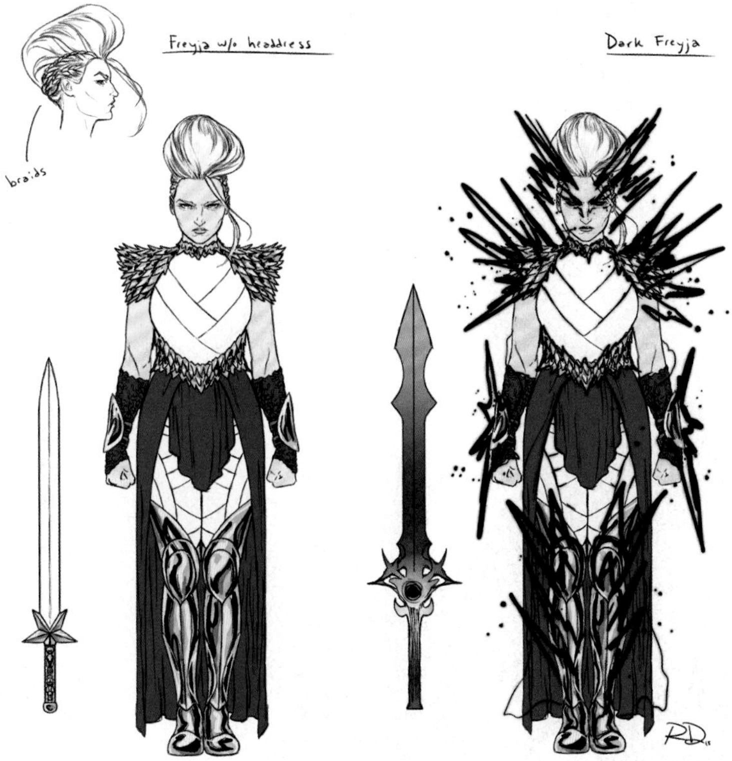
Freyja w/o headdress
Dark Freyja
braids

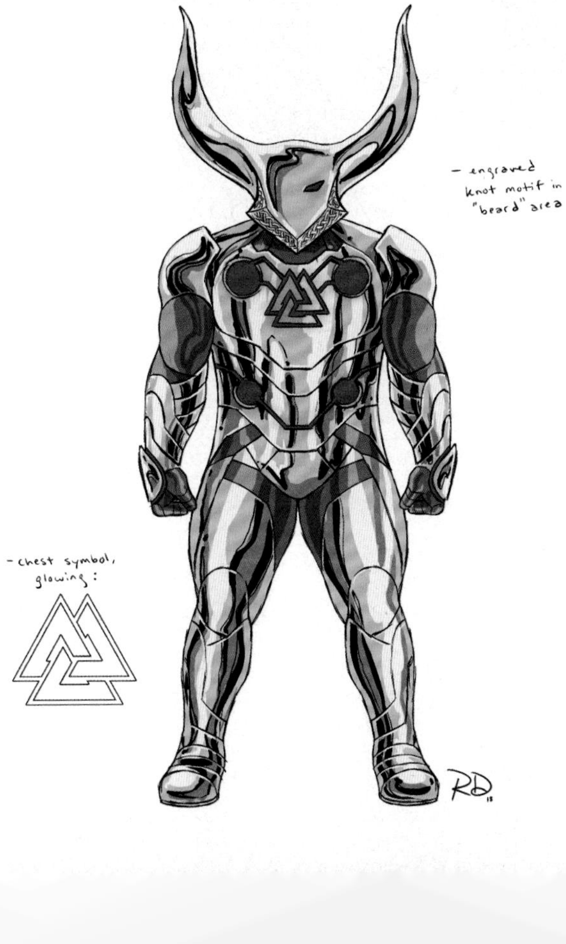
- engraved knot motif in "beard" area
- chest symbol, glowing:

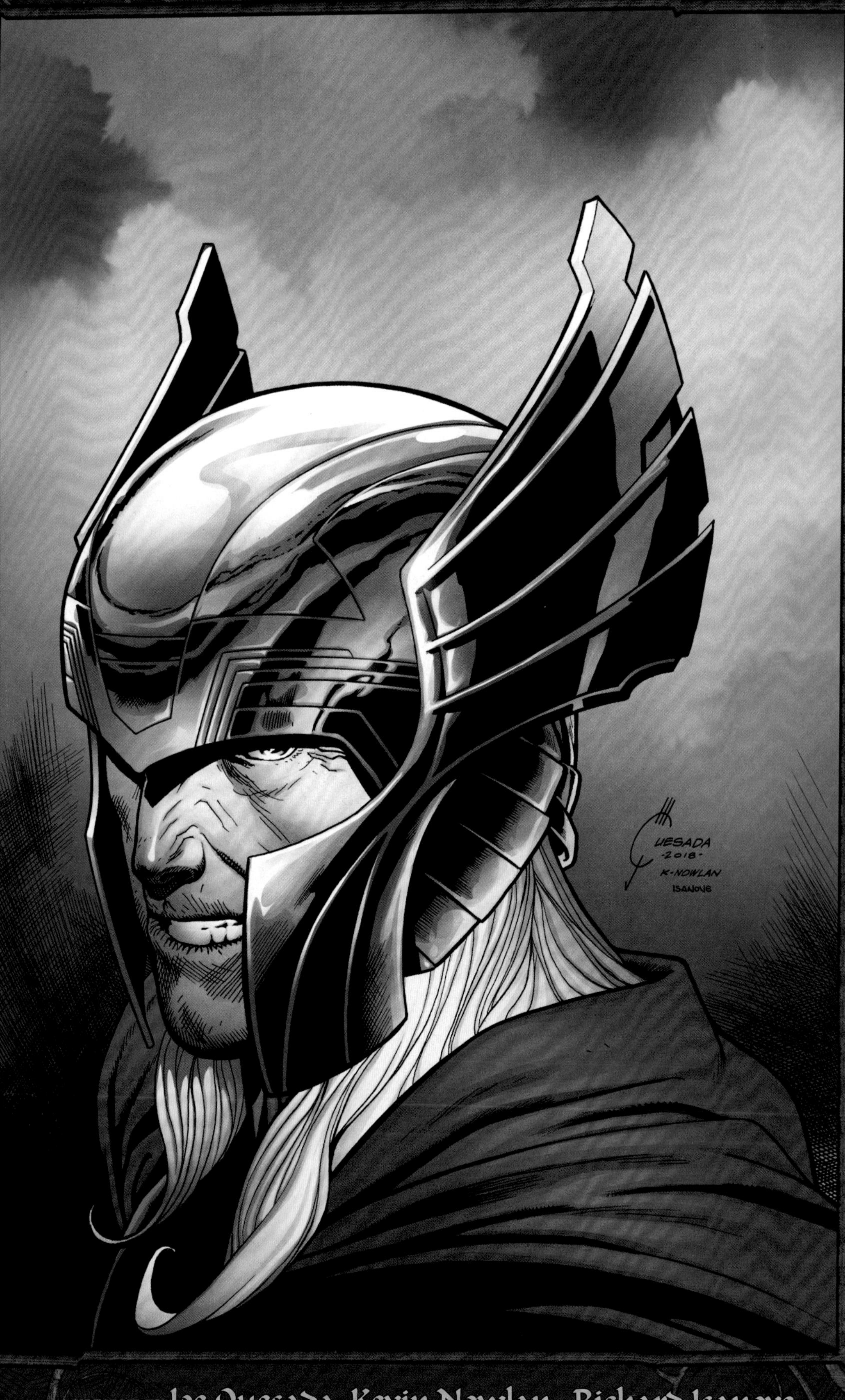

#1 VARIANT BY Joe Quesada, Kevin Nowlan & Richard Isanove

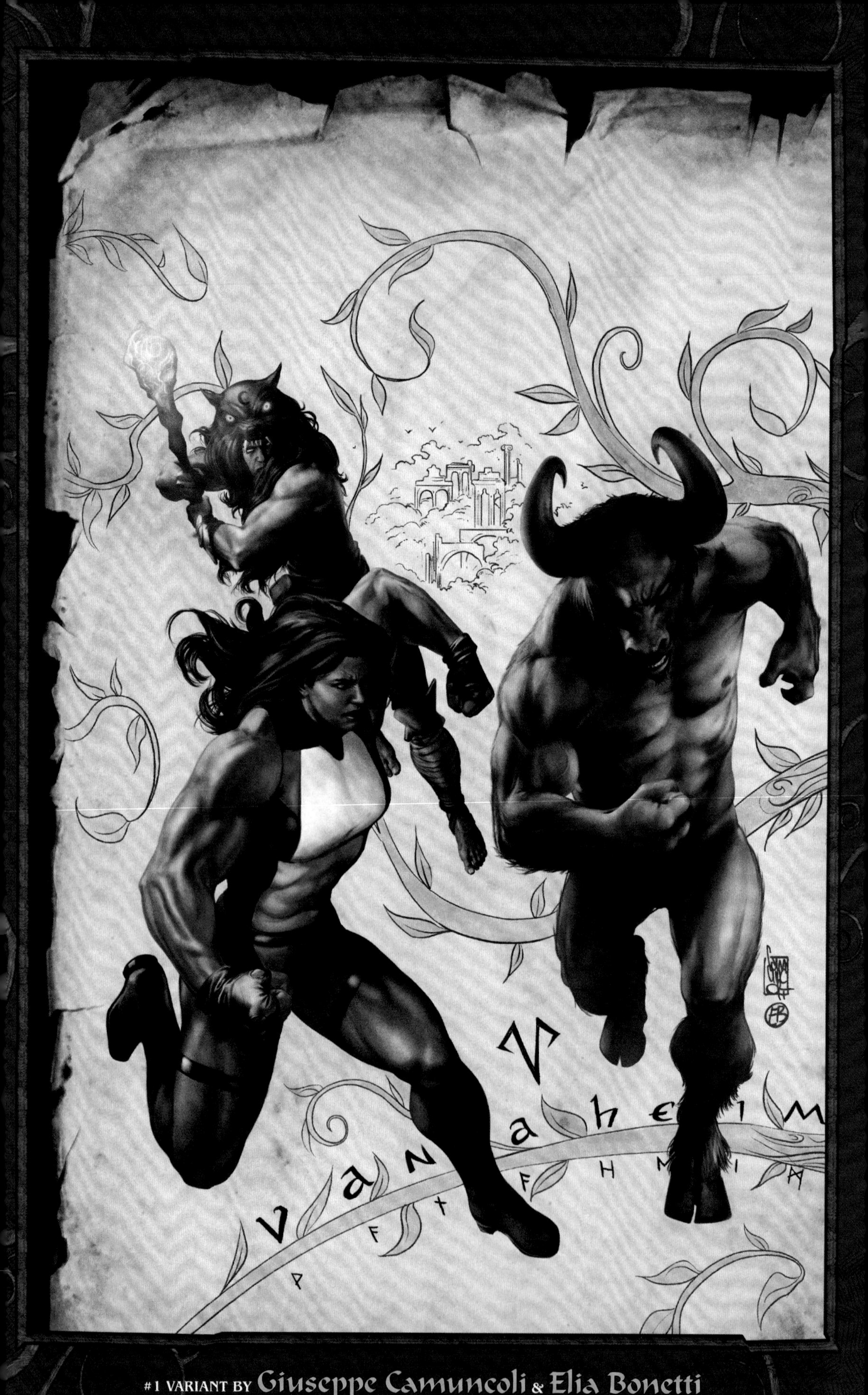
Vanaheim

#1 VARIANT BY Giuseppe Camuncoli & Elia Bonetti

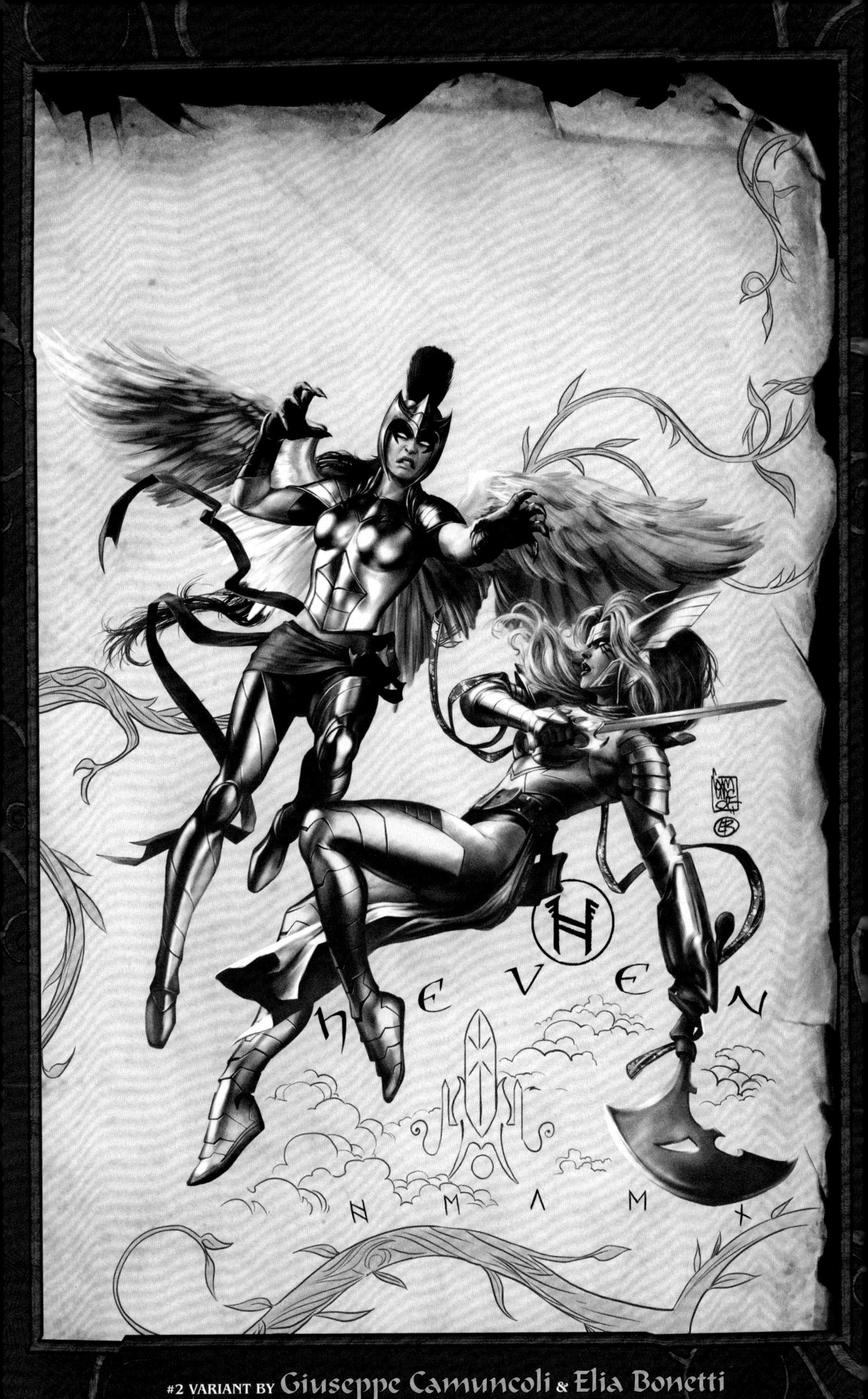
HEVEN

#2 VARIANT BY Giuseppe Camuncoli & Elia Bonetti

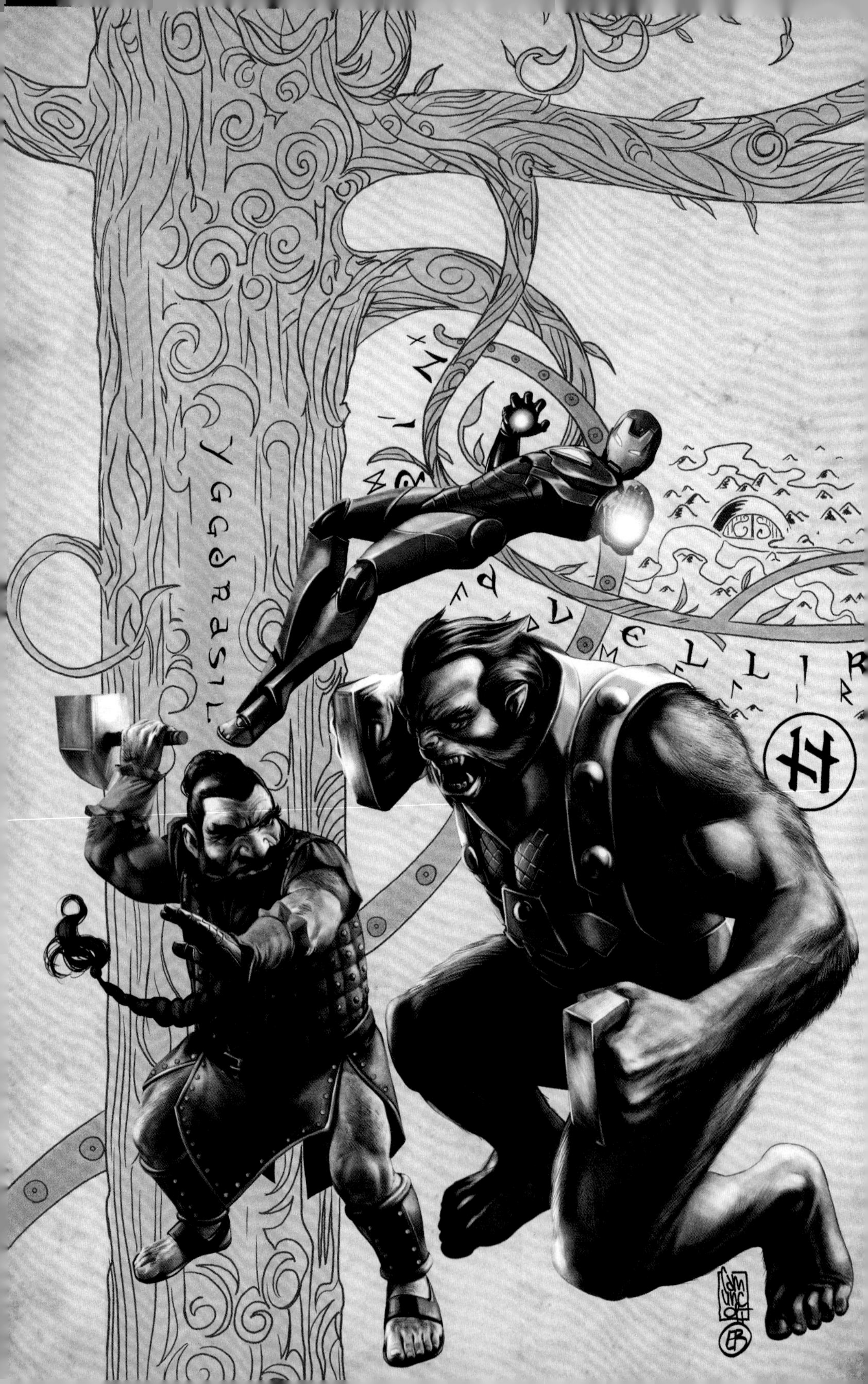
YGGDRASIL
NIDAVELLIR

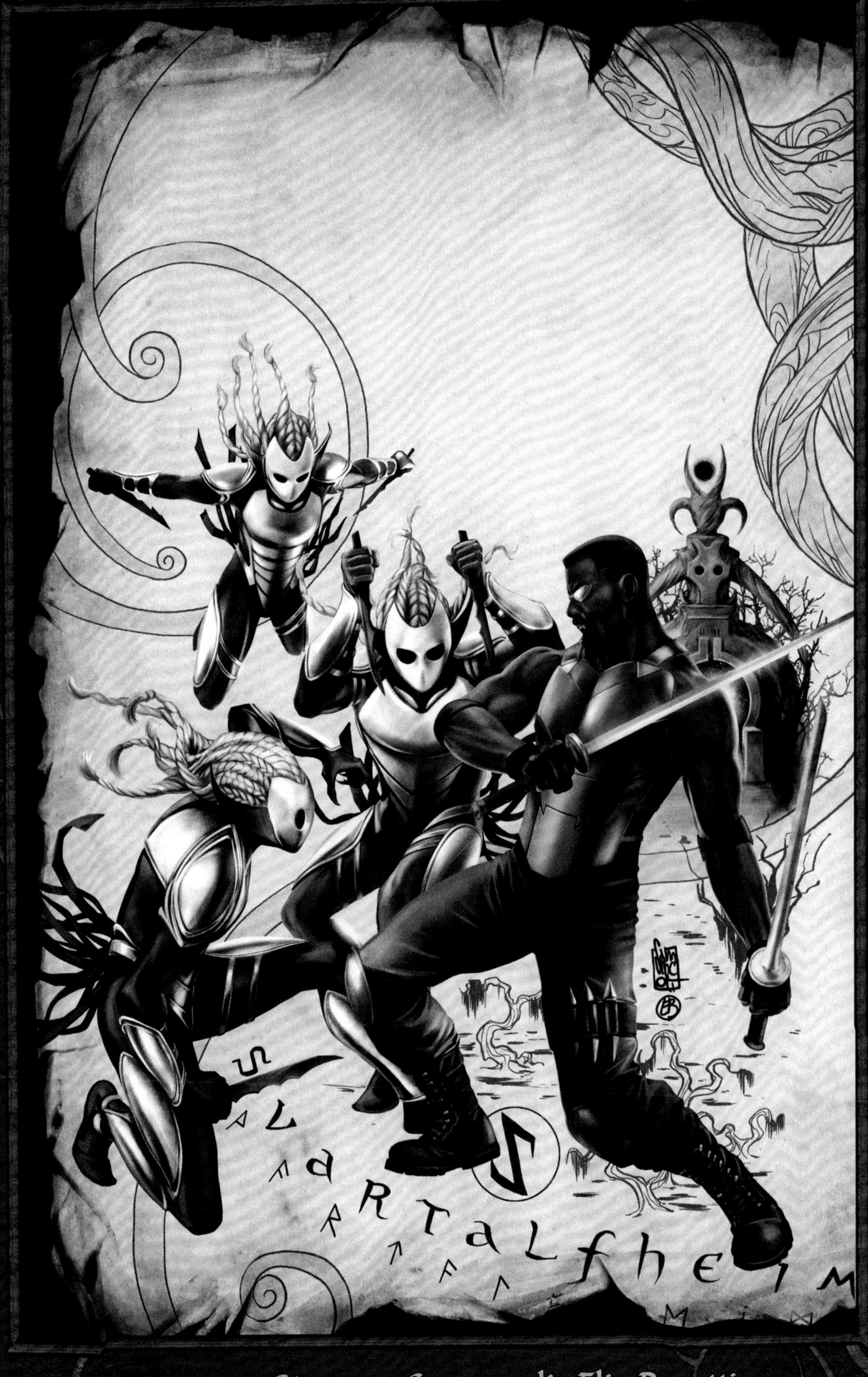
SVARTALFHEIM

#4 VARIANT BY Giuseppe Camuncoli & Elia Bonetti

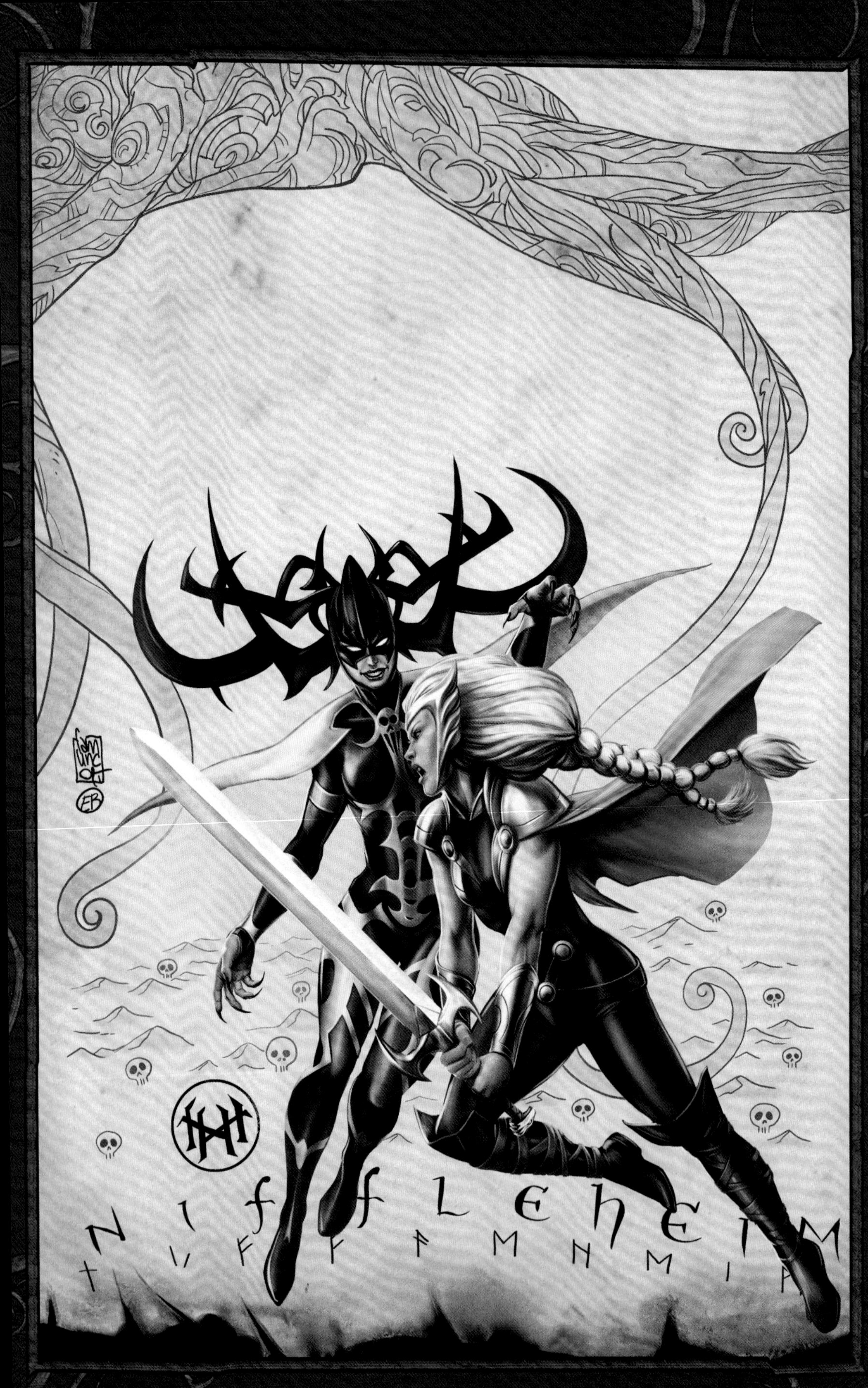
NIFFLEHEIM

#5 VARIANT BY Giuseppe Camuncoli & Elia Bonetti

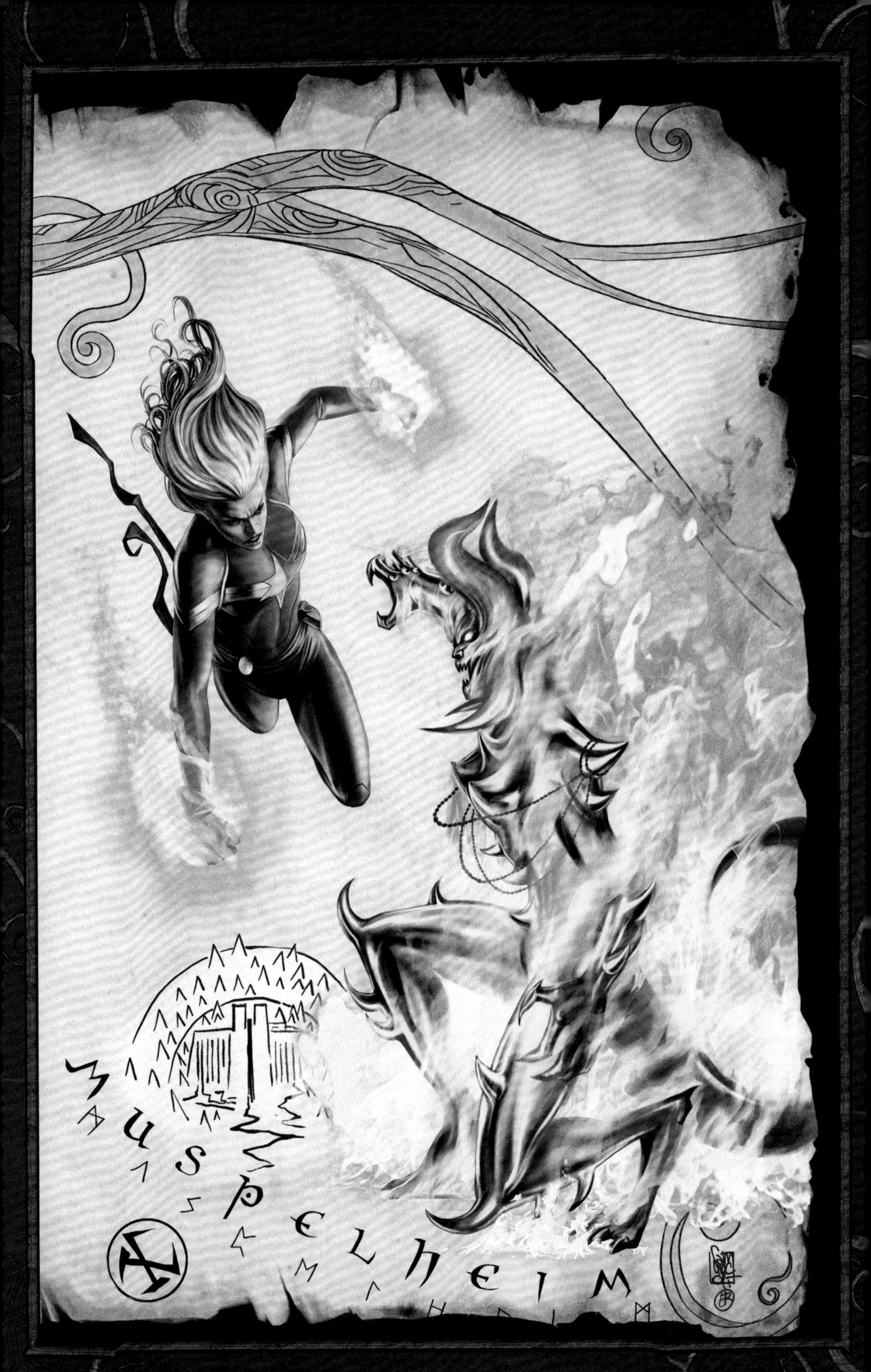
MUSPELHEIM

#6 VARIANT BY Giuseppe Camuncoli & Elia Bonetti

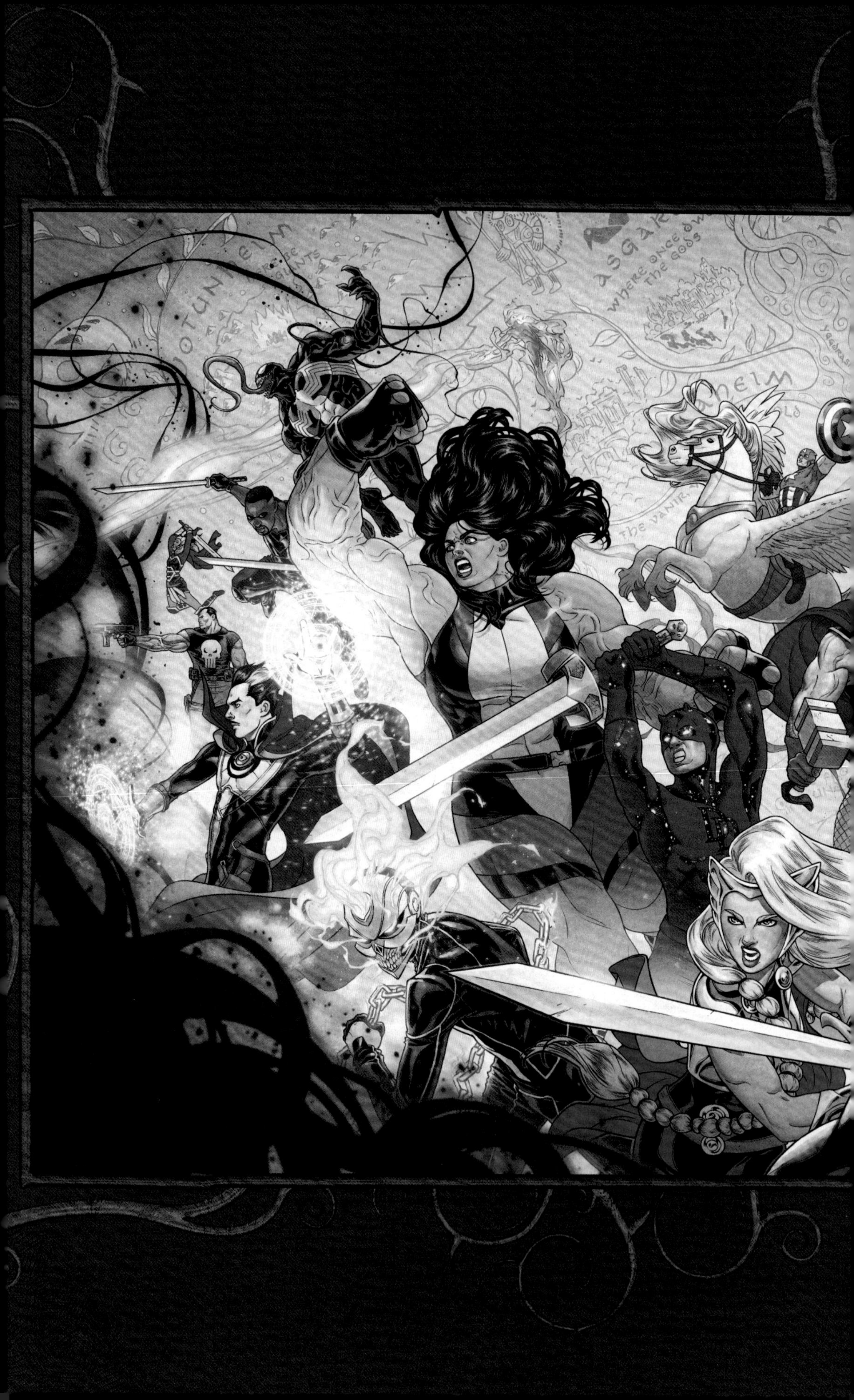
THE VANIR

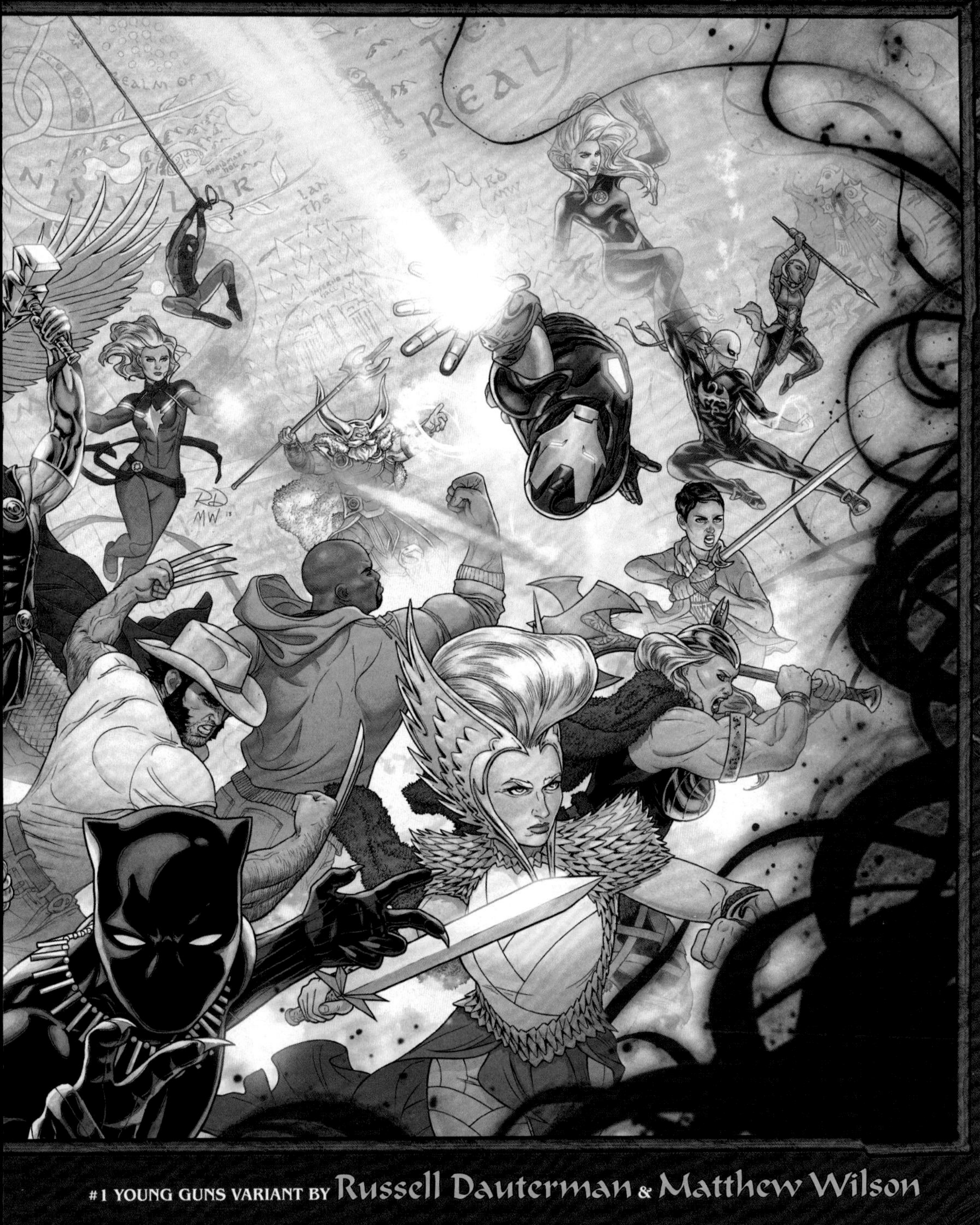

#1 YOUNG GUNS VARIANT BY Russell Dauterman & Matthew Wilson

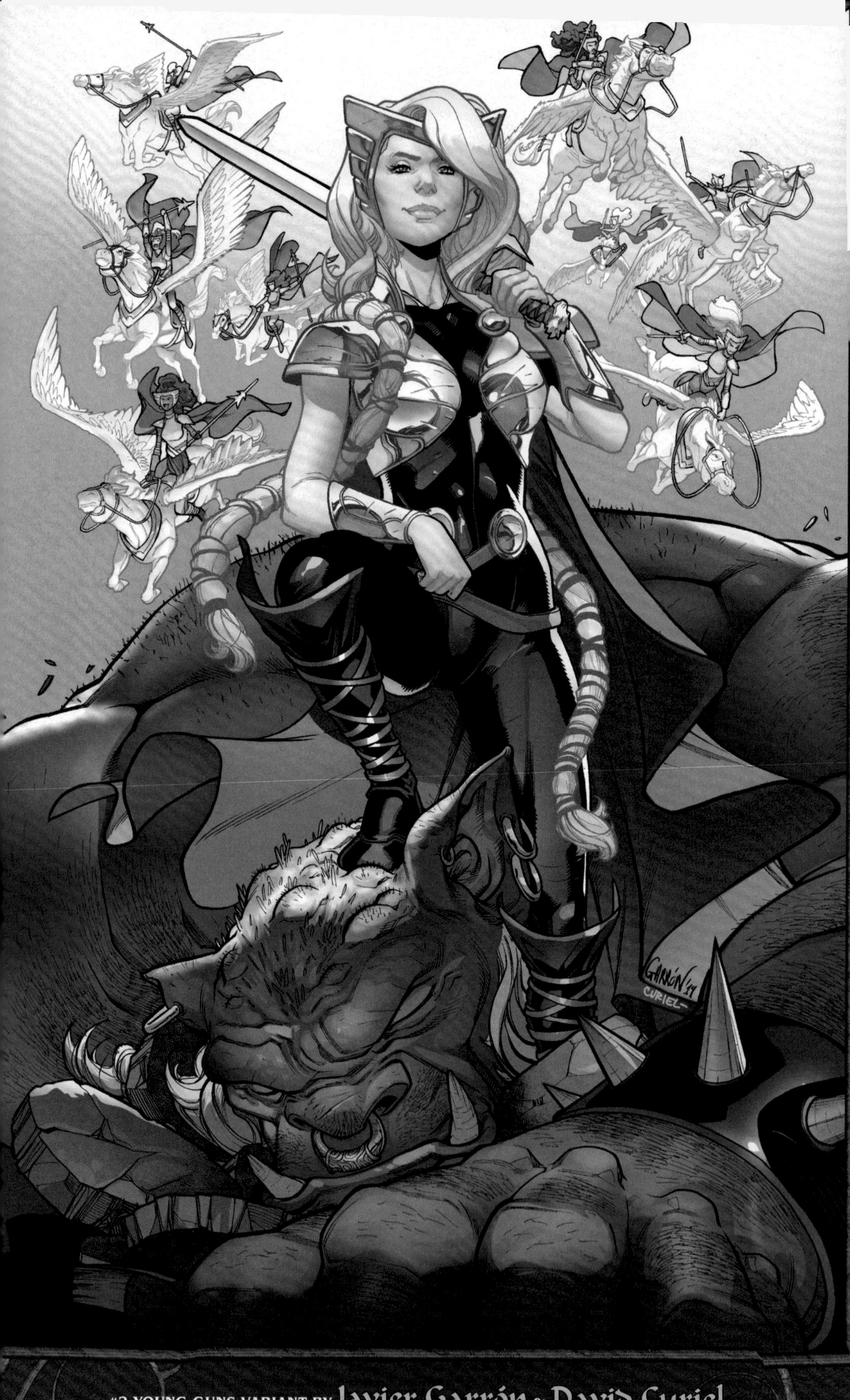
GARRÓN '19
CURIEL

#2 YOUNG GUNS VARIANT BY Javier Garrón & David Curiel

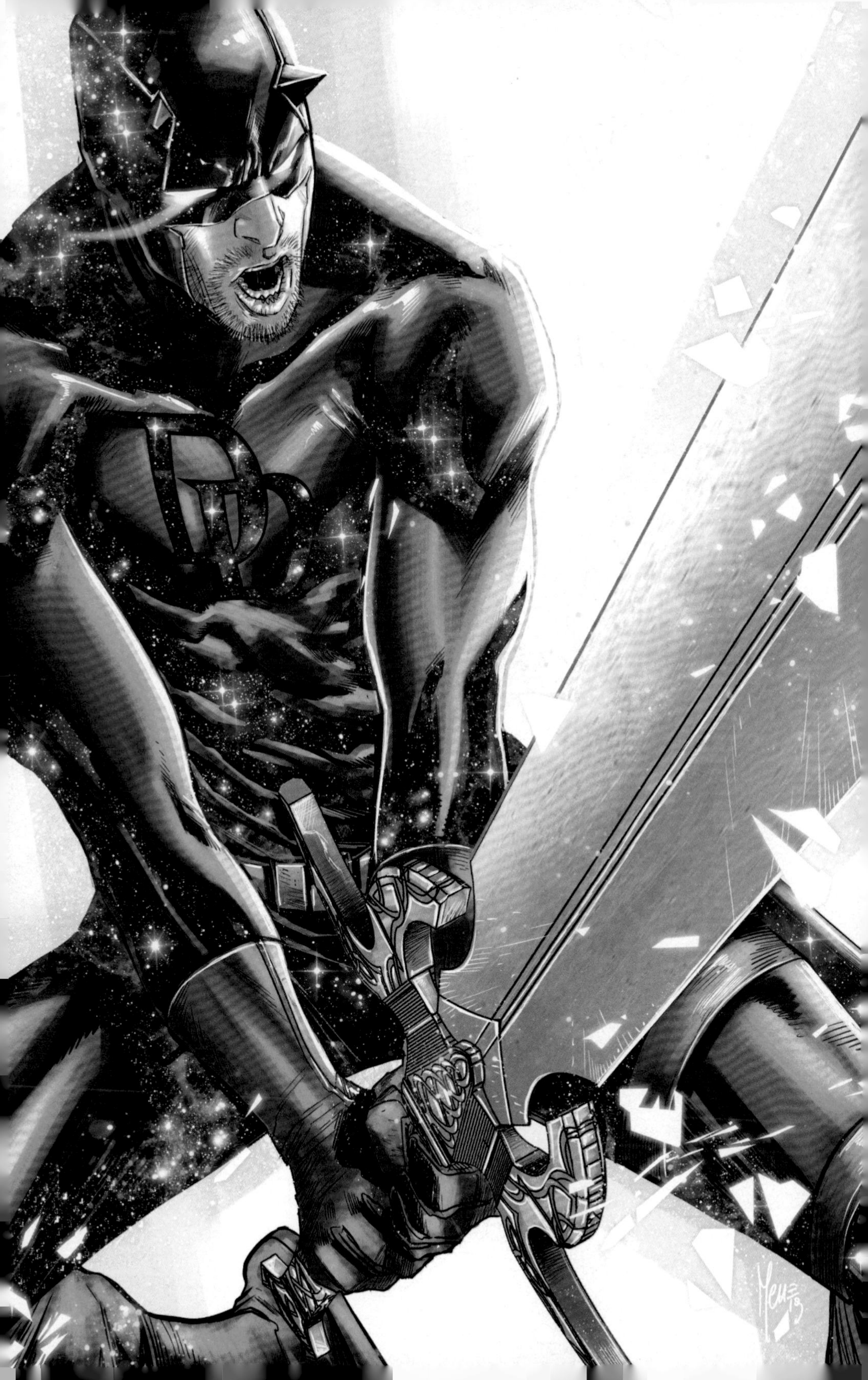

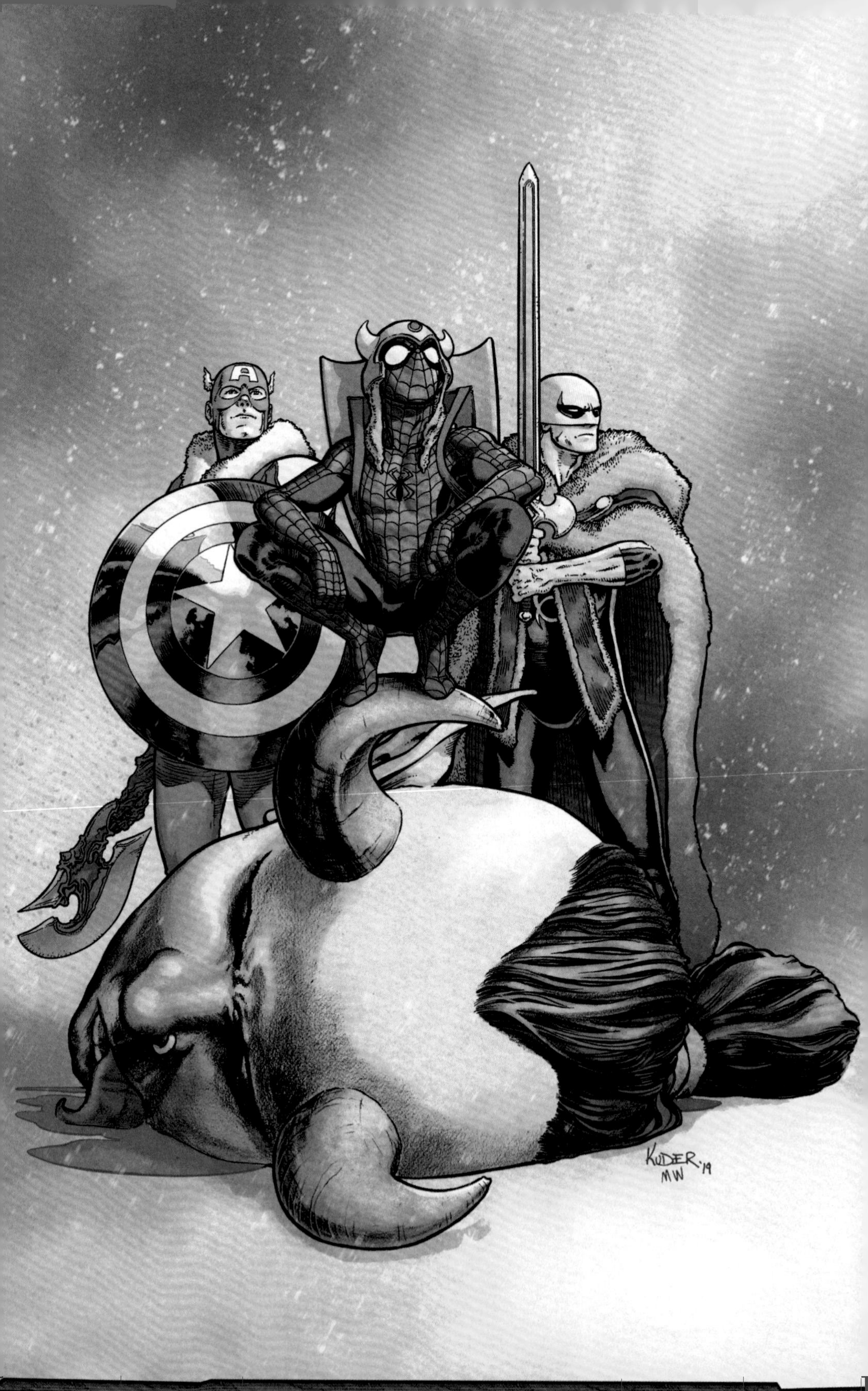
KUDER '19
MW

#4 YOUNG GUNS VA ew Wilson

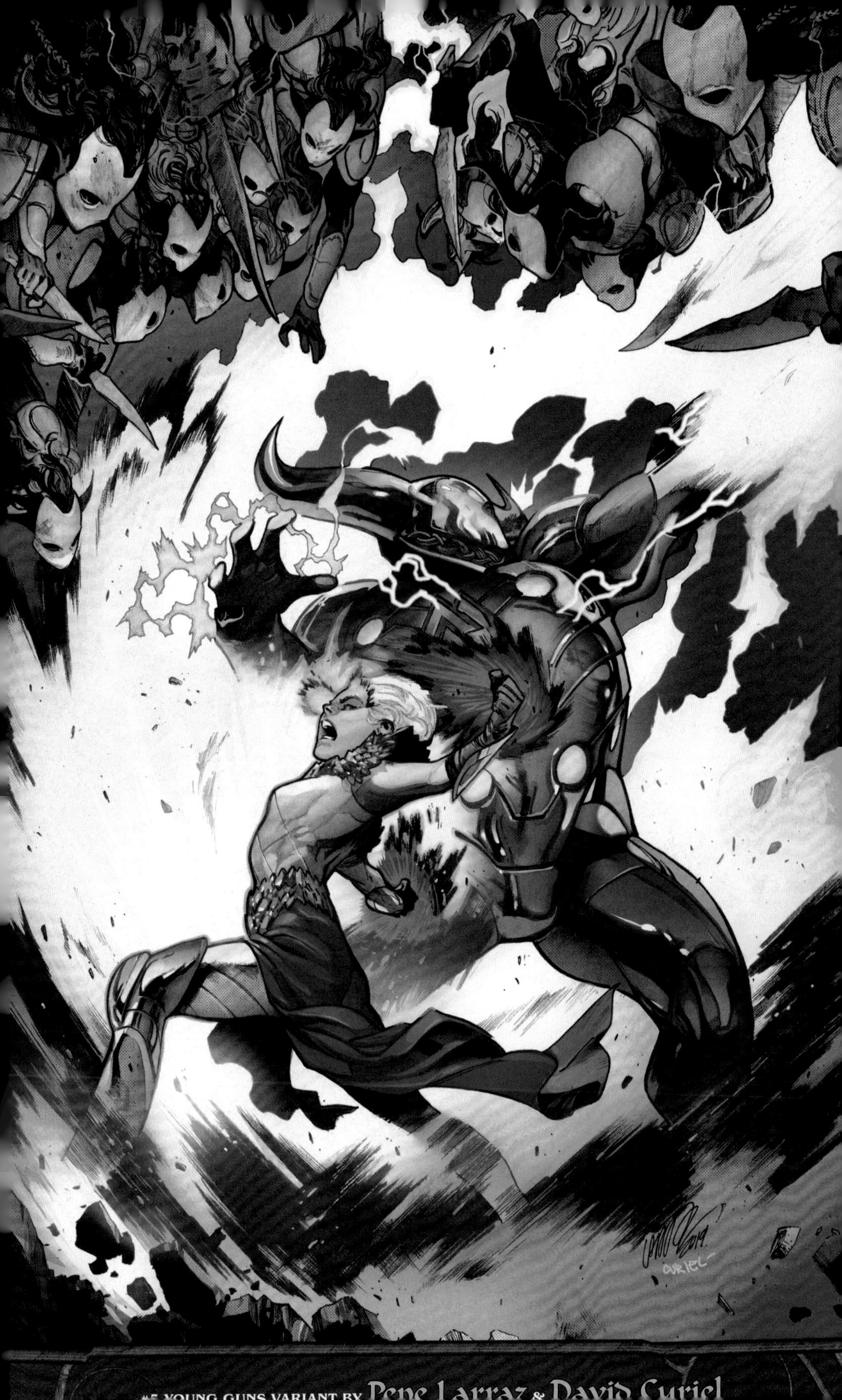

#5 YOUNG GUNS VARIANT BY Pepe Larraz & David Curiel

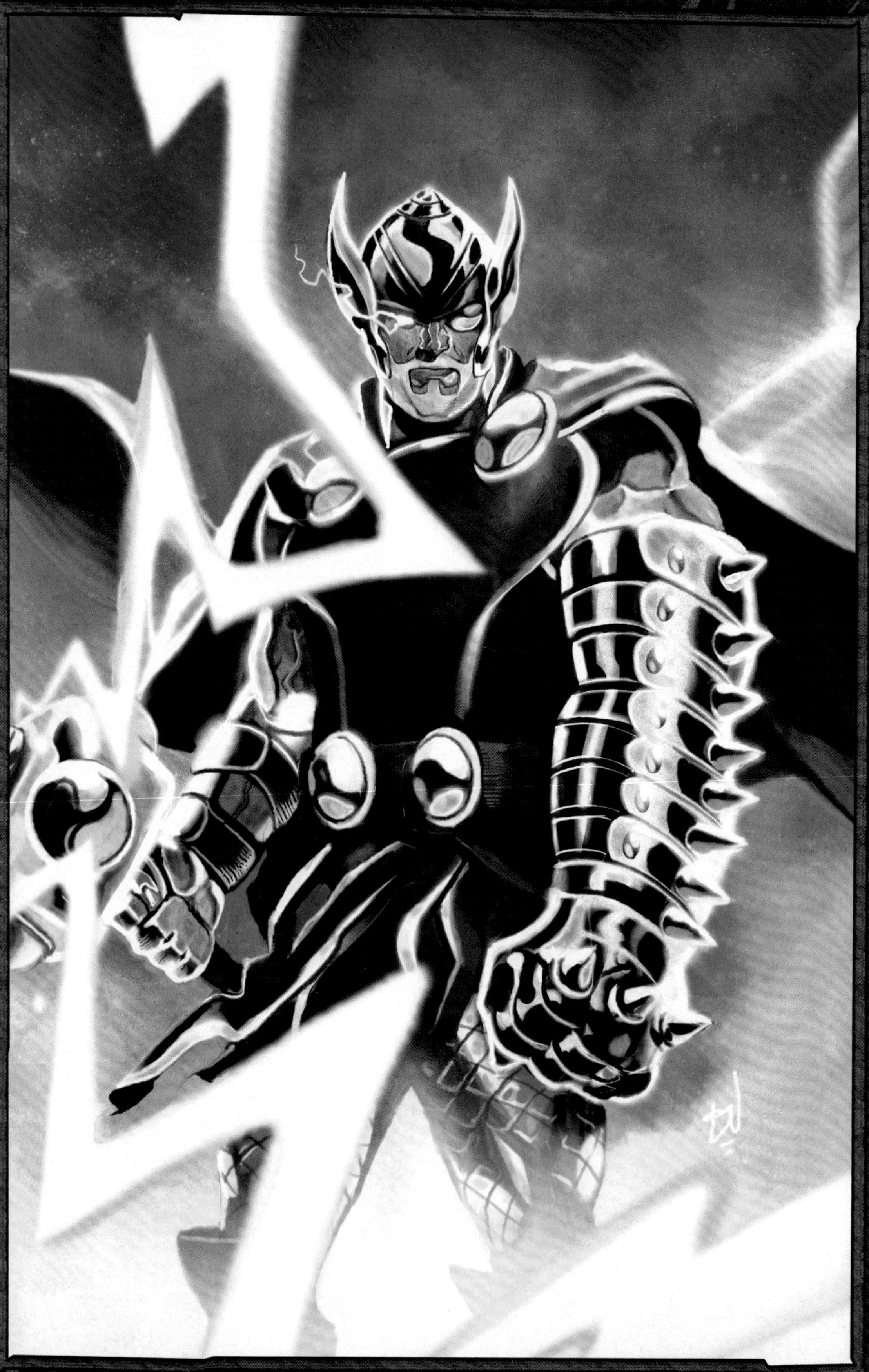

#6 YOUNG GUNS VARIANT BY Mike del Mundo

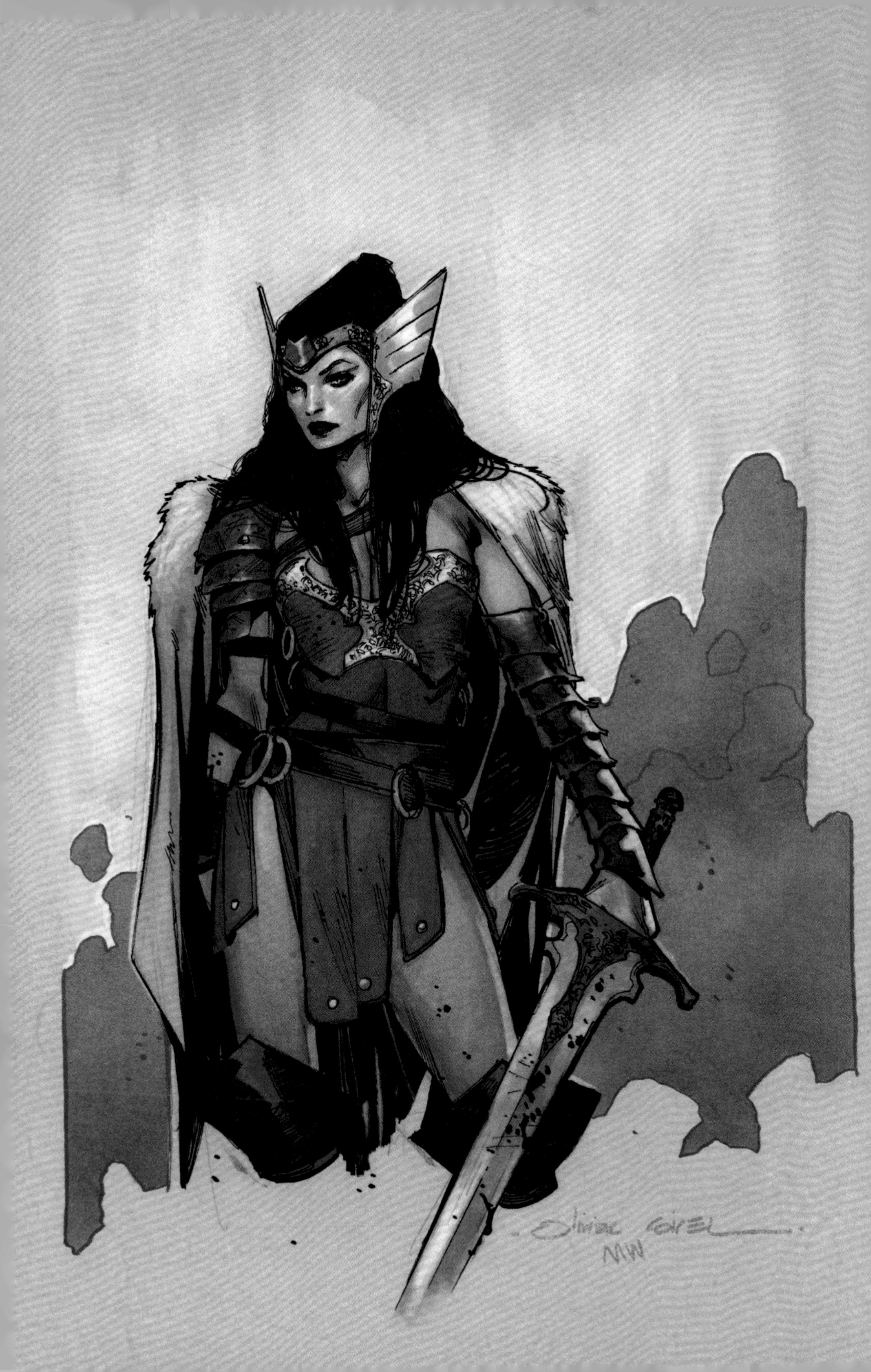

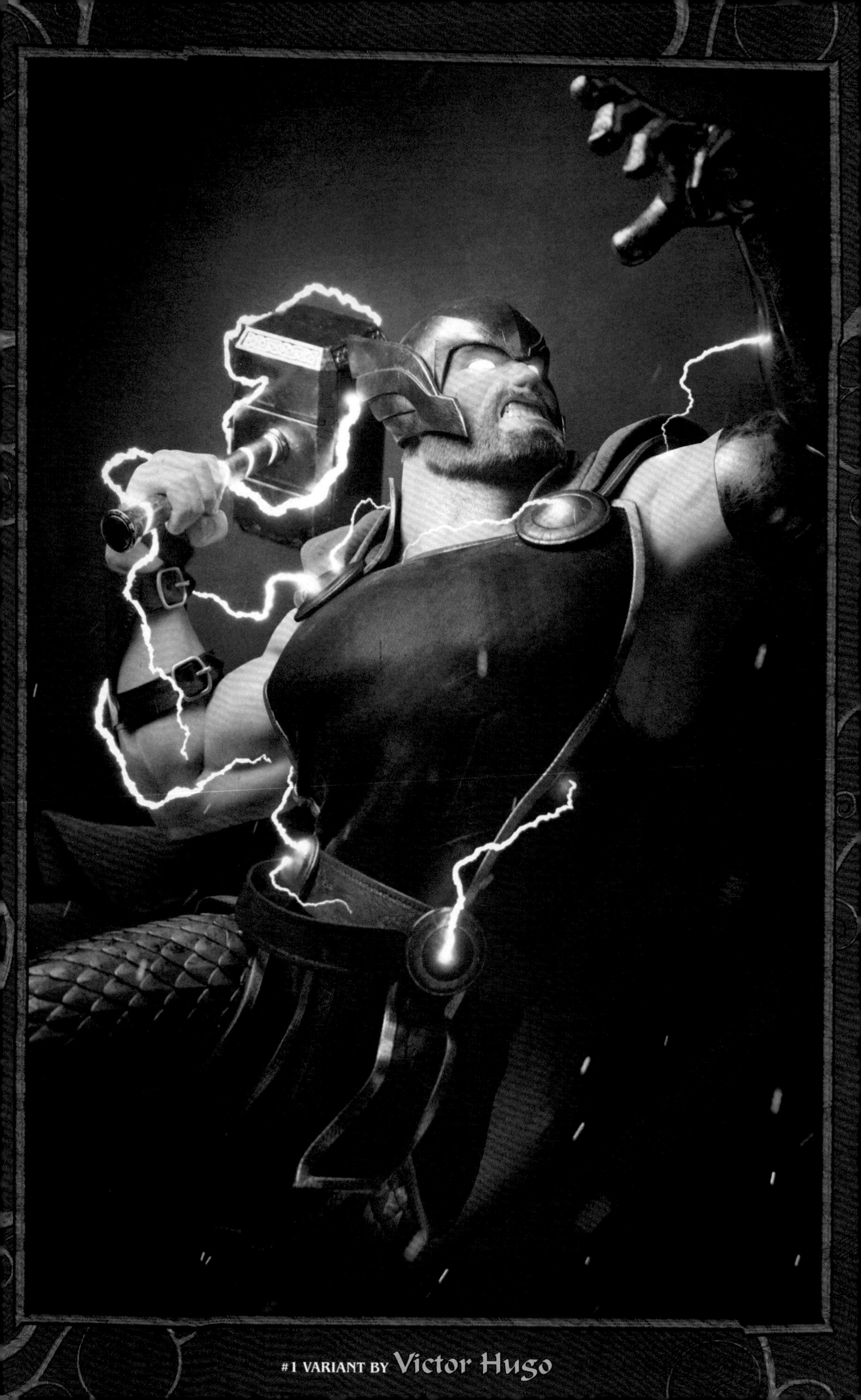

#1 VARIANT BY Victor Hugo

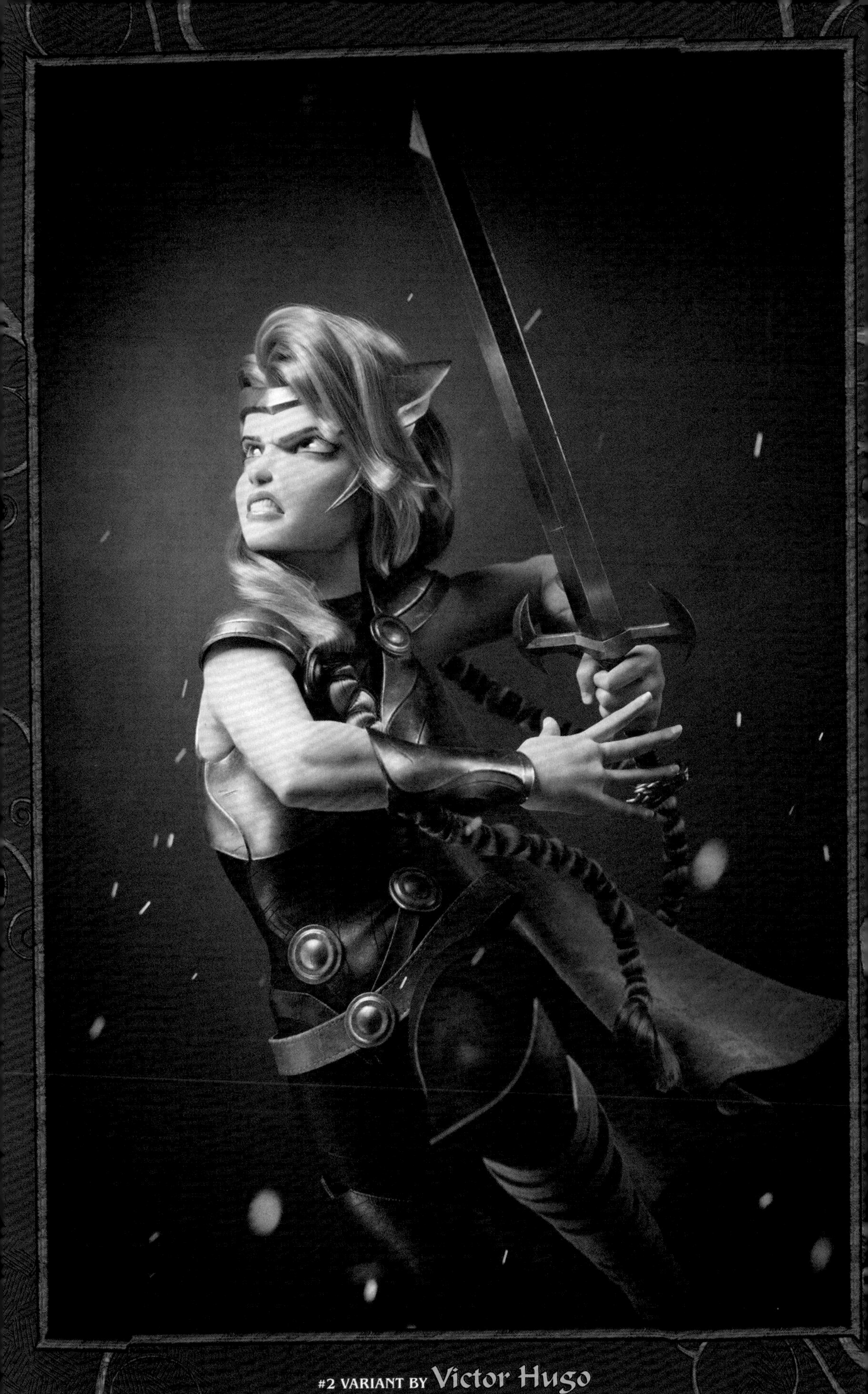

#2 VARIANT BY Victor Hugo

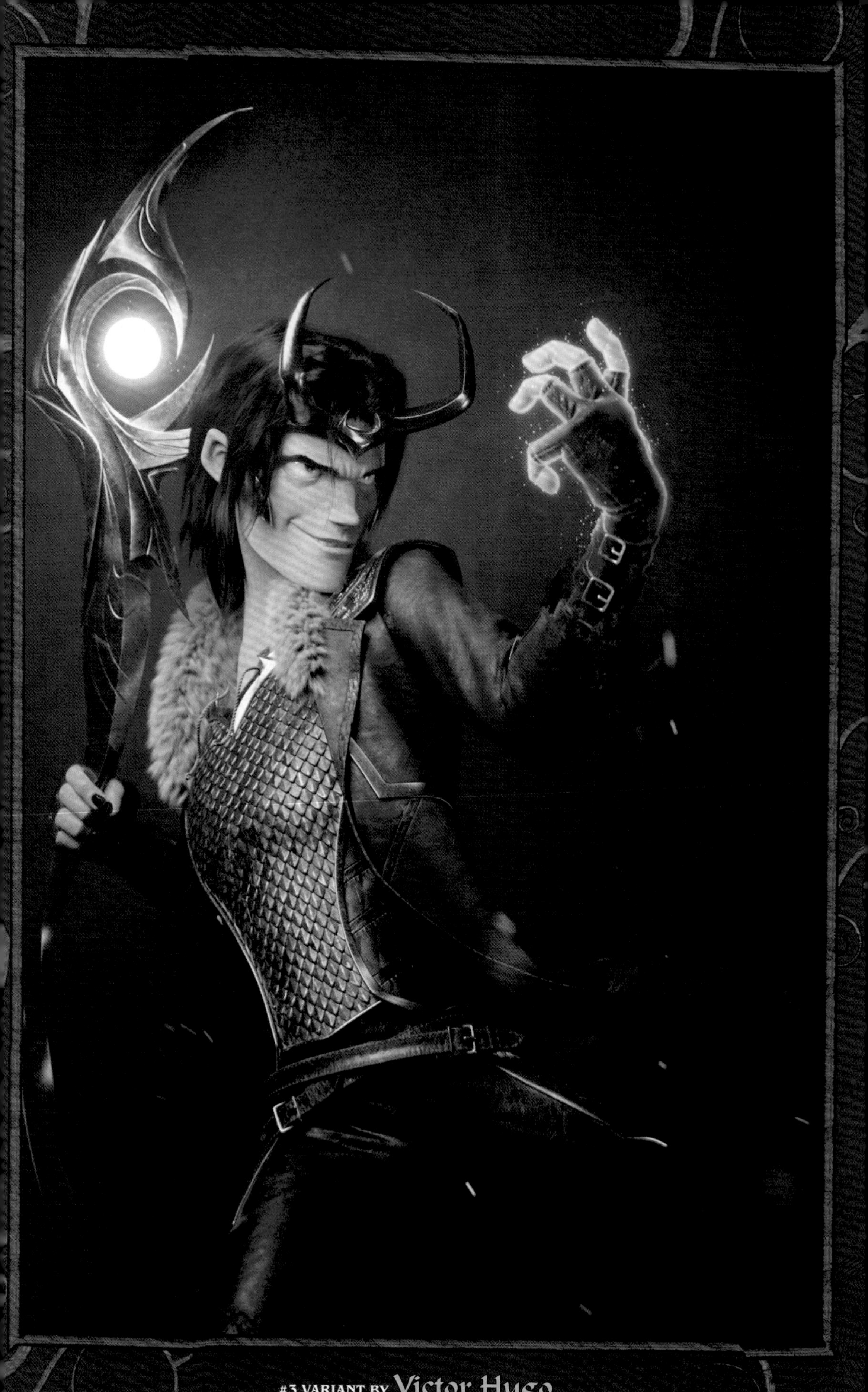

#3 VARIANT BY Victor Hugo

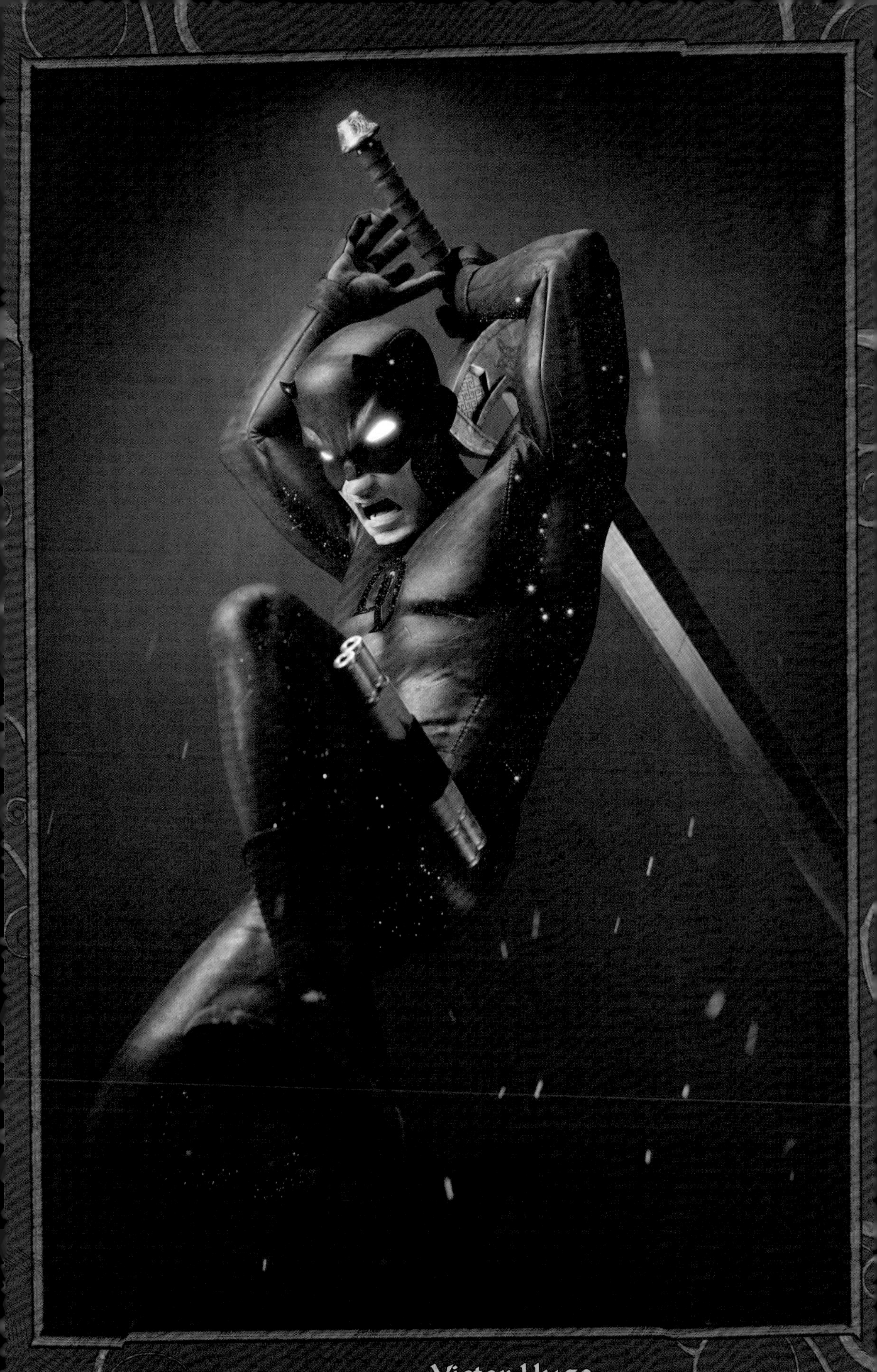

#4 VARIANT BY Victor Hugo

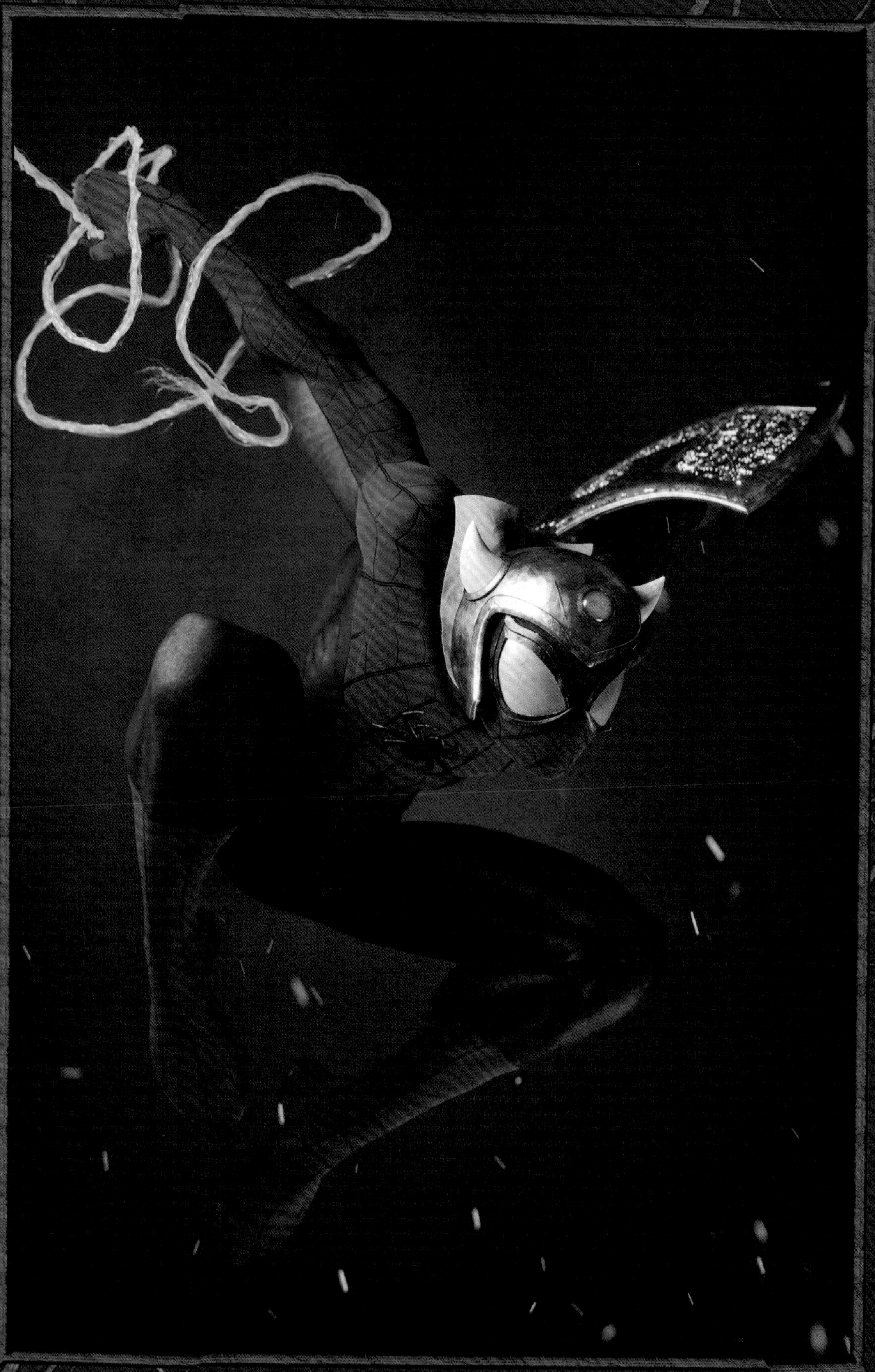

#5 VARIANT BY Victor Hugo

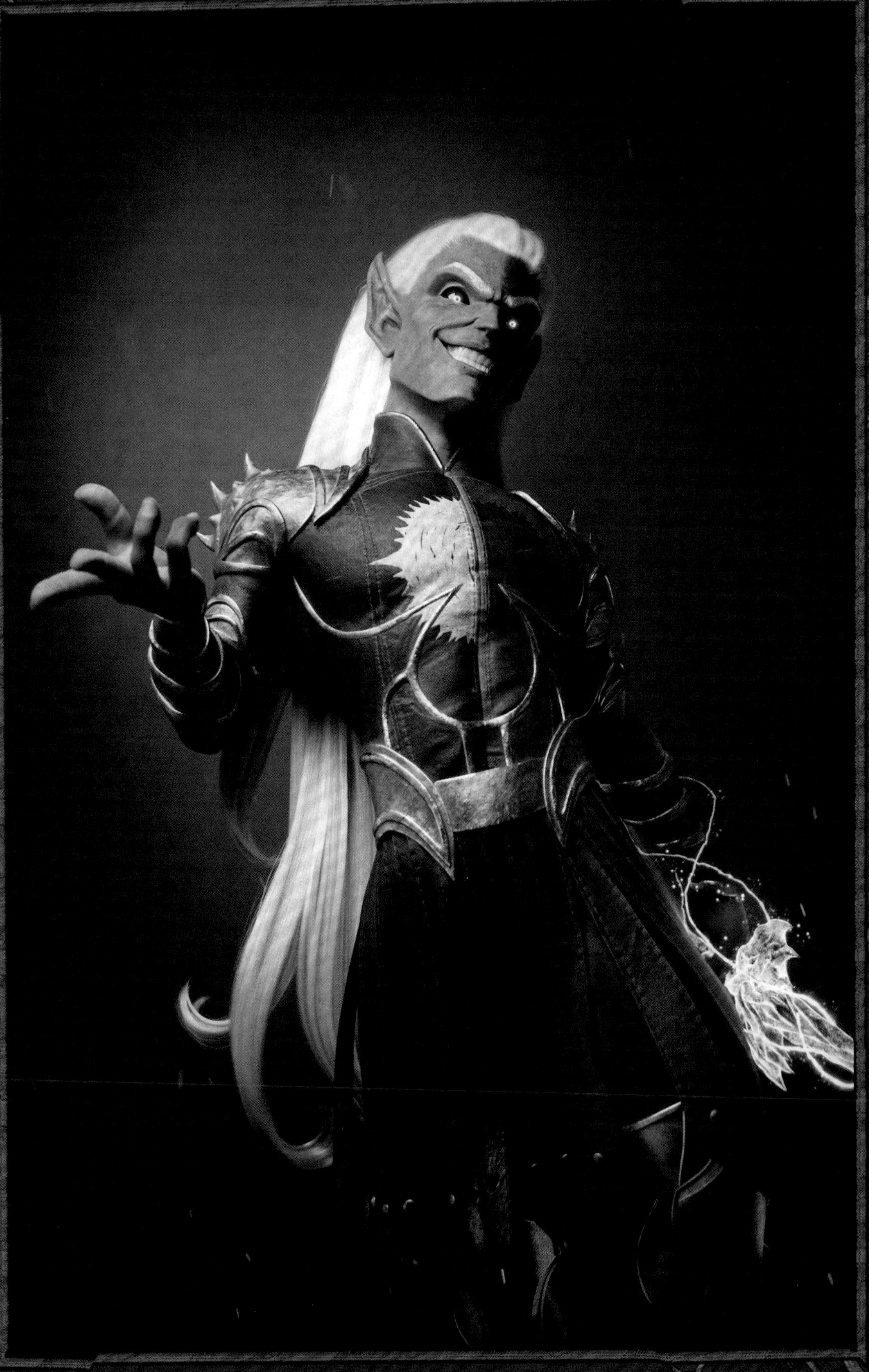

#6 VARIANT BY Victor Hugo

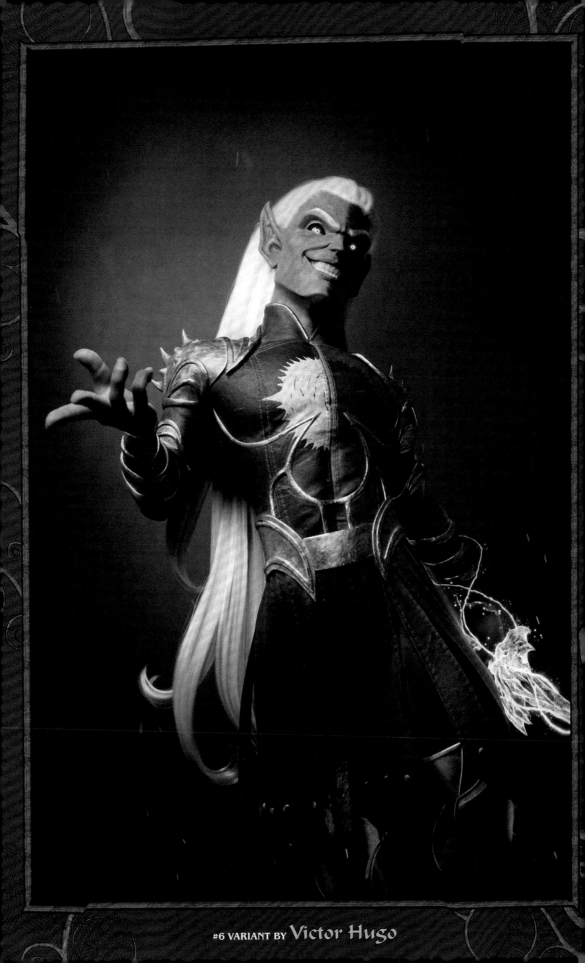

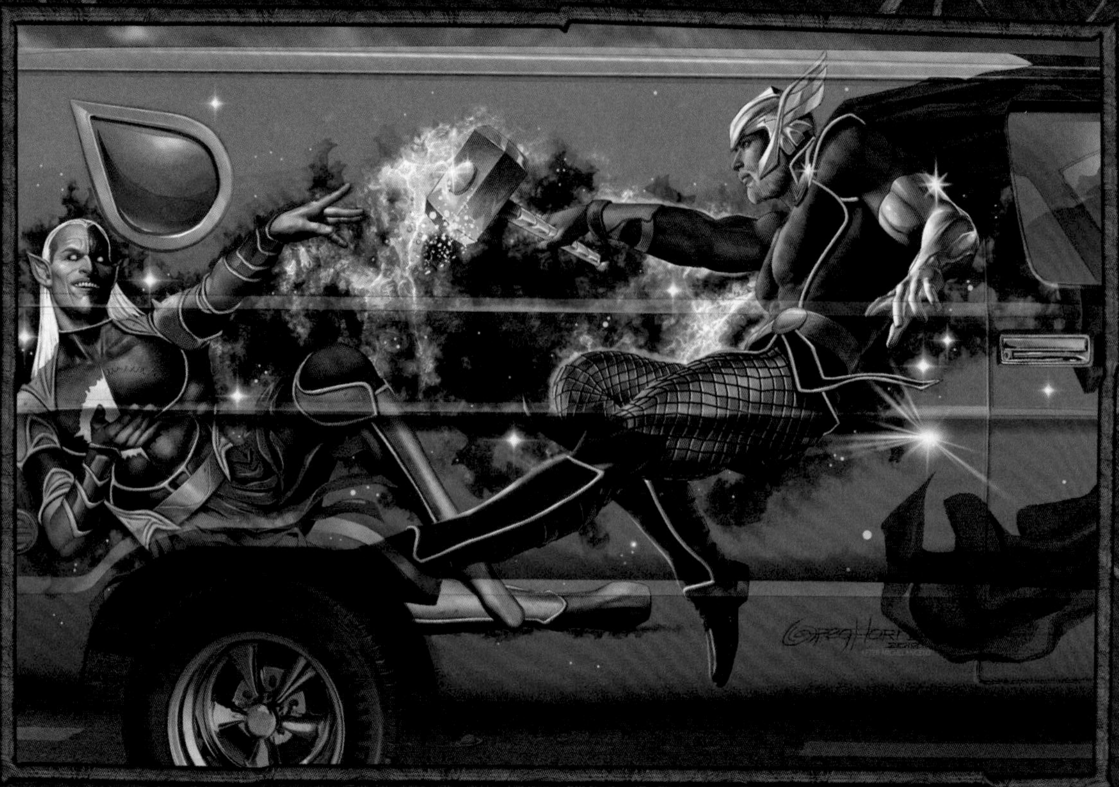

#1 VAN VARIANT BY Greg Horn

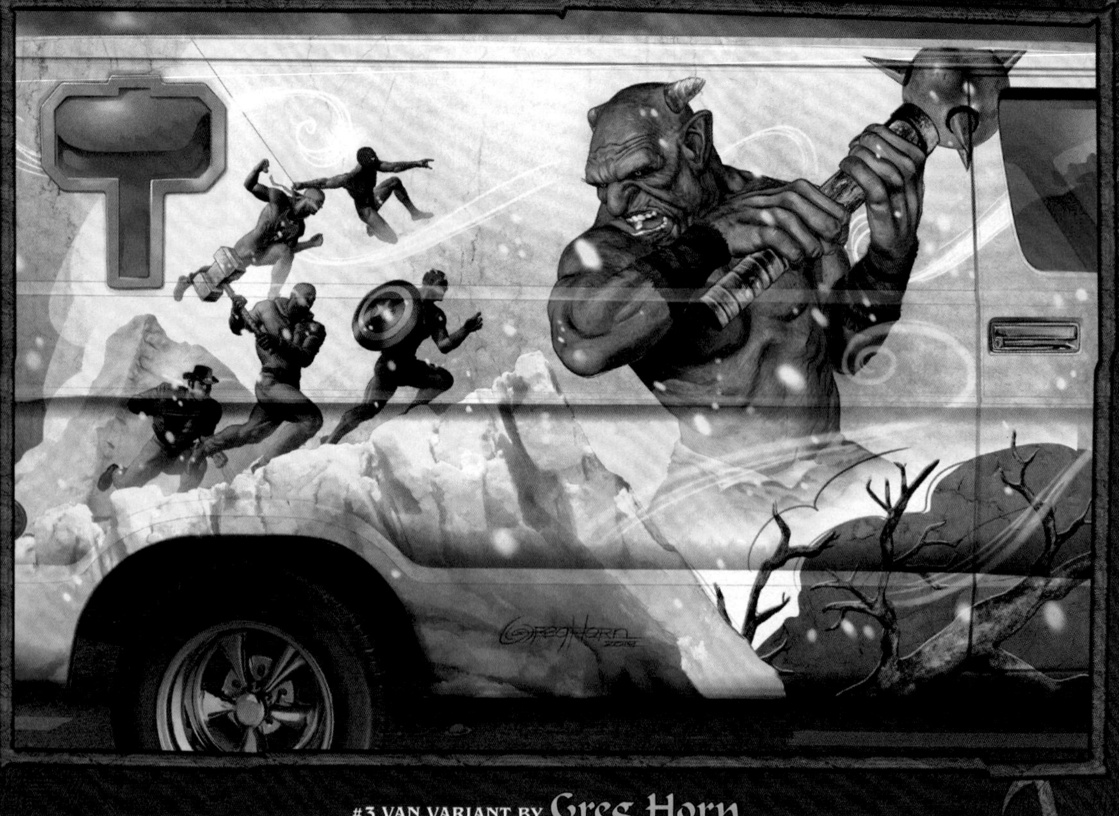

#3 VAN VARIANT BY Greg Horn

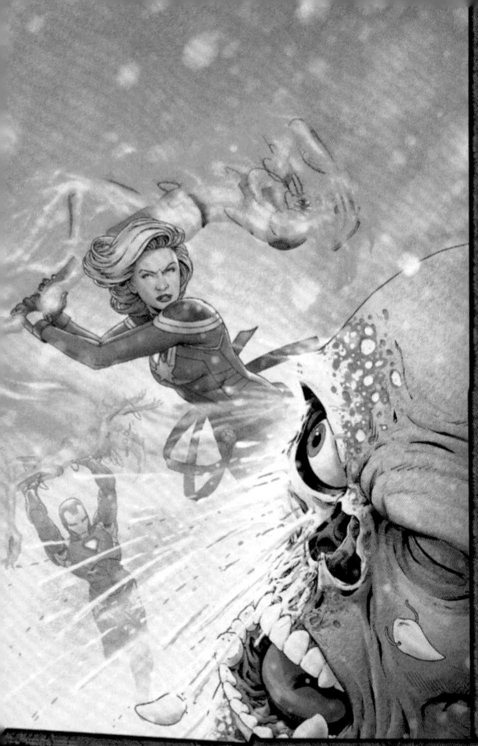

#1 VARIANT BY
John Tyler Christopher

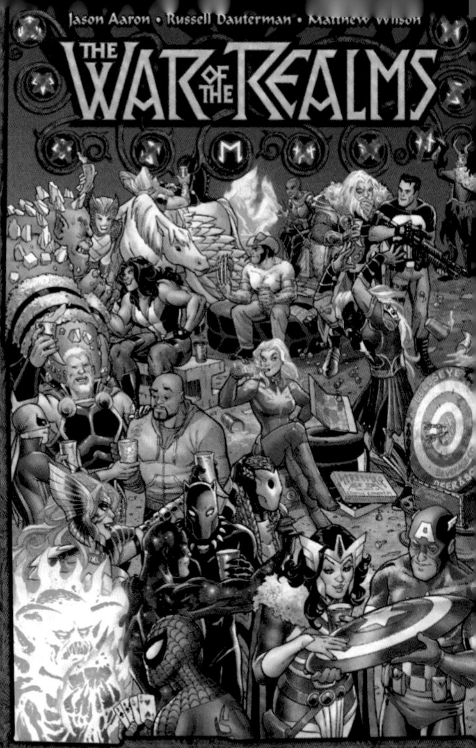

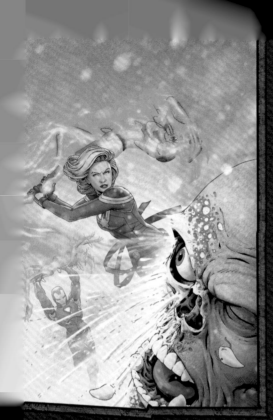

Jason Aaron • Russell Dauterman • Matthew Wilson
THE WAR OF THE REALMS

#1 PARTY VARIANT BY
Amanda Conner
& Paul Mounts

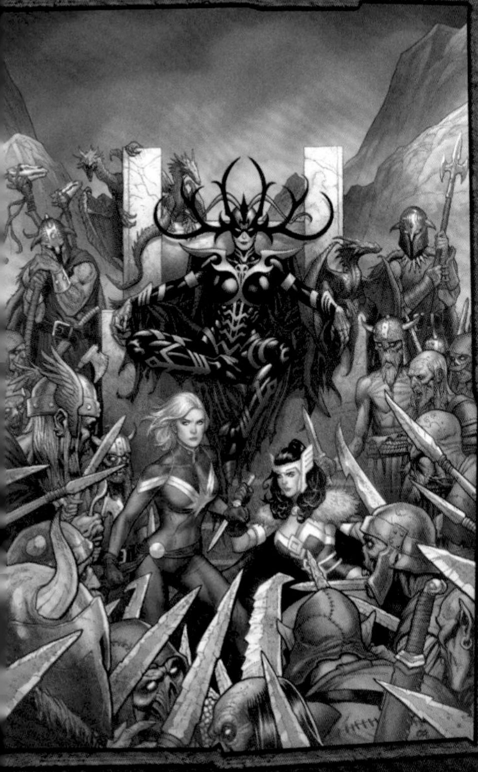

#1 VARIANT BY
Frank Cho & Sabine Rich

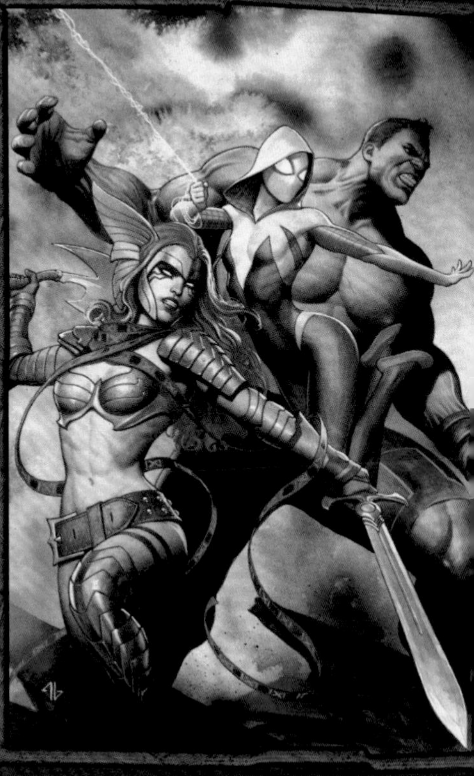

#1 VARIANT BY
Adi Granov

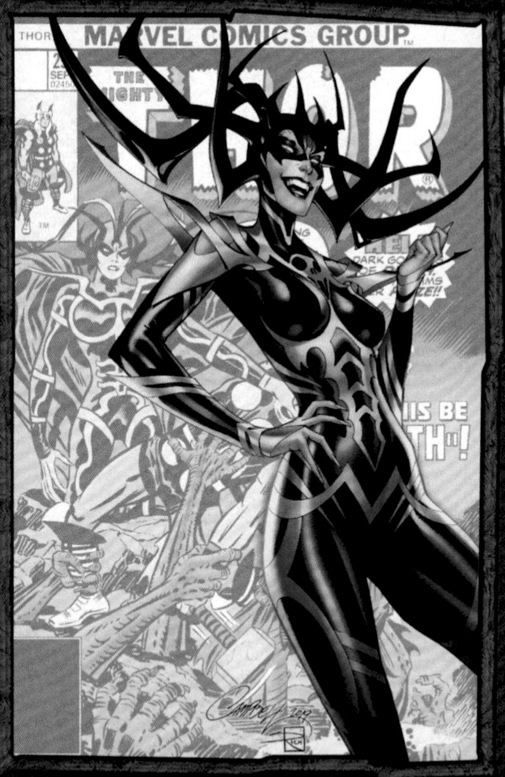
MARVEL COMICS GROUP

#1 VARIANT BY
J. Scott Campbell
& Sabine Rich

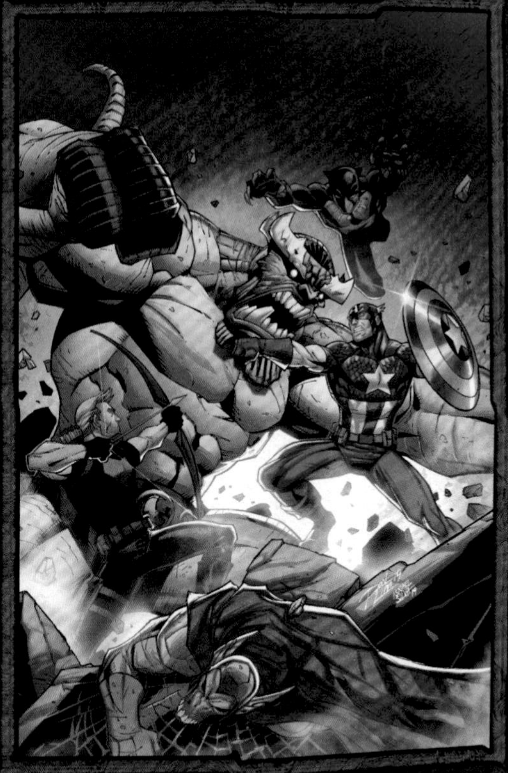

#1 VARIANT BY
Ron Lim
& Israel Silva

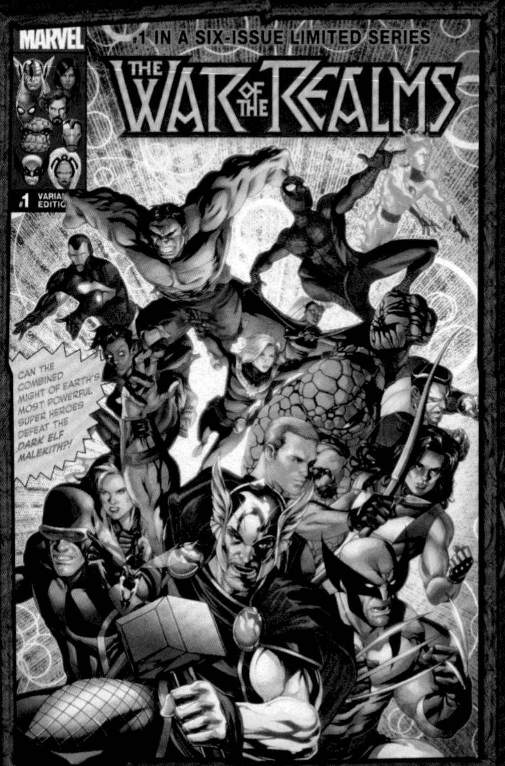
MARVEL
#1 IN A SIX-ISSUE LIMITED SERIES
THE WAR OF THE REALMS
CAN THE COMBINED MIGHT OF EARTH'S MOST POWERFUL SUPER HEROES DEFEAT THE DARK ELF MALEKITH?!

#1 VARIANT BY
Mike McKone

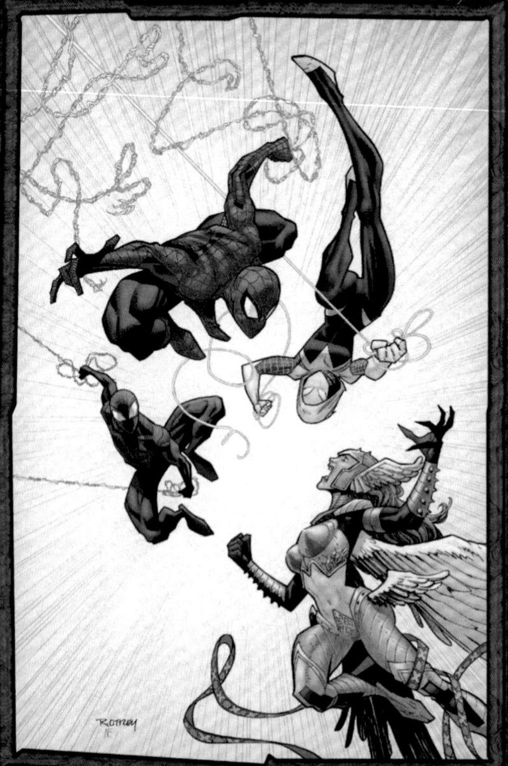

#1 VARIANT BY Ryan Ottley
& Nathan Fairbairn

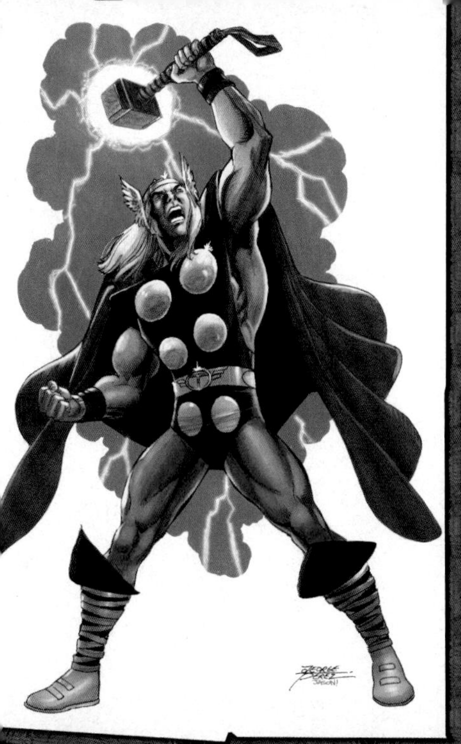

#1 VARIANT BY
George Pérez & Jason Keith

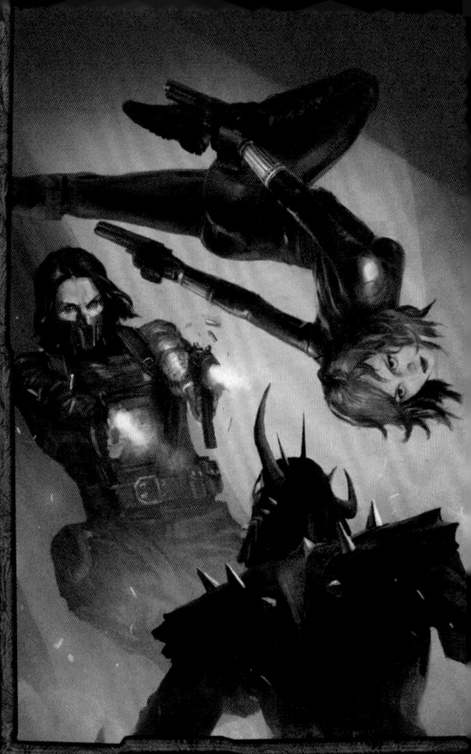

#1 VARIANT BY
Pyeong-Jun Park

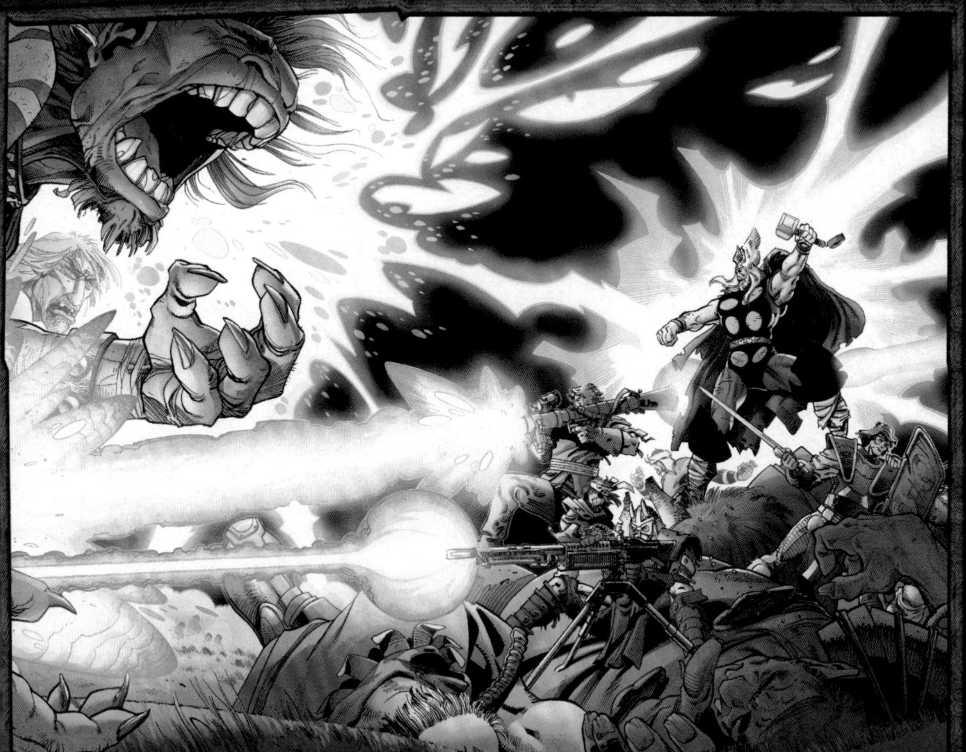

#1 HIDDEN GEM VARIANT BY Walter Simonson & Laura Martin

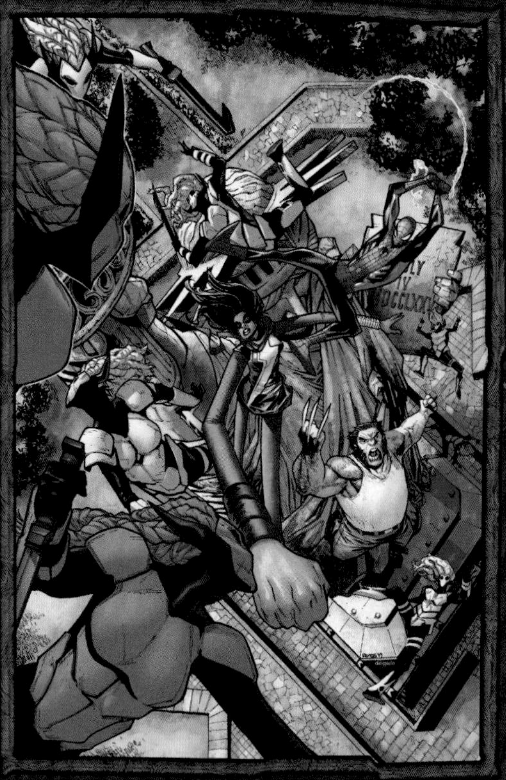

#1 INTERNATIONAL VARIANT
BY Humberto Ramos
& Edgar Delgado
WITH Mike Hawthorne

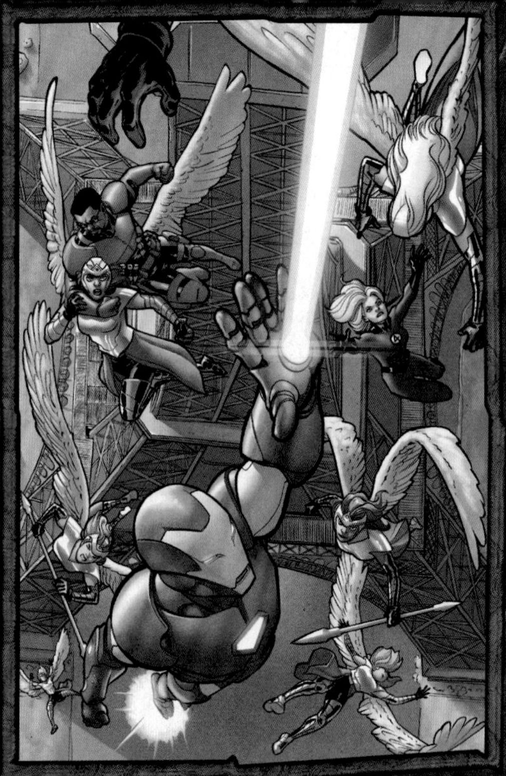

#2 INTERNATIONAL VARIANT BY
David Lopez
& Edgar Delgado
WITH Mike Hawthorne

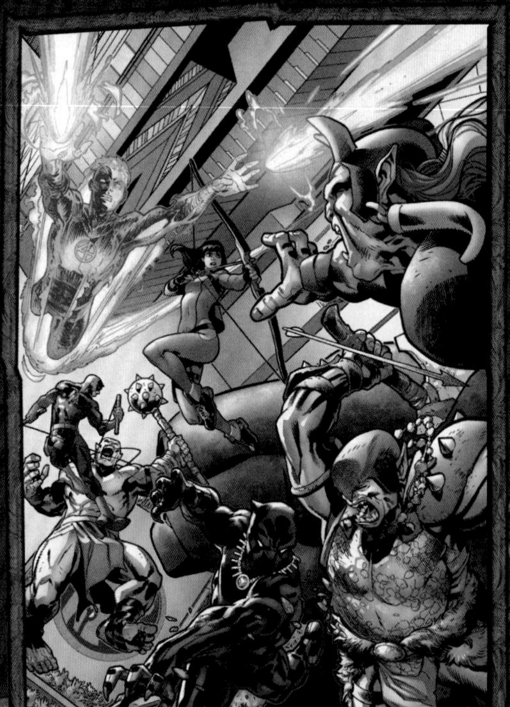

#3 INTERNATIONAL VARIANT
BY Sean Izaakse
& Edgar Delgado
WITH Mike Hawthorne

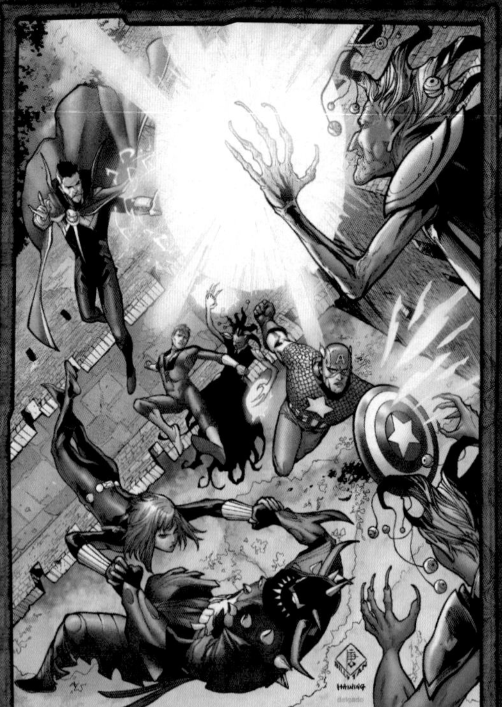

#4 INTERNATIONAL VARIANT BY
Billy Tan & Haining
OF Tan Comics & Edgar Delgado
WITH Mike Hawthorne

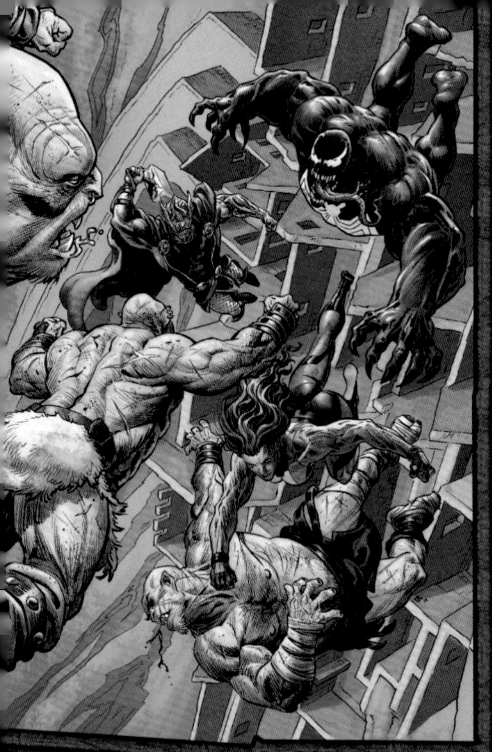

#4 INTERNATIONAL VARIANT
BY Luke Ross
& Edgar Delgado
WITH Mike Hawthorne

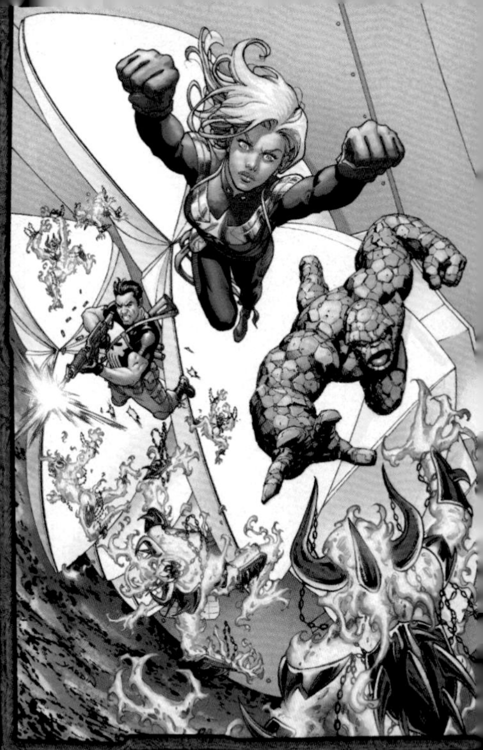

#5 INTERNATIONAL VARIANT BY
David Yardin
& Edgar Delgado
WITH Mike Hawthorne

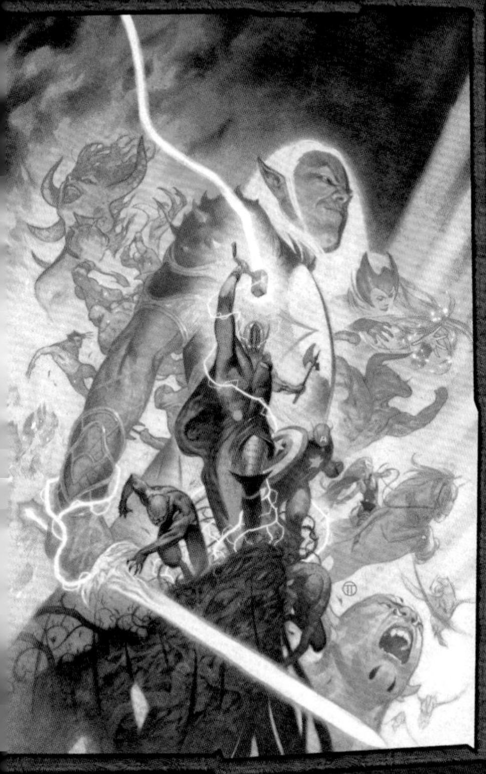

#2 VARIANT BY
Julian Totino Tedesco

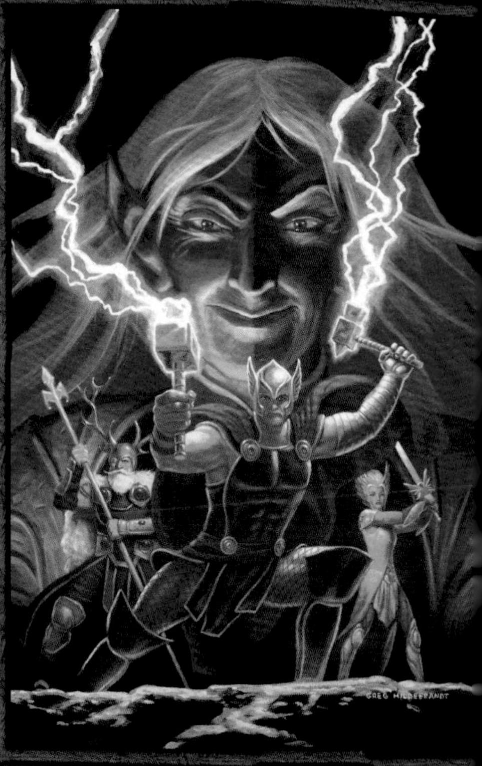

#4 VARIANT BY
Greg Hildebrandt

#5 VARIANT BY
Mark Texeira
& Rachelle Rosenberg

#6 SPOILER VARIANT BY
Terry Dodson
& Rachel Dodson

#6 VARIANT BY
Irina Nordsol